RELIGION AND POVERTY

Pan-African Perspectives

PETER J. PARIS, ED.

Foreword by
JACOB OLUPONA

Duke University Press
Durham and London
2009

D1572530

© 2009 Duke University Press

All rights reserved

Printed in the United States of America on acid-free paper ∞

Designed by Heather Hensley

Typeset in Quadraat by Keystone Typesetting, Inc.

Library of Congress Cataloging-in-Publication Data appear
on the last printed page of this book.

Dedicated to the memory of

REV. DR. LEWIN WILLIAMS, 1936–2006,

president of United Theological College, University of West Indies, and a pioneer Caribbean theologian

CONTENTS

Jacob Olupona | **UNDERSTANDING POVERTY AND ITS**

ALLEVIATION IN AFRICA AND THE AFRICAN

DIASPORA AN INTERDISCIPLINARY APPROACH

The essays in this volume critically examine the relationship between religion and poverty in African and African diasporic societies, problematizing the intersection of religion and poverty in the lives of the African peoples and their descendants in the Caribbean and North America. Emerging from a series of seminars and lectures held in several regions of Africa and the African diaspora over the past several years, the volume reflects the increasing convergence of theory, practice, and policy as it relates to the problem of poverty, its causes, and its alleviation. Though no central thesis guides the volume, it does suggest that, just as religious institutions and religious practices can contribute to and exacerbate poverty, religion can also play a potentially important role in poverty alleviation. Underpinning the evolving nexus between theory and practice is the difficult lesson that the academic pursuit of religious traditions must be seen in relation to the social and political situations under which faith communities live, flourish, and, at times, perish.

The volume sets out to provide an in-depth understanding of the problem of poverty in the experience of African people on both sides of the Atlantic, not only to examine the causes of poverty but also to provide answers for its alleviation in a way that will be beneficial to faith communities and the men and women currently struggling under the burden of poverty. In this volume, poverty as a concept and an analytical category is provided a broad, multidisciplinary focus in which phenomenological, theological, and sociological meanings and ethnographic investigation combine to provide an overview of the phenomenon. Though most of the scholars are theologians by training, the project is given a broader context than a purely doctrinal and scriptural investigation might have; it moves beyond the traditional notion of spiritual poverty set out in the Beatitudes: "Blessed are the poor in spirit: for theirs is the Kingdom of heaven" (Matt. 5:3).[1] Rather, the essays in this volume tackle the existential and substantial meaning of poverty understood as the lack of daily necessities such as water, food, and medicine and as a reflection of the hideous social crises of our time such as disease, crime, violence, war, and prostitution. Locating poverty within the broad nexus of the social, cultural, and religious nexus of the postcolonial era in Africa, the contributors provide a necessary sense of urgency and realism, arguing convincingly that poverty disproportionately affects peoples of color who are the poorest of the poor in the global community.

The Problem of Poverty

The phenomenon of poverty is often best grasped in relation to other highly pertinent issues such as violence, bribery, and corruption, as well as prosperity and riches. Paul Bouvier calls our attention to the social reality of our time that "today the poor are no longer individuals, but entire nations that become increasingly poor, while other nations become increasingly rich."[2] He sums up the most serious poverty predicament of our global world in these words: "today's proletariat consists of entire nations of victims of economic difficulties and the mechanisms of trade, carrying the burden of foreign debts and unable to overcome their lack of technological development."[3] No statement better sums up the conditions and contexts under which millions of people of African descent live today. Several of the case studies set out in this volume show that abject poverty in many regions of the world is intimately connected to environmental mismanagement and the exclusion of the very people whose lands and resources have made other nations rich from a share of the wealth. A classic case of widespread suffering brought on by environmental mismanagement is the situation of the Ogoni people of Nigeria's Niger Delta region. In order to maintain its high levels of oil exploration, the state forcibly acquired Ogoni lands, disabling an entire region of the local resources and livelihood. The Ogoni were denied access to and control over both material resources and the social resources, processes, and institutions that defined and reinforced their place. An integrative approach to alleviating poverty is, then, best suited to the project of understanding poverty, as it reveals the connection and causal relationship between poverty and environmental crises in many African and diasporic societies.

What, then is the nature of the poverty crisis? The comprehensive concept of poverty developed in this volume offers fresh insight and understanding into the problem of poverty in Africa and its diaspora. John Iliffe, who has written a substantial work on the African poor, classifies African poverty into two groups. One group comprises those who clearly "struggle continuously to preserve themselves and their dependents from physical want." Iliffe thinks that most Africans at some time fall into this level of poverty. The second group, fewer in number, is composed of the poorest of the poor and destitute, whose poverty has reached epidemic proportion. Facing starvation, they are beset by disease and malnutrition.[4] Paradoxically, it seems to us that disproportionately high levels of poverty occur in countries with great visible wealth and resources, such as Nigeria, South Africa, and the Democratic Republic of Congo. Such profound poverty in the midst of plenty engenders anger and frustration on the part of civil society, who watch helplessly as their nation's wealth is looted by a small number of so-called filthy rich individuals and powerful international conglomerates. Echoing several of the theologians who contributed to the present volume, Father E. Mveng, a Cameroonian Catholic theologian, provides an encompassing and insightful description of poverty, or what he calls "anthropological poverty," which goes beyond "economic or financial deprivation": a deeper condition of poverty, a psychology in which one's own humanity is impoverished and one's very humanity is denied.[5] A popular African proverb says that while "the poor person labors in the heat of the sun, the rich person enjoys the fruits of the labor under the shade" (*osise wa l'oorun, eni maje wa ni iboji*, as the Yoruba version goes). Found in various versions in other African societies, the proverb is a metaphor for the severity of the gap between the poor who work tirelessly to survive and the rich, the principal beneficiaries of the labor of the poor, who enjoy the enormous wealth generated from the fruits of the poor person's labor. The proverb further reflects the African and African diasporic condition and experience of poverty, the poor people's own understanding of their situation and lot in life under various historical and social situations, be they economic and social poverty and subhuman living conditions generated by the transatlantic and trans-Saharan slave trades, colonialism, postcolonial democracy, or military rule by African themselves.

As several chapters in this volume demonstrate, studying poverty in Africa and its diasporic communities requires that we begin with the poor's own description and understanding of their conditions and state of being. Whether these sources of knowledge are found in myths, rituals, metaphors, poetry, prose, or biographical narratives from the mouth of the common folks or from those Elizabeth Isichei calls "the village intellectuals,"[6] the narratives often describe the relationship between unequal individuals and peoples.

Historical Causes of Poverty

In analyzing the historical causes of poverty, we must look critically at the historical process and evolution of the continent from precolonial times through the colonial and postcolonial periods and examine the political economy of African states and the local and global forces that play central roles in the unfolding of the contemporary social life and situation of the people. No amount of synchronic understanding or ethnographic analysis on the present state of poverty on both sides of the African Atlantic society will do justice to the topic of our deliberation if we fail to acknowledge, even tangentially, the historical trajectory of poverty in Africa and African diaspora communities. While the centuries-long transatlantic slave trade laid the foundation for the current state of poverty in Africa and the African diaspora, the colonial legacy and the postcolonial condition of African people provide the background for the endemic nature of this crisis in Africa today. The slave trade led to the destruction of family, family values, communal and peaceful coexistence, and intergroup relations. As the demand for slaves increased exponentially in response to the insatiable demand in the Americas, warfare increased and the continent was deprived of its able-bodied men and women. The social disruption and depopulation that warfare and human trafficking wreaked on Africa over several hundred years gravely affected the human, social, and cultural development of the region. One can argue that Africa and the African diaspora people have not recovered from this human tragedy, a telling point that makes the request for reparations even more keenly felt.

There is no doubt that in the precolonial period—at least dating back to the early nineteenth century, when Africa had established empires, kingdoms, and states—there was both poverty and affluence. The poverty of that time, however, took a different form. As J. D. Y. Peel reminds us in the case of the Yoruba people, poverty as a social condition was intolerable and rejected as a way of life.[7] A Yoruba proverb portrays the stigma associated with poverty: "It is better to die young with dignity than to become old in abject poverty" (Ki a ku lo'mode yeni, ju-ki a d'agba ka t'osi). Old age typically signals respectability, comfort, and dignity; what the Yoruba saying underlines is that an old age that brings misery and poverty is disgraceful. The proverb also illuminates a cardinal element of Yoruba religious thought and practice: the Yoruba profess a this-worldly worldview, and the indigenous

Yoruba's religious quest to the *orisa* (gods) is that they provide to the supplicants the blessings of wealth, children, and long life (*Ire owo, ire omo, ire emi gigun*). The proverb's apparent rejection of the third of these blessings indicates the very high distaste the Yoruba have for abject poverty.

A more recent response to the crisis of communal and group poverty in African villages today is the growing link between ethno-religious identity and development. In Nigeria, Ghana, and other parts of Africa, for instance, village and town associations grow and meet in economic unity and social development. This often involves the reinvention of traditional value systems (of sacred kingship, totemic concepts, old lineage gods, and ancestors reinvented and reimagined in modern secular idioms). Although these groups are not necessarily linked to the worship of traditional gods, their members having largely converted to Islam and Christianity, they have established a platform for advancing economic unity and social development by appealing to the community as the sacred source of life. By invoking tribal myth and historic symbols and by galvanizing members of their communities at home and abroad to contribute to village, town, and community economic growth, they are responding to a crisis using their own metaphysical and epistemological worldview. Social, economic, and symbolic capital is rallied and tailored toward fighting communal poverty. These limited successes are unfortunately not matched by African governments, many of which have centralized control over natural resources. In general, traditional Africa was fairly well governed by traditional mores, customs, and laws that regulated the economy of the people and the nation-states in precolonial indigenous societies. There seems to have been greater accountability and greater commitment to the social welfare of the common people as well as significant checks and balances. Further, African beliefs and indigenous systems had real and symbolic meaning, and Africans were protective of children, women, the poor, and slaves. Reinvigorating these practices and traditions is an important aspect of long-term poverty alleviation in Africa and the African diaspora.

In the colonial period, as some of these traditions lost their power and as colonial rule and laws were introduced, Africans began to lose their sense of cultural identity and a new group of elites emerged to replace traditional rulers and to collaborate with the colonial powers. Although the colonial government reinvented aspects of indigenous culture that supported colonial rule, it also created new groups of elites from the natives. On a positive note, the tradition of market women's protest in colonial and postcolonial periods followed the traditional structure of ritual rebellion against what is perceived as oppression of poor people.

Though the 1960s brought the age of African independence, the magic of independence soon subsided as self-rule was haphazardly installed and the structures left by the departing colonialists undermined peaceful coexistence among different linguistic and ethnic groups that were forcefully situated under the jurisdiction of the same nation-state. In the first three decades of African independence, under systems of military rule, many African economies experienced significant growth as natural resources—particularly oil and minerals—were discovered. This was also a period when corruption was institutionalized and currencies were devalued to "inconvertible" foreign currency. Taking advantage of severely weakened developing states and the global economy, the World Bank and the International Monetary Fund (IMF) exploited conditions that turned these countries into the poorest in the world and developed nations into the wealthiest. The "structural adjustment policies" of the World Bank and IMF encouraged massive loans that, lacking alternatives, developing nations were forced to take for survival. Therefore, it is not surprising that throughout this period in Africa military coups were hatched, with new despotic rulers in khaki uniforms emerging. This situation continued into the late 1990s in most countries, when, with the support of the international community, many African states developed new democratic, though largely economically deprived, governments.

Given the complex historical experiences of the African peoples and African diasporic communities in the Caribbean and North America, the conversation on poverty calls for a radical rethinking of African philosophical, social, and ethical norms to understand how modernization, secular democratic ideals, and political transformation of the continent since independence, have impinged upon the norms, cultures, and indigenous African life today. For instance, as Elizabeth Amoah notes in her essay in this volume, one of the fundamental qualities of traditional African life is communal and common ownership of land and property. Following their colonial legacy, however, many African nations quickly adopted privatized systems at independence. Indeed, the breakdown of Africa's traditional common ownership of land and subsistence production is comparable to the massive closing of the commons in feudal England, when peasants were forcibly evicted from common lands and the commons were then used to develop agrarian capitalism, extend capitalist accumulation, and ensure a national wage-labor market. Privatization undermined the social welfare ethos predominant in rural African communities. The radical change from communal ownership to governmental control of communal properties provided the pretext for enacting many draconian laws and decrees by which very poor people in rural areas were deprived of their only earthly possessions: their lands. Lands were forcefully acquired for redistribution among the new rich and city entrepreneurs. Unfortunately, in places such as Nigeria and Kenya, this practice became a national program and many watched helplessly as millions of poor people were left destitute as the ethos of communal sharing gave way to complete deprivation. An exception was former Tanzanian president Julius K. Nyerere, one of Africa's most respected elder statesmen and peacemakers of the region, who established the *ujamaa* village program of community-based farming collectives. Its failure due to mismanagement, however, led Western critics and cultural despisers to conclude, as did Peter Berger, that socialism has always been a failed ideology whenever it was practiced. Father James Schall's famous study *Religion, Wealth, and Poverty* claims that the actual cause of poverty in the world is ideological and insists that the "last great hope for the poor" is "democratic capitalism." Citing Tanzania, Schall wrote, "The best way to discover why Tanzania remains poor and depends on handouts is not to examine its soil or its rainfall, but to read the collected speeches of Mr. Julius Nyerere."[8]

Judging from the poor assessment of Nyerere's program and Mugabe's current land redistribution program in impoverished Zimbabwe, one may conclude that African socialism and the adaptation of an indigenous African ethos to the fight against poverty are bound to fail. I am persuaded that this is not the case. The problem lies more in the implementation of the programs than in the ideological persuasion of these leaders. The partial success of Rwanda's ongoing National Poverty Reduction Program, based on *ubudehe*, "the traditional Rwandan practice and cultural value of working together to solve problems," clearly indicates how an indigenous-inspired poverty alleviation program can succeed. According to the architects of the program, "The objective of this *Ubudehe Mukurwanya Ubuduken* Program is to revive and foster collective action at community level. It is designed to work with and reinforce the on-going political and financial decentralizations process and to provide a direct injection of financial capital into the rural economy, aimed at overcoming one of the main obstacles to pro-poor economic growth."[9]

Responses to Poverty

A number of policy initiatives have recently been set forward to address the issue of poverty in Africa. Faith-based initiatives have proven particularly popular and deserve attention. Since 1960, membership in Christian faiths in Africa has increased over 80 percent, from 60 million (in 1960) to 300 million (in 2001).[10] Faith-based organizations in Africa are thus situated to take on significant roles in addressing underdevelopment and alleviating extreme crises. Many of Africa's most impoverished people are also deeply spiritual members of religious organizations. By joining religious social support networks, many achieve a sense of personal identity, unified community, and social solidarity and are able to call upon the combined resources of the faith organization to address the poverty and disease ravaging their communities. Using ancient religious teachings, religious denominations instill religious values as moral obligations to the faithful, who are obligated to alleviate poverty in ways that may be lacking in secular institutions, international development agencies, or local governments. Thus, on a global scale religious groups can serve as effective representatives for marginalized segments of third world peoples. Religious organizations can also compel national and local political leaders to discourage corruption in public, civic, and political life; to empower citizens to develop skills; to acknowledge rights; to elect responsible leaders; to address corruption of ethnic and political affiliations; and to dissuade Western governments from giving tax breaks to companies responsible for environmental disasters.

Indeed, in 2000 the Nairobi Conference entitled "Alleviating Poverty in Africa" was sponsored in partnership with the Council of Anglican Provinces of Africa and the World Bank, participating in a Council of Anglican Provinces of Africa (CAPA) training course for new bishops in Ibadan, Nigeria. The conference addressed the causes of poverty; political, economic, and social challenges; and ways to fight poverty by raising income and promoting empowerment, security, and opportunity in African nations. Seeing the spiritual as an essential component of development, these organizations committed to working with African communities to seek community-driven development, protect natural resources and environments, promote good governance by fighting corruption, and relieve debt. Further, some religious groups are directly embedded in the struggles against poverty by insisting through their lobbying groups that poverty be seen as a moral question of world economic policy. The Catholic social justice lobbying group, Network, for example, urges religious organizations to ask governments and corporations ethical questions regarding economic policy: How does policy affect the lives of people in poverty? How does policy improve the lives of people in poverty? How does policy affect their capacity to decide about their lives?[11]

Faith-based initiatives are not without problems, however. I argue that many Evangelical and Protestant groups should redefine their mission from one that focuses primarily on the saving of souls from eternal damnation to one that directly addresses the misery and poverty lived by many of their flock. They must address spiritual as well as material needs by cultivating a new mind-set similar to the notion of the "mission church" in the colonial era, in which the Bible and the plow were understood as mutually reinforcing. I understand faith-based initiatives as social programs developed by religious communities to eradicate and alleviate poverty, rejecting the popular understanding in the United States that faith-based initiatives, as defined by George W. Bush, are the state-sponsored redistribution of resources using the agency of religious communities. The latter understanding runs the risk of polarizing public opinion and engendering religious bigotry. Overall, however, religious bodies have long been involved in social welfare and charity without the support of the state. Beyond their peculiar meaning in America, faith-based initiatives imply the involvement of civil society at large, particularly in the postmilitary states of contemporary African nations.

The role civil society plays in poverty alleviation cannot be overemphasized. It has been widely argued that the chronic corruption in many failed African states has led to the growth of civil society. The excellent performance of the civil society in the postmilitary era, especially in the struggle for democratization, confirms that it needs to be strengthened today if nascent democracies in Africa are to survive. Progressive religious institutions constitute a significant segment of any nation's civil society, and developing programs to eradicate and alleviate poverty should be seen in that context. In the African situation, it is counterproductive to build a wedge between religious institutions and other civil society groups, such as trade unions, universities, and other nongovernmental organizations involved in the critical work of social change or social engineering. The Western notion of separating the spheres of influence of religion, state, and civil agencies may be foreign to Africans, hence the union of these spheres should not be assumed inappropriate in alleviating and eradicating poverty in Africa today through sustainable development.

An unexpected locus for poverty alleviation may be the international monetary bodies (the IMF and the World Bank) in partnership with religious organizations, particularly churches. Regarded as credible partners, many churches in Africa are forging new partnerships with the World Bank, and these partnerships may prove beneficial as the bank not only provides expertise in specific aspects of poverty and public policy but also has special access to national and international decision makers. The bank brings a global perspective and financial resources to alleviating poverty, as the largest source of multilateral development assistance to Africa.[12]

Though partnering with the World Bank may make new opportunities available, it is essential that the church always maintain its prophetic voice in such relationships or partnerships. Instead of denouncing partnership with the World Bank or the IMF as some churches have done, the church should insist on its prophetic tradition, which provides meaningful critique of global injustice while simultaneously sponsoring and collaborating with credible organizations. The story of the prophet Nathan related in the Old Testament book 2 Samuel illustrates the possibility of the prophet speaking truth to power. In 2 Samuel, the prophet Nathan was sent to reprimand King David for slaying Bathsheba's husband in order to take Bathsheba for himself to be his wife (2 Samuel 12:1–9). Nathan tells David the parable of a very rich man who had many flocks and a poor man who had only one precious little lamb and who raised the lamb lovingly as part of his family. Now the rich man, ignoring his many herds, took the poor man's lamb and had it prepared for dinner guests. On hearing the story, David became enraged at the perpetrator of this wicked deed, declaring that the rich man deserved to die because he showed no compassion. Nathan thus delivered the accusation to King David, "Thou art the man!" This old biblical story is useful in today's situation of unequal power among nations, corporations, and peoples. A skilled communicator, Nathan raised David's consciousness such that David was able, by acknowledging evil in one case, to recognize evil in himself.

The impact of poverty on gender relations in Africa, especially the status of women and the responses of women's religious, cultural, and social institutions to conditions of poverty is also profoundly important and is highlighted in Barbara Bailey's contribution to this volume. All available data suggest that poverty in Africa disproportionately affects women and children. The Council of Anglican Provinces of Africa in partnership with the World Bank issued a statement on gender and poverty in sub-Saharan Africa, declaring that if Africa is to achieve equitable growth and sustainable development, then women must have access to and control of productive, human, and social capital assets.[13]

The church sees the inherent partnership between men and women as originating in Creation and its breakdown as sinful. But the church's missionary heritage created structured, unequal gender roles. Thus, the church must now provide space for women to express and contribute their resources and gifts in a more participatory and equal manner, thus enabling the full range of Africa's human resources to alleviate poverty. The church must increase awareness of injustices against women through empowerment programs and gender training for all worshippers. The majority of church members in Africa are women, making gender equality a moral imperative as well as a developmental objective that is central to the church's survival. The church must remove the rigid structures of its community life in order to improve the status of women. Further, women must secure access to and control of a diverse range of productive, human, and social capital.

Religious groups can offer equitable provisions for women to articulate their resources and gifts, to address the female and child culture of poverty in Africa, to raise consciousness-supporting empowerment programs, and to offer gender-awareness training. Religious groups can change rigid structures of religious community life to promote women's leadership and to assess the impact of religious programs targeted to rural women, encouraging all segments of society to work together to alleviate poverty. Indeed, the Anglican Church's Mothers Union, the Women's Guild, and numerous other women's groups in many Christian denominations are doing precisely that. Peace depends on economic justice, social harmony, and spiritual sanctity of life. Religious groups identify the root cause of conflict in people's refusal to see any "good" in "the other" and its solution in the willingness to accuse and implicate one's self and one's own group as part of the problem. Forgiveness and reconciliation, based on this analysis, is the religious group's comparative advantage. In a conflict situation, religious groups can—and should—offer a permanent institutional framework that provides continuity and social stability.[14]

Conclusion

In 2005, when the developed world pledged to halve poverty in the world by 2015 and ultimately "make poverty history," there was a happy response from the African people that finally the developing world was awakening to its responsibility to aid the world's most impoverished peoples. All indications, however, suggest that not only has the developed world reneged on its promises, but it is not at all committed to "making poverty history." The Millennium Development Goals, as noble as they are, set a Herculean task for poverty alleviation because of the fundamental structures of the political, economic, and social orders that are entrenched in the world today, which render any meaningful reform improbable. All available statistics suggest that those who are most affected by the world poverty crisis are in the regions of Africa and the Caribbean, from where most of the case studies in the present volume originate. It is perhaps in the context of this crisis that the Pan-African approach and response to poverty was planned and carried out by some of the best scholarly minds living in the impoverished regions in question. *Religion and Poverty: Pan-African Perspectives* is a small but important contribution to the pressing challenge that poverty in Africa and the African diaspora present to the world.

Notes

1. Biblical quotations throughout this book are from the Revised Standard Version.
2. Paul Bouvier, "The Mission of the Churches amid the Social Reality of Rich and Poor Nations," in *God and Global Justice: Religion and Poverty in an Unequal World*, ed. Frederick Ferre and Rita H. Mataragnon (New York: Paragon House, 1985), 113.
3. Ibid.
4. John Iliffe, *The African Poor: A History* (Cambridge: Cambridge University Press, 1987), 2.
5. Bengt Sundkler and Christopher Steed, *A History of the Church in Africa* (Cambridge: Cambridge University Press, 2000), 914.
6. Elizabeth Allo Isichei, *Voices of the Poor in Africa* (Rochester, N.Y.: University of Rochester Press, 2002), 93 and 169. See also Steven Feierman, *Peasant Intellectuals: Anthropology and History in Tanzania* (Madison: University of Wisconsin Press, 1990).
7. J. D. Y. Peel, *Religious Encounter and the Making of the Yoruba* (Indianapolis: Indiana University Press, 2000).
8. James V. Schall, *Religion, Wealth, and Poverty* (Vancouver: Fraser Institute, 1990), 15.
9. Africa Forum, "Ubudehe to Fight Poverty," *Africa Notes*, November/December 2002, 1.
10. Deryke Belshaw, Robert Calderisi, and Chris Sugden, eds., *Faith in Development: Partnership between the World Bank and the Churches of Africa* (Washington, D.C.: World Bank, 2001), 3.
11. Neil Chethik, "Global Issues: Trends on Collision Course with Justice," *UU World* 14.6 (November/December 2000): 18–22.
12. Belshaw, Calderisi, and Sugden, *Faith in Development*, 8.
13. Ibid., 10.
14. Ibid., 14.

ACKNOWLEDGMENTS

First and foremost, I am altogether grateful to all the writers in this volume, who participated happily, faithfully, and tirelessly in the rigorous daily programs of this four-year collaborative project of Pan-African religious scholars. The scholars met annually for two-week sessions in five different countries: Ghana, Kenya, South Africa, Jamaica, and the United States. Special thanks are also extended to three members of our group, Rabiatu Ammah (Ghana), David Mosoma (South Africa), and Luiza Benicio (Brazil), who for various personal reasons were not able to continue to the end.

Our experiences together over the years of the seminar have resulted in relationships that will benefit us for all our lives. Further, our experience demonstrated that a community can be formed and sustained by a diverse group of people attending to a common project.

The four-year project was made possible by the cooperative support of two major institutions, for which we are most grateful. The Ford Foundation provided a planning grant to develop the proposal, as well as adequate funding for the program itself. Thus, we owe our most sincere thanks to the foundation's program officer, Constance Buchanan, and her staff for their helpful assistance throughout the entire process.

Princeton Theological Seminary provided oversight and administrative support for the business aspects of the project, which included annual financial reports. As the project's director, I am personally grateful for the relief of one course per annum in order to direct the project. Special thanks are due to President Thomas W. Gillespie, Dean James F. Armstrong, Vice President John Gilmore, Deadra Bachorik Ashton, Elizabeth Angelucci, Brenda Lucadano, James Morgan, and Teresa Reed, each of whom in different ways provided immeasurable help and support.

Numerous others made various contributions to the success of this project. Each of the following deserves special mention and sincere thanks for their efficient and generous support: student assistant Ray Owens, who made all the travel arrangements and traveled with the group to South Africa; student assistant Dante Quick, who coordinated local travel arrangements for the meeting in Princeton; local program coordinators J. O. Y. Mante, (Legon, Ghana), Mary Getui (Nairobi, Kenya), Takatso Mofokeng (Johannesburg, South Africa), and Joyce Williams (Kingston, Jamaica). The local coordinators were assisted by their respective staff persons and volunteers, each of whom graciously welcomed us. We are also grateful to their respective spouses, who warmly extended their hospitality: Florence Mante, Samuel Getui, Mampo Mofokeng, and Lewin Williams.

We are greatly indebted to a long list of lecturers in each of the countries visited, from whom we learned much. They include the following:

Ghana 2000: Joyce Wereao Broddy, Emmanuel Asante, Kwesi Dickson, Abraham Akrong, Elizabeth Amoah, Samuel N. Ashong, Rabiatu Ammah, John Pobee, Irene Odotey, Clara Fayorsey, Kwame Bediako.

Kenya 2001: Canon Clement Janda, Agnes Aboum, J. Ongong'a, Jesse Mugambi, Anne Nasimiyu Wasike, Cardinal Morris Otunga (Kenya's first Roman Catholic bishop and archbishop), Eric Aseka, P. N. Mwaura, Kennety Ombongi, E. Gimode, Violet Kimani, Njuguna Njoroge.

South Africa 2002: Samuel Malesi Mophokeng, Rev. Molefe Tsele, Mangezi Guma, Hon. Thoko Didazi, Samisani Hlopha, Mandla Seleoane, Samuel Buti, Itumeleng Mosala, Mahlornola Skosana, Mathole Motshekga, Puleng Lenka Bula, Tahir Sitoto, M. Motlhabi, T. S. Malukeke, Russell Botman.

Jamaica 2003: Errol Miller, Jennifer Martin, Suzette Martin, Garnet Roper, Portia Simpson, Ann Shirley, Elsa Leo-Rhynie, Michael Witter, Rex Nettleford (pro-vice chancellor, University of West Indies), Omar Davies, Paulette Chevannes, Marjorie Lewis, Evelyn Vernon, Maitland Evans, Roderick Hewitt, Tekla Mekfet, Mario Castillio.

United States 2004: Albert Raboteau, Vernon Mason (and staff Tiffany Taylor, Angela Moses, John Cardwell, Edison Jackson, Patricia Gatling, Lance Ogiste, Claudette Devonish, William Hunter, Julio Madina), M. William Howard (and assistants Junius Williams, Shirley Grundy, Roland Anglin), Lawrence Mamiya, Edward Hunt, Fred Davie, Garvester Kelley, Nimi Wariboko, Jacob Olupona.

Some observers attended either all or some of the seminars at their own expense. They were Angelin Simmons, Glenda Erskine, 'Bola Ilesanmi, Njuguna Njoroge, Maselele Masenya, and little Dora Hopkins.

I would also like to extend heartfelt thanks to all those at Duke University Press whose professional expertise and encouragement have combined to enhance the quality of this book. The associate editor Miriam Angress and the assistant managing editor Molly Balikov deserve special mention. It has been my pleasure to work closely with both of them on this project. Further, I wish to thank Jan Williams for her work in developing an excellent index.

Finally, but certainly not least, I extend a special word of personal thanks to my beloved spouse, Adrienne Daniels Paris, for her love and moral support throughout the program and beyond. The participants in the seminars appreciated her grace and enthusiasm so much that Elizabeth Amoah affectionately crowned her Queen Mother, the significance of which can only be fully appreciated by the Akan people of Ghana.

While teaching in Ghana in 1997 I was invited one evening to meet with a group of professors at the home of Dr. Irene Odotey on the campus of the University of Ghana to talk about the lack of meaningful relationships between African scholars on continent and those in the diaspora. During the conversation I asked the group to assess the value of a possible multi-year seminar that would comprise a number of African religious scholars for the purpose of studying some subject of common interest such as religion and poverty. All readily affirmed the idea and promptly offered many suggestions.

In due course, a two-week annual seminar was launched in Ghana in 2000 and met subsequently in Kenya, South Africa, Jamaica, and the United States. Those countries were selected because each, except for the United States, scored among the lowest third of the 175 countries measured by the United Nations Human Development Index (HDI).[1] Since 1990, when that index was developed by the Indian Nobel Prize laureate Amartya Sen and his colleagues, it has constituted the principal means for measuring human well-being globally. The index compares such variables as life expectancy, education, and access to health care, including such basic needs as safe drinking water, sanitation, and adequate daily nutrition. These measurements show that thirty of the thirty-two countries with the lowest HDI ranking are in Africa, which makes that continent the poorest in the world.[2]

Kenya was the only country we visited that was in the lowest HDI category, with a rating of 155 out of 178. Yet the others were not very far ahead: Ghana 139, South Africa 121, Jamaica 97.[3] Even though the United States scored 17 in the HDI with an overall poverty rate of 12.8 percent in 2004, a disproportionate 40 percent of African Americans were classified as poor.[4]

Much of the available data supports the claim that poverty in Africa has steadily increased since the dawn of political independence on that continent one half century ago. In spite of the apparent intractability of the continent's poverty, most African scholars and civic leaders reject deterministic conclusions. In fact, our learned informants at every seminar were hopeful that

Participants in Pan-African Seminar on Religion and Poverty, Observatory Ridge, Johannesburg, South Africa, 14–24 July 2002. Front row (left to right): Madipoane Masenya (South Africa), (unidentified guest), Takatso Mofokeng (South Africa), Peter Paris (Canada/United States), Elizabeth Amoah (Ghana);

Second row (left to right): Esther Mombo (Kenya), Barbara Bailey (Jamaica), (unidentified guest), Simeon Ilesanmi (Nigeria/United States), Nyambura Njoroge (Kenya), Adrienne Daniels Paris (United States guest);

Third row (left to right): David Mosoma (South Africa), Glenda Erskine (United States guest), baby Dora and Linda Thomas (United States);

Fourth row (left to right): Noel Erskine (Jamaica/United States), Angelin Simmons (United States guest), Ray Owens (United States staff), Dwight Hopkins (United States), Katie Cannon (United States);

Back row (left to right): Kossi Ayedze (Togo), Anthony Pinn (United States), Lewin Williams (Jamaica), Joyce Williams (Jamaica guest). Missing from photo, Laurenti Magesa (Tanzania).

with adequate help from the Western nations, poverty in Africa would be eradicated in time. Moreover, in the year that our seminar was launched, such a viewpoint had been proposed by the United Nations secretary general, Kofi Annan, in his document "We the Peoples: The Role of the United Nations in the Twenty-first Century."[5] That proposal gave rise to the Millennium Declaration, which was adopted by world leaders at the United Nations Millennium Summit that same year.[6] The principles of those documents have been fully embraced by the economist Jeffrey Sachs, who directs the Earth Institute at Columbia University. He makes the compelling argument that it is possible to solve the problem of poverty in Africa in a very short period of time.[7] His extraordinary optimism is good news to the ears of African peoples.

Everywhere that our group visited, we saw the devastating marks of poverty: major deficiencies in health, education, clean water, security, and political freedom, which prevent people from competing effectively for a higher standard of living. Clearly, those conditions constitute the breeding grounds for civil violence, wars, widespread corruption, and various pandemics of malaria, HIV/AIDS, and other diseases. Yet we also encountered countless signs of resiliency among local peoples who struggle fervently to eke out a living in the midst of immense adversity.

The second half of the twentieth century was dominated by various independence movements among African peoples, both on the continent and throughout the diaspora. As time went by, however, it became evident that the economic impact of colonialism and racial oppression had not been overcome by the various independence and civil rights victories. Rather, the majority of African peoples everywhere encountered new forms of social and economic impoverishment, which the Ghanaian historian A. Adu Boahen has attributed largely to the impact of colonialism:

> If colonialism meant anything at all politically, it was the loss of sovereignty and independence by the colonized peoples. This loss of sovereignty, in turn, implied the loss of the right of a state to control its own destiny; to plan its own development; to decide which outside nations to borrow from or associate with or emulate; to conduct its own diplomacy and international relations; and above all, to manage or even mismanage its own affairs. . . . [C]olonialism completely isolated and insulated Africa. . . . It is in this loss of sovereignty and the consequent isolation from the outside world that one finds one of the most pernicious impacts of colonialism on Africa and one of the fundamental causes of its present underdevelopment and technological backwardness.[8]

Further, Adu Boahen explained how colonialists intentionally delayed Africa's industrial and technological development, destroyed the traditional diversity of agricultural cash crops by demanding a single-crop economy for each colonial country, and eradicated preexisting industries by increasing the importation of cheap goods in their stead.[9] Thus he writes, "During the colonial period, Africans were encouraged to produce what they did not consume and to consume what they did not produce, a clear proof of the exploitative nature of the colonial political economy."[10]

Now, whenever African American scholars study the impact of colonialism on African and Caribbean societies, they readily observe that racial discrimination and segregation in the United States has had many effects similar to colonial occupation. As under colonialism, the ghettoization of African Americans in large urban centers has denied them equal access to the necessary resources for fair competition in the marketplace, which, by every social measurement, severely hindered their development for many generations. Thus, since African peoples have shared the common historic experience of oppression in one form or another, much common ground exists for moral discourse about these and related matters.

The ubiquitous presence of religion among African peoples is abundantly evident.[11] In its many diverse forms, religion constitutes their primary spiritual source of strength for survival, hope, and self-respect. Most important, whenever religious practices are under the control of African peoples, observers easily discern a holistic worldview that includes all dimensions of life. Thus, along with everything else, poverty among African peoples is quintessentially a religious concern.

The general purpose of this study was to develop a common moral discourse by studying religion and poverty through the multiple lenses of our respective academic disciplines.[12] Further, our group embraced a Pan-African consciousness similar to the one devised more than a century ago by various scholars and leaders from Africa, the West Indies, and the United States.[13] As those early Pan-Africanists eagerly nurtured and promoted African unity in their common quest for political independence from European colonialism, so we also share a common desire to eradicate poverty among African peoples everywhere. Acknowledging many differing understandings of an African consciousness, we share with other Pan-Africanists the desire for deeper and more expansive unity among African peoples while preserving their rich cultural diversity. Since the curricula of theological schools and religion departments lack a Pan-African awareness, we offer this book as a much-needed resource for teachers and administrators in schools, colleges, and religious institutions on the African continent and throughout the diaspora.

Methodology

Our group of sixteen scholars from Nigeria, Togo, Ghana, Kenya, Tanzania, South Africa, Jamaica, Canada, and the United States met with numerous well-informed specialists from universities, government, religious institutions, and nongovernmental organizations in each location for extensive fact-gathering and much intensive conversation. We also visited numerous programs in the respective regions to observe the various ways in which religious groups were responding to poverty and its consequences, the most prominent being unemployment, lack of access to education, the pandemic of HIV/AIDS, homeless orphaned children, and high infant mortality rates.

Admittedly, the difficulties of multicultural communication appear whenever Africans in the diaspora and on the continent come together. More often than not there is very little or no common ground among them. Usually, each strives to pull the other into his/her cultural orbit. Though such activity reveals a hospitable spirit, it alone is not a sufficient means for meaningful dialogue because the learning process is invariably one-sided. Clearly, the quest for unity among African peoples requires mutual understanding, which can be achieved only by respecting their diversity and relying less and less on the notion of common ancestral descent based on race or place of origin.

Apart from the negative experiences of oppression and poverty, what positive values do African peoples have in common? Elsewhere, I have explored that question in considerable depth by identifying and describing the basic moral and religious values widely shared by African peoples:[14] values that were not obliterated by the horrific experiences of slavery, colonialism, or racial oppression under the doctrine of white supremacy. Rather, I argued that the moral virtues shared by African peoples arise from their common understandings of the interrelatedness of God, community, family, and personhood.[15]

This particular inquiry about religion and poverty was rooted in the awareness that the cultural diversity of African peoples requires academic scholars to develop communities of discourse for mutual understanding and practical action. Thus, the format of this study was modeled after a program that has been well tested over the past half century, namely, Operation Crossroads Africa.[16]

Since scholars work best when they have the freedom to develop their work in accordance with their own perspectives, it was agreed from the beginning that the participants would have maximum freedom in writing their essays for this book. The editor's task would be that of bringing unity out of the diversity without sacrificing the latter. Thus, we sought to achieve with the essays what we try to do in our various disciplines of theological and religious studies: explore our subject matter through diverse perspectives. It should be noted, however, that all participants read one another's works-in-progress each year for the purpose of mutual encouragement, critical assessment, and common discourse.

In retrospect it was a good decision for the group to begin its travel and study in Ghana, formerly called the Gold Coast. That country not only has the distinction of being the first African nation to gain its independence from colonialism in 1957 but it is presently the site of two world heritage monuments, at Elmina and Cape Coast, which we visited. Built by the Portuguese and Swedes respectively in the fifteenth and seventeenth centuries, these monuments are massive castles, which for centuries constituted centers of European trade in gold and slaves. It is certainly fair to say that no part of our travels had a greater impact on the group than entering those castles and walking down into their dark, damp dungeons, where tens of thousands of slaves were warehoused while waiting for ships to carry them to a strange land where they would be permanently enslaved. Those fortresses stand today as vivid reminders of insatiable economic greed, unbelievable human suffering, and the complicity of Europeans, Americans, and Africans in the transatlantic slave trade.

Thus, part 1 of this book rightly begins with Katie Cannon, arguing that the deep roots of poverty lie in the slave trade. Barbara Bailey then demonstrates that the greatest impact of poverty is suffered by women and children.

Since poverty is both global and local, part 2 of this book analyzes the global challenges and local responses to poverty. Accordingly, Takatso Mofokeng carefully examines the nature of the so-called informal economy as an institutionalized local response, and Lewin Williams undertakes a theological analysis of the contemporary phenomenon of globalization.

Everywhere we went, we were concerned about the eradication of poverty. Thus, part 3 of this book presents analyses of four liberating strategies drawn from traditional religions, rituals of worship, biblical hermeneutics, and processes of decolonizing the mind. First, Elizabeth Amoah explains how poverty is understood in traditional African religions. Second, Linda Thomas and Dwight Hopkins demonstrate how religious rituals have the capacity to empower the poor. Third, Madipoane Masenya discusses her own *bosadi* method as a liberating hermeneutic for women reading the Bible in a patriarchal society. Finally, Nyambura Njoroge argues that the decolonization of the African mind requires the combined endeavors and insights of religionists, governmental policy makers, and literary writers in pursuit of genuine social transformation.

Further, our group was well aware of the ambiguities attending religion in general and Christianity in particular. Thus, part 4 comprises three analyses of the ambiguous dimensions of religion and its relation to poverty. First, Kossi Ayedze argues that since Christianity has often upheld poverty as a virtue, African Christians must now develop new understandings of the relation of wealth and poverty. Second, Esther Mombo argues that since the various programs for the alleviation of poverty in Africa are simplistic and ineffective, the true solution must come from Africans working cooperatively among themselves and with others. Third, Anthony Pinn argues that while poverty devalues the body and the various aesthetic acts of worship and celebration enhance it, religion in itself does not have sufficient power to eradicate poverty.

Part 5 of this book analyzes four theories for combating poverty that are deeply rooted in the cultural and political histories of African peoples. Laurenti Magesa critically evaluates the Tanzanian philosophy of ujamaa; Noel Erskine assesses the historical dialogical relations among African peoples in the Caribbean, the Americas, and Africa; Simeon Ilesanmi compares and contrasts civil and political rights on the one hand and developmental rights on the other; and Peter Paris argues for the primacy of the principle of self-initiation for all liberating struggles among African peoples, including that of poverty.

Now, let us look at each of the essays in a little more depth.

The Roots and Impact of Poverty

Clearly, no discussion of contemporary poverty in Africa can ignore the continuing impact of the horrific societal trauma of slavery on African peoples both on the continent and throughout the diaspora. Thus, part 1 of this book, "The Roots and Impact of Poverty," rightly begins by looking at the connection between poverty and slavery.

The opening essay, by the African American ethicist Katie Cannon, is entitled "An Ethical Mapping of the Transatlantic Slave Trade," a trade that she views as the originating cause of contemporary African poverty. She begins by discussing the way by which the fifteenth-century designation of Ghana as the Gold Coast lost currency when trade shifted in the seventeenth century from the exportation of products to the infamous buying and selling of human beings; Ghana then became known as the Slave Coast. Both enterprises deprived Africa of its wealth in both material and human resources. Most important, she outlines the process by which the European demand for slaves was accommodated by the African suppliers. Thus, those on both sides of that horrendous enterprise disrupted and corrupted the religious and moral fabric of traditional African societies to such an extent that it has had an enduring deleterious effect on their economies and social systems up to the present day.

A similar probing inquiry is seen in the essay by the gender analyst Barbara Bailey of Jamaica, "Feminization of Poverty across Pan-African Societies: The Church's Response—Alleviative or Emancipatory?" In defining poverty as material deprivation, social exclusion, and human degradation, she claims that its greatest toll is on women and children. She also observes that while most ecumenical initiatives tend to comprise strategies for reform, those at the local level are usually tactical responses to the immediate needs of ordinary people. She also discusses the plight of women and children, the HIV/AIDS pandemic, and some of the important changes in the United Nations Development Program. With strong criticisms leveled against the rate of globalization processes, she challenges theological seminaries to include gender studies in their curricula as a necessary part of ministerial formation and the quest for economic justice for both women and children.

Challenges of the Global and Informal Economies

Throughout our travels and study, we encountered in both Africa and the Caribbean abundant signs of two major economic realities, namely, processes of globalization on the one hand and informal market economies on the other. Two members of our group had a deep interest in those topics and wrote essays on them that have been grouped together in part 2 of this book. It should be noted, however, that virtually no one in our group, and only one of our numerous informants, had anything positive to say about the processes of globalization, largely because of the crippling conditions imposed on Africans by the loan programs of the World Bank and the International Monetary Fund.

In his essay "The Informal Economy and the Religion of Global Capital," the South African ethicist Takatso Mofokeng argues that the so-called informal economy was created by the poor throughout Africa and the Caribbean as a means of survival. Noting that traditional religious practices both resist and accommodate external intrusion and domination, he discusses how the processes of globalization strive to co-opt this local economy for their own purposes. Further, Mofokeng discusses this peculiar market's social organization, religious ideology, style of management, types of enterprises, and current means of promoting itself through music, song, dance, and language.

The Jamaican theologian Lewin Williams, in whose memory this book is dedicated and who passed away before its publication, entitled his essay "A Theological Perspective on the Effects of Globalization on Poverty in Pan-African Contexts." In his endeavor to see a positive relationship between the contemporary terms "globalization" and "global village" on the one hand, and the traditional Christian understanding of *koinonia* on the other hand, he carefully demonstrates how certain economic practices of globalization often result in divisions and impoverishment. In a constructive way, he discusses how koinonia could become a remedial factor if allowed to function as a normative theological principle in the Caribbean, where a dialogue has been in process between the Caribbean Community (CARICOM) and the Caribbean Council of Churches. He concludes that such a dialogue could constitute a necessary condition for the efficacy of a koinonia approach.

Religious Strategies for Liberating the Poor

Throughout our study it was assumed that all peoples respond to oppression in dialectical forms of adaptation and resistance. In our endeavor to discover how religion relates to such responses, we discerned various cultural factors that contained both debilitating and liberating potentialities. These included (a) the conflict between Western and African worldviews; (b) the pervasive nature of patriarchy and the gradual change in women's consciousness; (c) religious rituals as empowering resources; and (d) contemporary agencies for social transformation. The four essays addressing these concerns are presented in part 3 of this volume.

In her essay "African Traditional Religion and the Concept of Poverty," the Ghanaian religionist Elizabeth Amoah argues that poverty is a very complex subject in traditional African cultures because their holistic worldviews unite the material and spiritual dimensions of life, thus rendering everything sacred in some sense. Most important, since human well-being constitutes the subject matter of traditional African religions, poverty represents its antithesis. Thus the causes of poverty can only be combated by utilizing peculiar codes and rituals that undermine their efficacy. Amoah claims that traditional African proverbs comprise the locus for such practices. She concludes by calling upon Africans to look to their religious traditions for effective antidotes capable of restoring wholeness by delivering African peoples from the seductive powers of Western individualism and materialism.

In their jointly written essay "Religion and Poverty: Ritual and Empowerment in Africa and the African Diaspora," the African American theologians Linda Thomas and Dwight Hopkins discuss the findings of their comparative ethnographical studies of selected rituals in South Africa, Jamaica, and Chicago. Their study demonstrates that despite social fragmentation, political dislocation, and economic disparity, the poor are strengthened psychologically and spiritually by the various rituals of water, touching, music, dance, and song. Contrary to the disrespect accorded African beliefs by most Western philosophies, Thomas and Hopkins argue that African Christianity unites the material and spiritual realms of life, as evidenced in the Zionist, Apostolic, and Aladura churches in Africa, the Rastafarians in Jamaica, and the nascent Afrocentric churches in the United States and elsewhere.

The South African biblical scholar Madipoane Masenya argues in her essay "The Bible and Poverty in African Pentecostal Christianity: The *Bosadi* (Womanhood) Approach" that although the Bible is enormously important among women in her Pentecostal tradition, it does not help them overcome structures of domination either in the Bible or in their own lives. Thus, she constructs her own approach to Bible reading, which she calls the bosadi method. It helps women become aware of patriarchal domination present both in the Bible and in their own lives. Using the book of Ruth as an example, she illustrates how the women in the text accommodated themselves to the dominant cultural forces of gender, class, and ethnicity. In light of Jesus' actions of affirming and empowering women, her bosadi approach helps them discover how to emancipate their own consciousness while reading texts that are deeply rooted in patriarchal constraints similar to those in their own contexts.

Similarly, in her essay "The Struggle for Full Humanity in Poverty-Stricken Kenya," Nyambura Njoroge, ethicist and longtime staff member of the World Council of Churches, calls upon the Kenyan government, religious scholars, and the churches to become advocates for social justice and human dignity by developing a consciousness that is void of all vestiges of domination and control. She challenges her readers to assume a new appreciation for the historic freedom struggle in Kenya as seen in the Mau Mau freedom fighters of the last century and the contemporary literary writings of people like Ngugi wa Thiong'o. In short, Njoroge challenges all Kenyan leaders and especially educators to help decolonize African minds and work for constructive social transformation through interdisciplinary, holistic methods of teaching, research, and writing. She concludes that Kenyans themselves must become the primary agents in delivering the nation from poverty.

The Ambiguous Relation of Religion and Poverty

It did not take long for our group to see that religion is not a simple phenomenon. Rather, in all of its many forms, it is both diverse and complex. This is true of Islam, traditional African religions, Rastafarianism, and Christianity. For example, the diversity of Christianity is manifested in its denominational structures, cultural variations, and theological and ethical understandings. Relative to our inquiry, however, the complexity of Christianity is seen in its ambiguous relation to poverty.

In his essay entitled "Poverty among African People and the Ambiguous Role of Christian Thought," the church historian Kossi Ayedze from the Republic of Togo argues that Christian beliefs may lead to either improving or diminishing the lives of their adherents. This is vividly seen in the improved economies of Christian colonialists on the one hand and the oppression of Africans on the other hand. Ironically, however, Ayedze points out that while many colonial Christians accumulated much wealth for themselves, many Christian missionaries in Africa viewed poverty as a moral virtue. Unfortunately, many African Christians embraced that teaching, which, he contends, has helped slow down Africa's economic growth. Ayedze does counter such teachings, however, by appealing to such major Christian theologians as Saint Augustine and John Calvin, who did not condemn wealth as such but, rather, criticized its means of acquisition and the purposes it served. Thus, he concludes that African Christians should rethink their views on wealth and poverty as a first step in the process of eradicating poverty from Africa and throughout the world.

In her essay "Religion and Materiality: The Case of Poverty Alleviation," the Kenyan church historian Esther Mombo views reparations, debt relief, and fair trade as ineffective and simplistic solutions to the problem of poverty. Similarly, she criticizes the teachings of the so-called prosperity gospel and the charitable services of many churches as inadequate means for alleviating poverty. Instead, Mombo argues that the eradication of poverty lies in long-term strategies and cooperative interdisciplinary work with economics, science, and ethics. Though some Africans benefited economically from the colonial and missionary enterprises, Mombo claims that most did not. In fact, many corrupt rulers helped expand poverty after independence.

Thus, she applauds the efforts of churches and nonprofit organizations in striving to alleviate poverty through education, the self-employment system called jua kali, as well as various programs in health care, agriculture, animal husbandry, and social services. Following a detailed discussion of various debt relief programs, she concludes that since the problem of poverty is structural, the primary agents for its eradication must be Africans themselves, working cooperatively with others committed to that pursuit.

The African American religious studies scholar Anthony Pinn argues in his essay "Warm Bodies, Cold Currency: A Study of Religion's Response to Poverty" that there is a strong negative correlation between religion and economic poverty. He claims that even though the bodies of the poor are attacked by the conditions of poverty due to health issues and poor health delivery services, the aesthetic acts of worship, celebration, bodily purification, and spirit possession among the poor enhance rather than diminish the body. Moreover, he argues that when possessed by the divine, the bodies of the poor are infused with great value as compared with poverty's devaluation of the body. Yet, he concludes, religion as such does not have sufficient power to eradicate poverty.

Practical Theories for Combating Poverty

Our travel and observation also taught us that just as there are many theories about the causes of poverty, so too are there many understandings of how to combat it. Four such theories are the Tanzanian concept of ujamaa, the Caribbean spirit of resistance, the human rights tradition, and various self-initiated practices. Each is discussed in part 5 of this book.

In his essay "Nyerere on Ujamaa and Christianity as Transforming Forces in Society," Laurenti Magesa, a Roman Catholic Tanzanian theologian and priest, analyzes the theory of social change called ujamaa, which is an African philosophy of community that gained worldwide visibility under the leadership of Julius Nyerere, the first president of the United Republic of Tanzania, 1962–1982, and a devout Catholic. Magesa sees a close relationship between the ujamaa philosophy and the social teaching of the Roman Catholic Church. Accordingly, Magesa argues that Nyerere's legacy to the world is his conviction that Christianity and ujamaa are compatible because both hold that poverty dehumanizes people, who are made in the image of God and hence should be treated with dignity and respect. Magesa demonstrates how this view of humanity provides normative criteria for condemning the policies of the World Bank and the International Monetary Fund. After discussing the contours of the great class divide in Tanzania and elsewhere, he claims that Nyerere's policies failed because of the strident opposition to ujamaa by the economic and religious powers of his day. Magesa concludes that, like Christianity, ujamaa requires a conversation of the mind and the heart to desire human unity and equality among all peoples.

In his essay "Caribbean Issues: The Caribbean and African American Churches' Response," the Jamaican American theologian Noel Erskine compares and analyzes the cultures of resistance among African Americans and Jamaicans, both of whom endured centuries of enslavement and many other forms of oppression. They interacted with one another a great deal from the early nineteenth century onward, so their struggles became intertwined. He also discusses three important ventures: (a) the 1992 Caribbean/African American dialogue (CAAD), which identified three problems facing Caribbeans: racism, cultural identity, and the lack of democratic procedures in economic trade; (b) several consultations of African Caribbeans and African Americans in Cuba between 1984 and 1990 focusing on the work of the Pastor for Peace organization; and (c) the need for a revitalization of emancipatory partnerships between their respective churches.

In his essay "Africa's Poverty, Human Rights, and a Just Society," the Nigerian Christian ethicist and lawyer Simeon Ilesanmi argues that the protection of fundamental human rights is a necessary condition in all attempts to address poverty in Africa. Accordingly, he discusses the 1981 Banjul Charter adopted by the African heads of state, who affirmed the view that civil and political rights imply social, economic, and cultural rights. Subsequent to the adoption of that charter, "development rights" became Africa's contribution to the world's discourse on human rights. Following a discussion of Africa's extensive debt crisis, Ilesanmi's argument has three parts: the primacy of social and economic rights over civil and political rights, three objections to social and economic development rights, and the primacy of civil and political rights over development rights.

The volume closes with my essay "Self-Initiation: A Necessary Principle in the African Struggle to Abolish Poverty." Written from the position of an African Canadian–American social ethicist, it discusses the principle of self-initiation that has motivated all historic African struggles against oppression, including the independence movements in Africa, abolitionism, and the civil rights struggle in America. I conclude that since every significant gain in those struggles originated with the self-initiatives of African peoples, the eventual eradication of poverty among African peoples will be no exception.

Findings

The most important finding of this study was the discovery of much evidence to support the primary assumption underlying this project, namely, that African peoples share common concerns about the relation of religion and poverty in spite of the diversity of languages, regions, ethnicities, and theologies. Thus, we conclude that much common ground exists for continuing moral discourse and cooperative action on this crucial issue.

Second, the group's observations and discussions revealed that there are differences between Western and African understandings of poverty. The latter do not define poverty solely as a lack of material resources. In fact, many Africans who possess very little money or property do not consider themselves poor. Rather, they view alienation from families, friends, and communities as the state of true poverty, the intensity of which is increased by the lack of religious faith. Consequently, those who live in a family that is related to a larger community often do not think of themselves as being poor in spite of their lack of material resources.

Thus, it is amazing to see countless numbers of people working zealously and even joyfully in the midst of the densely populated squatter camps that are commonplace in so many African cities. It would be difficult for many outsiders to imagine the experience of living in such small, corrugated-iron-roofed dwellings, sharing communal latrines alongside public water pumps and open sewers, with children playing in stagnant pools of dirty water. Yet, in spite of the high infant mortality rate, the constant threat of disease, sickness, and death, the normal processes of living are sustained. One sees everywhere the hustle and bustle of countless numbers of people daily striving to eke out a living. Uniformed schoolchildren jostle one another in their daily walks from school as they happily hasten to their respective homes to assume their shared responsibilities of necessary work to sustain the family's life. Thus, many African people appear to be strengthened and even inspired by the habitual activities of their familial and communal life. They seem hopeful for a better day. Despondency and depression are overcome by the communal spirit of belonging, which fosters the virtues of compassion, sharing, and mutual respect for one another.

Clearly, the countless number of orphaned children on the streets of many African cities is a horrendous reality for all who have eyes to see. Separated from families and communities by the ravages of war and HIV/AIDS, a generation of children is growing up on city streets where they will never have known the loving care and protection of either natural or surrogate families. These are truly poor by African standards. Such a combination of material, familial, and spiritual impoverishment in the lives of tens of thousands of vulnerable children more often than not results in sexual abuse, forced conscription into military service, petty theft, drug dealing, prostitution, and even modern-day slavery.

A third finding of this study was the discovery that very few of the many and varied responses to poverty by either churches or community organizations had any strong advocacy program for social and economic justice. Rather, most responses attempted to provide various types of emergency services to the people in need. While those services are extremely important short-term prescriptions, they fail to address the basic causes of poverty and, hence, cannot in any way be long-term solutions. The lack of public criticism and advocacy may be due in large part to the slow development of democratic practices among the citizenry at large.

Though they are relatively few in number, we found that certain educational programs on HIV/AIDS led by young people appeared to be both creative and effective strategies for learning. Other creative programs are very much needed for addressing the root causes of poverty. For example, much advocacy is needed to help local business cooperatives to receive the support they need from government subsidies and loans. Some churches and other organizations have modeled this strategy by providing small loans to market women for the purpose of increasing their inventories and gradually empowering the recipients.

In conclusion, we join with numerous others in grieving the immense injustices that have been heaped on African peoples worldwide through the insatiable greed of their oppressors both within and without who enslaved, colonized, segregated, and abused African peoples for countless generations and thus contributed greatly to their present condition. Yet we celebrate the resilient African spirit that has often been broken but not destroyed.

Notes

1. A definition of HDI is given in the section "Poverty Overview" on the Thinkquest Web site, "A Dollar a Day: Finding Solutions to Poverty," at http://library.thinkquest .org/05aug/00282/over_measure2.htm.

2. Scholars agree that the causes of poverty in Africa are deeply rooted in the history of slavery, colonialism, widespread corruption, despotic political regimes, civil wars, and a lack of adequate infrastructure needed to inspire investment.

3. For data from the U.N. Human Development Index of 2003 see the following link: http://www.nationmaster.com/graph/eco_hum_dev_ind-economy-human-development-index.

4. See the report from the National Poverty Center of the University of Michigan's

Gerald Ford School of Public Policy at http://www.npc.umich.edu/poverty, taken from the United States Bureau of the Census in 2003.

5. See this millennium report of the secretary-general at http://www.un.org/millennium/sg/report.

6. See the Millennium Declaration at http://www.un.org/en/development/devagenda/millennium.shtml.

7. See Jeffrey Sachs, *The End of Poverty: Economic Possibilities for Our Time* (New York: Penguin Press, 2005). See comments on book cover.

8. A. Adu Boahen, *African Perspectives on Colonialism* (Baltimore: Johns Hopkins University Press, 1990), 99–100.

9. Ibid., 101.

10. Ibid., 102.

11. One limiting element in this seminar largely comprising Christian scholars was the absence of representatives from Islamic and traditional African religious traditions. Yet each of our seminars was addressed by scholars from those traditions. One member of our group was a scholar of traditional African religions. Also, since Africa now contains the largest concentration of Christians in the world, the broad ecumenical composition of our group (i.e., Baptist, Presbyterian, United Church of Christ, Pentecostal, Anglican, Roman Catholic, the Reformed Church in South Africa) enabled good interactions with our conversational partners.

12. With a couple of exceptions, each member of the study group is a specialist in theological and religious studies: the Bible, theology, ethics, history. The two exceptions are, respectively, specialists in gender studies and traditional African religions.

13. Some of the progenitors of that movement whose names have been immortalized in that quest were Kwame Nkrumah (Ghana), Nnamdi Azikiwe (Nigeria), Edward Blyden (Jamaica and Liberia), Jomo Kenyatta (Kenya), Leopold Senghor (Senegal), W. E. B. Du Bois and Rayford Logan (both from the United States), and George Padmore, H. Sylvester Williams, and C. L. R. James (all three from the West Indies), to mention only a few.

14. Peter J. Paris, *The Spirituality of African Peoples: The Search for a Common Moral Discourse* (Minneapolis: Augsburg Fortress, 1995).

15. Those virtues are beneficence, forbearance, practical wisdom, improvisation, forgiveness, and justice. For a full treatment of these virtues see Peter J. Paris, *Virtues and Values: The African and African American Experience* (Minneapolis: Augsburg Fortress Press, 2004).

16. Operation Crossroads Africa was founded in 1958 by the Reverend Dr. James Robinson, the distinguished African American pastor of Morningside Heights Presbyterian Church in New York. It continues to be a thriving program of bringing together international groups to live and work together on a common project, the realization of which makes a difference in the lives of others as well as one's own life.

THE ROOTS AND IMPACT OF POVERTY

| AN ETHICAL MAPPING OF

THE TRANSATLANTIC SLAVE TRADE

In this essay, I look at the religious, economic, and moral issues concerning West Africa's participation in the buying and selling of other Africans to work as slaves in the economies of the New World.[1] Most scholars who study the transatlantic slave trade talk about quantitative numbers and business transactions without any mention of the ethical complexities that characterize the quality of African life that was lost during four hundred years of slavery. Due to the slave trade, all kinds of divisions were taking place. One of the most basic was the gradual disestablishment of the transference of skills when the traditional exchange of mutual obligations between the elders and youth was disrupted, which in turn drained the profitability and energy of particular African industries. It is a central component of my argument that Ghana's descent from being the Gold Coast to becoming the Slave Coast is a foundational paradigm for exploring the multiple connections between religion and poverty in Africa and the African diaspora.

I will draw extensively on a lecture, "The Slave Trade and Its Continuing Impact on Ghana," by Dr. Akosia Makola (a pseudonym), in which she tells the story of Ghana's willingness to profit from the capture of massive numbers of women, men, and children who were sold as chattel property. A professionally trained historian, Dr. Makola begins her lecture with the following observation: "Ghana's participation in the transatlantic slave trade (1520–1860) is not a topic for tea."[2] She describes how she is often greeted with fear and hostility for challenging African politicians and journalists, who find it financially lucrative to jump on the more typical slave-export bandwagon. Most investigators of slavery in the Americas are familiar with enslavers who were Portuguese, Spanish, Dutch, French, and British, but Makola's claim of Ghana's willingness to sell other Africans as slaves almost always earns her harsh criticism.[3] She asserts, "As a person I am always in trouble with myself, because I must weigh how I present the facts so that I don't get in trouble with my people, and at the same time, I wrestle with presenting the materials so that I don't fall out with historians who will write me off as a charlatan."

The constant critique of her work creates this never-ending dilemma because, as a historian, she is compelled to present careful research and close reading of primary sources regarding the Ghanaian slave trade; and at the same time she is, as she notes, pitted against politicians and journalists who receive some gain for discussing Africans as enslavers, but who are easily forgiven for misleading impressions, half-truths, and unsubstantiated comments because they are not expected to have access to all the historical data. But we, the general public, consider historians obligated to present a systematic treatment of the information on record.

In order to explain the original texts of a wide variety of documents, Makola learned Danish and other languages. Aware of both the possibilities and pitfalls of this type of interpretative methodology, she then cross-checks the historical data in the Danish texts against British records and multiple Ghanaian rituals, festivals, and traditions. She pieces together a huge puzzle of Ghana's social history during the slave trade by drawing on correspondence between slave traders in the noble households of Europe, studying mundane details recorded in business transactions, especially bills of sale, culling legal petitions, and evaluating epigraphic evidence. She says, "When I was young, I used to travel to Denmark and read letters about slavery. And, I would come out of the archives so depressed with the materials I was reading. Imagine that you are twenty-one or twenty-two years old, and you are reading letters that were not meant for your eyes. The letters were written from European heads of state and sent to other European leaders, so they could really let themselves go. They used all kinds of foul language describing what they really thought about us."[4]

Makola then interpolates these written texts with philosophical wisdom from the Ghanaian oral tradition. Invoking a Ghanaian proverb as an organizing principle in this scholarly endeavor, she argues persuasively that suffering exists on both sides of the Atlantic Ocean: "My child is dead and you are calling me a witch." "It was a heart-wrenching loss of African sisters, brothers, fathers, mothers, and children. How sad it was for numerous loving relatives left behind. There is suffering on both sides of the ocean. So, if my child is dead, why are you accusing me of witchcraft? Unless you can unravel history and clearly delineate all of the culprits and all of the victims, then you may end up accusing the wrong person for the crime of slavery."

Especially given the growing demand by African Americans for reparation,[5] payment for the grievous crimes committed against black people and the incalculable damage they have suffered and continue to suffer as a result of nearly 250 years of chattel slavery and one hundred years of legalized racial discrimination, Makola maintains that the pressure is increasing for Africans to admit that they sold their own people into slavery. "Africans in the Diaspora should never think that your parents sold you into slavery. Someone stronger than your parents enslaved Africans. We may be of the same color, but African raiders and traders did not think of themselves as Black against Black selling their own." They thought of themselves as Abos people in the Cameroon; Conia people in Senegal; Kabiye people in Togoland; Gango and Mandingo people in Sierra Leone; Ibos, Nagaas, and Yoruba people in Nigeria; Pombo people in the Congo; Akan, Coromatin, Ashanti, and Wassa people in the Gold Coast. Anyone outside one's own people group was considered the enemy, fair game in procuring captives for the slave trade.

Whatever side of the reparation dispute one is on, or even if one is not invested on either side of the debt that America owes to Africans and African Americans, Ghana's participation in the transatlantic slave trade is worth paying attention to because the trafficking of millions of Africans to the Americas is one of the most dynamic influences in the life of the country, challenging both age-old religious customs and socioeconomic-ethical systems.

Age-Old Religious Topography

One of the most significant keys to mapping the transatlantic slave trade is the role of religion. The first things to note are religiously based initiatives on the part of European leaders. During this historical period the feudal states of European countries were beginning to unite and major religious wars were being fought between Christians and Muslims, especially Moors.

Religion was also key in motivating Prince Henry, later called "the Navigator" (1394–1460), governor of the Algarve and administrator of the Order of Christ, to send men from Portugal down the west coast of Africa in search of the limits to the Muslim world, in order to halt the Islamization of West Africa. Some of the Portuguese Christians who traveled to Ghana in the fifteenth century were trying to find the legendary Christian empire of the fabled priest-king Prester John. Legends of Prester John's devout Christian-ruled kingdom, which was strategically placed in Ethiopia to ward off Islamic influence, began to circulate in twelfth-century Europe. His persona, along with the image of Ethiopia as an awe-inspiring, much desired ally that was both peaceful and united, and inhabited by exotic animals and people, combined to create an image of Ethiopia that caught the minds of Europeans and prompted them to covet African resources.[6]

Religion did not motivate only the Europeans. It is also a key to understanding what was happening in Ghana during the era of the slave trade. The Ghanaian people are intimately influenced by traditional African religion and bound to ethical principles inherent in rituals, festivals, and oracle traditions that permeate the culture. It is not an exaggeration to say that West African oracles about spirit shrines represent specific beliefs. Spirit shrines were places where worshippers made prayerful requests for health, engaged in rituals of purification, mediated disputes, and greeted shrine spirits important to one's own household. For these reasons, shrine space was known as a sacred free zone. If women, men, and children captured in raids, marching in coffle caravans to the slave marketing centers on the coast, ran away to spirit shrines, they were declared free.

Admittedly, in order to make the point that the moral fabric was weakening, let us look at how religious shrines lost their significance due to the slave trade. According to old rules, traditional loyalty and customs, once targeted captives managed to reach the sacred ground of a spirit shrine, they could no longer be pursued as booty. This greatly handicapped slave-trading operations. The fact that slave raiders and trackers could not seize runaways once they reached the shrines converted shrines into havens of refuge. Slaves who became runaways, seeking sanctuary and security at the religious shrines, ended up in a lifetime of servitude to the priests and elders. They exchanged one form of slavery for another that was safer and supposedly more salvific.

Eventually, with the shift from small-scale mercantilist endeavors to large-scale ones, private traders of Europe, along with their armed African kidnappers who profited from the slave trade, realized that too many of the captured people were running away, seeking protection at spirit shrines, so the slave-raiding forces violently and brutally attacked the shrines. Driven by the motivation of profit, the raiders and trackers saw nothing reprehensible in violating sacred asylum space.

Makola argues that the breakdown of interpersonal relationships is of major importance. Families were broken apart. "The numbers of Africans who were enslaved, you can find in lots of books. Some people are saying at least ten million Africans were enslaved. Others say forty million. I haven't mentioned a lot about the depopulation of Africa because you can find those facts elsewhere. However, there is still too little evidence for what I am interested in, not the quantity of people enslaved, but the quality of life that was lost."[7] Cooperation and reciprocity between neighboring states could no longer be taken for granted. Fear mounted between coastal people and people inland that created a dependency upon the Europeans for military protection in the castles and forts. That families were divided and hostility developed between neighbor states is scarcely a new or startling point, and will probably seem obvious to any one who studies slave societies, but what has often been overlooked by the traditionalist leanings of many scholars is how the slave trade perverted Ghana's religious principles and ethical practices.

In an illuminating translation by Makola of a document published in Denmark in 1750, there is much talk about the erosion of moral values in Ghana. "Our people could not read and write, but fortunately, in 1738 a Ghanaian man on the coast gave this opinion to one of the European officers, and this is what he recorded":

> It is you, you whites they say, who have brought all of this evil among us. Would we have sold each other, if you had not come to us as buyers?
>
> The desire we have for your enticing goods and brandy has brought distrust between brothers and friends. So, alcohol has been a great enemy of mankind, since time immemorial—yes, even between father and son.[8]
>
> From our fathers, we knew in the past that anyone guilty of malpractice, who had committed murder twice, was stoned or drowned. Otherwise, the punishment for ordinary misdeeds was that the culprit should carry to the offended party's hut or house a big log of firewood for two or three consecutive days and beg him for forgiveness on his knees.
>
> We used to know thousands of families here and there on the coast in our youth. But now, we can hardly count a hundred individuals. That's depopulation. And the worst part is that you have become a necessary evil among us. For if you were to leave now, the Blacks up-country would allow us to live for a half-of-a-year, and then they would come and kill us, with our wives and children. And they bear this hatred because of you.

A disastrous consequence of the slave trade, and its corollary of slave raids, was a major shift of emphasis from forgiveness to punishment.[9] The spirit of reconciliation, which had been a cardinal principle in traditional communal relationships, was replaced with seriously aggravated vindictiveness. Even though the power brokers in the transatlantic slave trade neglected some regions of Ghana in favor of other, more productive ones, no part of the country remained untouched.

Another religion-related point that emerges from Makola's study is the fact that although African religion supposedly did not affect the lives of Europeans, when the Europeans got sick, the Africans took care of them.

Local African healers used their accumulated plant knowledge of millennia to cure all types of ailments, including those of Europeans.[10] Records show numerous transactions of Europeans paying African priests and medicine men for services rendered. Some of the best-known evidence for this is the numerous African talismans, charms, and amulets found hidden under the beds of European governors upon their death.[11] The factual dynamics and their practical implications can be assessed in this way: "The African belief system directly impacted the Europeans. However, the Europeans wouldn't dare come out openly and say so, because they were busy saying to the folks back home that the Africans were sub-species in order to justify slavery. Even when you read books about how Africans were primitive, barbaric, etc., you cannot say accurately, nor correctly accuse the Africans of not knowing God" (Makola).

The historian Barry Boubacar has noted that, "beginning in the second half of the seventeenth century, the development of sugar cane, cotton, and tobacco plantations in the New World led to an expansion of the slave trade. So from the eighteenth century to the first half of the nineteenth, slave trading became the center of Europe's trade with Africa. . . . In this slaving era, the continent of Africa went through one of the most massive processes of human transportation ever to have taken place by sea."[12] With the increase of external demand for wealth, more and more Africans were taken from Ghana to Spain and Portugal, especially Lisbon and Porto. Interestingly, it became fashionable for "exotic" Africans not only to work on farms, docks, and plantations but also to serve in the courts of the Iberian aristocracy. Perhaps the most remarkable shift in the Mediterranean world, beginning in 1501, is not the striking difference in the physiology of Africans and Euro-peans, but the awareness that African people could be differentiated from others according to their robust stature, hard work, and capacity to endure the chains of toil better than American Indians. Makola points out that it may sound surprising or far-fetched, but it was a reverend priest, Luis Rivera Pagan, who suggested that the Europeans should take Africans as human cargo to do the work in the New World in order to save the Amerindians, who were said to have had neither the numbers, the skills, nor the discipline to provide forced labor.[13]

We know from historical sources that the early Africans who were en-slaved in the Western hemisphere were often delivered in Dutch ships.[14] Dutch imperialists, who dominated the three-hundred-mile stretch of the West African coastline in the sixteenth century, used the same shrewd diplo-macy when they traveled to South Africa in the seventeenth century. In an attempt to understand how European religious authorities dealt with Africans, records indicate that there was a definite sense that being human and being Christian were interchangeable categories, and likewise being Christian and being Dutch. For example, an abundance of ecclesiastical evidence points to a supposed contradiction in the effort to bring the Christian gospel to Africa, since that implied an impossibility: that Africans could be fully human. The argument goes like this: "When Africans become Christians, they become Dutch. Africans cannot be Dutch, so we cannot make them Christian."[15] With few exceptions, the defenders of European Christianity, as aggressive perpetrators of violence, justified their theology of supremacy by describing African people as distinctly inferior to Europeans. African people were considered to be lower beings, with faces like tigers and teeth like swords, cunning man-eaters who supposedly lacked the fully developed capacities common to humanity.

Sociopolitical Economic Cartography

Perhaps not surprisingly, the castles and forts at Elmina and Cape Coast were not originally built for the slave trade. It is more accurate to say that in 1471, the first Europeans, the Portuguese, who landed in this country that is now called Ghana, were trying to find different routes to the Indian Ocean for easier access to the age-old spice trade in the East. Since the overland routes to Asia were blocked by Ottoman Turks, Portuguese mariners hoped to sail around Africa in order to secure some of the trans-Saharan trade in gold, ivory, pepper, gum, animal hides, dyewood, palm oil, and ostrich feathers. The Portuguese discovered that there was so much gold easily available where they landed that they named the place "Elmina," which means "the mine." At first sight, the whole stretch of coastline from Elmina to Accra was littered with so many gold deposits that the Portuguese called it the "Gold Coast."[16]

As one might guess, Europe was excited about the news of Elmina because with Portugal bringing in more gold, the value of gold coin increased as a medium of exchange. When the Portuguese left Europe on trade expeditions to Africa, the round trip required more than three months. Therefore, it must have seemed economically wise, given the European desire for a constant flow of African-produced goods (especially elephant tusks, grain, and gold), to build convenient depots where they could keep their goods in safe harbors and maintain supplies necessary to refit sailing vessels should their equipment need repair as they traded with African people. So, in 1482, the Portuguese built the first castle and called it Sao Jorge da Mina, Elmina.[17] Makola comments, "Now, if you think that the other European countries are going to sit down and watch Portugal get all the loot, then I am afraid that our interpretation of human nature is quite different. The other Europeans will not allow Portugal to enjoy such a monopoly. So others started coming to West Africa. You had the Dutch, the British, and the Germans coming in, and later the Swedes and Danes arrived. No one is going to sit around and allow Elmina to get all the loot. So, each group wanted its own trading post."

Originally, when the Portuguese built the fort at Elmina the Africans resisted. According to Makola, they said, in effect, "You have been coming here and silently trading with us and we are good friends and allies. We want it to remain that way. But if you come and build and stay permanently with us, we will end up fighting, so we don't want you to come." Up to this point, silent trading from the various outposts entailed leaving a quantity of trade goods at a coastal village, then sailing to the next one, where more goods would be deposited. When the entire cargo was landed, traders retraced their route, picking up whatever had been left in trade at each village. This was the essence of the straightforward African argument against the Europeans as permanent settlers in Africa.

However, over and against this, it became common for trade delegations from the Gold Coast to travel to Holland and invite merchants such as the well-organized and well-funded Dutch West India Trading Company to come and build forts and trading lodges in their states.[18] Many Africans from the interior wanted to have access to European goods such as muskets, gunpowder, and other commodities that the Portuguese were selling in Elmina. This commercial strategy marks a significant turn in Ghana's economy. Between 1612 and 1672 other Ghanaian states invited European trading monopolies such as France's Guinea Company (1651) and Britain's Royal Adventures in Africa (1660) to bring their commodities directly to them, so as to avoid the imposition of the higher prices, tariffs, and tolls that came with goods that had to pass through several hands. It was, after all, cheaper to buy European products in Ghanaian states that had their own secure castles and forts.

The mercantilist tradition of monopoly among the European expansionists was so strong that many Europeans could see no other end than the complete elimination of all commercial competitors, a territorial imperative that required a territorial base.[19] With the presence of the European force, Africans reasoned that they could get provisions at wholesale prices and avoid extortionist sea merchants, who frequently overcharged and substituted unwanted goods. At the same time, the towns that grew up around European trading posts increasingly looked to European supplies of ammunition and political and military support for intrastate problems and interstate warfare.

The matter-of-fact consequences of entrepreneurial, expansionist politics can be summed up in this way: when Europeans build trading depots, they always surround themselves with cannons, so there will always be lots of ammunition if, and when, war breaks out.

While it is true that some African leaders wanted European merchants to become outpost settlers, others did not.[20] So, in order to take a further step in this highly profitable, imperialistic endeavor, these subsidized European businesses did not hesitate at this crucial moment to receive permission from African factions who extended invitations to them. Acting swiftly, they built trading forts and set up their high-caliber, explosive cannon so that all opposition that was not in league and amity with their nation had to cease. Colonel John Biddulp says that such military might was needed by European mariners and adventurers because international arrangements in Europe were not regarded when the equator had been crossed.[21] As Makola points out, "Right from the beginning there were pros and cons regarding these matters. Like anywhere else, when you bring in something new, there will be people fighting against it and people who will accept it. And this is what happened at Elmina. So if you read anywhere that it was all about European imposition, and that the Europeans came and killed African people in order to build the forts, it is not true."

So, how did the mariners of Europe come in? Makola answers that it is important to establish the fact that they came in signing travel and trade agreements with local potentates, the state leaders of Ghana. The Europeans asked for portions of land that lay within reach of the ocean for a certain amount of money, which they paid monthly to the kings. Also, when there were festivals, the Europeans participated and presented the customarily expected gifts as a way of nurturing political friendships that might be of value some day against other dominant powers. The expansion of land for their dominions stimulated the wealth that would be obtained.

One might think that with signed treaties between the Ghanaian kings and the European traders, to arrive and depart without hindrance, that all was well. Not so. According to one scholar: "In the mind of the Europeans, they bought the land and possessed the proper documents to show their purchases. But lingering below the surface in the African mindset is the understanding that no land can be purchased because land belongs to the ancestors, the living, and unborn generations. From the African standpoint, they gave Europeans permission only to build on a designated piece of land, but not to own the coastline itself. This was a serious misunderstanding."[22]

Even more serious was the fact that there were political ramifications for the Africans living under the protection of the various fortified castles that were fighting each other. By the eighteenth century, the whole coast of Ghana was filled with European military posts.[23] So when the Europeans went to war against each other, it meant that the Ghanaian people connected to specific European trading stations also went to war. However, inland, where the Africans did not have much interference and had less fear of the Europeans coming in and dividing them, they were able to build their own states, such as the military empire of Dahomey and the great Ashanti kingdom.[24]

From evidence culled from her miscellaneous fifteenth-century sources, Makola says that Ghana operated an ingenious, first-class fishing industry long before the Portuguese arrived in 1471. The Africans used bark from trees to make fishing nets. Using an inherited compendium of scientifically informed traditions, the fishermen experimented with various trees in order to find the best bark for the most efficient results. Elders shared with younger fishermen their acquired knowledge of physics and chemistry, teaching them how to make different types of bark fiber nets for catching various species of fish.

Africans possessed extensive knowledge about environmental conservation and the ecological management of natural resources. And because they believed wholeheartedly that environmental conservation is tied to cultural survival, the elders created a careful, strategic fishing schedule, according to which they did not fish in particular stretches of the ocean between designated months and within seasonal time periods. At best, the people who were leading, organizing, and governing the society in matters of conservation were also deeply connected to a fundamental aspect of African traditional religion—"When people do not conserve, they will get in trouble with the gods." Time-tested religious sanctions were used in order to govern the people. If these fishermen had been situated in a culture of written literature, instead of living in an oral tradition, Makola says, we would be sitting down and reading books about their understanding of the interplay between earth ethics and political economy, and admiring them as great thinkers of Ghana.

Given what we now know about traditional Ghanaian fishing practices, we must not overlook the significance of the introduction by Europeans of imported sewing needles into Africa. The Europeans found a ready market for these needles among the Africans. The African fishermen shaped the needles into fishing hooks. The Europeans then saw a commercial opportunity in importing and selling ready-made fishing hooks and ready-made string to Ghana, so that the Africans would no longer need to make fishing nets from bark fiber. The recognizable and predictable consequence was that Africans bought imported ready-made hooks and imported ready-made nets, which meant that the Ghanaian fishing industry became more and more dependent upon European traders for its basic necessities. And, when it came time for fathers to pass on their skill of net-making to their sons, the slave traders had looted their villages, stolen the sons, the young, virile, skilled laborers, and, by causing the rapid depletion of industrial knowledge, set in motion the economic destabilization of a people and a region.

A nuanced critical analysis of the historical grounding of the Ghanaian fishing industry might result in the recovery of numerous aspects of African people's indigenous knowledge—science and technology—that had been thought lost forever, including also in the parallel areas of women's work that have been threatened with extinction.

When religious shrines lost their value as sanctuaries and the exercise of commerce became limited to private merchants, raiders moved in and seized and fettered nobles and commoners alike. The fact that African people were considered perishable commodities in a dominating cash market whose supply was always running short meant that queens and kings were herded and shackled together with tribal villagers in pitiable, horrifying, degrading conditions. As one historian documents, "Many fell ill; all had inadequate food. As a precaution against attempts to escape to their home country which was still not very far away, and in the absence of enough chains, slaves were fastened together by strips of raw hide, even those so physically weak that movement was difficult for them."[25] To render a voyage profitable, it was necessary for slave traders to revive captive Africans after the long march from the inland regions to the stretch of markets on the coast. When the shackled human cargo arrived at castles, forts, and dungeons, financial records indicate that local medicine men were retained, in order to make sure that each enslaved African could fetch the best price. According to the commercial structure of the slave trade, if an African person was missing a tooth, the buyer would deduct a certain amount from possible profit. As Makola observes, "on the day of the sale, they would rub Africans with oil so that their skin would shine. The Portuguese wrote descriptions about some buyers being so finicky that they even ran their fingers over the tongues of Africans to make sure that everything was in order. Europeans examined

Africans as if they were purchasing some kind of prize animal." Slave traders wanted to be assured of completing the transatlantic voyage successfully with profitable human merchandise filling the holds of their ships.

"Now if I were looking at the accounts of this period," Makola muses, "and if I didn't know that slave trading was going on, I would assume that this was a period of economic boom for Africa." This assumption is an understandable one, because when we look at the expense accounts we will see enormous expenditures on food and provisions for the governors and staff in the castles and the officers and soldiers in the forts. Makola continues, "If I didn't know that the economy during this time was based on the slave trade, I would have said that for farmers this period was a time of prosperity. When farmers took their corn to the castle, the corn was bought. When fishermen took their fish, their fish were purchased. African farmers and craft persons discovered new business possibilities with the sale of many gallon drums of palm oil and lots of handcrafted canoes." Unfortunately, this intricate web of lucrative economic activity was not proof of a thriving economy based on agricultural commodities, but one based on slavocracy and social death.

Moral Contours, Complicities, and Complexities

It is important to acknowledge that in various societies in Africa, Asia, Europe, and the Americas slavery appeared in many forms—small-scale domestic and artisan slavery to large-scale gang labor—throughout its long history. Therefore, we must not lose sight of the vital and enormous difference between chattel slavery in the largest forced migrations of Africans to American colonies, in comparison to the nature of slavery in European and Arab markets in precolonial Africa. The concept of "chattel slavery" refers to the stark racial component whereby enslaved persons of African descent were classified by Europeans as no longer members of the human race. Instead, the status of slave meant that an enslaved African was a nonperson, a mere piece of privately owned tangible, exploitable property.

Consequently, there were several distinct manifestations of slavery in internal African markets: as a slave, one's humanity was always intact, even when one was positioned marginally within the social unit; slaves were not acquired through purchase but through inheritance or family politics, and as punishment for misdemeanors, as pledges to creditors for major debts yet to be paid, or as captives of war. Prisoners of tribal wars who were not ransomed by their relatives were sold as slaves to traders.

There were some African states that refused to participate in the transatlantic slave trade because they had their own gold mines inland and wanted those defeated in war to intermarry among them in order to expand their lineages and increase the population, as a demographic resource. As Peter Haenger has noted, "Marriage between free individuals and slaves of the same household was customary, indeed even desirable: in time, marriage covered over the differences of unequal social backgrounds."[26]

In fact, formerly enslaved people were incorporated in varying degrees into the overall Ghanaian social system. After two or three generations, depending upon gender stratification and sexual divisions of labor, one's slave status was erased from one's background. Slaves were always part of the human family, even when forced to live on the fringes of society. In sharing the familial value of lineage in her own context, Makola says that in some places you do not even print out records of deeds which show the origin of a person, because you might find out that some of your leaders, who have been integrated into the family groups of their owners and lived as their social equals, have slave bondage ancestry.

By placing this contemporary social order alongside a much wider historical one, Makola invites us to wrestle with the fact that slave status, whether in matrilineal or patrilineal societies, is neither completely clear-cut nor without problems. She notes, "People who were taken as slaves from the coast of Nigeria and brought to Ghana, soon discovered that by the second generation their past was wiped clean. The only place where a rigid stratification of slave status existed was among those who were enslaved as laborers in the gold mines. There is also the point that in 1701, slave trading in Ghana was restricted to the Dagara tribe who had to pay to the Ashanti tributes in slaves due to their defeat in battle."[27]

During this time there was a raging malaria epidemic, which meant that Europeans, who were unusually susceptible to tropical fevers and other infectious diseases, could not travel inland.[28] So, the Dutch and other European expansionists sent embassies of African scouts and traders into the interiors to negotiate with local kings for the purchase of slaves. Many, if not most warring groups operating in highly stratified societies organized themselves as slave raiders. Armed by Europeans and hiding in large dugout canoes in salt marshes, they escalated raiding activities by ambushing other tribes working in fields or forested areas.

Sometime between 1742 and 1750 the Danes sent their own delegation to the Ashanti king to accelerate the establishment of a network that would bring slaves from the interior to the markets along the West African coastline for sale. The trek to the coastline has been described like this: "The slaves were brought from the interior, acquired often by raids especially for the purpose of taking people into bondage or through wars increasingly fought for the same purpose, and transported to the coast along river networks that served as the hub of internal trade. Frequently, such slaves changed owners several times in a series of transactions, and the trip to the coast could be very lengthy."[29]

Makola adamantly refuses to accept the current tendency wherein Africa, far too often, is presented as one huge, homogeneous black blob of similarity, a black hole where everything is the same—everyone looks the same, everybody acts the same. She sounds the trumpet-call to raise people's consciences in this way:

> If you travel to Europe and you tell Englishmen that they are the same as Portuguese or Italians, they will refuse such identities and connections because in their world they acknowledge their differences, especially their major cultural differences. But as soon as you enter the kingdoms of Black people, you assume that all Africans look alike and have the same mindset. Most people do not give recognition to the multitude of differences among people in Africa. Each nation-state is different and has developed along certain philosophical lines. Some are warriors. Others are not. These are some of the issues in the slave trade discourse that some groups refuse to accept as valid information.

Drawing on her extensive historical research of textual source materials, Makola elaborates the complicated interpersonal dynamics between the European soldiers who guarded the castles and the Africans who were housed in the dungeons underneath.[30] She maintains that we are perhaps so unfamiliar with the familial relationships that existed between those protecting the castles and those being guarded in the dungeons down below that we have ignored the conditions under which the Europeans had to depend on African people in order to survive. These professional soldiers of many nationalities were so underpaid that they ended up befriended by Africans who loaned them money. Their African friends would transact trade inland, advertising European merchandise so that the soldiers in the various brigades could supplement their income. Sometimes soldiers of one country who fought in the army of another European power married the sisters of their African acquaintances.[31] These facts do not in the least minimize the mercantile atrocities and the unusual harsh brutalities perpetrated against African people.

In focusing our attention on the complex human dimensions of slavery, Makola conveys a sense of empathy in regard to the excessive cruelty that Europeans inflicted upon other Europeans, especially servants and soldiers who labored in the castles and forts. The European governors, situated at the top of the ruling hierarchy, had all the privileges. There may have been some rare and partial exceptions, but by and large, the governors provided the workers with only just enough of the basic necessities to stay alive.

Administrators did not even trust work-worn Europeans to handle their own money because they felt that the soldiers would get drunk, continue to drink, and die. But, if the European overseers gave wages to African women,[32] who performed most of the labor-intensive agricultural work, they would make sure that their husbands had food to eat, herbal medicine for physical ailments, a roof over their heads, clean clothes on their backs, and religious protection within the realm of African traditional religions.[33]

Of course it is important to remember that until fairly recently a sense of human rights, labor laws, and rights for women and children did not exist. One need only study labor history in order to see how various administrators/bosses created an environment in which the culture of abuse thrived against disinherited peasants. "If we go to seventeenth-century Europe, we find severe mistreatment of workers. Children were being pushed up chimneys as chimneysweepers. Other children died from sheer exhaustion while working. As for women, women's rights did not exist. The governors, traders and colonizers who came here didn't treat their own people right. So arriving in Africa, and finding people who were different, they simply continued their patterns of maltreatment" (Makola).

In attempting to describe these dynamics of human relations, Makola asks us to pay attention to how Europeans working in government-chartered monopoly companies treated Africans as subhuman, on one hand, and as life partners, on the other. Pastors in the castles and forts left ample testimonies in the form of church teachings directed to those who were responsible for surveillance and discipline of enslaved Africans. Members of the lower-class citizenry who made up the soldier contingents did not know much, except to treat others the way they were treated. So, partly as rebellion against daily repression, and partly as survival strategy in a veritable climate of terror, European soldiers committed numerous acts of mutiny. Makola extends an open invitation for us to read the original documents so that we can see how the social fabric of the European castle societies in Africa was full of violence and corruption.

Conclusion

Ghana's descent from Gold Coast to Slave Coast is not at all pleasant to recall. In the 1400s West Africa had been a place where gold was abundant.

But, now in the 1700s, painful though it may be to admit it, Ghanaians had to face the truth that in order to make up for the shortfall that corresponded with the decreased value of the gold trade, they had been reduced from sellers of gold to consumers who actively traded other human beings into slavery in order to purchase imported gold from Brazil. At first, European traders, expansionists, and colonizers took Africans who were already living in Europe to their colonies in the Americas. Next, they renovated old castles and built new forts with the enslavement of Africans in mind. And as a consequence, the castles became dungeons for human cargo. It is not only regrettable that old forts were rebuilt, but because of the increase in supply to fulfill the increased demand, more and more new forts were built to stockpile people as profitable possessions in increasing numbers—so much so, that by the eighteenth century, the place once called the Gold Coast became known as the Slave Coast.[34]

Notes

1. Among the many works on this subject, see especially Allison Howell, ed., *The Slave Trade and Reconciliation: A Northern Ghanaian Perspective* (Accra: SIM Ghana, 1998); Benedict G. Der, *The Slave Trade in Northern Ghana* (Accra: Woeli Publishing Services, 1998); Paul E. Lovejoy, ed., *Africans in Bondage: Studies in Slavery and the Slave Trade* (Madison: University of Wisconsin Press, 1986); Anne C. Bailey, *African Voices of the Atlantic Slave Trade: Beyond the Silence and the Shame* (Boston: Beacon Press, 2006); Akosua Adoma Perbi, *A History of Indigenous Slavery in Ghana: From the 15th to the 19th Century* (Accra: Sub-Saharan Publishing, 2004).

2. The quotations are from a lecture titled "The Slave Trade and Its Continuing Impact," by a scholar who requested to be referred to by the pseudonym Dr. Akosia Makola. The lecture was given at a seminar in Accra, Ghana, on July 10, 2000.

3. According to the timeline created by the Gilder Lehrman Center for the Study of Slavery, Resistance, and Abolition at the Center for International and Area Studies at Yale University, the first organized Portuguese expedition to capture Africans and to enslave them in Europe occurred in 1441, when sea captain Antam Goncalvez returned from exploring West Africa with two Africans. In 1443, one of Goncalvez's men, Nuno Tristo, captured 235 Africans. This marks the beginning of the Portuguese as the principal carriers of enslaved Africans to Europe for the next four centuries. C. R. Boxer, *Four Centuries of Portuguese Expansion, 1415–1825* (Berkeley: University of California Press, 1969). In 1493 the Spanish began importing Africans to the Americas. Colin A. Palmer, in his essay "The First Passage, 1502–1619," in *To Make Our World Anew: A History of African Americans*, ed. Robin D. G. Kelley and Earl Lewis (New York: Oxford University Press, 2000), says: "In response to the request from the governor of Hispaniola for African labor in 1501, the Spanish Crown authorized the shipment of slaves in 1502. The slaves in this first cargo had lived in Spain for some time before they were shipped to the Caribbean. Not until 1518 would slaves be transported to the Americas directly from Africa." In 1565 the

Spanish took enslaved Africans to St. Augustine, the first permanent settlement in what would become Florida. The Dutch began in the early 1600s to arm their boats and capture Portuguese forts along the African coast. They dominated the transatlantic slave trade until the 1700s. Throughout the first half of the eighteenth century, the French and English, adopting Dutch tactics, built new forts and created companies for the organization of slave trade from Africa. The British took the Portuguese slave trade from the Dutch by way of Cromwell's Navigation Act, which forbade the importation of enslaved Africans into English and French colonies but did not prevent it in other regions. In the Treaty of Utrecht of 1713 the British won the *assiento*, or contract, the monopoly license to ship each year thousands upon thousands of African people as slaves to Spanish-controlled territories in America. After the Anglo-Dutch War ended in 1784, the British slave trade to the Dutch colonies became important. Profiles of the transatlantic slave trade can be reviewed in Hugh Thomas, *The Slave Trade: The History of the Atlantic Slave Trade, 1440–1870* (New York: Simon and Schuster, 1997); J. A. Rawley, *The Transatlantic Slave Trade: A History* (New York: W. W. Norton, 1981); and Colin A. Palmer, *Human Cargoes: The British Slave Trade to Spanish America, 1700–1739* (Urbana: University of Illinois Press, 1981); David Northrup, *The Atlantic Slave Trade* (Lexington, Mass.: D. C. Heath, 1994); David Brion Davis, *Inhuman Bondage: The Rise and Fall of Slavery in the New World* (New York: Oxford University Press, 2006).

4. Ifa Amadiume says, "To recover our culture, we often swallow our pride to read offensive works." *Meridians* 2.2 (2002): 45. See also Ifa Amadiume, *Re-Inventing Africa: Matriarchy Religion and Culture* (New York: Zed Books, 1997).

5. The U.S. government's first reparations plan to compensate African Americans for the legacy of slavery was forty acres and a mule apiece—that was General William Sherman's promise to former slaves shortly after the Civil War ended in 1865. His order set aside land on the Georgia and South Carolina coasts for the settlements of thousands of newly freed families. But the promise was quickly recanted and the land was taken back, with no plans for reparations. There is now an increased focus on getting compensation from corporations that once profited from slavery. Adjoa Aiyetoro, a legal consultant to the National Coalition of Blacks for Reparations in America, and Robert Sedler, a professor at the Wayne State University Law School, have filed a class action lawsuit to seek restitution. See W. E. B. Du Bois, *Black Reconstruction in America: An Essay toward a History of the Part Which Black Folk Played in the Attempt to Reconstruct Democracy in America, 1860–1880* (1935; reprint, New York: Russell and Russell, 1966); Randall Robinson, *The Debt: What America Owes to Blacks* (New York: Penguin Putnam, 2000); Clarence J. Munford, *Race and Reparations: A Black Perspective for the Twenty-First Century* (Trenton, N.J.: Africa World Press, 1996).

6. See James H. Robinson, *Africa at the Crossroads* (Philadelphia: Westminster Press, 1962), 5–6. Robinson says that after Islam consolidated its gain along the Mediterranean coast, the Muslims began a southward march across the Sahara. By the ninth century Islam had laid the foundation of great empires in Songay, Mali, Meli, and Ghana. Robinson argues that Henry IV of Portugal wanted to find Prester John because he hoped to make an alliance to help hold back the tide of Muslim penetration. Henry IV's sailors developed contacts along the west coast of Africa, down as far as the Congo River, and one of Henry's emissaries, in the same year that Columbus "discovered" the Americas, traversed the land mass of Africa in search of Prester John, until he reached an area we know now to be ancient Ethiopia.

7. On the depopulation issue, Makola cites Philip D. Curtin, *The Atlantic Slave Trade: A Census* (Madison: University of Wisconsin Press, 1969); and Walter Rodney, *How Europe Underdeveloped Africa* (Washington, D.C.: Howard University Press, 1982).

8. Peter Duignan and Clarence Clendenen write, "Although all sorts of trade goods were exchanged for slaves on the African coast, the principal medium of barter was rum. . . . The quantities of rum needed for the trade with Africa ran to fantastic amounts. To supply them, more than thirty distilleries operated in Rhode Island, as we have seen, and in neighboring Massachusetts there were more than sixty. Although huge amounts of rum were consumed in the colonies, the greater part of this liquor production was probably dispensed on the coast of Africa." *The United States and the African Slave Trade, 1619–1862* (1963; reprint, Westport, Conn.: Greenwood Press, 1978), 9–10.

9. See E. Meyerowitz, *The Akan of Ghana: Their Ancient Beliefs* (London: Faber and Faber, 1958); Benezet Bujo, *Foundations of an African Ethic: Beyond Universal Claims of Western Morality*, trans. Brian McNeil (New York: Crossroads, 2001); J. N. K. Mugambi and A. Nasimiyu-Wasike, eds., *Moral and Ethical Issues in African Christianity*, 2nd ed. (Nairobi: Acton Publishing, 1999).

10. The following titles are the best guides for understanding the essential role of a native pharmacopoeia in indigenous religions of Africa: A. K. Andoh, *The Science and Romance of Selected Herbs Used in Medicine and Religious Ceremony* (San Francisco: North Scale Institute, 1986); B. Oliver-Bever, *Medicinal Plants in Tropical West Africa* (Cambridge: Cambridge University Press, 1986); A. Sofowora, *Medicinal Plants and Traditional Medicine in Africa* (Chichester, U.K.: John Wiley and Sons, 1982); E. S. Ayensu, *Medicinal Plants of West Africa* (Algonac, Mich.: Reference Publications, 1978).

11. Jacob K. Olupona, ed., *African Spirituality: Forms, Meanings and Expressions* (New York: Crossroads, 2000); T. N. O. Quarcuopome, *West African Traditional Religion* (Ibadan, Nigeria: African Universities Press, 1987).

12. Barry Boubacar, *Senegambia and the Atlantic Slave Trade* (Cambridge: Cambridge University Press, 1998), 57.

13. On Amerindian slavery, see Gustavo Gutiérrez, *Las Casas: In Search of the Poor of Jesus Christ*, trans. Robert R. Barr (Maryknoll, N.Y.: Orbis Books, 1993); A. Marchant, *From Barter to Slavery: The Economic Relations of Portuguese and Indians in the Settlement of Brazil, 1500–1580* (Baltimore: Johns Hopkins University Press, 1942); J. Hemming, *Red Gold: The Conquest of the Brazilian Indians* (London: Macmillan, 1978).

14. See Johannes Postma, *The Dutch and the Atlantic Slave Trade, 1600–1815* (New York: Cambridge University Press, 1990); Johannes Postma and Victor Enthoven, eds., *Riches from Atlantic Commerce: Dutch Transatlantic Trade and Shipping, 1585–1817* (Boston: Brill, 2003); Harvey Feinberg, *Africans and Europeans in West Africa: Elminians and Dutchmen on the Gold Coast during the Eighteenth Century* (Philadelphia: American Philosophical Society, 1989).

15. Jonathan Neil Gerstner, *Thousand Generation Covenant: Dutch Reformed Covenant Theology and Group Identity in Colonial South Africa, 1652–1814* (Boston: Brill, 1991).

16. For the specific history of the Portuguese in Ghana, see John Vogt, *Portuguese Rule on the Gold Coast, 1469–1682* (Athens: University of Georgia Press, 1979).

17. Elmina, called "Sao Jorge da Mina" (Saint George's of the mine), was the first permanent structure south of the Sahara built by Europeans (1482)—and for centuries it was the largest. It also has the distinction of being the first of many

permanent "slave factories" (trading posts that dealt with the business of enslavement) that would be built along Africa's western coast. Elmina Castle saw several owners during the course of the transatlantic slave trade, including Portuguese, Dutch, and English. Deportation through outposts like Elmina continued for nearly three hundred years. See Tony Hyland, *The Castles of Elmina* (Accra: Ghana's Musuem and Monument Board, 1987).

18. According to Encarta, the Dutch West Indies Company was granted a charter of privileges and exemptions on 7 June 1629, and a monopoly of trade in the Americas and Africa, with the right of colonizing and maintaining armed forces. Pieter C. Emmer, *Dutch in the Atlantic Economy, 1580–1880: Trade, Slavery, and Emancipation* (Aldershot: Ashgate Publishing, 1998); A. Van Dantzig, comp. and trans., *The Dutch and the Guinea Coast, 1674–1742: A Collection of Documents from the General State Archives at the Hague* (Accra: GAAS, 1978).

19. Robert Harm says, "Mercantilists viewed international trade as a form of war in which the trading nations of Europe competed for shares of a relatively fixed supply of gold and silver. Each nation sought to maintain a favorable balance of trade in order to gain gold and silver from its rivals." *The Diligent: A Voyage through the Worlds of the Slave Trade* (New York: Perseus Basic Books, 2003), 35.

20. The distinctiveness of these dynamics is stressed by Robin Law, ed., *Correspondence from the Royal African Company's Factories at Ofira and Whydah on the Slave Coast of West Africa in the Public Record Office, London 1678–93* (Edinburgh: Centre of African Studies, Edinburgh University, 1990); and Ray Kea, *Settlements, Trade, and Politics in the Seventeenth-Century Gold Coast* (Baltimore: Johns Hopkins University Press, 1982).

21. John Biddulp, *The Pirates of Malabar* (London: Smith, Elder, 1907).

22. Jack Goody, *Death, Property and the Ancestors* (Stanford: Stanford University Press, 1962).

23. Albert Van Dantzig, *Forts and Castles of Ghana* (Accra: Sedco Publishing, 1980), 1–52.

24. For a more detailed account of the connections between Cape Coast Castle and the Ashanti Kingdom, see C. Reindorf, *The History of Gold Coast and Ashantee* (Accra: Waterville Press, 1895); J. K. Fynn, *Asante and Its Neighbours, 1700–1807* (London: Longman, 1971); Philip Koslow, *Centuries of Greatness: The West African Kingdoms, 1750–1900* (Philadelphia: Chelsea House, 1995); T. Edward Bowdich, *Mission from Cape Coast Castle to Ashantee, with a Statistical Account of that Kingdom, and Geographical Notices of other Parts of the Interior of Africa* (1819; reprint, London: Frank Cass, 1966).

25. Humphry J. Fisher, *Slavery in the History of Muslim Black Africa* (New York: New York University Press, 2001), 122.

26. Peter Haenger, *Slaves and Slave Holders on the Gold Coast: Towards an Understanding of Social Bondage in West Africa*, ed. J. J. Shaffer and Paul E. Lovejoy, trans. Christina Handford (Basle: P. Schlettwein, 2000), 3; see also Kwame Y. Daaku, *Trade and Politics on the Gold Coast, 1600–1720* (London: Clarendon, 1970).

27. Also see Ivor Wilks, *Forests of Gold: Essays on the Akan and the Kingdom of Asante* (Athens: Ohio University Press, 1993); Robert S. Rattray, *The Tribes of the Ashanti Hinterland*, vol. 2 (Oxford: Clarendon, 1932); Robert S. Rattray, *Ashanti Law and Constitution* (London: Oxford University Press, 1929).

28. Bruce L. Mouser, *A Slaving Voyage to Africa and Jamaica: The Log of the Sandown, 1793–1794* (Bloomington: Indiana University Press, 2002), xiii, says that "country fever" inevitably came with the rains, along with other fevers and diseases being spread by

caravan traders or ships that had stopped at numerous ports along the way. Poor knowledge about safe drinking water and food preparation meant that captain and crew would certainly encounter new parasites and bacteria.

29. William H. Worger, Nancy Clark, and Edward A. Alpers, eds., Introduction, *Africa and the West: A Documentary History from the Slave Trade to Independence* (Phoenix: Oryx Press, 2001), 4.

30. Kwame Daaku, *Trade and Politics on the Gold Coast, 1600–1720* (Oxford: Clarendon Press, 1970).

31. For an in-depth discussion about African kinship marriages, see A. R. Radcliff-Brown and Daryll Forde, eds., *African Systems of Kinship and Marriage* (London: Oxford University Press, 1950).

32. Christine Opong, ed., *Female and Male in West Africa* (London: Allen and Unwin, 1983).

33. Laurenti Magesa, *African Religion: The Moral Traditions of Abundant Life* (Maryknoll, N.Y.: Orbis Books, 1998); Robert M. Baum, *Shrines of the Slave Trade: Diola Religion and Society in Pre-colonial Senegambia* (New York: Oxford University Press, 1999); G. Parrinder, *West African Religion: A Study of the Beliefs and Practices of Akan, Ewe, Yoruba, Ibo, and Kindred Peoples* (London: Epworth Press, 1961); John S. Mbiti, *Introduction to African Religion*, 2nd ed. (Nairobi: East African Educational Publishing, 1991); Yusufu Turaki, *Christianity and African Gods: A Method in Theology* (Potchefstroom, South Africa: Potchefstroom University Press, 1999).

34. Willem Bosman, *A New and Accurate Description of the Coast of Guinea, Divided into the Gold, Slave, and the Ivory Coasts* (London: J. Knapton, 1705).

Barbara Bailey | **FEMINIZATION OF POVERTY ACROSS**

PAN-AFRICAN SOCIETIES

THE CHURCH'S RESPONSE—

ALLEVIATIVE OR EMANCIPATORY?

The Pan-African Seminar on Religion and Poverty brought a group of scholars together on a journey from Legon, Ghana; to Nairobi, Kenya; to Johannesburg, South Africa; to Kingston, Jamaica; and finally to Princeton, New Jersey, between the summer of 2000 and that of 2004. On this journey, the dialogue centered on the church's engagement with and response to issues of poverty in these various contexts. My personal interest in this journey was twofold: first, to determine the extent to which poverty could be described as a feminized phenomenon across the Pan-African societies visited; and, second, to evaluate the extent to which the church's response to situations of poverty was alleviative or addressed the structural roots of poverty and therefore had the potential to be emancipatory.

In this essay poverty is defined not so much in terms of material deprivation but more in terms of social exclusion and human degradation. In relation to the first concern, I posit that poverty is structural and in many instances results from hegemonic economic relationships at both the global and local levels and, in terms of impact at the local level, is mediated through social hierarchies of race, class, and gender—but with the latter having an overarching effect so that the face of poverty in many cultures is primarily female, as was the case in countries visited on this journey.

In relation to my second concern, based on observations made on the journey and secondary sources reviewed, I conclude that whereas ecumenical initiatives at global, regional, and local levels have been strategic in orientation, targeting structural and policy reform, those at the level of the local church are more tactical and practical responses to the immediate needs of the dispossessed. A concern that emerges is that in the face of unequivocal evidence of the feminization of poverty in the countries visited, for the most part, the discourse on issues of poverty was gender-neutral and few initiatives specifically focused on the unique needs of women. The catalytic effect of the international women's movement on existing gender relations in the social, economic, and political spheres, as well as women's access to social capital and personal agency, are therefore posited as alternatives that women in situations of poverty depend on to alleviate their plight.

Poverty Defined

Traditionally, poverty has been defined in terms of *absolute or primary poverty* and a lack of an adequate income to provide the basic requirements of sufficient food and adequate shelter to sustain physical life. On the other hand, *relative or secondary poverty* relates to the cultural needs of individuals and families relative to other members of society and therefore relates not only to provision of physical needs but also to needs based on the norms and expectations of society.[1]

A commonly used definition of income poverty is subsisting on one U.S. dollar or less per day. A problem in this regard is the use of a common poverty line in different countries, which, according to the 1997 Human Development Report of the United Nations Development Programme (UNDP), is misleading because of contextual variations in "necessary" commodities.[2] The use of a common poverty line to assess poverty in different countries can therefore distort the realities of a given context.

Consequently, this United Nations agency contends that poverty is contextual and that deprivations vary with social and economic conditions of communities: "The minimum income needed to escape social estrangement can be quite different between communities. . . . So, the assessment of poverty on the basis of a low minimum cut-off income used for poor countries fails to show any poverty in generally affluent societies, even when the relatively poor in those societies may lack social participation and may even suffer from hunger and malnutrition" (18). The UNDP report cites the United States of America as a case in point, where "incomes are high but inequalities generate a heavy burden of 'necessity' in the direction of socially obligated consumption often to the detriment of health and nutritional spending" (18).

A similar phenomenon is also evident in relatively poorer societies, such as Jamaica, where acculturation, particularly acculturation due to the reach of cable feeds of U.S.-based television programs and advertisements, creates a material culture and consumption patterns and preferences that result in a "heavy burden of necessity" for imported designer clothing and commodities. Persons in situations of poverty acquire these items for themselves and their children at the expense of provisions for basic nutritional, health, and educational needs. To the casual onlooker such persons would not be regarded as "poor" but, in fact, they lack basic necessities.

The more widely used method to assess the incidence of primary or income-based poverty in any given context is to set a "poverty line" relative to that society and determine the number of persons whose per capita income falls below this level. To arrive at this "a basket of goods and services is constructed corresponding with local consumption patterns. The value of this basket, at local consumer prices and satisfying a pre-set level of basic needs for one person, is called the 'poverty line'. If the per capita income of house-hold members is below the poverty line, the household and its members are considered poor."[3] The now more commonly accepted perspective of poverty is therefore in terms of personal income levels being below a defined poverty line, which then results in deprivation of material requirements for a minimally acceptable fulfillment of basic human needs.

In Jamaica, it was estimated that in 2001 the poverty line for a family of five (two adults and three children) was J$167,083.10 per annum (approximately US$54.50 per week at an exchange rate of US$1.00 = J$59.00). Based on this, the incidence of poverty was 16.8 percent of the population with persons in rural areas being more affected than those in urban areas.[4] This compares to the United States, where in 2004 the poverty line for a family of the same size was estimated at US$22,030.00, which, using the same exchange rate, equated to J$1,299,770.00, clearly illustrating that poverty is a relative concept shaped by normative expectations of the consumer culture.[5]

A number of indicators are presented in table 1, which deconstructs poverty in the African countries visited during the Pan-African Seminar journey and illustrates the extent to which the condition of poverty is related to factors of geography.

The poverty indicators included in table 1 clearly demonstrate that, overall, Kenya is more negatively impacted by poverty than are the other two countries in the table. The gross domestic product (GDP) per capita, as reflected by purchasing power parity (PPP) rather than official exchange rates, is lowest in Kenya. It is therefore not surprising that the highest level of persons (50%) living on less than US$1.00 is reported for that country. Data disaggregated by geographical location indicate that in all three countries poverty is more evident in rural than urban populations. The most

TABLE 1 POVERTY INDICATORS

Country	Ghana	Kenya	South Africa
GDP per Capita (PPP)	US$1,661	US$1,168	US$7,178
Percentage of Population Living on Less than US$1.00 per Day	N/A	50	24
National Poverty Head Count as Percentage of Population	31	42	N/A
Percentage of Population below 2/3 of Mean per Capita Income			
Urban	22	14	40
Rural	37	53	86
Share of Income by Population Group			
Richest 20%	41.7	50.2	64.8
Poorest 20%	8.4	5.0	2.9

Source: African development indicators, 2002. Drawn from World Bank Africa Database, World Bank.

dramatic indicator of poverty is the disparity in the share of income held by the richest 20 percent and the poorest 20 percent of these populations. The disparity is startling in all three countries and not surprisingly, given the political history of South Africa, is most marked in this country.

Indicators presented in table 2 serve to show the relationship between poverty and the social condition of a people. Given the poverty measures reported for Kenya, it is not surprising that, except for male/female illiteracy rates, this country scores lowest on the remaining indicators. These measures also reveal the particular impact of poverty on women and children as reflected in fertility rates, life expectancy at birth, infant mortality, and deaths in children under five years old, all of which are most marked in Kenya.

More recently, poverty has, therefore, been conceptualized as going beyond income poverty to include cultural poverty and ways in which economic deprivation results in the exclusion of individuals from opportunities and choices that are basic to human development. The United Nations Development Programme has therefore shifted its focus and now addresses poverty in relation to human rights and from a sustainable human development perspective: "Poverty can mean more than a lack of what is necessary for material well-being. It can also mean the denial of opportunities and choices most basic to human development—to lead a long, healthy, creative life, to

TABLE 2 SOCIAL INDICATORS, 1999

Country	Illiteracy Rate Male	Illiteracy Rate Female	Fertility Rate (children per family)	Life Expectancy at Birth (years)	Infant Mortality Rate (per 1000)	Mortality under 5 yrs (per 1000)
Ghana	21	39	4.3	58	57	109
Kenya	12	25	4.5	48	76	118
South Africa	14	16	2.9	48	62	76

Source: African Development Indicators, 2002. From World Bank Africa Database, World Bank.

enjoy a decent standard of living, freedom, dignity, self-esteem and respect for others."[6]

In its 1997 Human Development Report, the UNDP introduced the concept of human poverty and made a distinction between *income-based or consumption-based poverty*, on one hand, and *human poverty or poverty of lives and opportunity*, on the other, the latter being more closely linked to notions of human development.[7] This perspective relates not only to an impoverished state but also the lack of opportunity to lead valuable and valued lives due to social constraints as well as personal circumstances. Income and human poverty are therefore inextricably linked and mutually reinforcing.

The human poverty perspective is seen as being multidimensional and diverse in character, rather than uniform in content. According to the 1997 UNDP report, critical dimensions of human poverty that are difficult to measure and have therefore previously been excluded from measures of poverty include "lack of political freedom, inability to participate in decision-making, lack of personal security, inability to participate in the life of a community and threats to sustainability and inter-generational equity" (17).

In making assessments of human poverty the UNDP therefore includes deprivation in three essential areas of human life—length of life, knowledge, and standard of living. The last area is based on overall economic provisioning and takes into account access to health services and to safe water and malnutrition in children. The UNDP contends that these are more reliable indicators of real human poverty since private income is not an adequate indicator of an individual's access to economic facilities, which also include critical public services.

In addition to its material and cultural dimensions, poverty can also be seen as essentially racial, geographically circumscribed, and intergenerational and therefore an inevitable trap from which individuals rarely escape. This was the perception of persons from Etwatwa, a black township in South Africa, who participated in a study sponsored by the World Council of Churches (WCC) of the church's response to poverty and wealth: "There is a sense that poverty is something into which one is born. This is especially the case if one belongs to a racial group that is known to be poor, such as rural blacks. The identity between one's family and poverty means it is rare for someone to move out of poverty as an individual. Poverty is a shared life experience, and it stretches through generations. The poor are likely to be born in poor families. The condition of poverty is inherited and passed on to children and is perpetuated over generations."[8]

Theological Perspectives

Consumption and cultural poverty, which result in deprivation of basic needs and necessities for social participation, are typically associated with life-threatening consequences and therefore with negative connotations, but there is a sense in which there is a theological justification for poverty, which is addressed in a number of essays in this volume. I will therefore make reference only to the spiritual value of poverty as suggested in the Beatitudes addressed to the disciples and recorded in the Sermon on the Mount. Luke's version makes reference to the poor who will be blessed "for theirs is the kingdom of God" (Luke 6:20). One commentary points to the fact that although in Matthew's gospel the blessing is promised to those who are lowly and humble in spirit, in Luke's version the blessing is for those who are poor in the plain and obvious sense of economic poverty and for those who in actual circumstances of community life are the disadvantaged.[9]

Passages that speak to women as a specially disadvantaged group of the poor are also found in the gospels. Women from around the world who participated in a study of Christianity, poverty, and wealth identified a number of these biblical passages that make reference to widows and orphans.[10] The use of the Hebrew word *almamnah* for widow, a derivative of the word *alem*, meaning unable to speak, underscores not only the marital status of these women but also the voicelessness associated with their economic and legal status. The women in the study were equally clear, however, that the scriptures also pointed to God as protector and legal defender of these women and as one who would hear their cry. This idea of the compassionate and compensatory nature of God's love and his intervention in the reversal of the human condition of those in circumstances of poverty will be revisited in a subsequent section of this essay.

David Jary and Julia Jary give a succinct summary of one view of the poor: "The view that the poor are responsible for their situation due to some form of personal inadequacy fits into structural functionalist theory of social transmission where it is posited that individuals accept their role and position within the social structure of a society through the influence of socializing agencies such as family, church and school. In this paradigm success is presumed to be based on merit and the . . . positions which carry the greatest rewards and the highest rank are those which have the greatest importance for society and also require the greatest training or talent."[11]

Schooling plays a very important function in this regard. Functionalists argue that an economic function of schooling is to prepare students for later work roles. A meritocracy or a hierarchical social structure based on ability is created and, through a system of differentiation and sorting, individuals are prepared to fill the diverse roles required by society. In their book, K. B. deMarrais and M. D. LeCompte (1998) posit that "schools' stratification of students and creation of an ability-based hierarchical ranking serves to link occupational to social class differences in society."[12]

Through this mechanism, the school therefore functions to reproduce the social order and maintain the status quo. DeMarrais and LeCompte contend that in this way schools create a meritocracy, a hierarchical structure organized by ability that is based on the premise that no major external impediments stand in the way of success for able, hard-working individuals. On the other hand, Bernstein claims that lack of success and the inability to be socially mobile is attributed to motivational and cognitive differences acquired through socialization in the family.[13]

Functional theories of class stratification are often criticized on the grounds that they fail to take account of the exercise of power within structural hierarchies of nation, race, class, and gender that produce, among other things, asymmetrical, hegemonic economic relationships between countries of the North and South and between vulnerable and less vulnerable groups within populations. Poverty at the individual and household level therefore often results from these global economic relationships, with impoverishment in developing countries in the South being directly related to macroeconomic policies that facilitate accumulation of wealth in more developed countries of the North.

The industrialization of Britain, for example, was possible only by the flagrant ravaging of the human and natural resources of its colonies in Africa and the Caribbean, which were assumed to lack the industrial and technological knowledge to maximize use of these resources. The flourishing slave trade of the eighteenth and early nineteenth centuries and the movement of men, women, and children forcibly across the Atlantic from Africa to the Caribbean and the Americas are striking examples of hegemonic political and economic relationships and how the human and natural resources of subordinated groups were exploited to benefit the white plantocracy and its interests.

The gaining of political independence by many African and Caribbean countries including Ghana, Kenya, and Jamaica during the 1950s and 1960s has not significantly disrupted historical economic inequities. Neocolonial international financial institutions such as the International Monetary Fund and the World Bank have spawned more intrusive hegemonic economic policies and programs, which have produced new and more entrenched forms of economic enslavement and in many cases have eroded social gains and threaten the basic human rights of vulnerable groups.

Two economic policies that have had a profound effect on African and Caribbean countries over the last two to three decades are structural adjustment programs (SAPs) and the accelerated rate of globalization, both of which are supported by international financial institutions headquartered in Washington, D.C.

Grace Chang argues:

> Since the 1980s, the World Bank, International Monetary Fund and other international financial institutions (IFIs) based in the First World, have routinely prescribed structural adjustment policies (SAPs) to the governments of indebted countries as pre-conditions for loans. These prescriptions have included cutting government expenditures on social programs, slashing wages, liberalizing imports, opening markets to foreign investment, expanding exports, devaluing local currency and privatizing state enterprises. While SAPs are ostensibly intended to promote efficiency and sustained economic growth in the "adjusting" country, in reality they function to exploit developing nations' economies and peoples.[14]

Processes associated with globalization overlap with but go beyond policies associated with SAPs. There are two distinguishing aspects of the current process of globalization. In the first instance, there is greatly increased global mobility of capital in and out of currency and securities markets and shifts in liquid assets across international borders that bypass national government control mechanisms. The second feature is a transnational network structure of organizations engaged in production that is no longer geographically circumscribed. This international spread of production facilities is intended to encourage efficiency, international competition, and lower-priced, higher-quality consumer goods. The international division of labor is also a mechanism for utilizing low-wage female labor and identifying tax havens—and, in some cases, situations that require lower environmental standards.[15]

In his essay in this volume Lewin Williams postulates that the differential and negative impacts of globalization on third world countries, and particularly those populated by Africans on the mainland and in the diaspora, relate to the stratification of the global market and a preference for intellectual commodities and manufactured goods over and above agrarian products mainly from these countries and which have the lowest value.[16]

The condition of poverty can therefore be attributed to the dynamic interplay of a number of structural and personal factors operating at the macro and micro levels of state and family respectively. South African participants in the 2000 study *Christianity, Poverty and Wealth* identified factors related to both these dimensions.[17] State-related factors included unemployment, low wages, lending policies of banks, high cost of living, lack of infrastructure, conflict and wars, misappropriation of public funds, and the lifestyle of public officials. Personal factors advanced by the group included lack of knowledge and skills, having large families (once seen in Africa as a form of security and wealth), illiteracy and ignorance, laziness, and lack of discipline in use of income. Interestingly, the church was also incriminated as a causal agency in terms of demands made in the form of church dues and contributions. From a theological perspective, poverty was attributed to disobedience to God, a lack of faith, and failing to tithe.

Feminization of Poverty

In all the historical periods discussed in the preceding section, women in the South have been chief among those affected by hegemonic economic policies and programs orchestrated and managed by male economists and government bureaucrats in the North and South. According to Women Watch, a gateway for providing information and resources on the promotion of gender equality throughout the United Nations system, the majority of the 1.5 billion people living on US$1.00 per day or less are women, and worldwide women earn, on average, slightly more than 50 percent of what men earn.[18]

A study done by the United Nations Economic Commission on Latin America and the Caribbean (ECLAC) showed that in Latin America and the

Caribbean the incomes of women with nine years of schooling were lower than those of men who had only five years of formal education.[19] Further, although the female economically active population in the region is more highly educated than the male economically active population, at higher occupational levels women are subject to significant differences in remuneration, and that discrimination increases with age and with educational level.[20]

The economic deprivation that women in the developing world and parts of the developed world face on a daily basis has been exacerbated by macroeconomic policies promoted by the international financial institutions in relation to both SAPs and, more recently, the accelerated pace of globalization. Several interrelated issues are of relevance to this discussion: the changing patterns of women's work, the increasing incidence of female heads of households and the associated increased burden of work, the politics of migration, the new face of prostitution, and the increased rate of HIV/AIDS infection among women.

A briefing prepared by BRIDGE (Briefings on Development and Gender) at the University of Sussex indicates that in many parts of the world, including some African countries and the Caribbean, there is the strange paradox of rises in women's economic activity rates with more women working outside the household in paid work in the formal and informal labor force.[21] At the same time economic activity rates for men have been stagnating or falling in up to two-thirds of developing countries. There is therefore evidence that the increasing economic demands on households, precipitated by macroeconomic policies promoted by international financial institutions, are borne by women.

The BRIDGE briefing notes that the capacity of women to take on this added responsibility, however, is severely compromised by the fact that they are concentrated in the lowest status, lowest paying, and least protected sectors of the job market and therefore earn less than men. Additionally, a high proportion of economically active women are self-employed. In Africa this is estimated to be 53 percent, and in Latin America and the Caribbean 26 percent. In the informal sector women are, however, concentrated in a narrow range of occupations, particularly services and petty trades, while men in this sector are engaged in more diverse activities. In many developing countries a large proportion of economically active women are also engaged in agricultural work, but many do this as unpaid family labor.

Added to these distinct gendered patterns of work and remuneration, women also work longer hours than men. The briefing states that in Latin America and the Caribbean, on average, women work six hours more than

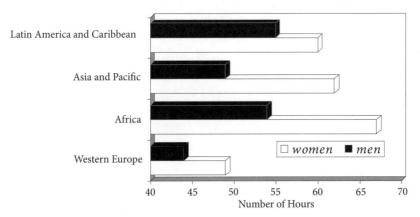

FIGURE 1 Average weekly hours worked by women and men, including housework, 1976–1988. *Source*: The World's Women, United Nations, 1991.

men per week, while in Africa the burden of work per week is twelve to thirteen hours greater for women than men (see figure 1).

The worsening economic crisis in many developing countries, coupled with cutbacks in social services, means that women economize on household expenditure in ways that require more domestic labor; in the late 1980s, in many developing countries, women were working sixty to ninety hours a week to maintain the living standards of the late 1970s. According to the BRIDGE briefing, this included meeting the gaps resulting from cutbacks in government expenditure on health and education and caring for children, aging relatives, and other elderly persons.

The burden of responsibility that women in poverty carry for households is compounded by the increasing incidence of households headed by females. The International Labour Organisation (ILO) posits that the process of feminization of poverty is linked with this phenomenon.[22] Data on living conditions show that households headed by women are more likely to be poor than those headed by men. This finding needs to be considered in relation to the fact that "the percentage of households headed by women increased world-wide in the 1980s and in the developing world varies from less than 20% in some Asian countries to almost 50% in some African and Caribbean countries."[23]

Female household headship is a sociologically distinctive feature of the Caribbean region's family structure dating back to the period of plantation slavery and has traditionally been a feature of the working class within the region, but with increasing proportions evident, in more recent times, among middle-class and economically independent women (see table 3).

TABLE 3 INCIDENCE OF FEMALE-HEADED HOUSEHOLDS IN THE CARIBBEAN

Country	Percentage of Female-Headed Households
Anguilla	32.2
Antigua and Barbuda	58.5
British Virgin Islands	28.7
Dominica	37.3
Grenada	42.7
Jamaica	44.7
Montserrat	40.0
St. Kitts and Nevis	43.9
St. Lucia	40.4
St. Vincent and the Grenadines	39.5

Sources: U.N. Economic Commission on Latin America and the Caribbean/Caribbean Development and Cooperation Committee (ECLAC/CDCC), "Poverty Eradication in Female-Headed Households in the Caribbean," POV/96/2, a paper presented at the ECLAC/CDCC Caribbean Ministerial Meeting on the Eradication of Poverty, Port of Spain, 28 October to 1 November 1, 1996; Planning Institute of Jamaica and Statistical Institute of Jamaica, Jamaica Survey of Living Conditions (Kingston: Planning Institute of Jamaica and Statistical Institute of Jamaica, 2002).

A more recent phenomenon, particularly in the African countries worst affected by the HIV/AIDS pandemic, is child-headed households resulting from the premature death of one or both parents. Other factors contributing to this phenomenon are family disintegration, disease, and conflicts such as the civil war in Rwanda. The majority of these children "have no access to health care or education, and lack sufficient food, basic household goods, or agricultural necessities. Without education, those assuming responsibility have limited choices as to how income is generated, and are frequently forced to prostitute themselves in order to provide for their families, exposing themselves to further risk and exploitation."[24]

In response to worsening economic conditions created by SAPs and globalization, many women in the South migrate to developed countries or other developing countries with stronger economies in a bid to support themselves and their dependents. The politics of the migration of women between developing and developed countries depends on a "food chain" relationship driven by domestic forms of structural adjustment in receiving developed countries. Grace Chang[25] argues that recession, cutbacks in health care, and lack of subsidized childcare in the United States contribute to increased demand among dual-career middle-class families for workers to care for children and the elderly and for housekeeping.

Chang also suggests that neoliberal economic policies promoted by international financial institutions are a snare from which women in developing countries cannot escape, whether they opt to remain "at home" or "go abroad"; she claims that

> in the Third World, women absorb the costs of cuts in food subsidies and health care by going hungry and forgoing proper medical care. Ironically, these same women continue to take up the slack for vanishing social supports in the First World, by nursing the elderly parents and young children of their employers for extremely low wages. Thus, there is a transferral of costs from the governments of both sending and receiving countries to migrant women workers from indebted nations. In both their home and "host" countries, and for both their own and their employers' families, these women pay most dearly for "adjustment." (2)

In spite of the vulnerabilities that these women face, they are kept malleable by the fact that their home countries and families, particularly children, depend on remittances for daily survival. Data from Jamaica indicate the importance of remittances to individuals, to families, and to the Jamaican economy.[26] In spite of a slowing in the United States economy, in 2001 private remittances to Jamaica grew by US$136.5 million to US$809.4 million, a significant proportion of which would have originated with migrant women workers in the United States.

Some migrant women turn to prostitution as a means of economic survival, while other women from a number of developing countries are trapped in this growing transnational industry either through deceit and promise of legitimate jobs or through coercion. Jyoti Sanghera writes that although prostitution is one of the oldest professions, under globalization it has taken on a new face and is now a profitable global industrial enterprise with a highly cohesive and organized set of principal players and beneficiaries.[27] The claim is that material benefits accruing to organizers of the sex industry equal those flowing out of the underground trade in arms and narcotics.

In many small island states, such as in the Caribbean, prostitution is part and parcel of the tourist industry. An international and national legitimacy is conferred on this aspect of the sex industry by the fact that under SAPs tourism is promoted as a viable development option for generating revenue and earning foreign exchange. A defining feature of the contemporary sex industry is the manner in which third world women's bodies and reproductive labor are commoditized, commercialized, and exploited by multinational corporations and are used to sell tourist destinations and tourist products. For this reason, Jyoti Sanghera argues, while the third world has been the principal source of raw resources, goods, and labor since colonial times, under the current wave of globalization "women and children from those regions of the world which have been under the grip of structural adjustments and economic liberalization are increasingly defined as the new raw resource. They constitute the prime export item for national development and international trade. This human cash crop is unique in that it offers a double-featured advantage: women's bodies are both goods and services at the same time."[28]

A 2001 study in Jamaica on the situation of children in prostitution reveals that children between the ages of ten and eighteen were involved in transactional sex activities in both private and public spaces.[29] The majority of the group was girls, and there was a gender division of labor in some activities.

In one of its reports, the International Labour Organisation notes that the sexual exploitation of children tends to lead to both emotional and physical consequences, among them loss of self-esteem, mental and physical illness, infertility, behavioral problems, substance abuse, and death.[30] With respect to these vulnerabilities there are, however, gender distinctions. First, more girls than boys are involved in these activities; boys are more at risk in relation to criminal and violent activities; and girls' reproductive rights and health are threatened. What is more, these forms of child labor fall outside of legitimate economic sectors and, in most cases, contravene the legal age for engagement in work and therefore are outside of any social protection or regulatory mechanisms.

A growing trend associated with the movement and engagement of women and children in the sex industry is the heightened rates of HIV/AIDS among girls and women. Data from the Ministry of Health, Jamaica, highlight the link between sex tourism and the region's increased risk of HIV/AIDS infection. While the risk is not gender-partial, females continue to be at greater risk of infection because of their generally greater participation in sex tourism. This has significant ramifications for the households that many of these women head and the children who may eventually become orphaned.[31] The heightened risk for women in the fifteen-to-twenty-four age group to contract HIV/AIDS is not limited to those in voluntary or forced engagement in the sex industry but is more associated with issues of sexual violence and control of women's bodies and their sexuality in their everyday sexual relations inside and outside of marriage. The impact of HIV/AIDS is greatest among the poor, who have no economic cushion and little support in terms of social nets and social networks. Several devastating impacts of

HIV/AIDS on the poor, particularly women and children, are identified in the United Nations Population Fund (UNFPA) *State of World Population, 2002* report.[32] The report points to the fact that inter alia:

Devastating Impacts of HIV/AIDS
—Almost 95% of persons living with the virus live in developing countries;
—More than 4 million children under the age of 15 have been infected with HIV;
—Infections in children have resulted in an unprecedented increase in infant mortality;
—Of the 580,000 children under the age of 15 who died of AIDS in 2001, 500,000 or 9 out of 10 were African;
—In surveys conducted in 22 countries young women knew less than young men about AIDS although young women are more vulnerable to infection;
—In the 1990s SAPs shifted much of the cost of care from the state to individuals, and girls are far more likely than boys to be kept home to care for sick relatives or do housework to free older women for nursing;
—Children become the household's only breadwinner if working age adults are sick and others are too old or young to work;
—AIDS deprives children of education because teachers and administrators are dying, draining education of its quality, increasing costs and weakening demand.

Data presented in this section point to the fact that poverty is a gendered phenomenon and that gender intersects with race and class to produce asymmetrical outcomes for women. As part of a project called Christianity, Poverty and Wealth in the 21st Century, which was aimed at revitalizing the debate about poverty and wealth within the ecumenical family, the World YWCA in Geneva carried out a study on women in poverty. The women in that study described poverty as dehumanizing, all-embracing, and all-encompassing, and as "an indivisible whole, an ongoing, day-to-day reality that cannot be simply defined by lack of a particular possession or amenity. Poor women experience not only lack of income and access to assets and basic services, but even more severe is the devalued social status which is magnified by various forms of violence and insubordination. Lack of dignity diminishes women more than the materials they lack. Poor women are those who are demeaned and have to struggle very hard to live."[33]

The Church's Response to Poverty: Alleviate or Emancipate?

The dismantling of slavery as a legal political system and the emancipation of the slave population in the Caribbean in the early 1800s did little to alter social and economic relations between colonizer and colonized. In fact, the very tool that was offered to the freed slaves as the means of economic and psychological liberation of the former slave population, primarily through the missionary enterprise, was also explicitly used as the means of social control and for reinforcing existing class, race, and gender stratification and for maintaining planter hegemony and the dominance of a white male minority.

Missionaries represented the interests of the colonizer and, whether in the Caribbean or Africa, a major intent of the missionary enterprise was to convert and control. In the pre-emancipation period in the Caribbean the main concern was maintaining a docile and pliable workforce. In the post-emancipation period this objective was effectively achieved through the establishment of a two-tiered education system managed by the church and intended to maintain social separation of the two populations, with one strand catering to the children of the former slave population and the other to the white population who could not afford to send their children to the metropole for a classical grammar school education.

In the Caribbean, popular education for the former slave population was established through a Negro Education Grant and the issue at stake was described in an 1835 report to the British Government by the Reverend J. Sterling. The burden of the report was the need to maintain the former slave population as a compliant laboring class through maintaining "power over their minds":

The Issue at Stake

About 770,000 persons have been released from slavery by the Emancipation Act, and are now in a state of rapid transition to entire freedom. The peace and prosperity of the Empire at large may be not remotely influenced by their moral condition; the care of this is in itself also a matter of grave responsibility; and lastly the opinion of the public in Britain earnestly requires a systematic provision for their mental improvement. It is plain therefore that something must be done; and it must be done immediately. For although the negroes are now under a system of limited control, which secures to a certain extent their orderly and industrial conduct, in the short space of five years from the first of next August, their performance of the functioning of a labouring class in a civilized community will depend entirely on the power over their minds of the same prudential and moral motives which govern more or less the mass of the people here. If they are not so disposed as to fulfil these functions, properties will perish in the colonies for lack of human impulsion; the whites will no longer be able to reside there; and the liberated negroes themselves will probably cease to be progressive. The law having already determined and enforced their civic rights, the task of bettering their condition can be further advanced only by *education*.[34]

This explicit colonial intent of using the missionary enterprise to ensure social compliance and maximum profit for the advancement of the metropole was not unique to the British Empire. In an essay included in this volume, Kossi Ayedze comments on a discussion between the minister of the colonies and the first missionaries to the Belgian Congo, where the injunction was to evangelize and to draw inspiration from the principle that they must act "first and foremost for Belgium's interests."[35]

Social class cleavage in postemancipation Caribbean society masked a gender differentiation consistent with hierarchical relations of gender marked by male supremacy and female subordination. This was effectively achieved through an intentional sex segregation of curricula offered in both tiers of the system which, in keeping with patriarchal norms and values, served to reinforce women's subordination and expected relegation to the private domain. Historically, schooling in most societies, particularly those with a colonial history, has played a pivotal role in channeling and socializing and reproducing social structure and order and thereby societies marked by hierarchies of race, class, and gender. The role of the school in this regard is reinforced and supported by a web of social and cultural norms and economic and legal provisions, the effectiveness of which is best represented by the system of apartheid established in South Africa in 1948.

Former slaves in the Caribbean, however, were not simply passive recipients of imposed race, class, and gender codes of behavior but in many ways exerted agency and exercised both covert and overt forms of resistance in relation to employment entitlements, the right of cultural and religious expression, and political participation, and, in this regard, women played a significant role.

S. Wilmot comments on ways in which Jamaican freedwomen featured in labor protests that challenged the political economy of the plantation system between 1838 and 1865.[36] He posits that one of the first issues to threaten labor relations in Jamaica was the withdrawal of women from regular field work and their determination for greater autonomy to focus on the cultivation and marketing of ground provisions to contribute to the needs of the family economy. This posed a serious challenge to the control over labor that slavery had guaranteed and therefore to the stability that plantation owners had previously enjoyed, and it resulted in counterresistance "bullying tactics" on the part of planters to enforce compliance. The dynamic cycle of resistance and counterresistance by freedwomen, on the one hand, and planters, on the other, in many instances forced planters to offer more conciliatory terms, which allowed women more time for attention to home and family.

These women were not only concerned about the emotional and economic well-being of their immediate families; issues that threatened the wider community of laborers also "attracted very impressive female response," as when, for example, men and women workers "threatened violent retribution when they believed that the British planters planned to kill the Baptist Ministers who had tried to negotiate wages and general working conditions for their congregations."[37]

The class, race, and gender systems associated with the plantation economy and constructed through the socializing and channeling function of state institutions and the supporting role of the missionary endeavor were still evident in the Caribbean up to the turn of the twentieth century. By the 1960s and early 1970s, however, many English-speaking territories had gained political independence from Britain. These independence movements and the quest for national identity and sovereignty were, in no small measure, influenced by other movements of the 1970s, which drew attention to class, race, and gender inequalities and brought into question the role of social institutions, including the church, in reproducing and reinforcing these inequities.

R. W. M. Cuthbert, writing in 1986 about the Caribbean Council of Churches (CCC), points to the impact of political independence movements in the Caribbean on the organizational structure of the historical missionary churches in the region, which began to recognize the need to reflect the national aspirations of Caribbean people.[38] This, he suggests, was also a period of transition in which the role of the missionary with strong links to the mother church was declining, and there was sharpening awareness among the indigenous leadership of the need for contact with fraternal organizations in neighboring Caribbean countries. In 1973, the regional ecumenical movement had come into being, and the Caribbean Council of Churches had been established, guided by ideological perspectives articulated at a precursor consultation of church leaders and laity, including women and youth, held in 1971.

Participants attending this early consultation, inter alia, called for greater attention to social justice and liberation and the creation of a new Caribbean person. Although no direct reference was made to class, race, and gender as major axes of social organization and the basis of social alienation in Caribbean societies, there was an acknowledgment that coming out of the missionary past, Caribbean churches had traditionally remained silent on the issue of foreign control of the economy and in many ways had served the interests of the establishment rather than those of the people. The mandate that emerged from the 1971 consultation called on the churches to develop a deliberate program to decolonize Caribbean theology. An important issue that came to the fore was the need to carefully examine the role of the plantation system in the development of Caribbean people and the ways in which the struggle for independence and the search for self-identity had been inhibited by the external control which multinational corporations exercised over their lives.[39]

In response to the critical analyses of the sociohistorical Caribbean context and mindful of the ideological perspectives that informed the dialogue, several programmatic ideas were identified in the 1971 consultation with the explicit intention of fostering more democratic processes and more equitable development and attacking some of the root causes of alienation in Caribbean societies. The most pertinent in relation to concerns of poverty was a call in a report on the 1971 consultation to the established missionary churches to "utilise their own resources, especially land holdings in rural areas where these exist, for the development of all the people and . . . to use the power which it possessed. . . . in its finances and its influence to help abolish the weakness in society. . . . such as racism, classism and landlessness and the domination of the poorer masses by systems which were basically un-sympathetic to the needs of the poor majority."[40] This was to be achieved through a Commission on Christian Action for Development in the Eastern Caribbean (CADEC) as well as through a Land and Food for the People program. In the first instance several grants and loans were disbursed to individuals, groups, and organizations in churches across the region to support a number of initiatives intended to reduce unemployment, increase productivity, and make a contribution to the livelihood of Caribbean people. Many project objectives related to economic activities and included employment creation, providing services and meeting infrastructural needs in identifiable communities, increasing income-earning opportunities, increasing productivity and rationalizing marketing, improving community nutrition, and changing the land tenure system.[41]

An evaluation of these projects revealed that those that espoused the rhetoric of the CCC, that had as their primary goal radical restructuring of Caribbean society, and that set out to challenge prevailing patterns of ownership and production and existing power structures, ran into difficulties and proved to be unsustainable. The implication was that dominant structures and systems were resistant to change. In a presentation to participants of the Pan-African Seminar in Ocho Rios, Jamaica, in 2003, Evelyn Vernon admitted that the work of the CCC has been considerably scaled down and that the ecumenical movement in the region had retreated into denominationalism and nationalism and was in need of renewal.[42]

The irony is that, as far back as 1986, Cuthbert admitted that the ecumenical movement was viewed with skepticism and was often labeled as being elitist, as being neither relevant nor grounded in local realities, and therefore not responsive to the very issues that it sought to challenge:

> The persons involved in the movement are still a small minority, and are often regarded as being alienated from the historical reality of Caribbean life. They are seen to be escaping into a sphere of abstraction where unique concepts, colourful jargon and stirring rhetoric characterise the field of discourse and where reference points and criteria of validity are not subject to objective analysis and testing. The ecumenical circle is seen as being closed and self-contained, set apart from institutional church life at both the regional and local levels, where the agenda and frame of reference is far removed from the ecumenical debates on development and liberation."[43]

As Konrad Raiser notes, even as the Caribbean ecumenical movement and its agenda for social reconstruction are in decline, the general secretary of the World Council of Churches (WCC) notes that fighting poverty has moved back into the center of the international agenda, conceding that "traditionally, the churches' response has been characterized by the work of charity without challenging the political, social and economic structures that are the root causes of poverty."[44]

Raiser went on to suggest, however: "The geo-political changes during the last decade of the 20th century and the accelerating process of economic globalization have obliged the churches and ecumenical organizations to rethink the principles, objectives and methodologies guiding their participation in development."[45]

In the year 2000, the WCC in collaboration with its partners in the Association of WCC-related Development Organisations in Europe (APRODEV) engaged in a process of case studies in a number of countries, including Ghana and South Africa, and Jamaica and Grenada in the West Indies, designed to "gain a better understanding of how churches, agencies and ecumenical organizations could respond more effectively to poverty in the 21st century." The study included special sector studies of the labor movement, transnational corporations, and the especially disadvantaged position of women.

Following on from these studies, the Pan-African Seminar also set out to reach an understanding of the role of churches and related organizations, and considered particular cases and countries. The limits of this essay do not allow for a full discussion of the case studies, but based on the outcomes, five priorities and a number of programmatic elements that churches might adopt to combat poverty and wealth were identified, as were targets intended to complement the United Nations Millennium Development Goals aimed at cutting global poverty in half by the year 2015. Priorities included drawing attention to excessive wealth and greed as well as poverty; directing resources to advocacy on a more equal footing with that for projects and programs; building a strong and effective global alliance to combat poverty and greed; strengthening and renewing local churches and Christian communities to combat poverty and greed and promote social transformation; and clarifying an ecumenical theology of wealth, poverty, and justice.

The perspectives undergirding these priorities seem directed at structural change and social transformation. Although there is no suggestion of any intentional correspondence, elements of these priorities are discernable in national-level initiatives visited during the seminar's study tour. The Ecumenical Service for Socio-Economic Transformation (ESSET), an arm of the South Africa Council of Churches, for example, seeks to promote socioeconomic justice in church and society; facilitate visible, competent, and effective church action in economic life; affirm the wholeness of life; acknowledge God's preference for the poor; and encourage responsible stewardship of resources.[46] Through its work ESSET assists churches to attain a level of economic literacy that enables meaningful participation in economic discourses in the country. A practical expression of its thrust was the hosting of a conference in 2002 to assess the impact of trade liberalization on the garment industry and the launching of a research project on how these impacts affect women's sustainable livelihoods—a critical undertaking given the impact of SAPs and globalization on free trade zones located in developing countries, and therefore on employment opportunities for women from lower socioeconomic strata.

Another of the national-level initiatives studied was that of the Centre for Community Change of the National Council of Churches in the United States (NCC USA), which asserts that in the last three decades economic security has declined for most workers and has set itself the task of advancing a collective agenda to ensure access to basic needs of food, health care, education, employment, and housing regardless of income, geography, citizenship, or any other condition. The organization aims to achieve this goal through an advocacy program called Let Justice Roll, designed to influence and shape public policy that assures the well-being of those living on the margins of society.[47]

In its quest for greater social and economic justice NCC USA recognizes that disadvantaged women and their families are more dramatically affected by poverty, and through its Justice for Women Working Group it has called for an acknowledgment that most contemporary families no longer fit the mold of the two-parent nuclear family. The group questions government welfare family-related policies that assume that marriage is a cure-all for systemic social problems and boldly asserts that marriage will never be a substitute for necessary social programs or for addressing the injustices of the economy.[48]

All countries visited as part of the Pan-African Seminar on Poverty and Religion were replete with examples of social ministry programs geared at meeting immediate needs related to the existential condition of the poor in specific locations. These included, for example, the Potter's House in Pretoria, offering refuge to women who were victims of domestic violence; the Orlando Uniting Reformed Church in Soweto, which was an advocate for economic justice and supported the government's Basic Income Grant program, intended to reduce destitution and poverty and provide minimum support to the poorest 10 percent of households in South Africa; the Salvation Army Home for abused children and HIV-infected children from three to ten years old in Soweto; the Mustard Seed Community in Kingston, Jamaica, operated by the Roman Catholic Church and catering to physically and mentally challenged children; and many others, too numerous to list.

Judging by the material referred to in this essay and what I saw as a participant in the Pan-African Seminar, I have the sense that, even as initiatives at the global, regional, and local levels seek to achieve a common goal, there is no intentional coordination of activities at these various levels and each initiative therefore is inherently autonomous. At all levels, however, ecumenical initiatives appear to adopt a more strategic orientation targeting structural and policy reform, whereas initiatives at the local level are more practical and tactical responses to the differential impacts of economic and political structures and systems on men, women, and children.

A particularly worrying concern for me, however, has been that even in light of evidence that unequivocally points to the feminized nature of poverty, particularly in countries of the South, the ecclesiastical and secular discourse that we have engaged in around issues of poverty, for the most part, has been gender-neutral and few initiatives have specifically targeted the needs of women and their dependents. I am also acutely aware that on this journey there have been limited structured opportunities to hear the voice of the most destitute. More often we have observed their plight "from a distance," engaged in discussions about factors that affect them and ways in which church and state have sought to combat poverty in the various contexts.

As a result of this "othering" of the dispossessed, an experience common to most minorities, women also have to exercise personal agency in a search for solutions to their situations of hopelessness. In this quest, women—who are the most affected and who constitute the majority in their churches—find support through social capital networks or "an economy of affection" in church, family, and community that function outside of a monetary system. In some churches women (and men) also "demonstrate [a] resistance to the dehumanizing consequences of poverty" through engagement in healing rituals and spirit possession.[49]

These practices and their liberating effect are fully explored in sources already referred to, two of which are included in this volume: one by Anthony Pinn, and the other by Linda Thomas and Dwight Hopkins. I will therefore describe only the encounter I had with a Shangaan woman from Orlando East in the Soweto Township. She was a member of the Zion Christian Church and sold cakes, peanuts, oranges, and packets of cheese crackers from a tray under the shade of a tree, an image that was replicated in every country we visited. She told me that she was married and had four children and was able to realize about 10 rand (US$1.65) a day from her enterprise and used this to help with the education of two of her four children, who were still attending school. The other two had already completed their schooling. Although she received no tangible assistance from her church, she was very clear about the importance of selling her wares each day because this allowed her to "buy" holy water, which helped to bring her customers and which was therefore critical to her continued survival and that of her family. For her, as for many women in all our contexts, her church gave her a sense of hope but was doing little to change her circumstance of abject poverty.

A Concluding Comment

One can hardly discuss the situation of women in poverty without taking note of the impact of the international women's movement, and the several associated conferences held over the last four decades, which have focused the world's attention on critical issues facing women, including the need for economic and political empowerment within a framework of human rights and the dismantling of male hegemony. The women's movement, I would contend, is presenting a challenge to prevailing gender ideologies and gender role assignment, as well as existing relations of gender in social, political, and economic spheres, and therefore to traditional patterns of access to productive resources including women's access to education and employment in both the formal and informal sectors of the labor market. Gender systems, however, are not static, and even as driving forces are exerted for change by state and church, opposing and constraining forces operate to maintain the status quo and sustain the project of patriarchy. A major way in which this is achieved is through male control of the governance of social, economic, and political—and, I would add, theological—institutions. In my opinion, the limited capacity of "the church" to attack the root causes of poverty in any significant way may be due, in no small measure, to the fact that it is part of the establishment that it seeks to reform. This was most eloquently expressed in Peter Maurain's short essay "Out of the Temple": "Christ drove the money lenders out of the Temple. But today nobody dares to drive the money lenders out of the Temple because the money lenders have taken a mortgage on the Temple."[50]

As a participant in the Pan-African Seminar on Religion and Poverty, I see two possibilities for enhancing the church's impact in situations of poverty. Essentially, conversations have consistently traversed three domains of knowledge: theological studies, economics, and development studies, and on occasion there is a fourth, gender studies. Issues related to governance and citizenship also surfaced on a number of occasions. This suggests that theologians, and particularly those who subscribe to a theology of liberation of the oppressed, must find creative ways to reinterpret vision and inform action with reference to these knowledge domains. One speaker suggested that, if the church is to effectively respond to issues of poverty, there needs to be a change in the "knowledge culture" of ministerial formation and ways need to be found to bring theological studies into a more direct relationship with other domains of knowledge.

Broadening of the curriculum used for ministerial formation to ensure that basic economic, development, and gender issues are integrated in the program of study would then become necessary. In South Africa reference was made to a WCC initiative already under way to introduce gender studies in the curriculum of theological institutions. In her essay in this volume, Nyambura Njoroge makes a similar suggestion but in terms of the need for religious scholars to adapt an interdisciplinary, holistic approach to fighting poverty, which would require reaching out to other professionals, sharing information, creating networks around issues, and being socially engaged with the poor in their own context.[51]

Second, if the welfare approach, as reflected in the social ministries offered through our various churches, proves to be the more common and effective response to immediate needs of women, men, and children in situations of poverty, these programs need to incorporate opportunities to build awareness among participants of "not only the nature of the structures creating poverty for some and wealth for others, the mal-distribution of social wealth and capital, the unbalanced distribution of political power, but also the structures of inequality between men and women which weaken both in their common struggle for survival and for betterment. Such work has to include the importance of organising, of creating alliances and coalitions, of exerting influence, of communication and public education."[52] Awareness of these issues would prepare women to exercise greater agency in the identification of coping strategies and solutions to problems related to their situation of impoverishment. Church leaders who act on behalf of the poor also need these understandings and skills.

Notes

1. David Jary and Julia Jary, "Sociology," *Collins Dictionary of Sociology* (Glasgow: Harper-Collins, 2000).
2. United Nations Development Programme, *Human Development Report, 1997* (New York: Oxford University Press, 1997).
3. United Nations Population Fund, *State of the World Population, 2002: People, Poverty and Possibilities* (New York: United Nations, 2002), 17. Available at http://www.unfpa .org.
4. *Jamaica Survey of Living Conditions, 2001* (Kingston: Planning Institute of Jamaica and Statistical Institute of Jamaica, April 2002).
5. The figure for the U.S. poverty line was supplied to me by Rev. Rodney Rogers, executive director, Christ of Calvary Community Development Corporation, Inc., Philadelphia.
6. "Overview: Human Development to Eradicate Poverty," *Human Development Report, 1997*, 5, available at http://hdr.undp.org/en/media/hdr_1997_en_overview.pdf.
7. United Nations Development Programme, *Human Development Report, 1997* (New York: Oxford University Press, 1997).
8. Ibid.
9. *The Interpreter's Bible: A Commentary in Twelve Volumes*, vol. 8, *Luke and John* (Nashville, Tenn.: Abingdon Press, 1952).
10. World YWCA, *Project 21: Christianity, Poverty and Wealth in the 21st Century*, draft report (2002), available at http://www.aprodev.net/files/CPW/WYWCA.pdf.

11. Jary and Jary, *Collins Dictionary of Sociology*, 234.

12. K. B. deMarrais and M. D. LeCompte, *The Way Schools Work: A Sociological Analysis of Education* (New York: Longman, 1998), 10.

13. B. Bernstein, "Social Class, Language and Socialization," *Current Trends in Linguistics* 12 (1974): 1545–62.

14. Grace Chang, "Structural Adjustment Undermines Social Welfare around the World: Women in the Global Labour Market," 1, *NNIRR*, Network News: National Network for Immigrant and Refugee Rights, available at http://www.nnirr.org/news/archived _netnews/strucadju.htm.

15. "African Women, Globalization and Poverty," Initial Position Paper (CSW, 2002), available at http://www.femnet.or.ke/documents/CSW_2002_position_paper.pdf.

16. See Lewin Williams, "A Theological Perspective on the Effects of Globalization on Poverty in Pan-African Contexts," in this volume.

17. Molefe Tsele, "Etwatwa: South Africa, Project 21: Christianity, Power and Wealth in the 21st Century," 6, available at http://www.aprodev.net/files/CPW/SAfrica.pdf.

18. United Nations, Department of Economic and Social Affairs, Division for the Advancement of Women, "The Feminization of Poverty," available at http://www.un .org/womenwatch/daw/followup/session/presskit/fs1.htm.

19. ECLAC, "La mujer en América Latina y el Caribe en el marco de la transformación productiva con equidad," LC/L.618 (MDM.12/3), Santiago, Chile, May 1991.

20. A. Sojo, "La intersecion laboral de la mujer latinoamericana: entre la crisis económica y los ratos de la transformación productiva con equidad," manuscript, Santiago, Chile, 1992.

21. BRIDGE, "What about Women? Why We Need a Gender Perspective in Development Policy: Work and Incomes," briefing prepared for Office of Development Assistance (Norwich, U.K.: Institute of Development Studies, University of Sussex, April 1995).

22. J. Heintz, "Globalisation, Economic Policy and Employment: Poverty and Gender Implications, Employment Strategy Papers, Employment Policy Unit, Employment Strategy Department, available at http://www.ilo.org/public/english/employment/ strat/download/esp2006–3.pdf.

23. H. B. Morado, "Female-Headed Households in the Philippines," available at http:// www.bles.dole.gov.ph/download/fhhp.pdf.

24. Viva Network, "Risks Facing Children—Child Headed Households," available at http://www.viva.org.

25. Chang, "Structural Adjustment Undermines Social Welfare."

26. Planning Institute of Jamaica, *Social and Economic Survey, 2001* (Kingston: Planning Institute of Jamaica, 2001).

27. Jyoti Sanghera, "Globalization and Trafficking in Women," Global Policy Forum Web site (1998), available at http://www.globalpolicy.org/socecon/inequal/prostitu .htm.

28. Ibid.

29. Leith Dunn, *Situation of Children in Prostitution: A Rapid Assessment*, Investigating the Worst Forms of Child Labour, Jamaica, no. 8 (Geneva: International Labour Office, 2001).

30. International Labour Office, *A Future without Child Labour: Global Report under the Follow-up to the ILO Declaration on Fundamental Principles and Rights at Work*, International Labour Conference, 90th Session, 2002, Report 1 (B) (Geneva: International Labour Office, 2002).

31. B. Bailey and H. Ricketts, "Gender Vulnerabilities in Caribbean Labour Markets and Decent Work Provisions, *Social and Economic Studies*, 52.4 (2003): 49–82.

32. United Nations Population Fund, *State of the World Population*, 2002, 43–44.

33. World YWCA, Project 21, 3.

34. Quoted in Shirley C. Gordon, *A Century of West Indian Education: A Source Book* (London: Longman Group, 1963), 20–21.

35. See Kossi Ayedze's essay "Poverty among African People and the Ambiguous Role of Christian Thought," in this volume.

36. S. Wilmot, " 'Females of Abandoned Character'? Women and Protest in Jamaica, 1838–65," in *Engendering History: Caribbean Women in Historical Perspective*, ed. V. Shepherd, B. Brereton, and B. Bailey (Kingston, Jamaica: Ian Randle; London: James Currey, 1995).

37. Wilmot, " 'Females of Abandoned Character'?" 284.

38. R. W. M. Cuthbert, *Ecumenism and Development: A Socio-Historical Analysis of the Caribbean Conference of Churches* (Bridgetown, Barbados: Caribbean Conference of Churches, 1986).

39. Ibid.

40. Ibid., 79.

41. Ibid.

42. See Evelyn Vernon, "The Caribbean Conference of Churches: A Philosophy of Sustainable Development," paper presented at the Pan-African Seminar, Kingston, Jamaica, July 2003.

43. Cuthbert, *Ecumenism and Development*, 109.

44. K. Raiser, foreword to *Christianity, Poverty and Wealth: The Findings of Project 21*, by M. Taylor (London: Society for Promoting Christian Knowledge; Geneva: World Council of Churches, 2002), ix.

45. Ibid., x.

46. For information on ESSET, visit http://www.esset.org.za/about.html.

47. For more information on the *Let Justice Roll* program, see http://www.letjusticeroll .org.

48. Justice for Women Working Group, *For the Good of All Families: Affirming Our Interdependence* (New York: National Council of the Churches of Christ USA, 2004).

49. The phrase "economy of affection" is from Linda E. Thomas and Dwight N. Hopkins, "Religion and Poverty: Ritual and Empowerment in Africa and the African Diaspora," in this volume; the comment about "resistance to the dehumanizing consequences of poverty" is from Anthony B. Pinn, "Warm Bodies, Cold Currency: A Study of Religion's Response to Poverty," also in this volume.

50. P. Murain, *Easy Essays on Catholic Radicalism*, 3rd ed., rev. (Kannapolis, N.C.: Omega Graphics, 1976), 2.

51. Nyambura J. Njoroge, "The Struggle for Full Humanity in Poverty-Stricken Kenya," in this volume.

52. Kate Young, "Gender and Development," in *The Women, Gender and Development Reader*, ed. V. Visvanathan, L. Duggan, L. Nisonoff, and N. Wiegersma (London: Zed Books; Dhaka: University Press; Bangkok: White Lotus; Halifax, Nova Scotia: Fernwood Publishing; Cape Town: David Philip, 1997), 54.

CHALLENGES OF THE GLOBAL AND INFORMAL ECONOMIES

Takatso A. Mofokeng | **THE INFORMAL ECONOMY AND**

THE RELIGION OF GLOBAL CAPITAL

In this essay, I look at the informal sector of the economy in Ghana, Kenya, South Africa, and Jamaica. My thesis is that this subeconomy, which operates in all these countries and many others in Pan-Africa, is the black poor's own creation and that it functions as their economic instrument of survival. In it the poor use their creativity and ingenuity. I will also investigate the social organization of the participants (the participation of nuclear and extended family in the enterprise), the ideological, religious roots of the informal economy (what role tradition and religion play in the enterprise), and its management in order to determine its resilience. I argue that the global market economy's disposition is to absorb this resilient economy by exploiting the philosophical, religious, and cultural resources of African people, which provide ideological support to it for maximization of profit for the global economy. Finally, we shall look at ways in which the informal economy can defend and protect itself against the imperialism of global capital.

The Informal Economy: Hope of the Struggling Poor; The Case of Ghana

The first economic analyst to use the concept "informal sector" in reference to economic activity was Keith Hart.[1] He used the concept in his discussion of the historical origins of what he calls the "distortions" in the economy of Ghana that caused the informal economy (popularly known as the makola market) to become larger than the formal economy. This sector, which the poor of Ghana created in the colonial period and which extends to all trade (local and international) and manufacturing, presently constitutes the largest informal economy in Africa, with the Nigerian one being the second largest on the continent. The poor of Ghana created this economy in the rural as well as the urban setting, as people who were entering the industrial economy from two different entry points. Some poor people entered as laborers who had been thrown out of a constantly shrinking formal economy (retrenched laborers), the growth of which could not keep pace with the growing urban and rural population. Others entered the already saturated industrial labor market as redundant laborers from the agrarian hinterland, who came from a shrinking agrarian economy (a subsistence agrarian economy), as well as from commercial agriculture in the rural areas. In the case of rural workers, their subsistence economy had been progressively reduced in size by the introduction of formal commercial agriculture and the introduction of mechanized production. Kenneth King says that this economic sector reflects a "crisis of the state and of formal public sector of the economy, especially in Africa."[2] What he means is that the state, both colonial and modern, failed to create employment by expanding the formal economy, which could have absorbed the growing working population of Ghana.

As far as Ghana is concerned, we have to trace the fundamental weakness of its economy to the depopulation of Ghana through the slave trade, which robbed Ghana of millions of young and able-bodied people who could have contributed to the economy. Their permanent removal from the Ghanaian economy damaged it irreversibly. In the case of the colonial state to which King refers, it should be said that it never was its objective to grow the Ghanaian economy into a large and vibrant one; its objective was to extract raw materials for the British economy and to extract profits from Ghana through the mercantilist economy. This meant that there was no way in which Ghana could accumulate capital reserves for the future development of its own economy. It also meant that when the nation-state was formed at independence, there was no capital to ground a formal economy on a firm foundation. One cannot but conclude, on the basis of the length of history of this crisis (which, as we have pointed out, started during the colonial era) and the size of the sector in question, that we are here dealing with a permanent economic crisis, which continues to worsen at both the national and continental levels.

World Trade Organization statistics (2001), which state that Africa's share in the world trade accounts for only 1 percent of the entire world trade, attest to the enormity of the crisis. The United Nations Human Development Report of 2001, which also defines the Human Poverty Index, states that "the 25 countries at the bottom of the index are all in Africa, and 30 of the 34 classed as low human development nations are in Africa."[3] The second conclusion we can draw is that the poor of Ghana are in a perpetual crisis that can only be arrested if they receive urgent economic attention from all people of goodwill in the world. The question is, does that goodwill exist? This I doubt.

The informal economy of Ghana is not a pure and clearly delineated sector. I concede, however, that there are inherent distortions in it. These distortions were introduced during the course of history, and they persist in the economy of Ghana up until today and continue to worsen. They were introduced by traders in the makola market who, in terms of the size of their enterprises and the level of accumulated capital they own, ought to graduate to the formal economy. Instead of doing so, they continue to operate in this less regulated sector of the economy. Some Ghanaian economists are very pessimistic about elements in this sector voluntarily graduating into the formal economy and thereby reducing the size of the informal sector.

Further distortion is caused by operators in the formal economic sector who operate clandestinely in the informal sector to avoid high taxation, which is levied in the formal economy. These distorters of the informal sector and thereby the national economy as a whole lead also to constant weakening of the currency, by keeping large sums of their earnings from the informal sector out of circulation. This they do to evade the tax system. Their operations in the formal sector lead to a weakening also of the true and legitimate operators in the informal economy, by offering them uneven competition that the legitimate operators are unable to win. The legitimate operators end up falling out of the informal economy into the large pool of destitute unemployed people. It is important to note that when Keith Hart was discussing the crisis in the Ghanaian economy, he was referring to the economic crisis of a postindependence nation state. The new state at independence inherited a situation that it did not have the capacity to handle.

POVERTY IN KENYA AND THE STRUGGLE AGAINST IT

In order to show the gravity of the Kenyan economic situation, I will cite some statistics and information derived from the *Interim Poverty Reduction Strategy Paper, 2000–2003* of the Kenyan government, issued on 13 July 2000. According to this paper, the overall national incidence of poverty stood at 52 percent. This translated into 5 million Kenyans, the overwhelming major-ity of whom are women, most of whom live in rural Kenya and work as subsistence farmers. In Kenya, one can thus justifiably talk about the femin-ization of poverty and the struggle against it through the informal economy, a topic that is discussed in the next section.

JUA KALI: AN ECONOMIC INSTRUMENT OF STRUGGLE IN KENYA

The type of economic activity that we observed in Ghana also obtains in many African countries, including Kenya, though it may bear different names. In Kenya, which the Pan-African Seminar participants visited, it is called *jua kali*, a Swahili term meaning "a hot sun." One can already understand that this is an economic sector without the statutory "shelter"—literally and figuratively —that should have been provided by the Kenyan government. It is a sector in which the participants, the poor of Kenya, the overwhelming majority of whom are rural and urban women, literally eke out a means of survival in the hot sun. Jua kali has several characteristics within the Ghanaian informal economic sector as well.

Like the Ghanaian informal economy, the jua kali exists on different scales in rural and urban settings. In 1993 a report sponsored by the U.S. Agency for International Development (USAID) put the size of the Kenyan jua kali at 900,000 enterprises employing some two million people. In other words, the jua kali serves as the poor's own economic instrument of struggle for survival in a hostile economic atmosphere. Most analysts agreed then and now that the formal economy of Kenya was expected to grow at least sufficiently to cater for the expected employment needs of the Kenyan people. In fact, in 2001 this formal economy experienced a negative growth (-2%), hence the massive and rapid growth of the jua kali. In both cases, this economic sector, contrary to logic, does not serve as the first step, or practicing ground, that prepares the participants for a smooth and successful entry into the formal economy. Instead, according to Keith Hart (writing about Ghana) and Kenneth King (writing about Kenya), the long history of the existence of this shelterless economy is evidence that there is a permanent and deliberate separation of the formal and informal economies. This separation is due to several weaknesses in the informal economy, namely, the lack of formal production skills and managerial expertise, and a lack of capital and an identifiable market segment. As far as the Kenyan jua kali is concerned, it is common knowledge that participants in it depended on the resources they had saved when they were still employed in the formal system. King, attesting to the separation of the two economies, states that the International Labour Organisation in its report also recommended that, instead of destabilizing this economic sector by destroying its self-constructed shelters in which creative activities take place, and instead of having its practitioners generally harassed by the Kenyan police, the government should provide serviced sites and security with a view toward a formal linking of the two economies through subcontracting. These actions would send signals to the banks to enable the jua kali easier access to production loans. In the absence of such positive signals, and taking into account the persistent expansion of the jua kali as a result of the continual shrinking of the formal economy, one can only conclude that the necessary conditions for increased savings, which could translate into capital and hence entry into the formal economy, do not exist.

Here again, we must note that there is a distortion inherent in this jua kali economy. This distortion is introduced by some participants in the formal economy who take advantage of this less-regulated sector to operate parallel ventures in order to evade taxation. The social effect of their intervention is the destabilization of this sector by their offering unfair competition to financially weak enterprises in this sector. As in the case of Ghana, many of the legitimate operators end up closing down their operations and increasing the pool of unemployed people.

ORGANIZATION OF THE JUA KALI

The jua kali is organized along traditional African social-systemic lines, since the owners and producers of capital are one and the same, and they come from both the nuclear and the extended family. Even children assist the parents, when they return from school and during weekends. Some children combine schooling with this form of income earning, while some parents combine working in the formal sector with jua kali activity. This household economy also includes maids and servants who comprise the poorer members of the extended family. It is in the course of production that skills are acquired and passed on. In some cases skills were acquired in the formal sector by those who were retrenched and who decided to enter the jua kali.

HOW JUA KALI SURVIVES AND THRIVES

Since Kenya is 70 percent rural, we can rightly assume that African culture and philosophy are still strong and influential in that setting and in Kenya generally. No wonder that jua kali economic activity relies very strongly on traditional philosophical, cultural, and practical resources. Examples include the *aegesangio* practice, in which the community comes together to assist a household to complete a task and expects reciprocity, and the *aahoi* practice, whereby a destitute household is given a new start with a loaned cow, sheep, or ewe, or loaned land. Some resources are drawn from forms of African Christian faith or Islam for encouragement and impetus.

Since there is a very thin line between African culture and religion, we can also conclude that this economic enterprise is being resourced by elements of African religion. Muslims in the jua kali benefit from Islamic economic ethical teaching (*azakat*), the giving of which translates into distribution of capital without expectation of interest from the recipient; it is mandatory for all Muslims who possess money beyond a certain minimum established in the sharia, the Islamic ethical code. All these resources, individually and collectively in some instances, create a spiritual and ethical universe that enables the jua kali to keep on growing and expanding its economic survival network for the ever increasing number of poor people.

Poverty in South Africa

According to the South African National Development Agency, a governmental body set up to combat poverty, in a population of about 45 million people, 20 million South Africans live below the poverty line. In 2003, the national unemployment level stood at between 25 percent and 35 percent. In "informal settlements" (a euphemism for squatter camps) it stood at 60 percent. Of this figure, between 60 percent and 70 percent comprised black youth, some of whom were university graduates. It is conceivable that the majority of the people in the above statistic were female. The formal economy has not grown sufficiently since the 1990s because of after-effects of the earlier economic isolation of apartheid South Africa. This lack of growth led to ever spiraling unemployment. When the apartheid government realized that it would never be able to provide employment, it introduced the strategy of deregulation of the economy. It is that strategy which allowed for the creation of the informal economic sector in South Africa, which did not exist prior to that decision. Many of the unemployed and retrenched women and men ended up in the informal sector, or what in South Africa is called the *spaza* economy.

SOUTH AFRICAN SPAZA ECONOMY

"Spaza" means "not genuine," and "spaza economy" refers to the many trading efforts along pavements in the cities, squatter camps or informal settlements, black townships, rural villages, and white-owned farms. It consists of small manufacturing enterprises (crafts, woodwork, trading in all sorts of consumer items, etc.) in small shelters built out of corrugated iron and wood, which are sometimes donated by international donor organizations as well as service industries located in poor black people's homes. "Spaza economy" also refers to efforts by the black poor to substitute for the banks and other financial service providers that are not accessible to spaza operators. Money pools are also created among social circles and friends. The purpose is to enable one another with interest-free loans for different purposes (*mogodisano*).

In some of the undertakings, the purpose is to accumulate profit for purposes of growth and entry into the formal economic sector. For those who operate with that profit motive, more often than not, the objective is never attained. The participants cannot win in the competition for a sizeable market share with formal sector participants. Instead of becoming competitive, their market share shrinks as more and more unemployed blacks enter this sector. In some cases, the motive is mutual assistance for mutual survival. In other cases, the participants strive to acquire money, which they need to purchase commodities for family use, which can only be bought from the formal economy with money. In other words, if the old traditional barter system still operated, they would still be resorting to it. In its absence, however, they have created something similar and use it effectively.

SOCIAL ORGANIZATION OF THE SPAZA ECONOMY

The greatest number of participants in pavement trade are individual women who accept the challenge of struggling for the economic survival of their families. More often than not, these women's husbands are underemployed in the formal economy and that compels their wives to sell something on the pavements to augment their husbands' income. In some cases, their children would also be selling at different spots in the township or on city streets. These different roles of the members of the same family are planned and decided and agreed on at home. In service and manufacturing spaza industries, households participate. In other words, children and even grandparents play a role in this struggle for economic survival.

In financial mutual assistance schemes, groups of closely related people constitute a society. In some cases a group of friends or fellow employees constitute an economic fellowship. In other words, an economic activity simultaneously operates as a social event. The involvement of children in such struggles for survival would not be seen as unjust child employment.

SPAZA ECONOMY AND IDEOLOGICAL RESOURCES

Every economic mode operates with an ideological superstructure that consists of ideas, values, and a culture. A dialectical relationship exists between it and the superstructure of ideas and ideology. Religion always forms a part of that superstructure. This has been the case since the existence of economic markets during different epochs of human history. Many sociologists of religion have established this fact. In an important essay, Eduardo Mendieta argues this same point.[4] The economies in Africa, formal and informal, are not an exception to this reality. The same applies to the informal economies generally, and especially those economies being considered in this volume. Wherever an informal economy operates, whether in Kenya,

Ghana, South Africa, or anywhere else in the Pan-African world, these efforts by the poor draw on philosophical, cultural, and religious resources for their organization, coherence, management, and energy. These are readily available in the community of the spaza economy, in both rural and urban settings. That does not mean, however, that every cultural, philosophical, or religious resource can and does serve as a positive resource in the struggle for economic survival. Some are counterproductive and only serve to subvert that struggle, as is evidenced by some forms of Christianity, Islam, and African religion prevalent in the rural areas of Ghana and elsewhere. Similar exploitative practices occur in the ghettoes and shantytowns of Nairobi and in the South African townships, in large cities such as Johannesburg and Pretoria, and in smaller towns and rural areas. A critical attitude is necessary in the discernment of useful forms of cultural, religious, and philosophical resources. Contemporary sociologists of culture like Amilcar Cabral and those of religion like Peter Magubane have done a sterling job in developing critical analytical instruments for such a task of discernment. We can also refer to Max Weber, who recognized that there was an absence of innocence in Protestant Christianity and that this played a role in the emergence and success of capitalism.[5] In Ghana and Kenya biblical names, themes, and texts are widely used in support of these small enterprises. Madipoane Masenya mentions some of these names and themes in her essay in this volume.[6]

Culture, Religion, and Philosophy of the Poor: Opium or an Instrument for Survival?

I have stated that the informal economy, as the last resort of the poor, draws very crucial nonmaterial resources from the rich ideological chest of those battered communities for its sustenance and survival. If its success depends largely on resilience fueled by these resources, as I contend, how do we deal with a socialist ideological critique of this ideological realm? Karl Marx's widely known reference to religion as the opium of the people has unleashed an unending debate on what he meant by the phrase. If he was implying that the people chose it freely, that would not be so bad, because it would be chosen because it is of some use to them. On the other hand, as some have argued, if Marx meant it was an opium "for the people"—something imposed on them for reasons that are not theirs and for the achievement of purposes that are not theirs either—it is certainly harmful. Whichever way we look at the issue of religion, whether it be Christian, Muslim, Hindu, or traditional African, we have to admit that it sometimes operates as an opium for the people and has disastrous consequences. There are numerous examples in many parts of the world, including Africa and the diaspora. In the case of Ghana, there is something called the *trokosi* system, in which young girls are sent to serve in temples; the religion that underpins that system clearly has a negative impact on the families and lives of the poor girls who become servants to the priest. It destroys the social fabric of the families and weakens them by removing some economically productive forces from the families. At a psychological level it is clear that those girls will be scarred for the rest of their lives.

In Kenya, the prevalence of Pentecostalism cannot escape a similar critique. In South Africa, distinctions must be made among the different forms of Christianity and their function in the nation's society, such as state Christianity, church Christianity, and liberation Christianity. In the *Kairos Document*, issued by a group of South African theologians in 1985, at the time of apartheid, state Christianity as well as church Christianity were criticized for blunting the sharp edges of people's anger, while liberation Christianity was praised for energizing the creative imagination of oppressed people.

In the distant past, some forms of traditional religion required an annual sacrifice of people in order to gain a blessing for the community. It was a practice that violated the human rights of the victims and their families, let alone the integrity of the social fabric, and the victim's ability to contribute to the family economy. In our day, however, African religions and cultures, whether Muslim, Christian, or traditional African, have a potential for good and have proved to be sources of inspiration and fountains of creative thought concerning the delegitimation of the oppressor as well as the legitimation of liberation struggles. There are ample examples to prove this. They can be found in Ghana, Kenya, South Africa, the Caribbean, and in the United States, and there is no way we can talk about the resilience of the informal economy without bringing them into the picture and acknowledging their positive role.

Poverty in Jamaica

Jennifer Martin opened her description of Jamaican society by saying: "A race has been freed but a society has not been formed."[7] The race referred to is of Africans, who constitute the largest part of the 2.5 million people of Jamaica. The other citizens are Tainos and Europeans. Fifty percent of the people of Jamaica live and work abroad. Their remittances to Jamaica add up to about 50 percent of the budget of Jamaica. While the financial benefits of living and working abroad are large, the social price is not negligible.

As Martin said, "a society has not been formed." She added that instead of the formation of a society, the absence of about 50 percent of the heads of families, whether they be mothers or fathers or both, has resulted in the large-scale destabilization of the Jamaican family. Forty-five to 50 percent of Jamaican families are now headed by women. In addition, there are many other types of families, including some headed by children. The absence of fathers and mothers has led to the large-scale migration of children, abandoned in their home villages, who seek refuge in the cities where they live on the streets. There, they swell the numbers of desperate city dwellers. Those who remain in the rural areas form part of the 70 percent of people who live in poverty in the rural areas of Jamaica. Thirty percent of the children in the growing population of Jamaica are born to teenage mothers. HIV/AIDS is also rampant in this age group; a consequence is an increase in abandoned babies, some of whom are also HIV positive and who cause a strain on national resources. One of the results of the social dislocation of society is escalation of different types of crime, including violence in which guns are being used.

A positive development lies in the educational sphere. Government and the churches regard education as an important instrument that can contribute to the improvement and strengthening of the social structure. The general emphasis on the education of girls is bearing fruit in that at present, 70 percent of graduates with university degrees are women. It is hoped that they will contribute to the strengthening of the Jamaican society and the broadening of its economic base.

ECONOMIC ORGANIZATION AND POVERTY

According to Michael Witter of the University of the West Indies, the informal economy of Jamaica, which constitutes 33 to 40 percent of the economy, is the actual economy in the hands of Jamaicans.[8] The rest of the economy (60 to 67 percent) is owned by multinationals and transnational cartels, which are based in the Western metropolitan capitals and which operate especially in the mining sector. Jamaica imports 90 percent of its oil and depends a great deal on food imports. The net result of this economic domination is the outflow of needed capital, the growth of the national debt (60 percent of the national income goes to international debt repayment), and the continuous shrinking of the Jamaican economy, which results in growth of unemployment. According to the 28 July 2003 issue of the Jamaican national newspaper The Gleaner, the national herd of beef- and milk-producing cattle was shrinking at an enormous rate. This situation was leading to the increase of labor migration to Western metropoli and the further weakening of the fabric of the Jamaican society.

THE POOR AND THEIR RESPONSE TO POVERTY

The poor people of Jamaica, like their counterparts in Ghana, Kenya, and South Africa, have also created small enterprises in both rural areas, where the poor constitute 70 percent of the population, and urban areas in an effort to address poverty and unemployment. These enterprises are the 40 percent of the economy mentioned by Michael Witter in his talk to the Pan-African Seminar in Kingston. They are in many sectors of the economy including agriculture, crafts, and services. Omar Davies, the Jamaican minister of finance, drew attention in the same seminar to distortions in the informal sector.[9] They consist of traders in the formal sector of the economy who evade taxation by operating in the informal sector as well. The result is—as in the other countries I have described—that they compete against the naturally weak operators in that sector and squeeze them out, driving them deeper into poverty. The minister also referred to the illegal drug trade, which is run by very powerful and wealthy cartels. The political and social impact of the intervention of the drug lords in the informal sector lies in their control of the residential areas where the poor live. It is for this reason that Rev. Garnet Roper referred to the withdrawal of the state and the absence of politics from these areas.[10] Omar Davies argued that neither economic growth nor the eradication of poverty could be achieved without the strengthening of the informal sector of the economy by the government through training its participants in skills required to run successful enterprises and through financial assistance. In that way, he believes, small enterprises would graduate into the formal sector of the economy. In The Gleaner of 28 July 2003, Errol Ennis, the minister of agriculture, was reported to be taking similar steps, encouraging the practice of group farming in place of subsistence farming in order to curb soil erosion; with this training and assistance, the lot of poor farmers would improve and they would eventually join the formal economy.

RELIGION AND ITS RESPONSE TO THE SOCIOECONOMIC SITUATION

Jamaica is populated mainly by the descendants of Africans whose ancestors brought with them to the New World the religions of Africa, as well as the rich cultures of Africa; these practices and beliefs permeate the entire society on the island and influence all facets of life. It would therefore not be wrong to assert that Christianity, which is undoubtedly the most prevalent religion in Jamaica, is also greatly influenced by these African religions to a greater or lesser degree, depending on the class of people one is dealing with. Scholars of religion say that there are more churches in Kingston per square meter than anywhere else in the world. The strongest of these churches are organized in an ecumenical body called the Jamaica Council of Churches. It is through this body that they devise strategies for dealing with the many problems of society, including urban and rural poverty, with the limited means at their disposal. Yet one also finds churches that uphold and preach the so-called prosperity gospel. They simply preach a gospel of individual effort, which appeals to the middle classes in society, and are therefore not influential as far as the poor are concerned.

The most pervasive religious influence in Jamaica is exerted by the Rastafarian religion, with its emphasis on peace and sobriety.[11] Through reggae music this religion has spread throughout the Caribbean, Africa, and large parts of the Western world. The culture of Rastafarianism, which is based largely on a conservative interpretation of the Old Testament, mixed with elements of African culture, is also as widely spread as the reggae music. Though its adherents are found in the various classes of society, the vast majority come from the lowest classes, namely the poor and the less educated. It is difficult, however, to measure its impact on the economy of the poor, that is, on the informal sector. While the influence of Rastafarianism cannot be accurately gauged, there is still a sense that Christianity has been less effective as an influence on this sector. Garnet Roper claims that Christianity has not succeeded in exerting comparable influence because it has not succeeded in translating itself into an ideology. This assessment is shared by Omar Davies, who during the Kingston seminar leveled criticism against the training of pastors, which avoids serious attention to economic issues. Another critique came from Rex Nettleford, who is convinced that a greater impact would be achieved in the struggle against poverty if theology and theologians would concentrate their efforts on the informal sector of the economy.[12]

The Global Market and Its Interest in the Informal Economy

The global market economy, through the local and regional economy as its agency, is interested in the informal sector for three reasons. First, the informal sector is an area of production and trade where money circulates that could be transformed into capital for the benefit of the formal sector. More often than not it circulates without entering the banks and also eludes the tax system. The banking system, as a financial wing of the global economy, always wants to siphon away the accumulated income of the informal sector without returning any of it to the people. Instead of doing that, it puts capital beyond the reach of the informal sector. This can be seen in the many advertisements that are put out by banks, which clearly target the accumulated finances of the informal sector. Some banks and insurance companies even go to the extent of sending agents to convince the operators of the spaza economy to deposit their incomes with them. The draw is clearly the attraction of that accumulated income. The operators of the informal sector are encouraged to deposit their money in the banks and other financial institutions, but when they try to secure loans, they are suddenly confronted by collateral requirements that they cannot satisfy. These loan conditions include for example, formal qualifications in managerial skills and experience in running an enterprise in the formal economy, financial literacy, and a clearly determinable market share. Such requirements lead them to put their own collective savings in the banks, insurance companies, and other financial institutions beyond their reach and exclusively within the reach of the formal sector. This is the reason why the Department of Finance in South Africa supported a bill that would force the banks to reserve an agreed and determined percentage of their loans for the informal sector, with softened collateral requirements.[13]

The second reason why the global market economy is interested in the informal economy is the size and capacity of the informal sector as a large pool of potential consumers of certain commodities, which could enlarge the global economy's profits.

Third, the global market, through its consumer market arm, is interested in the informal sector as a small-scale creator of consumer items that do not go through the national bureaus of standards but are able to slow down the growth of the formal sector while satisfying the basic needs of the general poor population. This way of operating enables the poor to survive further impoverishment. We should note that in many cases, these informal-sector workers are self-trained and pass on their skills to other operatives in the sector who do not go through formal training and education. This means that their education does not cost the state and the formal sector much of anything. In some instances, the operators in the formal economy do finance the establishment of platforms where new or even foreign commodities are tried out. Whenever that is the case, the spaza activities are throttled out of existence when they have served their usefulness.

The global market economy is also interested in the poor, and in poor operators of the informal sectors, as potential consumers. It intends to transform them from free users of commodities and turn them into real consumers as it does with everyone else, including the workers in the formal economy. As consumers, they will be totally subjected to its ideological and material power. Alternatively they will be turned into commodities themselves if they have the potential to maximize profit for the global economy. This is what happens to many people who acquire celebrity status in the eyes of the general public. It happens to many creative people, some of whom come from very poor families and communities: artists, sports people, and other professionals. As commodities or celebrities, they will be bought at a price, owned, and their use value managed, marketed, and consumed at a high price by other people who have been turned into consumers. More often than not, these celebrities tend to lose their humanity and their freedom in this process. They become unrepentant worshippers of this god (global capital). Either (or both) of these eventualities leads to the shrinkage of the informal sector. It is therefore incumbent upon those who believe in the survival of the poor to strengthen the poor's own defenses.

THE GLOBAL MARKET AND LEGITIMATION

The global market is an old economic formation that has been operating for as long as markets were formed. Still, it has regularly changed its form throughout the ages and in different circumstances and geographical areas.[14] In other words, it is adaptable and flexible. It is because of these attributes that it has been able to weather the storms of time and continue to thrive. The academic study of the global market has also established that it uses different ideologies in different areas of the world as long as it can succeed in maximizing profit and achieving hegemony.

If, as I allege, the global market is interested in the growing informal sector in our countries, what instrument will it use to make itself attractive to this economic sector where these informal sectors are large and well established? An observation of the language of the global market economy shows that like all new modes of production, this one is in dire need of an appropriate language for self-justification, self-articulation, and self-propagation. Since its global nature means that it has no home soil even though its center is well known to be the G8 nations, it must indigenize itself everywhere on the globe. There is consequently a concerted effort on the part of global capital to search for and use effective language to promote and legitimize itself if resisted and defend itself if attacked. In secular cultures, it adopts the language of the local secular culture. In religious cultures, it has no choice but to adopt the language that is heavily influenced by the local religious ethos. This is noticeable for instance in Ghana, where "Lord" is the name of a cigarette brand; "Grace," a brand name for butter; and "obedience" is used to advertise Sprite. From that perspective, one can say the commercial sector, through advertisements, has converted religious rhetoric into economic sales language. In the case of Sprite ("Obey your thirst"), business supplants the religious talk and advertises its own message (products) to consumers, effectively asking them to "obey" and buy its product (Sprite). The consumer's desire to obey God and elders is replaced by the desire to satisfy thirst. The abstract thing called obedience is replaced in the citizens' consciousness by the tangible thing called Sprite, sold by Coca-Cola and marketed through ads. The religious persona (believer) is thus turned from a consumer of God's words to an economic consumer, a buyer of Sprite, and his or her desire to obey God is exploited. The same argument can be used for a cigarette called Lord, and other related brands. In this regard, one may argue that these ads ride on the wave of religious discourse and take advantage of it and its symbols—and consequently have a greater impact than those that stand in isolation lacking context. Global capital is able to operate flexibly in this because according to the scholars U. Ulrich Duchrow, Julio de Santa Ana, and Bob Goudzwaard, global capital itself operates with a religious logic.[15] In areas where Christianity is the dominant religion, the global economic market has chosen a Christian language to legitimate and market itself. In areas where other religions are dominant, it uses the most prevalent one. In Europe and North America, it has chosen church theology in its search for relevant theological concepts with which to legitimate, entrench, and expand itself.

Why does global capital relate so comfortably to religions, ethnic or otherwise? The answer can be found in its nature and character. It is itself a religion and it projects itself as such.[16] It has a god, as seen in its devotion to monopoly finance capital. Dwight Hopkins says the following about this: "The god of globalization embodies the ultimate concern or ground of being where there is a fierce belief in the intense concentration, in a few hands, of monopoly finance capitalist wealth on the world stage."[17] Like every religion, it demands a faith response from its adherents after a concerted campaign. They end up accepting its confessional statement that, inevitably, builds sacrifice in its operations. The poor and the weak are always the first to be sacrificed. Bob Goudzwaard states the issue this way: "They [our gods] require sacrifices in exchange for providing us with material prosperity—mounting poverty, the destruction of health and the environment, the relentless elimination of jobs and the quality of work and the perpetual return of the threat of war. Yet time after time we are told in tones borne up by the weight of 'self-evidence' that these sacrifices are necessary, if not 'preordained.' "[18]

How Global Capital Roots Itself among
the Poor in Africa and the Diaspora

Those economists who study strategies of global capital agree that absorption and homogenization are its major strategies for penetrating new and virgin economic areas. Global capital aims at homogenization of culture, consumer patterns, consumer items, and the absorption or destruction of ethnic foods and drinks. It always replaces ethnic economic items with synthetics to achieve homogenization. Ghanaian kente cloth will be substituted by kente prints made outside of Ghana, and genuine dreadlocks are replaced with synthetic dreadlocks, for example. Sometimes in order to lay legal grounds for these strategies to be achieved, copyright laws are invalidated and new ones drawn by the World Trade Organization. At other times, blatantly military strategies are pursued and invading armies are indemnified by international institutions. In Africa and the diaspora, where an indigenous African Christianity that employs African cultural and religious elements in its expression holds sway, the global economic market has chosen that religion as the area of search for concepts and practices that it can use to win the hearts and minds of African people, especially the poor among them. Once won over, African people will become uncritical consumers and praise-singers as it expands throughout greater Africa. As I concede above, there are negative elements in African culture and religion that do not promote life and equality between the sexes or the equality of people generally. These elements should be identified, criticized, condemned, and discarded in order to make it difficult for the global market economy to swallow the informal economy of the poor in our countries.

As I have already stated with regard to the practice of trokosi in Ghana and the charismatic church religion that is widespread in Kenya and South Africa, both are notable examples of religious traditions that are not helpful in the economic struggle of the poor. But even other traditions can be subverted to harm the poor. The ideologues and strategists of the global market economy have come to realize the resilience and pervasiveness of the positive in the cultures and religions of the people of the third world, as well as their potency as instruments of both survival and liberation. But they have begun to absorb them into their linguistic universe in order to mediate the absorption of spaza economies and poor people of Africa (on the continent and in the diaspora) into the global market as consumers of finished products, but also to contain the possible anger and protest action against the *comprador* capitalists. Since much of culture and religion is expressed through language and music, the language and music of the poor in Africa and the diaspora have become the focal point in the spread of global capital throughout Pan-Africa. We can see that the melodies and lyrics and sounds in ethnic music are being replaced by those in the global capital centers in order for homogenization to be achieved.

In this entire process of co-optation, a new religion of the global market economy is constructed and marketed to the poor for consumption. It goes without saying that this exercise can only be achieved through the domestication of those indigenous concepts, because they are alien to the language of global capital. It is clear here that religion, philosophy, and culture of the poor of Africa and the diaspora are a terrain of struggle in which no neutrality is possible and the poor themselves are challenged to defend their heritage if their makola, jua kali, or spaza economic efforts are to survive. The pertinent question at this stage is how the poor can resist further impoverishment in their struggle for the betterment of their condition. What cultural and religious instruments of struggle do they use in the different dimensions of human existence, social, political, and economic? What concepts and practices that are fundamental to African social structure and philosophy remain to inform the economic struggle of the poor in Africa and the diaspora? It is my contention that the answer lies in continuous renewal of the culture and religion of the poor in Africa and the diaspora, because their language is gradually and systematically being absorbed into the arsenal of global capital and used against them. If this is the case, how can these key cultural practices and concepts be protected or renewed for purposes of resisting the further impoverishment of the poor?

There is a growing school of economics that argues that the resilient cultures and traditional religions of Africa and the diaspora, which were responsible for their survival as a people, could serve as a defense against further erosion of the economy of the poor.[19] George Soros, head of the Soros Fund Management, who acquired his enormous wealth from gambling in the global finance market, claims that the weakness that causes instabilities in the global finance market lies not in the economic sector but, rather, in the political. For the moment, this is the sector that still eludes the global tendency of homogenization, because a global political system that harmonizes with the global economic system does not exist. The world still has nation-states and national governments that adopt different and sometimes conflicting laws, policies, and regulations relating to the global economy. In that context George Soros has made a very important statement, which identifies the weak underbelly of the global market economy, in his book Crisis *of the Global Economy*. In it, he says: "If I had to deal with people instead of markets, I could not have avoided moral choices and I could not have been so successful in making money."[20] In other words, people and their morality—in our present case, poor people of Africa in Africa itself and in the diaspora, their cultures and religions, are the weak underbelly of the global economy. But precisely because they are a weak point in this system, they are the strength upon which the oppositional discourse should concentrate and ground its struggle for the survival of the poor and their economies.

Notes

1. Keith Hart, quoted in Kwame Ninsin, *The Informal Sector in Ghana's Political Economy* (Accra: Freedom Publisher, 1991).
2. Kenneth King, *Jua Kali—Kenya* (Nairobi: EAEP, 1996), 11. Another very useful book on the political economy of Kenya in general, and jua kali in particular, is Peter Coughlin and Gerrishon K. Ikiara, eds., *Industrialization in Kenya: In Search of a Strategy* (Nairobi: Trans-Africa Publisher, 1984).
3. *United Nations Human Development Report* (Oxford: Oxford University, 2001), 143.
4. See Eduardo Mendieta's "Society's Religion: The Rise of Social Theory, Globalization and the Invention of Religion," in *Religions/Globalizations: Theories and Cases*, ed. Dwight N. Hopkins, Lois Ann Lorentzen, Eduardo Mendieta, and David Batstone (Durham: Duke University Press, 2001).
5. See Max Weber's classic *The Protestant Ethic and the Spirit of Capitalism*, trans. Talcott Parsons (New York: Scribner, 1958), 37–46.
6. Madipoane Masenya, a biblical scholar at the University of South Africa, addresses this issue in her essay "The Bible and Poverty in African Pentecostal Christianity: The *Bosadi* (Womanhood) Approach," in this volume.
7. Jennifer Martin was one of the speakers who addressed the Pan-African Seminar group in Kingston, Jamaica, in July 2003.
8. Michael Witter, an academic at the University of the West Indies, also addressed the Pan-African Seminar in Kingston, Jamaica, in 2003.
9. Omar Davies was the minister of economics in the Jamaican government when he addressed the Pan-African Seminar, Kingston, Jamaica, 2003.
10. Garnet Roper, a minister of religion, also addressed the Pan-African Seminar, Kingston, Jamaica, 2003.
11. See J. Owens, *Dread: The Rastafarians of Jamaica* (London: Heinemann, 1979).
12. Rex Nettleford is the vice chancellor of the University of the West Indies; he addressed the Pan-African Seminar, Kingston, Jamaica, 2003.
13. *Pretoria News*, 7 July 2003.
14. See Ulrich Duchrow, *Europe in the World System, 1492–1992: Is Justice Possible?* (Geneva: WCC Press, 1992).
15. Ibid. Also see J. De Santa Ana, ed., *Sustainability and Globalization* (Geneva: WCC Press, 1998); B. Goudzwaard and H. de Lange, *Beyond Poverty and Affluence: Toward an Economy of Care* (Geneva: WCC Press, 1986).

16. Goudzwaard and de Lange, *Beyond Poverty and Affluence*.
17. Hopkins, Lorentzen, Mendieta, and Batstone, *Religions/Globalizations*, 9.
18. Goudzwaard and de Lange, *Beyond Poverty and Affluence*, 106.
19. Ibid., passim, esp. 106.
20. George Soros, *The Crisis of Global Capitalism: Open Society Endangered* (London: Little, Brown, 1998), 196.

Lewin L. Williams | **A THEOLOGICAL PERSPECTIVE**

ON THE EFFECTS OF GLOBALIZATION ON

POVERTY IN PAN-AFRICAN CONTEXTS

The phrase "global village" bears such a positive ring that people hardly hesitate to warm to the echoing of it, when the echoing is done in a world that seems to be so otherwise separated by exclusive borders and rules and regulations. "Global village" suggests links of understanding and caring among the worldwide human family. The phrase seems to have originated in the religious community, where the hope for a better world was seen to be able to exist in a kind of human cohesiveness. This is not to say that religious people thought in naiveté that there was this singleness of experience in the human condition all over the world, but that there exists the potential for relational benefits in the whole peopled world. When the term "globalization" became a primary term in neoliberal economic vocabulary, the religious community was not immediately suspicious of it. One of the reasons for that was that the unexamined suggestions of globalization can resemble the positive aspects of the "global village" of the religious community, even though the differences between them are extreme. The chief contention of this essay is that aspects of globalization not only cause separations among the peoples of the world, but by their processes of stratification also cause underdevelopment and poverty in the already weak sections of the global community. Prime examples of this may very well be observable in Pan-African situations.

Some questions are being asked of globalization:

(1) What does "globalization" mean?
(2) Whose process is it?
(3) Who stands to benefit more from it?
(4) What if it causes more disruption than cohesion?

(5) What would be the recommended remedy for the disruption?

(6) Who then provides, or at least suggests the recommendation for change?

What the religious community brings to the table where globalization is being discussed is not simply based on the unsentimentality of neoliberal economics. Here, economics assumes its own transcendence, and for the religious community, that is anathema. It is not even based on the new ethics of the social scientists' "cultural anthropology," which comments on cultural stratification as something that is no longer tolerated. While it is true that the religious community appreciates this new ethic whenever it is observed, its roots may be merely humanistic as the community sees it. In fact that ethic may even owe its origins to the religious community, which sees positive globalization from the perspective of the global village as totally related to the concept of the Imago Dei. According to Walbert Buhlmann, the idea of the creation or world covenant that holds all of humanity together hinges upon the fact that we are all created by God and in the image of God.[1]

It is plausible then, that when globalization causes disruptions among human beings, the religious community could be an agent for the provision of remedial considerations of globalization. On becoming aware of these shortcomings, it is the religious community that perceives clearly that that which may serve as the agent of cohesion to make globalization a positive force for all is not at all humanistic. It is something of divine contrivance. Since people fail, on mere human terms, to create the kind of sociocentrism that itself fosters the desire for level playing fields concerning human dealings, we need to seek divine intervention. This, then, is the avenue through which the term koinonia enters the discussion.

"Koinonia" specifies the area of the religious community (referring to the Christian church) that has utilized it. Yet while the term emerged as an egalitarian effort within the early Christian church, the principle it represented, and other like principles, have been universalized throughout the ages. It is not a stranger to some socialist structures and even to indigenous African traditions such as Nyerere's ujamaa in Tanzania. In any case koinonia, which here appears as a suggested response to globalization, is a much broader application of the principle observed in the early church. After all, the community that is its focus is larger and wider than, and contextually different from, that of the early church. It therefore will seek to cover more that exists, to the detriment of people in more involved situations, such as African unity and Caribbean integration.

Poverty in the Pan-African Situations

It is not unusual to find in neoliberal economic thought the assessment that poverty is only a minor irritant in society. Behind that notion are two basic factors. One is the fact that poverty is often intellectualized out of all proportion to its immobilizing reality. The other is the complications that arise when poverty itself calls for its own contextual definition.

The intellectualization of poverty is easy when the interest in poverty is purely academic. Economists may even list figures representing high, medium, and low monetary value without the slightest experience of how it affects the life of those who encounter the systems in the real world. For example, victims of poverty are often blamed for being in the situation they are, probably because of laziness or because they are without the capacity to recognize any path of achievement of upward mobility. So then, poverty can be mentioned as listed statistics without identifying itself with any particular human community.

Poverty, defined, can cause confusion in how people understand it. The reason for this is the problem of relativity. There are several things to be taken into consideration when an answer is provided to the questions, who are the poor? or what is poverty?

In most cases poverty is judged by the availability of wealth within the context. Thus the poverty line may not be the same representative figure from context to context. Rich countries would have a higher poverty line than poor countries. Sometimes it is judged as the point below which people cannot feed themselves and literally starve. Yet in a place like Jamaica in the Caribbean, while some people who are considered poor may not starve, they may be unable to pay for health costs. They do not have enough to pay either for physicians' services or for the prescribed medication. Since these variables cause complications in defining poverty, it is often treated as the unexamined "lumpen."

It is quite obvious now, that poverty in its multidimensional state may not be defined in simple single dimensions. We have seen, for example, that it is not enough to say poverty is the inability to feed one's self. It is quite possible for a family to feed itself from the produce in a kitchen garden, and yet be unable to pay for medical care. Even so, there are further complications with definitions of other entities that will include, how is "feed" defined? How balanced must the kitchen garden produce be, before it can be considered to be of the kind of nutritional value warranting identification as food? Hence, if what is eaten in such conditions provides no nutritional value, can it be said that people are able to "feed" themselves? Notwithstanding this, the actuality is that there are those who may be able to afford nutritious food but eat junk food anyway.

We have seen also that poverty may be relative, given the context in which it exists. The complication here is in finding some kind of consensus for the designation of it. The testimony of many persons considered poor is very often that they are oblivious to the fact of their poverty. This indeed suggests that there are different standards to the judgment of poverty even by those who are poor. It goes without saying that a certain kind of nonchalance may very well be the guiding principle for those who make decisions that will affect the poor. A case in point may lie in the eagerness to solve welfare problems in the so-called welfare states. Sometimes the welfare recipient is judged to be poor by choice, and with the kind of poverty that is not as real as it is being made out to be. The assessors seldom speak to the culture of poverty, which often means that there are people, who in the totality of family circles, seem unable to escape the cycle of poverty. Parents are poor, their children are poor, and so are their children's children. It seems as though powerful psychological forces are at work and are hard to overcome. However, here very little attention is paid to the evaluation of systemic impediments to upward mobility.

Generally speaking, poverty has to do with all those things and conditions that rob persons of a certain quality of life, of dignity, and of well-being. Of course, what is true of persons is true also of nations. The designations for rich persons/poor persons work for rich countries/poor countries. And the question as to the reason or reasons that people of African descent fall into the category of the world's poorest people must be processed through the idea of the rich nation/poor nation. In the same sense that in a particular context, systems at work make some people rich while keeping others poor, there are countries which in their drive to stay rich and powerful make others poor and keep them so. One of the means by which this position is maintained is the process of globalization.

One would think that with the concern of globalization being human cooperation, poverty, in whatever context, would be the concern of the entire world. This is true if a religious point of view is taken at this juncture, that the emphasis on human cooperation amounts to a covenant. Indeed the religious community would see it thus. Walbert Buhlmann, in agreement with that position, would argue that the entire world is indeed a covenant (creation covenant) into which people enter simply by birth.[2] "Covenant" suggests egalitarian cooperation in which people naturally look out for the welfare of one another. It makes very little sense then, that in the world of commerce, a continent as large as Africa is forced into the position where it controls only 2 percent of the world's export market. The converse is also true. Much smaller entities walk away with giant shares in the same market.[3] When the situation is examined, it is seen quite readily that the kind of poverty that such divisions cause is apparent not only in continental Africa but throughout the African diaspora.

Globalization

Globalization may be a relatively "new" term in our vocabulary, but the principle has existed for as long as there has been the notion of "here, and out there." That concept must have stimulated the human instinct from the very beginning, to engage the "out there." This is not to say that this engagement is always in operation as a negative force. Interest in "out there" can be as positive as a genuine desire for human cooperation. Expeditions across borders for positive reasons may very well result in positive exchanges in which cultural blends occur to the benefit of all concerned. This is true, not only of some political and cultural expeditions, but also of religious ones. Those who in contemporary times query the validity of the fifteenth-century and later missionary thrusts argue often, not against the movement as such, but against the cultural stratification that it encouraged.[4] The problem is that in most cases in the North-to-South thrust, for example, the South was treated to the bottom level of cultural acceptance.

However, there is the negative side to the crossing of borders, whether it concerns politics or religion. Expeditions for the purpose of forced acculturation have been an impediment to human development throughout all times.[5] The economic gain to the powerful, who base their own survival strategy on empire philosophies, has always been lopsided. They plunder and subdue those they consider inferior. They take their land and their goods and often enslave them. And the conquering zeal of religious bodies is often no less vicious because the cultural misunderstandings are the same.[6] The early missionary thrusts into places like the Caribbean made it easier for the intrusions of gluttonous colonial seekers of power and wealth.

Globalization is an evolving process among peoples and economies. Some argue that it is governed by a few wealthy nations who benefit by setting the rules for its operation then leaving the system to run by itself—in which case, when lopsidedness develops in the rewards the system offers, there is no one to blame, because systems may not be charged with sentimentality of caring concerns, or cruel biases.

To describe "globalization in the world today" is not as easy as the phrase may suggest at face value, because the world itself is in a state of flux in which societies pose and oppose systems of operation, whether of economic dealings or religious influence. Given globalization as a force within the world, some societies experience positive results and some are devastated by it. This is the reason that globalization presents such ambivalent prospects as it does. So while the conditions cause some societies to succeed at economic ventures, raising their standard of living in dramatic ways, others meet with economic failures and political woes beyond reason. The leaders of societies in the latter situation find that their initiative is met always with futility.[7]

In addition to what seems like economic and political involvement, there is the dimension of globalization in its more contemporary sense. We take up the religious case, bearing in mind the view that it is a religious point of view we will call upon to provide a remedial input for all the ill will of globalization. Yet we open with the confession that religion is not always the glorious answer in all of its operations. If the general world looks bad, as it is impacted by globalization, in some cases, the religious world is often no better. For example, those religious leaders who claim to care very little about the socioeconomic development in this world, but only about spiritual success for the world to come, are usually successful in this world. Their popularity expands into global fame and their "this-earthly" coffers get full. Yet those who are saddled with the healing of the dysfunctions of society have very little with which to provide remedial solutions, and life for them is not as rosy. When some of the "spiritualists" get involved in the economic environment in the world, it is merely to promote a gospel of individual success. In the theology that supports these theories of personal success, there is no engagement with nation building. Televangelists fly around in private jets to preach "the Word" and while they get richer, the world gets more violent. They argue that every person was meant to be as wealthy as they are, but since it is the faith of the individual believer that brings the reward from God, the reward is meant to be treated as a personal achievement. Ironically, this theology aids and abets the globalization trend, which is built up around a kind of exclusive competitiveness. Those who are unable to name things and claim them in the spirit of Christ have a faith problem that they alone can remedy.

In a sense, these religious systems operate much like the economic and political systems of the world. In the economic and political arenas there are no level playing fields in the world, though all are being asked to begin to operate as if there were. We are being asked by the system called globalization to be open to new and dynamic intrusions and thereby reap the great benefits. But there is much to consider as the variables come to light. Perhaps the main variable is value. Do all societies operate on the same set of values? How will globalization get around things differing in different societies? That kind of question does not escape the religious community with a "name it and claim it" attitude, because it does not take into consideration the individuality and variety of religious experiences. However, in the final analysis, because "economy" and "economics" are akin to certain religious dimensions, we shall take the liberty to turn to religion for answers to the problem of globalization. M. Douglas Meeks even dares to speak about "God the Economist," basing this characterization on the fact that the word "economy" derives from *oikonomia*, which covers both financial and household management to the extent (he argues) where it spans the globe to make it the "household of God."[8] That indeed is globalization at its very best. Of course, for the neoliberal economists, globalization is supposed to be the integration of all national systems of operation (especially economics) into one system that is controlled by a single unit of operation. While this speaks to the economics of the world, there are conversations over the globalization of other spheres of activity among nations. For example, there are attempts at global standardization of educational and other methods, the rules governing communication, and so on.[9] And there is no doubt that much about globalization has to do with methodology, but a methodology that is tested more systematically in the area of economics. So if economics is taken as the most important issue, it is being argued here that at the center of this issue is the "global market." In globalization as it is understood in the world today, there are specific items that are being addressed as a means of development: unrestricted market for goods, labor, communication, and investments; less political governance; easy movement of goods, services, and investments across borders.[10] All of the above are pursued through a system called the market, which cannot afford to be sentimental about the business of nation-states. It is the case, therefore, that those who had more lucrative frontiers all along are better poised to do well in the market. Those who are not so blessed find that it is hard to begin, let alone catch up with the major players in this system.

The Market

Theologically speaking, globalization through the market presents the world with a problem. The market as the centerpiece in globalization seems to take on a kind of autonomy that mimics divine transcendence. It takes on the responsibility of controlling human behavior in every sector of the human endeavor. As stated before, the global market claims that it cannot be expected to be sentimental, but it creates its own preferences for certain types of goods. Such activity indeed stratifies what the world produces and puts some societies at a disadvantage. For some time the market's first preference has been manufactured goods. However, manufactured goods in recent times are losing their position to the so-called intellectual commodities. According to the stratification of the market, the groupings of goods the world produces are: (1) intellectual commodities (communication, etc.), (2) manufactured goods, and (3) agrarian products. This stratification has significance for the understanding of the creation of poverty, and contexts that tend to be devastated by poverty. The problem for contexts such as those peopled by continental Africans and Africans in the diaspora is that their production is mostly agrarian. The stratification extends to stratification of products and makes agrarian products of least value. This may partially explain why this context is constantly besieged by poverty. In addition to the fact of the value placed upon agrarian products by the will and whim of the market, the perishability of these products weakens the bargaining power for good and fair prices.

Positive Assumptions about the Market

We admit that not everything about globalization is absolutely negative. Yet globalization, as an unstoppable process, has its best effects on those societies that already possess both the infrastructure and superstructure to be called developed, to the benefit of such societies. In general terms:

(1) It has caused the speed and space of international commerce to develop beyond all expectation.
(2) The market continues to move forward globally in excess of its own standards.
(3) Investment incomes shatter prior records by quantum leaps.
(4) The flow of foreign direct investment from the major economies amounts to trillions, most of which is directed to less developed countries, though expressly for the gain of the developed countries.
(5) Daily transactions in the United States have reached $1.5 trillion. Other countries beside the United States that are mentioned in this miraculous surge of benefits are Japan and the Asian tigers—Hong Kong, Singapore, Taiwan, and South Korea.
(6) Of course, those who sing the praises of globalization declare that the

benefits are for all countries who open their doors to the speed and volume the process offers, and what they gain amounts to economic growth, poverty reduction, and better democratic politics.

The Negative Aspects of the Market

1. Because money can travel faster electronically, and business transactions have so multiplied, the crime of money laundering has become a "global" problem. It is estimated that at any given time there is about $5 billion in the world that the owners are trying to launder,[11] and billions more are actually being laundered. What this does is pump large sums of money into the world economy—a situation that accentuates the drug problems of the world, as these funds are directly related to the drug trade. This cannot be considered a blessing for the third world or any other world.

Some people cast morals aside and argue that the drug trade does bring wealth to less developed countries. Such conclusions should come under very serious evaluation. Notably,

(a) There is the question of values, when the argument for gain by any possible means arises. Nation building must include not merely economic growth but also personal development. And personal development involves body, mind, and spirit. In the argument for gain at any cost, where does conscience fit?

(b) In recent times it has been assessed that drugs such as marijuana are not produced in less developed countries as much as formally estimated.

2. Economic growth itself is said to come by a certain openness to foreign trade as opposed to the protectionism of closed economies. This is far more complicated than it sounds:

(a) While it is true that the less developed countries benefit from the technology that has already been developed by the wealthier countries, they must purchase such equipment as they need, at prices that are beyond their control (farm implements and machinery, computers, medication). Often the national income is such that there is not enough purchasing power for such "necessary" goods.

(b) There are other infrastructural difficulties, such as in the provision of roads, electricity, water, and shelter. These, for some nations, are not easily provided but are necessary for processing, developing, and transporting goods.

(c) Openness in the market should apply not only to importation but also to exportation. In Ghana, as in Jamaica, some very special problems have been developing in this area: the development of synthetic production in the industrial countries has curtailed the need for some raw materials from these countries. As a result, reciprocity in the import/export system is becoming nonexistent. Developing countries must always purchase from the developed. The developed ones are always searching for ways to purchase less, while selling to developing ones. So although the champions of globalization argue against closed systems in the market process, such lessons may be meant only for the poor and dependent countries.

3. Perhaps the most devastating of the negative factors in globalization are the recommendations for rectification of the inevitable depression resulting from the unfair dealings in the market with the poorer economies. To say the least, these recommendations come out of major power situations that impatiently ignore the dictates of culture and the particularity of contextual needs. In this respect, the function of the International Monetary Fund in the process of structural adjustment for "third world" countries is a prime example. The usual recommendation in the case of the International Monetary Fund is the devaluation of the local currency and the curtailing of spending by laying off government workers. Such recommendations create two problems:

(a) National debts escalate simply because the local currency is worth much less than the foreign (U.S.) currency. Since the debt is serviced through foreign currency, the local economy, in one stroke of the devaluation pen, sees its debt double or triple or even quadruple. Instead of being able to concentrate on development, these countries never get to do more than debt servicing.

(b) Without the facility of unemployment insurance, the government workers who are laid off are laid off to "die." They lose livelihood without the power to recoup. The eventual consequence is that these people fall behind the contextual poverty line and the cycle of poverty continues.

The Remedial Factors

The antiglobalizationists are not necessarily contextual purists. Contextual purists tend toward closed dealings at national borders. The globalizationists, on the other hand, are against closed economies, being in favor of free movement of goods and services across borders. In between those poles, there are those who are contextually sensitive but who argue for both the autonomy of individual context and the right to the ability to choose self-inclusion in the globalized dealings.

In any case, since the process of globalization has the inscrutable power of co-optation, none is able to successfully resist. Yet when the process works to the disadvantage of many, where do they turn for rectification?

Basically, there are three ways to look at globalization, in terms of the response it may demand. They are called the Washington consensus, the development consensus and the people-centered consensus.

(1) The Washington consensus is so called by researchers because of the major power stance it takes. Big nations and big businesses are most favored in this position, and always stand to benefit from political graces such as less government interference, fewer environmental safety conditions, and less minimum-wage control. The consensus promotes the rationale that when major powers, be they nation-states or businesses, are successful, then smaller, poorer states and people will reap trickle-down benefits. In addition, with such freedom of operation, the competitive spirit will ensure the survival of the fittest. The weaker competitors perish, leaving the stronger to provide the best for unaffordable yet unavoidable consumption.

From the underside, however, the objections and warnings are many. Bigger nations and businesses tend to become blinded with excessive power and thus act with great arrogance in their self-interest. Danger to self-interest is often more contrived than real; thus, for example, foreign policy is skewed in support of those perceptions. The "trickle down" favors only those who surrender to the dictates of that kind of foreign policy. In fact the Washington consensus simply endorses a triage in which the weak are bound to lose.

(2) The development consensus is not necessarily predetermined to be detrimental to persons, for in fact it is organized with the poor in mind. Development is meant to lift the poor to a higher level of existence, and redirect the marginalized toward the center. The problem is that organizations such as the United Nations, which have the will to assist the weak, are without the clout to take the theoretical themes into practice. They are unable to fight the major power's foreign policy machinations. So, they may provide some handouts that address the immediate infrastructural needs of the poor, but they are unable to address the superstructural deficits that cause poverty in the first place. Ultimately they do more harm than good

because the handouts salve the consciences of the benefactors at the infrastructural stage, and numb their consciences toward superstructural adjustments for the eradication of poverty. Here again it is the poor and the weak who lose.

(3) The people-centered consensus is a virtual withdrawal from the high intensity of the global "rat race" into a kind of subsistence value base. It is a far more radical approach than when taken at face value, because it defies the market's insistence upon a certain kind of openness. Chief among the variety of advice the people-centered consensus provides for itself is "produce what you consume, and consume what you produce." This advice is not merely in reference to a few food items that people grow in a kitchen garden for the benefit of the family. It has potential for the curbing of international debt. It also provides incentives for innovation in the area of technology necessary for production. Where the market enforces the language of "bigger" and "more," the people-centered consensus would develop a new value system in which people and their needs would be placed much above the profit motive. The main difference between the Washington consensus and the people-centered consensus is that the former is a profit-driven organization, while the latter focuses directly on people development. Nor does the people-centered consensus seek to ignore its responsibility to a global community. It simply must relate to it in the way that its humanitarian philosophy will allow.

But how does a world whose dominant inhabitants are so steeped in the profit philosophy change its ways so drastically? Perhaps the answer lies in the theological encouragement toward some disengagement with the Cartesian split between the sacred and the secular, where secularization will come to mean that the transcendent spirit of God permeates all of human society, including the so-called secular world. With the belief that we share a common spirituality, we may begin to address radical change at a global level. Here then we interject the koinonia principle.

Koinonia as an Alternative Remedial Factor

There are no greater themes in religious dealings than the themes of "love" and "justice." These provide the underpinnings for any reasonable expectation of peace and sociality in a world in which people tend to be aggressively at odds with one another. Surely there are acceptable differences among the many cultures that make up life's collage, but for the collage to be meaningful, a certain sociality must exist within it. This is why, among some of the ancient observers of life, "righteousness" became such an important concept. In that it meant "right relations" it addressed the regulatory factors of life, demanding a kind of koinonia principle by which people must live, if they are to find, or better still, create equilibrium in the global village.

It is not by accident then that the early Christian church, in its attempt at the equalization of its community, chose "koina" over "idione" because koina contains the sociality that is built on egalitarian principles. Idione is a concept that favors the individual. It goes without saying, of course, that while the individual is of enormous importance to society, the individual who chooses competitiveness that excludes any egalitarian principles is probably courting a proneness to rugged individualism and greed, which are factors present in globalization as it exists today. On the other hand, koina, cognizant of the fact of the divine source of all the world's goods, expresses itself through the awareness of the connectional worth among the peoples of the world. It functions under the auspices of "right relations" in its most egalitarian significance. It sees to the formulation of covenantal-type community, held together by love (chesed). Furthermore, it is only when the principle of right relations is broken, creating observable incidents of injustice, that the idea of justice becomes a crucial entity in the covenant. It is indeed by the application of justice that rectification comes to the broken covenant relationship that koinonia has come to represent.

The function of a world so described should be synonymous with what is being termed globalization, because koinonia takes on the notion that the globe is the "household of God." It recognizes that there are many kinds of cultural systems at work in a kind of covenant where God is at the center. Because these different kinds of systems relate to God at the center, all cultures then relate to each other. The sociocentric lifestyle of many African communities is a good example of how it works. People live together in communities that take care of one another's needs to the extent that no one suffers when resources are available within the community. Indeed, one African definition of community is "people are people because of other people."

As koinonia seeks to address wholeness in the human being, so it addresses wholeness in the human society. Consequently the macroeconomic analyses and sectorial studies done over the world can be translated into policies regarding the living conditions of real people, whose existence is based on the holistic notion of emotional, cultural, and spiritual values. And people who have such holistic concerns for the world work at the creation of a better world, one in which poverty is nonexistent.

Although koinonia is being posed as a corrective principle for the lop-sidedness of the process of globalization, it would be naive to believe that the world of commerce could be easily induced into its acceptance. Suggestions of such a kind will be viewed as curtailment of laissez-faire systems and therefore curtailment of "democratic" freedom. However, if it is worthy of demonstration, facets of it could be applied in contexts of weak economies such as the Caribbean, where people suffer from the strength of the opposite. Koinonia applied in such contexts is not for exclusivity, but for survival in the first place, and second, as demonstration of the possibility of a global trend.

Koinonia in Contextual Praxis

It is now taken for granted that the centerpiece of capitalist philosophy is self-interest. Adam Smith claimed the proof of the concept. It is just as true that there are many articulations as to how self-interest may be transferred into communal concerns. Others, indeed, are convinced that there are no reasonable transfers. The argument is that while there are wealthy organizations that make generous donations toward needed assistance, there is usually no egalitarian concern. Most of the organizations that get assistance operate in nonprofit situations. Nobody helps the competitor to succeed. In any case leaders of some countries with smaller, weaker economies have consistently argued that their expectations have very little to do with charity. Handouts are not among their chief desires. Their chief concern is fairness in the marketplace.

Fairness in the marketplace is not based on the same ethical principles that the small economies argue for. It is not unusual for the large business conglomerates to swallow up smaller ones without a sentimental thought because there is "nothing personal" about such transactions. It is business, and in business, the strategies employed are based on the self-interest prin-ciple. This is one of the foremost reasons for the development of negotiating bodies such as the African Caribbean Pacific (ACP) organization, to see whether the traders represented in these countries can get a fair deal in the marketplace. Yet in recent times these organizations seem unable to broker any great deals with the World Trade Organization. Cases in point include the handling of bananas in the Caribbean, the handling of debt crisis in Jamaica and sugar quotas in the Caribbean sugar belt, and the Caribbean Ship Rider Agreement.

Some of the European countries, in recognition of the fact that they were once colonizers of the Caribbean territories, made an effort to place less tariff on the importation of Caribbean bananas into their countries. This "courtesy" for specific reasons was not extended to others such as the United States' banana companies operating in Central America.

(a) One reason for not including these other companies is that the ACP operating out of Brussels negotiates for African, Caribbean, and Pacific countries, which are under the LOME Treaty, which gives them the right to strike bargains with European countries.

(b) The banana companies operating in the Central American countries are a part of giant conglomerates not considered to be in need of concessions.

(c) While banana production in the Caribbean is done by manual labor, the big companies in Central America produce by automation. The Caribbean companies are unable to afford automation. This means that they produce much less than the others. What the European market allowed them in concessions was meant to help boost their earnings to compensate for what they lost in the manual process.

(d) One of the most important reasons for the tariff concessions was the conscience imperative. Much of the wealth gained by some European countries came through the colonization and enslavement of these countries in the African diaspora.

By ordinary ethical assessment these tariff concessions would seem fair for no other reasons than those given. However, the United States has sought to have those concessions abolished as bargaining rights, because, according to the United States' claim, since they were not extended to the United States conglomerates operating in Central America, the "playing field" is not level. That appeal was made to the World Trade Organization and that organization now supports the claim of the conglomerates to the point that the Europeans are being forced to withdraw their concessions.

The debt crisis in Jamaica forced a number of transactions, some of which have been detrimental to the nation's efforts at economic survival. One of these efforts was an appeal to the International Monetary Fund (IMF). Perhaps it needs to be said at the very outset that the IMF was set up after World War II to be a type of insurance that countries that met devastatingly unusual situations could draw on for temporary assistance. It unfortunately lost most of its salvific effects for small countries when it became politicized. Countries count their votes by how much financial responsibility they take to it, thus the bigger and richer the participating country, the more votes it has. Such a country therefore can force the political conditions under which a smaller country gets a loan through the IMF. Jamaica, for example, could be denied a loan, or receive it under unusually harsh conditions, if it maintained any kind of relationship with Cuba, which is deemed to be an enemy of the United States. Here major-power politics would determine by neocolonial means what happens in a less developed and dependent country.

While the situation described above is more than a surmise, a real case worth mentioning is the milk situation in Jamaica. The IMF often makes suggestions, which in fact are dictated, as to how borrowed money may be spent. In one case some was to be spent on imported milk powder. It was more nutritious because it contained added nutrients. It was cheaper because the country it came from (United States) had the government subsidize the farmers who produced it. All of that transaction seems fair, except that it put the Jamaican farmers out of business. It completely destroyed the market for their milk. In fact the reality unfolded so suddenly that thousands of gallons of milk had to be dumped. It goes without saying that the fact that the milk powder is imported accommodates the globalization philosophy of open borders to trade in goods. Consequently, in this case it is only the Jamaican border that gets opened to receive foreign goods and there is certainly no reciprocity. The IMF, which acts as policy enforcer for the major powers, hardly listens to an organization such as the ACP.

Older people in Jamaica, like the older people anywhere, look back at the time they refer to as "the good old days." A salient marker of the times called the good old days is a Jamaican phrase "when sugar was king."[12] That phrase suggests that the importance and popularity of the sugar trade spans a pretty long period, through colonialism and slavery, To this day mercantilism exists in sugar production. The sugar factories are closing in the areas where they function to provide the raw material for the exotic things that are shipped back to the underdeveloped for consumption. Even when sugar was king, the profit did not remain in the places where the factories are situated. They were owned by foreigners who sent those profits back home, where the wealth accumulated. And the profit becomes excessive when they "refine" the sugar and send it back to the local situations to be sold for enormous prices. Unfortunately, "refine" means the extraction of the nutritious part of the raw sugar (molasses) for other sales. At present, where the factories are operated by local concessionaires the particular weakness in the transactions is that, despite the ACP, the price of sugar is fixed to the detriment of the seller. The sellers cannot fix their prices, because they are not allowed. They are fixed by the buyers, and often below the cost of production. And this is the reason for the factories closing. The mills, the tractors, the trucks, the factory equipment are produced abroad, and the sugar producers who are not allowed to set their price for sugar are also not allowed to quote their price for the material they purchase. So movement takes place across borders but certainly not equitably. And it is the weaker economy that suffers.

The major-power domination across borders is not always strictly related to straight business. On the occasion of what is called the Ship Rider Agreement, the real problem was illegal drugs. The United States drug enforcement organizations determined that the Caribbean was a lucrative transshipment point for illegal drugs traveling from Colombia to the United States. As a result the United States requested that the countries of the Caribbean give up their sovereign rights to their waters, allowing United States surveillance vessels to travel through them with the occupants having the authority to detain, arrest, and bring to trial suspicious persons. All of this was to be done without reference to the relevant country and its own laws. The strategy the United States employed was not to consult the region as a whole. It approached one country at a time to propose it, and offered aid in the process as payoff for the inconvenience to their sovereignty. It is only when Barbados and Jamaica refused to give up their sovereign rights that the whole Caribbean realized how much it would have lost by insidious means.

Globalization does not seem geared to temper the power of political imperialism. It is therefore necessary to find the means by which Jamaica and the other territories may benefit from the principle "business is business."

Critical Evaluation of Local Context

Although many of the economic woes of small nations are due to the dealings of the global market, it would not be true to say that contexts such as Africa and the Caribbean hold no responsibility for their condition of poverty. The failure to establish cohesion among states that share geographical location and a sameness in economic predicament is a major deterrent to development.

A case in point is the apparent inability of CARICOM (Caribbean Community) to establish integration: jealousies and the lack of trust have so prevailed among the Caribbean people that time and time again, CARICOM has failed to create an atmosphere of trust through fairness in their own regional market. Even the creation of the Multilateral Clearing Facility in 1975, regulating fairness in free trade, had to be abandoned. Some territories tried to force too much of their products on others, while making decisions to accept too little from others. It was when this free trade agreement failed that it was decided that since integration in the marketplace did not work for this community, integration in production should be tried.

Integration in production proved to be futile as well. In one instance, bauxite producers in Guyana and Jamaica developed with Trinidad a plan for an aluminum smelting plant. Guyana and Jamaica would supply the bauxite; Trinidad would supply the gas for smelting. It did not move beyond the plans because Trinidad judged that the demands made on its gas supply were unfair. When it pulled out of the agreement, the scheme failed.[13]

Trinidad is the only territory in the Caribbean with oil, and when crude oil prices are high it enjoys a better economy than most of the other territories. Since the new and recent effort of CARICOM toward free trade, Trinidad has often been charged with being uncaring because it refuses to sell oil to the other territories at special concessionary rates. On the other hand, although it had been bargained that Trinidad would refine oil for the whole region, other territories such as Jamaica installed their own refineries. In other instances, it has been charged with unfair practices and excess aggressiveness in the way it forces its goods onto other territories, its insistence on selling more and buying less.[14]

In the common market agreement, the territories should purchase available goods within the borders of CARICOM while goods are available; it is only by special concessions that a territory may purchase outside these borders. Quite often, a contentious problem develops when some territory chooses to buy from outside the borders. The agreement is surely tested when Jamaica, perhaps to honor some old International Monetary Fund agreement, seeks a concession to purchase rice from the United States. Guyana and Suriname, the chief rice producers in the region, do not merely question the loyalty of Jamaica to CARICOM, but also the validity of the organization itself.

By these examples, and many more, it is obvious that although the territorial links exist geographically, it takes much more than the superficiality of geographical links to cause and sustain integration for regional development. In 1973, because of the fermentation of some political radicalism in the Caribbean, the global scanning spotlight that determines worth and importance to major-power concerns fell on the region. By that scrutiny, it was judged that by its resources and people, the Caribbean could be a case to ponder if its people recognized the power of unity. Since then, territoralism continues to take a toll on attempts at unity. A functional case of sociality would not only demonstrate what true globalization might be like, but also the contributions of regional value that the Caribbean might make to the world. The case, then, for koinonia as an applied regional principle is clear.

In 1958, the Caribbean established an organization called the West Indian Federation, which failed by 1961. One of the postmortem assessments claimed that it was a body trying to exist without a soul. Perhaps that statement sets the parameters for what is needed among the peoples. As has been pointed out, koinonia's most important characteristic and essence is sociality, but it suggests that for sociality to be cohesively cemented, it must acquire an element of the divine character. There is a definite need for a social contract within this situation, and it must possess more than economic binders. Religion must play a major role.

Jamaica developed a social contract that purports to be a kind of koinonia. It takes into consideration the links among persons—employee and employer, businesspersons and consumers, the trade unions between employee and employer. It then asked all the players to consider themselves nation builders in commitment to Jamaica. The one mistake that was made in that venture was that the religious community was not included. The government forgot that the values that influence attitudes toward human cohesion have their genesis in religion.

Of course, if a social contract can make development work in a single traditional setting, it may be workable for the total Caribbean. It is the failure of the West Indian Federation that suggested the development of CARICOM, which is an organization to promote unity. At the same time the Caribbean Conference of Churches could present CARICOM with an important positive core called its soul. In a sense, it may be considered an exclusive Christian community, which does not cover all that koinonia is meant to remedy. However, there is encouragement in the fact that the Caribbean Conference of Churches, existing in a community of multireligiosity, is including in its theological consideration deep thoughts about interfaith dialogue. The focus of Caribbean theology in this area is clearly defined. This then will help to promote the integration of development for this community.

Notes

1. See Walter Buhlmann, The Chosen Peoples (Middlegreen, U.K.: St. Paul's Publications, 1982), chap. 1.
2. Ibid.
3. See The Call for a "Processus Confessionis" by the World Alliance of Reformed Churches (WARC) (Debrecen, Hungary: WARC, 1997). Also see subsequent confessions of the World Alliance on the economy and especially the one entitled "Covenanting for Justice in the Economy and the Earth Project."
4. See Lewin Williams, Caribbean Theology (New York: Peter Lang, 1994), 5–7.
5. Ibid., chaps. 1 and 2.
6. Ibid.

7. Joseph Stiglitz, *Globalization and Its Discontents* (New York: W. W. Norton, 2003), 5ff.

8. See Douglas Meeks, *God the Economist: The Doctrine of God and Political Economy* (Minneapolis: Fortress, 1989).

9. See Dafne Sabanes Plou, *Global Communication: Is There a Place for Human Dignity?* (Geneva: World Council of Churches, 1996).

10. See "*Processus Confessionis*," in ibid.

11. See the following book by an international expert on money laundering: Jeffrey Robinson, *The Laundrymen* (New York: Simon and Schuster, 1995).

12. See the Jamaican daily newspaper *The Herald*, "US$25M for Sugar at Stake," 15 August 2004.

13. See Christoph Mullerleile, *Caricom Integration Progress and Hurdles* (Kingston: Kingston Publishers, 1996).

14. Ibid.

RELIGIOUS STRATEGIES FOR LIBERATING THE POOR

Elizabeth Amoah AFRICAN TRADITIONAL RELIGION AND

THE CONCEPT OF POVERTY

In choosing the theme "Religion and Poverty" this group of Pan-African scholars from Ghana, Togo, Nigeria, Kenya, Tanzania, South Africa, Jamaica, Canada, and the United States agreed on two basic things.

First, they agreed that there is a relationship between religion and poverty. Second, they agreed that Africans both on the continent and in the diaspora have had common experiences that affected and shaped the poverty situations in which they find themselves. For example, they have all experienced colonialism, missionary activities, and the slave trade, which have left in their trail structures that have produced vicious and seemingly inescapable forms of poverty among them everywhere. In relating poverty to religion the scholars probed the crucial question, what have religion and poverty got to do with each other? The assumption here is that religion and poverty are connected insofar as religion generally concerns the spiritual as well as the material well-being of humanity.

There are several ways of dealing with such an important question, especially when the major concepts, poverty and religion, have several implications and can be looked at from different perspectives. This essay looks at the question from an African perspective. Specifically, it inquires into some of the insights from traditional African religion on the various ways of dealing with the issue of poverty. African traditional religion focuses on wholeness, the well-being of people, and the community at large. The traditional African concept of well-being comprises everything that makes life worth living. It ranges from good health, peace, and harmony within individuals, with the spirits and the entire society, to the material or physical resources that seem to give comfort. Well-being as seen in this sense has both external (material) and internal (psychological and spiritual) dimensions.

The holistic nature of African traditional religion has crucial implications for our subject. For example, it implies that the sacred and the secular complement each other. A further implication is that poverty in this context is seen in not only material and physical terms but also spiritual, thus making poverty a broad and complex issue. Consequently, within a typical traditional context realities such as the careless use of money, alcoholism, or the lack of money are seen in spiritual terms. For example, among the Akan peoples of Ghana, the condition of a hard-working person who is constantly in need of money is often explained in terms of witchcraft or some other evil spirit, which has put an invisible hole in that person's pocket or palm. Such a condition is rarely seen in terms of harsh economic conditions but, rather, in spiritual terms while ignoring the physical realities on the ground.

In looking at the complex issue of religion and poverty from the traditional African perspective, we must not look at the spiritual dimension alone. There is the need also to look at other dimensions such as the economic, moral, philosophical, and social in order to capture the holistic nature of traditional African understandings.

Objective

My essay seeks to explore the African mechanisms, based on traditional African religion and other social structures, that have been put in place for dealing with poverty. Any serious discussion on religion and poverty from the African traditional perspective cannot ignore the African traditional concept of well-being because within the traditional African heritage the three concepts of religion, poverty, and well-being are integrally related. Thus, the search for traditional African models for dealing with poverty is, to a large extent, the search for codes or models that either undermine or foster well-being, the lack of which leads to poverty. This is the main goal of my essay.

Methodology

For this essay I first collected and critically analyzed some traditional African proverbs and sayings, which have direct bearing on the concept of poverty. That is to say, I focused on proverbs that make direct reference to the local words for poverty. I am very much aware of the problem associated with the use of oral materials such as proverbs when these are critically analyzed. Normally, they tend to have multiple interpretations and meanings. Some proverbs not only have opposite meanings but also lose their meaning and relevance when they are taken from their cultural and historical context. These problems become apparent when proverbs are seen as statements of public opinion, which unlike absolute truths are likely to vary.

These African proverbs and maxims are repositories of the accumulated knowledge and wisdom of Africans. Thus, a better understanding of poverty from the African perspective requires an examination of the African proverbs on poverty, because they express the traditional opinions and views of Africans on the subject.

Second, besides analyzing proverbs and sayings on poverty I also looked at some traditional African rituals, as enacted in some of the traditional festivals, specifically, the *homowo* festival of the Gas of Ghana to unearth its significance in dealing with poverty. The aim is to look at ritual performance and the underlying beliefs that deal with basic physical needs such as the lack of food.

Third, I collected and analyzed beliefs and social practices in relation to the acquisition and use of property, communal relation, wealth, morality, and values, as well as positive and negative sanctions governing human interrelationships. Some of the traditional moral values that govern the equitable use of resources were also examined. In addition to this, a selection of people were interviewed for their views on the concept of poverty and how people deal with it currently. Finally, I drew on the various experiences and knowledge gained from the seminars during our travels to the various countries.

On the whole, the basic data for this discussion are predominately cultural materials with rich verbal and nonverbal variation. I am very much aware of the problem of interpreting and translating oral and cultural materials, but I strongly believe that these materials contain a whole range of information on the traditional concepts of poverty. My objective in this essay is to explore through oral traditions the interplay between religion and poverty and how it is dealt with from traditional African religious perspectives.

Definition of Key Concepts

Given the complexity and size of Africa and the rapid changes that are going on in the continent, it is necessary to clarify the key words used in the title of this essay because it is problematic to assume that the word "tradition" implies that much has remained unchanged here. Obviously there are variations in African traditional religion, which has not remained pristine, because it has an accommodating nature. In fact, traditional African religion has been going through constant change, which has resulted at times in the exchange of African and non-African ways of thinking.

In other words, some African traditional systems have been affected by other systems, and vice versa. By "tradition" I mean anything that is very resilient and that has been passed on from generation to generation. That is to say, despite the changes there are certain basic core elements that continue to persist and influence the lives of Africans. Such essential and enduring elements constitute traditional features that continue to influence the lives of Africans wherever they find themselves. Thus, any search for viable ways of dealing with poverty among Africans cannot ignore those elements.

AFRICAN TRADITIONAL RELIGION

In the traditional African worldview, religion is not an abstract intellectual construct. Thus African religion exemplifies the view that religion is about people acting and living out their faith. In this sense African traditional religion, with its wide range of beliefs (in which people continue to have strong faith) and practices, is a way of life. African traditional religion is so all-encompassing that it is not possible to cover all aspects of it in this essay. Instead, I shall concentrate on some of the essential elements that have direct bearing on poverty. However, I need to emphasize the fact that the underlying belief in traditional African religion is a strong faith in what many scholars are presently calling a "community of spirit powers," which is in a reciprocal relationship with human beings, each group—spirits and humans—having duties and responsibilities toward the other. The spirits range from the creator spirit, the numerous gods and goddesses, and the ever-present ancestors to the several other spirit powers that harmoniously exist and work together for the well-being of the entire community. Appropriate communication mechanisms have been devised to establish the continual relationship between the people and the spirit powers.

Religion in this sense is seen as a tool for survival, dealing with and solving basic human needs and problems, which are seen to be material and spiritual. As I have already noted, traditional religion is holistic. The sacred and the secular in fact merge in the African belief system. Its central core is the pursuance of life (material and spiritual) in abundance, here and now. This implies that anything that is contrary to the abundant life or well-being of people has to be drastically dealt with through the use of rituals, moral practices, and other social mechanisms. Poverty is one such contrary matter that concerns traditional African religion.

However, there is also a general belief in spirits that use their powers negatively on the lives of people. An example of such evil spirit activity is witchcraft. At the Pan-African Seminar meeting in Jamaica, for example, we learned that such an evil spirit is commonly referred to as the "evil eye." Many believe that witchcraft can make people poor. The belief in the destructive nature of witchcraft is so strong that some Africans even today desist from accumulating material wealth for the fear of being harmed by witches.

Another essential element in the traditional African belief system that is relevant to our discussion on religion and poverty is the source of creation and the nature of being human. In the African traditional religious system, creation including humanity and the environment has a sacred source and this implies that all people are interconnected and that human beings are custodians of natural resources. Since human beings have a sacred source, each and every person should be treated with care, dignity, and respect. The Akan of Ghana have a saying that "all people are children of Onyame [God], and no one is the child of the earth." The implication of this saying is that people by virtue of being children of God are endowed with dignity and respect. Poverty, as portrayed in some of the African proverbs, degrades and dehumanizes people. Their common humanity demands that those in poor situations must be helped to regain their dignity in order to become human beings again.

The traditional belief in the concept of the ancestors is also very crucial to the discussion of poverty from a traditional African perspective. In the traditional African religious system, the dead continue to live. Some of the dead who are honored as role models are raised to the status of ancestors, the highest position a person can attain after death. These ancestors become the custodians of natural resources such as land, an important economic asset in traditional African communities. As such, land was not sold and was judiciously used for the benefit of the members of the community.

Again, there is the general belief among some Africans that people should be encouraged to be fertile and reproduce to ensure the reincarnation of the ancestors. Thus, within traditional African communities some people have a strong desire to have many children, whether they have the means to take proper care of them or not. It is not surprising that in some of the countries that participants in the seminar visited there are a lot of children, either living on the streets or being cared for by religious and charitable organizations.

Poverty is a common feature in human society. However, poverty can be defined in many ways. Sometimes it is defined by comparing the material conditions of two or more societies. Normally, the resources enjoyed by one community may be used as a measure of what is considered poverty or wealth, For example, people from a context where it is normal for one person to have a fleet of cars may describe those who do not have any such items as being poor. As a concept, poverty is culture- and time-specific and may change from time to time. For this reason it is difficult to give a precise definition that will suit all people in different historical and cultural contexts.

Yet most people readily identify poverty with the lack of basic needs and a certain level of comfort with regard to clothing, food, shelter, and a general feeling of well-being in terms of material, psychological, and spiritual satisfaction.

According to Peter Townsend, "Individuals, families and groups in the population can be said to be in poverty when they lack the resources to obtain the type of diet, participate in the activities and have the living conditions and amenities which are customary, or at least widely encouraged or approved, in the societies to which they belong. Their resources are so seriously below those commanded by the average individual or family that they are, in effect, excluded from ordinary living patterns."[1]

However, the material aspects of poverty are less problematic than psychological ones, in the sense that they are more easily identifiable. The difficulty in addressing the material aspects lies in a culture's level of technology: that is, its development and advancement with regard to how these material needs are dealt with. Every community has specific ways of dealing with poverty in accordance with its level of technological advancement.

Though the psychological aspects of poverty are internal, in contrast to the material aspects, there are good reasons to believe that, whatever the technological level might be, a certain basic feeling of comfort and well-being is universal, though it is reflected upon and experienced differently in various societies. Further, the spiritual aspect of poverty is reflected in the different religious traditions in the world.

POVERTY IN TRADITIONAL AFRICAN PERSPECTIVE

As a concept, poverty is so complex and multifaceted that it cannot be measured in only material terms like the gross national product. The complexity of poverty is highlighted in many African proverbs.

Among the Akan proverbs for example, the subject of poverty is ubiquitous, and it cuts across cultural, economic, and social boundaries. The universal nature of poverty is expressed in the following proverbs, most of which were selected from J. G. Christaller's *Dictionary of the Asante and Fante Language*:[2]

> *Ohia te se owo onno faako.*
> Poverty is like honey; it is not found in one place.

> *Ehia batani hia paani.*
> Both the employer and the employee can be poor.

> *Ohia na ɛma obroroni si ne ntoma wɔ aborekyire bɛhata wɔ abibiriman mu.*
> It is because of poverty that the white man washes his clothes in Europe and dries them in Africa. (The proverb says that poverty is not

only a problem in Africa; it is also a problem of the West—with Westerners exploiting resources in Africa to enrich themselves.)

Poverty in any circumstance is seen as evil and undesirable. This view is clearly indicated in the following proverbs:

Ohia nam yɛ wen.
The meat of poverty is bitter.

Ohia ye musu.
Poverty is evil and undesirable.

Ohia nnye ade pa.
Poverty is not a good thing.

The evil nature of poverty is concretized in specific ways in proverbs. We learn from the proverbs that poverty specifically is a lack of the basic necessities in life such as food and shelter. The lack of the basic life sustenance as an essential aspect of poverty is seen in the following proverbs.

Chia onipa a ɔda wuramu.
If a person becomes poor he/she sleeps in the open forest.

Chia wu a na wurwe sumina-due.
If you are poor you eat from the dung heap.

Chia wu a wurwe aberekyi were.
If you are poor you eat goat's skin.

The symbolism of sleeping in the open forest and eating from a bin is very significant. Normally, wild animals live in the forest, while human beings live in homes. And scavengers such as vultures, which are considered dirty creatures, eat from waste dumps.

One may infer from the symbolism in these proverbs that in the Akan system of thought, poverty reduces human beings to the status of animals. Thus, it has a wider implication than the deprivation of material goods. It completely destroys the dignity of people.

Poverty transcends material wants. It has social, economic, political, and health dimensions as well, as expressed in the proverb "Nnyɛ ohia nko ni ka" (Poverty is not only being in debt). The loss of dignity and personhood is illustrated in other proverbs too:

Ohiani bu mfu.
The poor person has no right to be angry.

Ohiani bu bɛ a ennhyɛ.
A poor person's proverb does not go deep. (A poor person's intelligent contribution is never accepted by anyone.)

Ohiani mpow dabrɛ.
A poor person has no choice in deciding where he or she sleeps.

Ohiani hyɛ sika a yɛbu no sɛ awowa.
If a poor person puts on gold ornaments they are considered brass.

Ohiani tumi nnyɛ tumi pa.
A poor person's power is no power. (The poor person is powerless.)

Poverty does not imply only a loss of identity, self-esteem, and power, but also alienation and loss of community. This is implied in the following proverbs:

Ohiani nni yonko.
The poor person has no friend.

ɛhia wo a wo da wuram.
When you are in need you sleep in the bush.

All these proverbs illustrate that poverty is also the lack of things considered basic to human survival. Even though these needs are basic, the lack of wherewithal to solve the basic needs does not make those who lack them useless. There was always a way out of poverty. Hence it was often said, "ɛhia wu a nnwu" (You should not die when you become poor).

As such there was an element of hope in poverty situations. This is because the traditional institutions were effective enough to help people out of poverty. However, the major question is, as traditional societies change and the scope of poverty expands, are the traditional institutions—especially traditional African religion—sufficient to help people effectively deal with poverty? To answer such a question we need to look critically at traditional African religion in search of effective codes or keys in the search for viable ways of dealing with poverty.

THE USE OF LAND AS A COMMON RESOURCE

One of the means of dealing with poverty in traditional African society is to ensure an equitable distribution and judicious use of land as a basic resource. This is based on the strong belief that the ancestors are the owners of the land, which means that the land should not be sold outright to anyone. Ideally, the land is leased to those who need it for some years and then returned to the owners after the lease expires. Even though this is the ideal, in practice, some members—especially men—have more access and control with regard to the use of land than women. In such situations, those who have direct access to the use of the land are obliged to use the produce of the land to take care of those who do not have direct control and exclusive access. However, in communities where men own the larger and sometimes more fertile parts of the land, the women are allowed to have their vegetable farms around their houses.

From our visit to the Masai land in Kenya we learned that, in the case of pastoral communities, the situation seems to be that men, again, have the direct control and exclusive access to the needed resources such as land and grazing fields. The men move around to look for pastures for the animals to graze, leaving the women and children behind. Such practices put the control over the resources directly in the hands of men to the exclusion of women. Again, an implication of this is that there is a potential situation for differential poverty between men and women, since the women become economically dependent on men. Even in such cases the situation demands that no persons should be left without the minimum requirement for life. In fact, among the Masai, we learned that before leaving for the fields the men make adequate provision for the upkeep of the women and children they leave behind. The point is that the African traditional way of land use has its own internal mechanism for ensuring that no one lives in abject poverty.

Unfortunately, with the new economic and religious systems that confront many African nations, the traditional use of land has changed. Many people do not accept any longer the belief that the ancestors forbid the outright sale of the land. Multinational corporations have bought large tracts of land from Africans for farming, mining, and other economic activities and, consequently, they make huge profits that do not benefit the local people. In Kenya we saw large tracts of fertile land used mainly for tea and coffee plantations that do not really profit many Kenyans. The result is that many Africans, the original owners of the land, have little or no land for themselves. This has resulted in the increase of poverty for those Africans whose economic survival is centered on the land.

THE PRINCIPLE OF SHARING AND RECIPROCITY

The principal of sharing and reciprocity, which is a typical feature of the African way of life, operates in such a way that the community's resources (material and nonmaterial) are mobilized to ensure the welfare of all the members of the community. In fact, in some situations the community's resources of food and shelter are shared with people outside the community.

The practice is widespread, as seen in the practice of leaving cooked food in certain places for those who may be in need.

Also, access to health delivery is a shared resource. That is, healers and all those who care for the health needs of the members of the community charge very little or nothing for such services. In a way, they see their services as contributing to the total healing of the community. The services rendered toward healing are seen to be a communal obligation. Any member of the community may be called upon to perform some service or another for an ailing member. Similarly, in times of crises such as bereavement or debt, the entire community pulls resources together in the form of money, food, time, energy, and other services to help those in need of such services. Thus individuals are not left entirely on their own, feeling helpless and hopeless in times of need.

CONCEPT OF WEALTH

Another related issue in dealing with poverty in the African traditional context is the concept of wealth. Wealth in the traditional African system is not merely acquisition or piling up of material things for individual use. Rather, it is community-centered. By this I mean that the emphasis on wealth is on its use to promote the welfare of the community. In this sense, the idea of sharing is an integral part of the concept of wealth. Thus wealth by itself is worth very little if it is not used to advance or promote human welfare. In other words, the essence of wealth does not lie in mere individualistic accumulation but in the requirement to use it for communal welfare.

EMPHASIS ON HARD WORK

One of the sure ways to get out of poverty is through hard work, and so people are encouraged to do so. Through proverbs the elders in the community keep teaching the youth accordingly:

Edwuma mmbu kon.
Hard work does not break one's neck.

Edwumma pa wo aketua.
There is dignity and profit in hard work.

The perceived lazy people in the community are advised against laziness. They are often told, "Anihawmu nni biribi sɛ ohia" (There is nothing in laziness but poverty). Discouragement of laziness among the Akan finds an echo in the Kenyan proverb that says, "Visitor status is enjoyed for only a couple of days; on the third day the visitor should be given a hoe."

EMPHASIS ON RESOURCE MANAGEMENT

Great emphasis is placed on resource management. This is implicit in sayings such as "Wo nya sika a sie bi" (If you have money, save some of it).

People are encouraged to be thrifty with their resources such as money. This underlies the saying "Sika wo antaban, out se anoma" (Money has wings; it can fly as a bird does).

Taking good care of one's investments and property is very much encouraged. Farmers, for example, invest in large farms so that they can take good care of themselves and others. It is important that one does not spend everything one has, not saving for the future. Resource management is not limited to money only. It extends even to ecology considerations. In slash-and-burn farming, as practiced traditionally, leaving giant trees to serve as soil-retaining trees helped nature to regenerate itself during the fallow period. Such indigenous and prudent, ecologically friendly farming practices in the face of the limited wants of the society—which then could be identified as the pursuit of biological necessities of food, clothing, and shelter—thus ensured a better level of well-being than what is prevailing now.

In the present time, land for either grazing or farming is constantly being taken away from the people and given to corporate entities for large-scale farming or mining activities under the guise of investments. In the unlucky event of a community's land being found suitable by a corporate entity, that community—including its values, social systems, and ideals—would all belong to history. The youth drift to make a living in the cities, dwelling in slums and ghettoes, and leaving the aged to fend for themselves. This could be said to be the common denominator for most cases of poverty in Africa.

EMPHASIS ON MODEST LIVING

Traditional society believes strongly in modesty and humility and therefore frowns on reckless living and the irritating display of wealth. The need to be modest and humble in life is enforced by the traditional belief in witchcraft. There is a general belief that witches punish people who live ostentatiously.

THE SACREDNESS OF ALL LIFE

The resources for life are said to have a divine source. Indeed, many essential natural resources are considered to be sacred gifts to humanity. These include land, rivers, sea, trees, animals, and minerals. Thus, these resources should be properly cared for and used in ways that enhance the dignity and well-being of people for the following reasons: (a) humanity as a whole is interconnected because of its common source, and the actions of individuals affect not only themselves but also the entire human race; (b) the divine element in everyone suggests that all human beings have dignity and respect, which should be upheld at all cost.

These conceptions of what it is to be human imply that equal rights are given to everyone by the common divine source of all. Most important, these traditional beliefs reinforce a general concern for the welfare of poor people. In fact, the whole basis of human nature is questioned if other parts of humanity suffer indignity as a result of poverty. Here, we are reminded of an Akan saying, which literally translates as "The day a friend dies is the day when one dies."

TRADITIONAL MORALITY

This call to be concerned for others is an essential element of traditional morality, which is necessary for social relationships. Human activities that affect each other are firmly rooted in moral principles and other values that constantly remind the members of the society of their interrelatedness and connectedness. Such moral principles make people transcend self-centeredness and unhealthy competition to outdo one another.

TRADITIONAL VALUES

In the traditional African society there is an acceptance that material things are useful insofar as they enhance the well-being and survival of people. That is to say, greater value is placed on human beings and their dignity than on mere acquisition and possession of material things. The high value placed on human beings is portrayed in the Akan saying

Onipa ne asem,
Mefere sika, sika nnyeso,
Mefere dan dan nnyeso,
Onipa ne asem.
A human being is of value,
If I call on money (wealth) it will not mind me,
If I call on building, it will not mind me,
A human being is of value.

Even if for a moment it may look disastrous and gloomy, a lack of material things is not the end of human life. The element of hope in the situation of poverty is also highlighted in the saying "Ehia wo nnwo" (Do not die because of poverty). There is always a way out of poverty.

NEGATIVE AND POSITIVE SANCTIONS

Traditional African societies require every member to come to the help of the needy. Those who do not do so for one reason or another are looked down upon and stigmatized. In traditional societies stigmatization often leads to guilt, which serves as a very potent and negative sanction. On the contrary, those who are known to be ready to help others in situations of need are held in high esteem and praised. In traditional Akan society, for example, such people are referred to as model human beings.

AFRICAN TRADITIONAL FESTIVALS

Apart from these underlying philosophies, periodic festivals mirror the importance attached to human relations and the concern for the other person's welfare. These are practical and institutionalized activities in many traditional African communities, and they also deal with poverty. Examples are periodic ceremonies and traditional festivals. Many of these festivals focus on instilling in the people the necessity to remember always to make provision for one another's basic needs. In agricultural communities this is reflected in the various forms of ceremonial and ritual activities associated with harvest.

For example, the *odwira* festival among the Akan of Ghana generally focuses on the harvest of root crops such as yams. The *aboakyere* festival of the Effutu of Winneba, a town on the central coast of Ghana, focuses on hunting; and the *bakatue* festival of the people in Elmina, a predominantly fishing community, honors fishing. The homowo festival among the Gas celebrates the production of corn.

The homowo festival is said to be a memorial to remind the Gas of a period of severe hunger that occurred in the past, when there was a failure in the production of the main staple food of the people, corn. It is said that that hunger was so severe that people became very poor; some even died because of hunger and poverty. It was viewed as a major societal disaster. Consequently the homowo (or hooting at hunger) was constituted to ritually hoot at hunger and poverty and to remind the people of the need to consistently work hard to produce what they need for living. This festival continues to be observed and has instilled in the Gas the need to work hard at all their endeavors, on land or sea, in order to achieve bumper harvests every year.

The need for hard work for sustainable prosperity that drives away hunger supports the traditional view that poverty is a temporary situation that can be dealt with and that need not be the cause of people's death. Again, it is a clear demonstration that the frontal attack on poverty in traditional African society is essentially a community issue. Some of these periodic festivals, which end with communal feasting, allow everyone, including the poorest, to participate. Indeed, in some cases a conscious attempt is made to encourage the poor to participate in the feast.

On such occasions libation is poured and special prayers are said to invoke the various spirits to ensure good health, protection, and energy, and to prevent people from getting into trouble and doing anything that can spell doom to the society. The gods are always pleaded with to prosper the works of the people's hands so that they will not suffer poverty.

LEAVING FOOD AND OTHER ITEMS AT SHRINES AND SACRED PLACES

In many traditional communities it is a practice to leave food and other items periodically at sacred places. Such items are believed to be for the gods and other spirits, but in reality they are left for people in need. Items given to the gods are exclusively theirs, and supernatural sanctions apply to any breach of their preserve. However, the belief is that no harm can come to needy people if they feed on food left for the gods. In the situation of poverty, the gods and the spiritual agencies themselves are believed to relax such sanctions, emphasizing their own concern and interest in ensuring that those in dire need relieve their poverty.

Traditional ways of dealing with poverty fitted in very well with the specific context of traditional society, which was small in size. In such a context, the understanding of poverty related to the narrow range of physical, material needs with which existing traditional institutions (political, social, religious, and economic) easily coped.

Yet African traditions have never remained static. Through contact with other societies and the encounter with new and different institutions, there have been far-reaching changes. These changes have shaken the foundation of traditional social systems.

Consequently the concept of poverty has changed. New needs and ideas taken from Western and other societies continue to define and influence such needs and the choices that people now make toward providing for them. For example, when asked, most Ghanaians today define a poor person as one who lacks modern amenities such as refrigerators, modern houses, money, imported food, clothing, cars, computers, and access to modern health facilities and educational institutions.

This view is echoed in the definition of development adopted by international economic systems, which also use quantitative measures as indicators of wealth and poverty. One can discern a progressive decline in traditional support systems in African societies because of the alien emphasis on competition, individualism, acquisitiveness, consumerism, and self-assertiveness, all of which undermine the values and ideas of traditional economic, social, and religious systems.

The castles along the coast of Ghana are examples of European contact with Africa that brought in a new set of economic, social, religious, and political structures. These new systems introduced new market approaches that were dictated by Europeans. They brought in values that viewed material things as more valuable than human beings. In fact, they viewed Africans as commodities, as evidenced in the slave trade. Again, the trend toward competition for individual wealth, acquisitiveness, and consumerism ignored the traditional African spirit of communal concern for the needs of all.

Another significant legacy of such contact between Europeans and Africans was the introduction of gunpowder in weapons of destruction. The effect of that commodity has been devastating; it is one of the major causes of the continuing cycle of poverty, exacerbated by wars, refugee displacements, and the upsurge of interethnic and religious conflicts.

A further consequence of these conditions is the phenomenon of children thrown onto the streets, increased incidence of HIV/AIDS, mass unemployment of both men and women, increased criminality, and generally a sense of hopelessness in getting out of the vicious cycle of poverty.

In this brief analysis I have raised some important issues in relation to poverty. I have argued that if we honestly want to deal with poverty we cannot avoid the issue of equitable distribution of resources and we cannot avoid moral principles that emphasize a sound understanding of our common humanity. In brief, we cannot avoid challenging the understanding of wealth that focuses attention on individuals rather than communities.

Again, we cannot ignore religious issues that undergird human living and the dignity and respect due to all. We have also seen that it was these values that in traditional African contexts ensured that poverty was not such a divisive force in society. Rather, these religious values gave hope to the poor and enabled the society as a whole to see poverty as a temporal human condition that could be overcome in the context of the ideals and the supportive system that traditional culture provided.

The crucial question in all this is, what is the place of traditional beliefs, practices, and value systems with regard to this new phase of poverty? The question is even more urgent in a situation where poverty within Africa has international repercussions and has become very complex and vicious. Can traditional coping mechanisms effectively deal with poverty today?

One is inclined to be pessimistic. especially since some of these traditional ideals are in decline. First, persistent wars in places such as Sudan, the Democratic Republic of Congo, Liberia, and Sierra Leone continuously displace and destroy people, as well as destroying facilities for living. In such contexts the traditional sense of community that encouraged members to be one another's keeper is gradually breaking down.

Second, we have already touched on the fact that indigenous people are losing arable land to multinational corporations in mining, agriculture, and other economic activities that do not directly benefit the land's original owners. With increases in population the natural resources become increasingly scarce for everyone. New religious and other systems that have been introduced to Africans directly or indirectly erode some of the traditional religious and moral values that once preserved the environment and encouraged the responsible use of land and wealth. These and other factors militate against the traditional coping systems with regard to poverty.

Fortunately, even though new systems and values seem to be overtaking traditional values and ways of coping with poverty, there are still a number of discernable elements from the traditional systems that give some hope for reconstructing ways to deal with poverty. One cannot fail to see examples like the communal sense of sharing in the tasks of dealing with human needs. For instance, in Kenya, there is the system of *harambee*, in which the members of the community come together to offer gifts and other support to needy members of the community.

In Ghana and other places in Africa, one comes across countless numbers of young persons selling foods on streets, forming small groups in the informal sector to make crafts, baskets, sandals, and traditional clothing, all to ensure survival for themselves and the family they might have left in the rural areas. Further, one can cite numerous cases of economic migrants scattered all over the world who send goods and hard currency and other necessary items to support both the nuclear and extended families that would otherwise be in dire need.

Further, religious groups and women's and other organizations are creating centers where people with different needs can go for comfort. Many African governments are seeing the need for developing the private sector and encouraging voluntary organizations and nongovernmental organizations in supporting the poor and the needy in various ways. Some governments offer grants of various types and have instituted training centers at local levels.

All these attempts derive from the traditional African view of care and concern, which sees poverty as a communal rather than individual issue. Indeed, it could be considered that even this Pan-African group of scholars is itself an indication of the traditional Africa spirit of communal care and concern for the poor.[3]

Notes

1. Peter Townsend, *Customs and Activities* (London: Alan Lane, 1979), 31.
2. J. G. Christaller, *Dictionary of the Asante and Fante Language Called Tshi (Twi)* (Basel: Basel Evangelical Missionary Society, 1935).
3. For more on these issues, and for background and sources, see the following works: W. E. Abraham, *The Mind of Africa* (London: Weidenfeld and Nicolson, 1962); E. Y. Amedekey, *Cultural History of the Akans: A Bibliography* (Accra: Ghana University Press, 1970); E. Amoah, "Moral and Social Significance of Proverbs among the Wasaws—An Akan People," M.A. thesis, University of London, 1974; K. Antubam, *Ghana's Heritage of Culture* (Leipzig: Koehler and Ameland, 1963); A. F. Banahn, " 'Kyiriba': Tradition, Change and Anomie in Puberty Rites," *West African Journal of Sociology and Political Science* (1974/76); K. A. Busia, "The Ashanti," in *African Worlds: Studies in the Cosmological and Social Values of African Peoples*, ed. D. Forde (London: Oxford University Press, 1954); J. B. Danquah, *The Akan Doctrine of God: A Fragment of Gold Coast Ethics and Religion*, 2nd ed. (London: Frank Cass, 1968); H. W. Debrunner, *Witchcraft in Ghana: A Study of the Belief in Destructive Witches and Its Effect on the Akan Tribes* (Accra: Presbyterian Book Depot, 1959); K. A. Dickson, introduction to J. B. Danquah, *The Akan Doctrine of God: A Fragment of Gold Coast Ethics and Religion*, 2nd ed. (London: Frank Cass, 1968); S. A. Dzeagu, "Proverbs and Folktales of Ghana: Their Form and Uses," in *Traditional Life, Culture and Literature in Ghana*, special issue, ed. J. M. Assimeng, of *Conch* 7.1/2 (1975): 80–92; A. B. Ellis, *The Tshi-Speaking Peoples of the Gold Coast* (London: Chapman and Hall, 1887); E. E. Evans-Pritchard, *Witchcraft, Oracles and Magic among the Asante* (Oxford: Clarendon, 1962); M. Z. Field, *Religion and Medicine of the Ga People* (London: Oxford University Press, 1937); M. Z. Field, *Search for Security: An Ethno-psychiatric Study of Rural Ghana* (London: Faber and Faber, 1960); E. Bolaji Idowu, *Olodumare: God in Yoruba Belief* (London: Longman, 1962); E. Bolaji Idowu, *African Traditional Religion: A Definition* (London: S.C.M., 1973); E. L. R. Meyerowitz, *The Sacred State of the Akan* (London: Faber and Faber, 1951); E. L. R. Meyerowitz, *Akan Traditions of Origin* (London: Faber and Faber, 1952); E. L. R. Meyerowitz, *The Akan of Ghana, Their Ancient Beliefs* (London: Faber and Faber, 1958); E. L. R. Meyerowitz, *The Divine Kingship in Ghana and Ancient Egypt* (London: Faber and Faber, 1960); Geoffrey Parrinder, *West African Religion* (London, Epworth Press, 1949); John S. Pobee, "Aspects of African Traditional Religion," *Journal in the Sociology of Religion* 37 (1976): 1–18.

Linda E. Thomas
Dwight N. Hopkins

RELIGION AND POVERTY

RITUAL AND EMPOWERMENT IN AFRICA

AND THE AFRICAN DIASPORA

This essay utilizes a cross-cultural contrasting methodology to reflect on and analyze the means by which peoples of Africa and the African diaspora deploy religious rituals to cope with systems of poverty.[1] Specifically, our thesis is that, within disadvantaged communities, religious rituals are evidence of empowerment among the poor in African indigenous churches or African independent churches. Furthermore, cognizant of ambiguous beliefs and contradictory practices, we engage the ways in which rituals both empower African and African diaspora peoples to deal with structures that cause them to be adversely affected by race, gender, and class, and encourage these peoples to participate in the development of a positive sense of the black individual self and black communal selves.

Our research investigations and immersion experiences in South Africa, Jamaica, and the United States provide the following definitional intent. For our purposes, religion indicates institutionalized manifestations of belief in the sacred—the interaction of spirituality with humanity and all of creation. Ritual suggests repetitive practices to harness the presence of the sacred. Empowerment implies how impoverished people perceive their positive agency resulting from their experience of the sacred. Finally, African indigenous churches signify Africans and peoples of African descent who reinterpret the Christianity brought by missionaries and combine it with a reinterpretation of African cultures.

Notions of Poverty

At this juncture, we identify at least two forms of poverty—structural and spiritual. Structural or material poverty is most clearly what we peoples of African descent are faced with today. For instance, in the United States, structural and institutional poverty are such that the majority of black, working-class people living in systemic poverty are worse off than they were before the civil rights movement of the 1950s and 1960s. They suffer more in quality-of-life indicators such as health care, education, collective ownership of land and other forms of material wealth, employment, and general standard of living. The rise of a small, elite stratum of black upper-income people has helped to mask the plight of the majority of poor and working-class people. Even middle-income blacks suffer due to racial discrimination, another systemic mechanism subordinating the full potential of black people. And, of course, outside the United States, the globalization of U.S. monopoly capitalist corporations has intensified structural and institutional poverty for peoples in Africa and other parts of the third world.[2]

Structural or material poverty has intensified the division between the "haves" and the "have nots." In the United States, the ruling elite argues that the nation's health should be determined by the rise of Wall Street's stock market and the success of venture capital in Silicon Valley. However, if the nation's well-being were examined by the status of the least sectors of society such as working-class people, those caught in structural poverty, farm laborers, and other vulnerable citizens, we would discover that most people suffer increasingly downward marginalization due, in great part, to more and more mergers and consolidation of real wealth into fewer and fewer hands at the top of U.S. society.[3]

Moreover, structural or material poverty not only impacts greatly the economic asymmetry among classes within the United States, it also places black folk or peoples of African descent into disproportionate levels of material poverty. Thus structural poverty has a racial and cultural dimension to it. Probing further along this line of investigation, we discover the intensified racial feminization of poverty among black women forced into adverse economic and social conditions. To appreciate the grueling daily impact of material poverty in Africa and throughout the African diaspora, it is important to find out where and how black women live.

Regarding material or structural poverty and religion or spirituality, we suggest that systemic poverty offers Africans and peoples of African descent the possibility to develop a spirituality of fortitude and an ethic of resistance. In other words, though the wealthy of this world use structural poverty as a means to demolish the energies of people at the bottom of society, the poor who have faith in a sacred being believe God uses these situations to build character and long-term endurance in an ongoing struggle against evil. If one is capable of surviving catastrophes, one has the potential to translate the sacred-human connection into strategies of survival and positive actions and energies to construct a better individual self and a new commonwealth of communities.

After structural poverty, we look at spiritual poverty. This concept has often been ridiculed or condemned by progressive or justice-minded, religious people of African descent. Such reactions are understandable because both white Christian preachers during American slavery and white missionaries to Africa and the diaspora have reinterpreted and hence manipulated the notion of spirituality as an opiate of poor and working-class communities. Generally, missionaries in the early United States and those abroad told black people to rely on a spiritual Jesus and not to worry about material white supremacy, economic inequality, and gender discrimination. Here spirituality serves as a drug because it does not focus oppressed people on the structures of capitalism and heinous forms of human poverty. However, we would suggest that the idea of spiritual poverty offers a very important heuristic even for justice-minded and progressive Christians.

By spiritual poverty, we mean two things.[4] First, we underscore the harmful emotional and psychological scars that we all carry as a result of negative childhood or adult experiences. One does not have to be a formally trained psychologist, licensed therapist, church counselor, or twelve-steps expert to realize that we all embody, at different levels, the crying voices of the wounded children within us. These psychological injuries exemplify one form of spiritual poverty.

The second manifestation of spiritual poverty is the tendency to forget what our African and enslaved ancestors taught us, specifically, the belief that spirituality pervades all dimensions of African peoples' lives. Our African ancestors did not recognize a separation between sacred and secular. Rather, they acknowledged that God's spirit and our ancestors' spirits accompany us at all times and in all situations. But those of us with an African heritage who are educated with advanced graduate degrees too often buy into the European practice of separating our African spiritual beings from other parts of our identities.

These nuanced definitions of poverty allow us to engage our two case studies of South Africa and the United States, and one general study of Jamaica. Drawing on textual and direct experiences in South Africa, Jamaica, and the United States, we will explore a number of important questions: What is the relation of religion to the constitution of the cultural systems of race, gender, and class in each of these contexts, and what are the ritual modes that African communities and African diaspora peoples mobilize to deal with these forces in their everyday lives? This overarching query, which emphasizes the ways faith communities sustain and support their people, will be supplemented by posing additional issues: In the new millennium, what are the effects of deleterious racial, gender, and class differences among peoples of African descent? How do African and African diaspora people, who have been historically oppressed, make their lives work on a day-to-day basis? What is it about who they are, what they do spiritually, that assuages the rawness of oppression as well as the hustle and bustle of life? How do the politics of religion and racial discrimination, gender oppression, and class exploitation manifest themselves in South Africa, Jamaica, and the United States? And in what ways do they affect the poor?

The social environment in each of these countries is such that a significant number of peoples of African descent fall well below the poverty line, thereby giving them a sense of inadequacy in their lives—a lack of well-being that is manifested spiritually, culturally, physically, socially, and psychologically. We assert that for many, relief is found in religious dynamics with the following characteristics: a biblically based Christian theology, a sense of personal empowerment by the Holy Spirit, certain African retentions in sacred life, community support and concern, vibrant music, and a focus on material and spiritual healing. All of these religious practices give members a sense of hope.

In this essay, we seek to explore what draws people to these types of ecclesial institutions. One hypothesis is that the cultural construction of oppression, including hardships such as unemployment or familial instability, contributes to members' malaise and affects people's sense of wellness and safety. This is true for middle-income families as well as for the poor. Material, cultural, and emotional dislocations force people to pursue new avenues for resolution and stability—both of which are support systems provided by the church. Thus, people who are supported by faith communities enthusiastically share their experiences with others. Those who have heard about the support the community provides come to these faith communities seeking the same spiritual and physical healing and assistance received by their friends.

In addition to worship gatherings, churches and faith associations provide food, shelter, childcare, spiritual healing such as exorcisms of spiritual-physical "demons" from the body, and most important, a feeling of community. By offering some basic resources, these spiritual institutions help to meet people's needs and empower them. Through community support, a commitment to a holistic life, and healing (material and spiritual), members achieve a more fulfilled life. Such churches and believing groups seem to grow as the message spreads that new life and health can be found in these cultural systems of sacred space and ritualized practices.

Method

This essay utilizes fieldwork, interviews, immersion experiences, secondary literature, and participant observation approaches to two case studies—South Africa and the United States, and one general study—Jamaica. Each country confronts unique day-to-day questions while sharing some general commonalities. Contextual material and spiritual poverties have birthed the necessity of rituals for survival and empowerment. However, ritualizations differ. We will show how, in South Africa, rituals flourish within worship and as an extension of the worship services. In Jamaica, it is clear that ritual has become part of everyday life. And in the United States, ritual occurs in monthly repetitive sacred routines.

We argue for empowerment because these rituals actually embolden adherents to maintain spiritual sanity and material advancements, individually and collectively. We are aware of other notions of empowerment such as organized struggles to confront state power and macroeconomic monopolies. (One encounters such examples in the history of the 1960s decolonization and liberation movements in Africa and the Caribbean, the African American civil rights movement, and the black power and Pan-African offensives.) However, all phenomena are particular, fluid, and dynamic. So too is the concept of empowerment. Empowerment and its ritualized revelations configure differently in varying epochs depending on the balance of forces contending for dominance within specific societal historical junctures. From our observations and analysis, the two case studies and one general study meet the definition of empowerment given the preponderance of evil spirituality's attack on poor people at the beginning of the twenty-first century. These rituals engender proactive agency for the poor and the disadvantaged. Perhaps in the future another flow of resistance led by black and African indigenous churches will occur in these three models under discussion.

Obviously, one can detect the ambiguous beliefs and contradictory practices of these churches. They embody the tensions of two cultures and two political economies—the legacy of communal Africa and the press of global monopoly capitalism. Concomitantly, they bring to the surface the precarious and, too often, oppressed status of women by drawing on negative traditions of patriarchy from Christianity and African traditions. Still, what we want to point out is the potential empowerment that rituals of healing can provide for poor Africans and African Americans in these ecclesial formations.

South African Immersion

Since its colonization by white Europeans in 1652, South Africa has suffered contentious racial discord.[5] In the beginning, the colonizers—Dutch, French, and German—were concerned neither with peaceful coexistence with the Africans nor with their conversion; the European colonizers were interested in their enslavement and their extermination.[6] In the nineteenth century, with the progression of the colonialists eastward, European treatment of the Africans changed. At the behest of many Christian missionaries horrified by the inhumane treatment of Africans, the colonizers started to use education as a weapon to subdue the indigenous populations. The missionaries argued that Europeans had a duty to bring Christ to the "pagan" peoples so that they could be elevated to the "elite status" of European civilization.

The belief in a humanitarian, Christianizing effort subsequently became a justification for colonial expansion, African land dispossession, and segregation. In 1948 with the election of the National Party to power, segregation laws were aggressively enacted and segregation became the official "law of the land" in a system known as apartheid. Apartheid resulted in grave economic, educational, health, and life-expectancy discrepancies between the black South Africans and the white ruling minority. It was not until the 1990s that segregation laws began to be overturned and the black South Africans would be given the right to vote.

Though apartheid has officially ended, it has left its legacy on black South Africans. Millions still live in poverty. To combat their oppression, many Africans turn to religion as a source for healing.

The South African St. John's Apostolic Faith Mission Church, the specific African independent church we are analyzing, is one of several such churches founded in 1892, when Africans rebelled against their treatment in European mission churches (Methodist, Presbyterian, etc.). Because Europeans thought their culture superior, white missionaries frequently attempted to stamp out any vestiges of African indigenous culture and religion maintained by Africans who converted to European Christian denominations. Africans' spiritual needs related to ancestors, and precolonial religious practices were regarded by whites as unimportant if not demonic.[7] This advocacy of cultural superiority on the part of many missionaries meant that Africans were seen as inferior to whites.

Within this broader African independent church movement, St. John's Apostolic Faith Mission was founded by a black woman named Mother Christina Nku, who received a "vision" from God that inspired her to launch her own church in 1938. Her faith community grew so rapidly that congregations developed and spread throughout southern Africa. Presently, St. John's is a denomination whose total membership exceeds two million. Most of the individual congregations of St. John's have no more than twenty-five to sixty members, who express a strong sense of collectivity, focus on mutual aid, and use 90 percent of their church's income to assist members who are in need.

One particular St. John's church is located in the township of Gugulethu, outside of Cape Town. Forty-eight members make up this local church, and they are overwhelmingly poor. The religious cosmology of St. John's derives from a synthesis of Protestant Christianity and precolonial African religion. For instance, members of the church underscore biblically based prophecy on the part of the leadership and the laity. This prophetic practice also has roots in an African indigenous way of life, which includes diviners—people who offer prophecies to the community. Prophetic revelation plays an important role at St. John's because members believe in personal transactions between God, who reveals, and human beings, to whom disclosures are made. The church members go to designated prophets to discern why a particular circumstance has taken place, why a sickness has developed, or why a death has occurred. The church members call these revelations "propheting."

In that universe, if one wants to fulfill one's destiny, one needs the support of the ancestors. This is due to the prevailing sense that alone, human beings are fragile. Members of St. John's are constantly aware of their ancestral spiritual beings and of their position in the foreordained cosmos. In addition to the ancestors, use of the Bible and the ability to tell the person about his or her past life and future are key elements of prophetic revelation in the Christian context at St. John's. Ritual, prophecy, and divining are part of a healing formula in which the prophet and sick person begin to develop a symbiotic relationship.

In addition to prophecy and diviners, the belief in spirits and ancestors indicates the syncretic theology of St. John's Apostolic Faith Mission. Church members assert the continuation of the spirit after death; this conviction influences members' faithfulness to ancestor veneration. They also view their ancestors as the trustees and conservators of ethical behaviors. The departed members of the family suggest moral values that are associated with ideal conduct. Kinship ties through the clan bind people to one another, and ancestor veneration marks commitment to the moral standards and ethics of the family group or community. Consequently, St. John's members approach the ancestors as often as they call upon God.

Healing occurs at St. John's through the means of *umoya* (spirit), which empowers the church in all aspects of its life. The spirit usually takes possession of persons during worship services in a spontaneous and unpredictable manner. When the Holy Spirit descends upon an individual believer, rarely is the person isolated by himself or herself. Indeed, spirit possession functions as a ritual of performance amidst the public arena of fellow believers testifying before God. Similarly, in the open space of the St. John's blue-and-white sanctuary, a possessed individual typically enacts a regular stylized dance during times of communal a capella singing.

The climax of every Sunday morning worship service at St. John's is a healing ritual. After the sermon, the minister usually proclaims: "It is time to prepare to go to the lake [*ichibi*]." To "go to the lake" is symbolic language that signifies the commencement of the ritual drama of healing. The drama unfolds in the following way. First, a member, routinely a woman, begins to sing a hymn called "Se teng sediba sa madi," meaning "There is a fountain of blood."[8]

The words of the hymn are rich in symbolic meaning. An exegesis of the text suggests that the fountain of blood represents an altar of atonement symbolizing Jesus' sacrificial death. The fountain of blood serves metaphorically as medicine that gives power to life. Thus, the blessed water that the members drink stands for the blood of Jesus.

During the singing of this hymn, the sanctuary is transformed to represent a lake that symbolically portrays the pool, Bethesda, where Jesus cured a man who had been an invalid for many years (John 5:1–8). The lake, like its counterpart in the New Testament (John 5:3), is reputed to heal persons who drink its water and receive prayer during the service. To construct the lake, members of the congregation raise above the center aisle a large, spotlessly clean, white cloth, six feet in length and three feet in width, with blue borders. The aisle has a cross outlined in spotlessly clean white tiles, placed against a solid blue background. Above the aisle is a fluorescent light bulb that is also shaped as a cross. Consequently, symbols of the cross completely surround the blue-and-white canopy.

Next, two members bring water in a large container to the front of the sanctuary, which, after being blessed by the pastor, is poured into little plastic cups and handed to those who stand in line to receive it. Having swallowed the water, people move quickly under the blue-and-white cloth to be blessed by the ministers and their spouses, who lay hands upon them. After everyone has partaken of the water and received a blessing, the pastor walks through the church and sprinkles the healing water in an act of final cleansing and blessing. Members believe that the blessed water and the healing rituals change their lives because the Holy Spirit, which comes from a powerful God and Jesus Christ, was present. Throughout the extended ritual, congregants fervently sing hymns and they display a manifestly happier state in their impoverished lives.

The blessed water is not only used for drinking; its other uses include bathing, emetics, and enemas. For example, usually on Saturdays, male and female ministers take women and men to gender-segregated shacks on the church property. Here, the unclothed bodies of spiritually and physically wounded "patients" from the township and rural communities undergo a thorough religious bathing. Spiritual and psychic demons from which the people must be healed include internal anger, low self-worth, feeling a lack of control over one's life, marital discord, general malaise in the soul, and so on. All of these forms of "dirt" that enter a person's body from foreign sources have to be removed, thus the use of enemas and vomiting as central ritual activities. However, it is not simply a question of removing physical dirt. Fundamentally, adherents believe the blessed water embodies the power to remove unclean spirits. To remove these unwanted spirits and injuries, the female or male clergyperson blesses the person and calls out the troubling presence within the soul and body of the individual. Surprisingly, most of the participants in healing practices are not members of St. John's. This signifies how the broader population perceives the church as a religious and social service agency even for the nonmember.

Baptism indicates another type of water ritual healing. Massive communal baptisms take place in the cold water of the ocean. Usually, the baptismal ceremony is preceded by an indigenous religious practice—animal sacrifice. The use of the Christian sacrament of baptism after animal sacrifice represents the syncretism of diverse religious sources. The traditional sacrificial animals are a cow and three sheep. In order for the ceremony to be performed correctly, the cow must bellow in a specific manner once the knife enters its head. It is believed that the ancestors are present only when the cow cries out in a particular fashion. Concomitantly, spiritual actions complement physical needs. For many participants, the food they receive from the cooking of sacrificed animals and distribution of meat, vegetables, and drink is a rare complete meal. And poor people, by creating their alternative leadership to apartheid and the postapartheid legacy coupled with their own sacred, separate African space, foster the growth of new leaders as well as suggest how self-confidence in their own rituals could spread to self-confidence in the broader civic realm.

St. John's evinces one way that black South Africans dwelling in township poverty respond to apartheid and the continuation of postapartheid challenges. Members, as "liminal personas" living in apartheid and postapartheid culture, are constantly at risk. This betwixt-and-between status compromises and jeopardizes their sense of well-being, as many must endure chronic violence and/or devastating unemployment. Apartheid and its legacy precipitated a state of uncleanliness that frequently manifests itself in sickness, violence, and systemic deprivation of those things (land, quality housing, health care, education, and employment) to which white South Africans have virtually automatic access. St. John's Church fought this devastating attack on black humanity. Historically, members contested the status quo upheld by apartheid society by refashioning it into a system of meaning that made sense to them as marginalized persons. Members still continue to do this today in apartheid's aftermath.

More specifically, the rituals provide a means for poor, black South Africans to turn to a comforting community and to a respected holy leader when sickness (ukugula) surfaces. The healer, who lives in the same local context as the patient, provides a source of support that could not be duplicated by an outsider. When sickness is acute, members go to clinics and hospitals but, in most cases, they consult initially with the pastor and follow his or her prescribed healing applications.

Another form of resistance apparent at St. John's is support networks. Mamphela Ramphele notes that a communal survival strategy among hostel dwellers in South Africa is an "economy of affection," which includes relatives, "home-people" (abakhaya), and acquaintances.[9] In like fashion, St. John's members forge an "economy of affection" at the church. For instance, when people are too sick to work, those who are healthy and employed share their income, food, and services. Those who were well but unemployed care for the children of those who work. Thus the sharing of resources, both material and spiritual, is a communal benefit.

Women display similar ritual resilience to garner collective resources. Groups comprised of community and church members form all-women "clubs" where the religious participants deposit monies on a monthly basis. Each month, a different woman uses the total funds for her household food, rent, clothing, and other survival necessities. During the female gatherings, oftentimes secret, the women engage in ongoing and spirited dancing and singing. Songs refer to both Jesus and the ancestors. In this sense, women hybridize Christianity and indigenous religiosity to survive and resist structures that keep them oppressed and, at the same time, create a uniquely feminine solidarity and spirituality.

An additional survival strategy among St. John's members is the sharing of stories for strength and renewal. Since potential initiates usually come to the church in crisis, members regularly talk about the reasons they joined St. John's and their personal experience of healing. Those who have been healed assist the inexperienced novices in the ways of the St. John's ritualized regiment. St. John's minimizes individualism by quickly incorporating people into a conversation of love and support. Members believe themselves to be a transformed collective because of their relationship with a liberating supernatural source. Through shared ritual activity they overcome the devastating effects of ill health and societal conditions. In so doing, members create an emancipatory space in which to exist.

Ultimately, St. John's Apostolic Faith Mission Church evidences a dissenting, syncretized Christianity that can empower its members in sacred space so they can live emboldened lives in secular space. The cosmology of St. John's is a ritualized midpoint between the local order and the macro-level world of apartheid and apartheid's legacy. The ritualized space, betwixt and between worlds, serves to rejuvenate people. While the healing rituals do not reverse the powerful and informal structures of apartheid's legacy (especially a seeming perpetuation of economic apartheid on the part of whites), they enable poor blacks, the most vulnerable within the system, to live as liberated a life as possible under the press of macro structures. The establishment of an institution independent of colonial control demonstrates an act of resistance. African peoples crafted a new cosmology in separate sacred space to practice religion on their own terms.

Indeed, the micro-level symbolic order of the St. John's healing rituals stands in stark contrast to the entrenched patterns of the macro level. As such, the micro-order symbols work to disempower the legacy of apartheid structures, assist marginalized persons to assert their own self-determined religious identity, and carve out an order in a chaotic macro, white-dominated political economy.

Jamaican Immersion

The African diasporic experience in Jamaica has evolved out of a complex history that includes colonial occupation, the decimation of indigenous populations, the encroachment of Christianity from Europe and the United States, the rape of enslaved African women that produced the country's mulatto population, and the resulting majority of citizens of African descent.[10] This history began in 1492, when Columbus first made contact with the indigenous Tainos peoples of Jamaica (the Arawak Indians). From 1492 to 1655, Jamaica was a colony of the Roman Catholic country Spain. As happened in other Spanish global expansions, effected by force and biblical imposition, in Jamaica the missiology of Christian discourse and the violent rule of military might resulted in the genocide of the original peoples of the island. The year 1655 witnessed the transfer of colonial military and theological power from Spain to Britain at the time of the ascendancy of the British Empire, which kept control of Jamaica from 1655 until 1962. The slave economy, during the period 1655 to 1838, took on a distinct Anglican flavor. Africans, imported through the international slave trade and accompanied by European Christian missionaries, gradually converted from their African indigenous religions to Christian beliefs and practices.

Yet, even in the midst of intense Christian oppression, enslaved Africans, like their proselytized sisters and brethren throughout the Americas, reappropriated the Jesus narrative imposed on them by their slaveholders and incorporated it into their own African cosmology of human wholeness, dignity, and attenuated ritual practices. African Jamaicans seized upon the Baptist denomination as their primary mode of an expressed religiosity of survival and resistance. African religion met European opinions of Christian norms, and a specific Afro-Jamaican Christianity was born. Hence Africanized Christianity matured within a process of forced dependency on external superpowers while maintaining efforts of independent self-authentication and African cultural retentions.

Such a legacy of colonial occupation, contested notions of Christianity, and lack of economic self-determination continues to haunt Jamaica today. More particularly, in the contemporary period since World War II, United States monopoly capitalist corporations act in concert with the growth of new waves of (predominantly) white, evangelical, Pentecostal missionaries. Though these missionaries profess the love of Jesus Christ as a spiritualized savior, they also offer a theological rationale for North American capitalist consumer culture, patriarchal hierarchy, and white-skin privileges. These new preachers recruit members based on a "prosperity gospel," advocating accumulation of consumer goods as signs of Jesus' blessing. And the aesthetics of whiteness has created a hierarchy of skin color among Jamaicans: white, Chinese, Indian, mulatto, and black African. Indeed, alien Pentecostal, neoevangelist Christians have colonized Jamaica to such an extent that these foreign religiosities now constitute 30 percent of the country's churches.

An island nation of 2.5 million people mainly of African descent, Jamaica signifies intense manifestations of oppression exacerbated by stringent demands, beginning with the 1977 "structural adjustment" and "liberalization" initiatives. That is, U.S. monopoly capitalist businesses (and their influence in the World Bank, the World Trade Organization, and the International Monetary Fund) imposed oppressive, immoral conditions. They demanded removal of public transportation, and the decrease in or elimination of water, electricity, housing, mental and physical health care, education, welfare, and necessary job opportunities for the majority of the population in order for economic imperialism to own increasing wealth and reap skewed income benefits from the Jamaican masses. In hindsight, structural adjustment and liberalization continue to transfer massive amounts of wealth and income upward.

For example, in 1977, the Standby Agreement, foisted on the nation by U.S. monopoly capitalist businesses, was made between Jamaica and the International Monetary Fund. This agreement consisted of a loan of $75 million to help restore Jamaica's failing economy. The agreement required, among other things, that Jamaica meet certain quarterly payments. Often, Jamaica could not make these payments, and so the Western nations shut down parts of the Jamaican infrastructure. Today, structural adjustment and liberalization continue to transfer massive amounts of wealth and income upward into the hands of wealthy North Americans.

For the everyday people who own no land in their own nation, the effects of such poverty literally are life-threatening. Sixty percent of the poor live in rural areas; 53 to 80 percent of poor households are headed by women; and 60 percent of all poor are children and the aged. Sixty-five percent of murders per year result from the sale of firearms to Jamaica by U.S. companies—a multibillion dollar industry. Eighty-five percent of the gun-crime perpetrators come from urban areas and squatter camps. Second to South Africa, Jamaica and the Caribbean have the fastest growing incidence of HIV/AIDS in the world. Girls between fifteen and nineteen years of age constitute the most at-risk social sector. In all these negative categories, blacks and Africans comprise the largest proportion by far.

Spiritual poverty among Jamaicans accompanies their dire material predicament. Crime and murders among the people indicate external violence and anger turned inward, both against their own self-esteem and against their neighbor. Another source of diminishment comes from imported culture, food, music, and other objects of consumption, which many Jamaicans acquire a taste for because they are constantly bombarded with advertisements and products of U.S. capitalist firms. In adopting these imports, the people unwittingly turn away from the spiritual legacy and creative genius of Jamaican collective culture. Authentic Jamaican traditions privilege sacrifice and solidarity for family and community, sharing with and protection for the vulnerable, and a compassionate and collective justice sensibility in all matters, sacred and so-called secular. Spiritual poverty may also lead to family illnesses and disequilibrium, which point to an insufficient means of material and psychological stability. Such an inclusive, intense attack yielding profound suffering reveals raging warfare on the systemic level and in the spiritual realm for the masses of ordinary people.

Contemporary religious expressions offer a variety of institutional and ritual responses to material and spiritual poverty. In particular, the Rastafari movement is the fastest growing religion in Jamaica. Rastafari demonstrate versatility in faith. No headquarters exists. They demand a minimum of allegiance and allow diversity; thus they accept whoever comes. Moreover, they have crossover impact, as Rastafari enter and survive in mainstream Christian churches. They worship a black God, who accepts black people fully. Rastafari employ music as a means of communication in which anyone can participate. With their strong emphasis on black solidarity and African nationalism, they offer an umbrella for panracial unity. Class distinctions, moreover, have begun to complicate the picture with more middle-income people becoming Rastafari. And, finally, the Rastafari movement has globalized to such a massive extent that one does not have to be in Jamaica to become Rastafari.

Rastafarianism is an indigenous Jamaican spirituality that originated in the early 1930s in the midst of the Great Depression. It consisted mainly of peasant migrants to the Kingston urban area, and drew heavily on Marcus Mosiah Garvey's Pan-African back-to-Africa repatriation movement (Garvey held a 1929 convention in Jamaica), and the installment of Ras Tafari (Prince Tafari) as Emperor Haile Selassie I of Ethiopia in November 1930. The Rastafari movement, a syncretism of co-opted Christianity, African political solidarity, and Jamaican cultural particularities, grew out of Jamaican religious traditions. One Jamaican religious tradition it drew from was the Myal religion, founded in the 1760s. Myal was the first Pan-African religion that enabled the various enslaved African language groups in Jamaica to come together as one African people in resistance to the white supremacist slavocracy. Myal wedded central African religious beliefs and rituals with its own adaptation of Christianity. It replaced Jesus with the Holy Spirit as the essential medium between God and humanity and likewise substituted missionary dogma with reliance on the spirit's instructions. Spirit possession became the pivotal mark of the Myal form of Christianity.

Rastafarianism also drew from Jamaican revivalism. In the 1860s, the formal leadership of the Jamaican church embraced a wave of revivals throughout the island. However, to the chagrin of official ecclesial hierarchy, the masses of black folk soon incorporated their own culture into the Christian revival movement. In a word, under the impact of revival fervor, Myal was transformed into revivalism with its own subsets, called Zion and Puku-mina. The former (Zion) adhered to more evident Christian ritual. The latter (Pukumina) expressed more African indigenous religions. Both, however, recognized good and bad spirits, divine representations through thunder and lightning, the importance of the Bible, dead ancestors' spirits, and dreams and visions conveying supernatural communications. In addition, they believed in natural healing of physical, mental, and social illness, Jesus the good spirit, Holy Spirit possession, and *obeah* as knowledge of inanimate and animate objects with evil and sacred supernatural powers, angels, arch-angels, and prophets. Despite white missionary efforts and their black Ja-maican representatives' struggle to stamp it out, revivalism, though modi-fied, persisted, and some of its adherents joined the Rastafari peasant and working-class movements.

Rastafarianism has grown into a diverse group of spiritual and religious dynamics today, with disparate attitudes toward the Bible, hierarchy, and religious organization. Still, there are generalizations that can be made par-ticularly with regard to how Rastafari respond to black spiritual and material poverty in Jamaica. Central to Rastafari theology is the belief in a black Jesus as Christ and Emperor Haile Selassie I as fulfilling both the second coming of Jesus and the messiah prophesies of Garvey concerning the crowning of a king. Therefore the emperor is divinity and Christ is black. The association of black bodies with divinity gives Jamaicans a savior image with which they can identify and fashion a strong self-identity.

Another theological tenet central to Rastafari spiritual uplift is connec-tion to land. Rastafari believe in repatriation to Africa, specifically Ethiopia, often referred to as Zion. All Rastafari understand themselves as exiles from their homeland and only Jah (God) can realize the diaspora's transfer back to its land of origin. Rastafari assert they are exiled in "Babylon," the Rastafari word for any form of oppression. Psalm 68 and the Hebrew exodus narra-tives underscore the biblical warrant for this forced-removal, voluntary re-turn motif. Indeed, the Bible provides ample evidence of Ethiopia's primacy and includes a plethora of African and black personas.[11] By using the exodus story and various biblical passages as a model for their own restoration, the Rastafari glean a comfort and peace that carry them through their oppres-sion by knowing that God will eventually bring them "home."

Another uniquely Rastafarian practice that contributes to spiritual uplift is the wearing of dreadlocks. This tradition began in the 1940s and arose from biblical imperatives for Nazarites, Israelites who were not allowed to cut their hair because they served the Lord (Num. 6:5). It was also inspired by the appearance in the Jamaican press of Africans who wore a similar hairstyle.[12] Dreadlocks have several levels of significance. First, they serve as a political and cultural statement against the dominant white image for men of straight, cropped hair and a shaven face. They also counteract white images of beauty (e.g., straight, light hair) by elevating the tight curls as sacred features. Dreadlocks also strengthen the connection between Rastafari and the natural world. Because they view Babylon as unnatural, Rastafari, by letting their hair grow naturally, are fighting against Babylon. Moreover, dreadlocks connect Rastafari with God and God's natural power or "earthforce." Since Rastafari connect themselves with this earthforce, "the shaking of the locks is thought to unleash spiritual energy which will eventually bring about the destruction of Babylon."[13] In essence, the locks are symbolic of Babylon's impending doom. The name *dreadlocks* appropriately reflects this belief. Dreadlocks ultimately provide Rastafari with both a positive aesthetic image and a spiritual awareness that God's justice will eventually conquer Babylon and its oppression.

Another ritualization of their self-conscious outcast status is the smoking of ganja. Smoking serves profound spiritual purposes. Rastafari believe the Bible points to the divine ordination of ganja use. Genesis 1:29 and Revelation 22:22 both reference the value of herbs and tree leaves for eating and healing. For Rastafari, ganja provides spiritual illumination and assists in inducing sacred dreams and visions. It provides access to a deep, "inner and worldly knowledge by helping the user to look past whatever is currently distracting him or her. Since the oppression of Babylon is a major distraction for the Rastafari, smoking the ganja helps them to move beyond their current oppression and decolonize their minds. Ganja smoking is also a source of community because a bond generally develops between those who share the pipe."[14]

Another way in which Rastafarianism has brought spiritual uplift is through its own particular religious tongue. Rastafari believe that their native African languages were stolen from them when they were captured as slaves, and that English is an imposed colonial language. To counteract the language of their oppression, the Rastafari have developed a new, sacred language. This language is exemplified by the usage of "I" which is similar to the Roman numeral "I" after the emperor's name. Accordingly, with their personal pronoun "I," Rastafari are part of God—that is, the Roman number "I" of the divinity Selassie. All Rastafari are "I"; consequently they utilize "I and I" for "we."

Perhaps the biggest critique of Rastafari lodges on the gender question. Women remain subordinate to men, for theological reasons: Eve and Delilah both tricked men; women are unable to receive complete divine knowledge

(Jah's enlightenment)—only her "king-man" has such capability. Yet a woman's equality movement has begun among the Rastafari; it challenges the mandatory covering of women's hair and other unbalanced gender practices, such as men's absolute leadership over and authority in all matters Rastafari.

The U.S. Experience

The first group of twenty enslaved Africans arrived in Jamestown, Virginia, in August 1619.[15] They did not arrive as indentured servants; rather, they were violently removed from their original continent, herded onto a Dutch man-of-war, and brought to an English-speaking colony. There, they were subsequently sold as privately owned objects to the English colonists in Jamestown. Unlike white indentured servants, Africans did not come voluntarily, under a contract to pay off their indenture once they completed a certain period of forced labor.

After slavery's end (in 1865), roughly 4 million southern black folk were now able to move their previously secret African-Christian syncretized worship (known as the underground "invisible institution" during the slavery period) to the public arena. At the same time, about 2 million northern African Americans had moved into Christian institutions. The majority fashioned their own independent, syncretized religiosity in African Methodist Episcopal, African Methodist Episcopal Zion, Colored (now Christian) Methodist Episcopal, and African Baptist churches. Still, a small set of northern African Americans remained within white churches. Blacks in the current white-dominated United Church of Christ hail from this final historical trajectory.

Today, the United States of America has a population approaching 300 million people, 40 million of whom are of African descent. The overwhelming majority of black people are structurally unemployed, working-class, and in financially at-risk, middle-income, and professional sectors. Most own homes or rent living spaces in the urban areas of America. Blacks make up one-quarter of all American poor communities, and the majority of the people in these impoverished communities are black women. In this dire context, poverty and crime are married. For instance, the United States has the highest incarceration level in the world, and African Americans account for 28.1 percent of those arrested but over 50 percent of persons convicted and actually admitted to federal and state prisons. Disproportionately, black inmates serve time for nonviolent crimes related to drug use and addiction. On the state level, prison expenditures are the third largest state cost after education and Medicaid. Consequently, even though overall crime statistics appear to have declined, the prison system remains a multibillion-dollar, profitable industry for white corporations and communities.[16] An egregious corollary to the megadollar drug trade is the increasing reality of black drug addicts stealing from their neighbors and family members. This form of low self-love and low self-esteem indicates an expression of negative spiritual poverty.

With a focus on inner-city African Americans, Trinity United Church of Christ in Chicago is one paradigm of an African indigenous church in the African diaspora. Located in a depressed, black urban section of Chicago, Illinois, Trinity is the largest local church in the entire United Church of Christ national denomination. Trinity consists of a mixed African American population comprised of working-class, middle-income, and professional black people. Its vision and mission embrace the materially disadvantaged, the emotionally bruised, and the spiritually troubled of all races and ethnic groups, yet it underscores the unique plight of black folk. Though technically Trinity is part of a predominantly white North American denomination, it intentionally seeks to combine a new religious interpretation of Christianity with a novel understanding of how to be African diaspora peoples. In this manner, it is a type of diasporan African indigenous church that contributes to the empowerment of African Americans.

One of the ways in which Trinity connects with the spiritually disenfranchised is through its public outreach. For example, its theological slogan is "Unashamedly Black and Unapologetically Christian," and its new members' class title is "Black and Christian." Likewise, the standard documents presented to those who enter new members' classes state that blacks are African people. Among its local, national, and international outreach, one finds active African and Caribbean ministries. Its different choirs even wear African dress.

Trinity offers a normal paradigm of the predicament of most global descendants of African peoples. Blacks who endured the European slave trade have undergone a severe dislocation from the particular land, language, clothing, foods, traditions, rituals, names, ancestors, grave sites, worldviews, lifestyles, and so on that their ancestors had in Africa. Thus the Trinity congregation, like so many diasporic Africans, selects and combines an array of traditions from all over Africa. Consequently, unlike African indigenous churches of the continent, Trinity syncretizes rituals, languages, and perspectives on life from different communities representing West, East, North, and South Africa. This forging of an African American identity from an eclectic range of traditions from disparate African nations contrasts with the fact that the majority of today's black Americans come from distinct language and clan groups from the west coast of Africa.

Nonetheless, Trinity represents a viable, new-world, African (American) indigenous church, one that has arisen from conscious self-naming and self-understanding. Some of those names and understandings are "It takes a village to raise a child"; "I am because we are"; the notion of the extended family; perceiving all adults as uncles and aunts and each church member as a brother or sister; the welcoming of spirit possession and holy dancing during worship services; the essential role of vibrant music in celebration; heavy reliance on biblical instruction; ministerial laying-on of hands of individual members who seek specialized prayer and healing; ongoing political and cultural analysis from the pulpit and in church publications; faith in a God of love, compassion, and justice for the disadvantaged; a deep sense of African and black American ancestors; the sacredness of children's total well-being; belief that the God of black Americans' African ancestors is the same God of Jesus and this God is black and African; and the foundational tenet of God ruling over all of God's creation, and hence, no firm separation between sacred and so-called secular realities.

Trinity implements these indigenous beliefs in several ways. Wanaume Kwa Sala (WKS, from the Swahili for "men at prayer") is one of many ritualized men's groups established by Jeremiah A. Wright Jr., Trinity's former senior pastor.[17] Men's groups seek to bring together small assemblies of (Trinity and non-Trinity) African American males in a spiritual formation to improve black men, their families, church, the community, and whatever paths they feel called to pursue. Twelve to fourteen men make up WKS, and it meets every first and third Saturday of the month from 7 AM to 1 PM at a member's home. With men ranging from their early thirties to early sixties, WKS has been functional in various incarnations since 1993. The overwhelming majority originate from working-class or working poor backgrounds. Yet all have defied the inherent adverse odds of poverty and racial discrimination in America and have attained at least an M.A. degree. Also, the standard wisdom that negative sociological predictors would work against the WKS members—several grew up in homes without their biological fathers or mothers—does not prove true: all can claim positive outcomes.

WKS commences and ends each gathering with prayer. To begin, men hold hands in a prayer circle in order to invoke the presence of the Holy Spirit and the spirit of their ancestors. "Brothers" bring food to the meeting, in a potluck. Throughout the session, soft gospel, spirituals, and jazz music envelope the sacred space in a subtle manner. The basic purpose of this monthly ritual is to yield spiritual growth; emotional support; political analysis; self-help processes; the exchange of skills and advice; fundraising; cultural affirmation; therapy; the construction of a new, more healthy African American male; and healing. For the participants, the holistic ritual serves to cast out emotional and psychological "demons" linked to stress engendered by material challenges and assaults on the psyche in the white and black worlds. Aiding this process are Bible readings and other related written materials, recordings and videotapes, and the theoretical and practical discussions that ensue. At the end of the meeting, the men close with prayer as a way to give each other comfort and guidance until the next gathering.

The men of WKS participate, either as a group, in subsets, or as individuals, in disparate other ministries. Some are in the leadership of the church's job fair and employment ministry; others run Trinity's annual black college tour; and some work in the leadership of the annual weekend men's conference. Still, a few engage in the church's Isuthu ministry, offered to teenage boys as a "rite of passage" process. One member heads an urban HIV/AIDS organization; another leads a community organization that reaches out to the Chicago ghetto. Still another has organized an international network of black religious and spiritual professors and activists. Whatever one member does, the others lend their assistance.

In additional efforts, WKS undertakes regular collective work and responsibilities. First, the group believes in modeling a liberating power for black children (girls and boys) so the youth can see positive, successful, and spiritual African American men and fathers who have overcome poverty and racial disadvantages in America. To this end, various activities pertain to members' children. When children graduate and go to college, WKS acknowledges their achievements (for example, by giving the graduate a gift or announcing the graduation in a church bulletin). Likewise, when their children preach or perform some other function in church, the members of WKS attend to show their appreciation as well as a physical sign of their support for the young people's effort. Children of the group who have special needs are the recipients of periodic annual fundraisers that include catered soul and/or Caribbean and African food and drinks, a live band and church dancers, men from church trained to do security, poets and singers, and other types of volunteers from Trinity who can make up an entire day of activities.

WKS also emphasizes saving, nourishing, and enhancing the family. In fact, the group helped to support one member through his divorce, healing, and subsequent remarriage back with his divorced wife. In the same spirit, members participated in another man's wedding. Afterward, this newlywed held his reception at a member's home. At least once, but usually twice a year, the men hold special gatherings with their wives, fiancées, and girlfriends. Inevitably, the get-togethers include food and drink, complemented by an outing to a black play or the viewing of a video and subsequent frank conversations at a member's home.

With accumulated regular dues, wks also provides supplemental funds for different members who occasionally confront financial difficulties. This could range from inability to pay bills or to travel during a family emergency, to covering the costs of the annual Trinity men's conference registration and hotel expenses.

We mention one other wks activity: its participation in rigorous political debates on local, state, national, and international political and economic topics. Its politics, moreover, extend into the electoral arena and petition signing, boycotts, and protest activities.

What undergirds Wanaume Kwa Sala is its deep spiritual glue, persistent awareness of being descendants of Africans in America, and a conscious belief in laying a foundation for the next generations.

Conclusion

This essay engaged notions of material and spiritual poverty. Material poverty embodies the physicality of oppression resulting from, in large measure, the effects of colonialism and now a globalized economy dominated by one superpower (the United States). Obviously these macro negativities have had local support among some government and church leaders in each of the countries studied here. With globalization, the ever increasing levels of poverty among those of African descent have reached crisis levels. There exists a sense that impoverished Africans, Jamaicans, and African Americans are dispensable and do not matter to the world.

This crisis is not merely physical, it is also spiritual. There is a feeling of "anthropological poverty," where African communities and large sections of the African diaspora are perceived as not quite fully human.[18] Lack of humanity, in this perception, invokes an array of negative characteristics upon black peoples. Unfortunately, too many people act out these harmful emotional and psychological demons. Following the perspective of most African and African diaspora cosmologies that the physical and the spiritual are interwoven as a dynamic unit, we believe that to heal from dehumanization, African peoples need to deploy simultaneous healing on both the natural and the supernatural levels.[19]

Enter the syncretist religious formations of Africa, Jamaica, and the United

States. These sacred institutions, in the main, bridge forms of reformulated African indigenous cultures and religions with a reinterpreted Christianity.

In South Africa, one finds Africans who broke away from European missionary churches physically and/or ritualistically in the second half of the nineteenth century over the issue of Christianity's antagonistic placement within African culture and the necessity of African leadership. The new denominations continue to accent the power of healing and prophecy and the role of the Holy Spirit and African ancestors' spirits. Here one still finds a strong presence of African traditional expressions.

The rituals performed by these churches, at least on the micro, everyday level, can supply a sense of community and home amid economic and political dislocation. Disparate healing rituals, especially ones comprising water usage, spiritual touching, and uplifting music, have physically and spiritually transformed many poor people. Once transformed, they have the potential to see beyond the immediate survival constraints to larger, macro exigencies impacting their lives.

While South Africa's hybridized form of African indigenous church performs water rituals on Sunday and extends them into the rest of the week, Jamaican rituals are part of everyday life. Rastafarianism lacks a headquarters, but globally, if one participates in the daily Rastafari spiritual routines in one's diet, clothing, and hairstyle, and looks to the land of Africa, a black God and black Christ, and a divine Haile Selassie I, then one joins the worldwide movement of the Rastafari.

The United States case exemplified, likewise, a melding of reinterpreted types of African culture with a refashioned Christianity. The history of the Trinity United Church of Christ of Chicago originates in the efforts of white Christian missionaries to reach out to black people in the United States. Though Trinity is part of a larger white denomination, it is a local black church in Chicago's ghetto area. It sees itself intentionally combining African culture and religion with belief in Jesus Christ and the Holy Spirit. This essay focused on the men's group Wanaume Kwa Sala as an instance of monthly, repetitive, sacred routines at Trinity.

Ultimately, from our perspective, one needs to focus on the rank and file of all of these movements. Here are the possible glimmers of prophetic remnants that can effect a transition from micro change to macro reconstructions. It seems to us that such a vision signifies the best of an African worldview and the message of Jesus. The hybridization of these two religious cosmologies already prevails in churches created by Africans in Africa and in the diaspora. And their rituals provide aspects of empowering agency for oppressed communities on the continent and beyond.

Notes

1. We thank Emily Einstein who helped research and edit this essay. We are especially thankful for her research and language for the Rastafari section.
2. For an analysis of how globalizations impact Africa, Asia, Latin America, and the United States, see Dwight N. Hopkins, Lois Ann Lorentzen, Eduardo Mendieta, and David Batstone, eds., *Religions/Globalizations: Theories and Cases* (Durham: Duke University Press, 2001).
3. The downward trend of farmworkers' wages is exemplified in the case of the tomato pickers of Immokalee, Florida. In 2003, workers there received 40–45 cents for every 32-pound bucket of tomatoes, amounting to an average annual income of $6,574. This was below the U.S. minimum wage standard of $5.15 per hour or $10,712 annually. The wages of the farmworkers had remained the same since 1980 even though the cost of living had increased. It would be necessary to raise the price to 73.5 cents per bucket to bring it to the same rate as in 1980. See John Bowe, "Nobodies: Does Slavery Exist in America?" *New Yorker*, 21 and 28 April 2003, 106–33; and Coalition of Immokalee Workers, *Facts and Figures on Farmworker Wages* (Washington, D.C.: U.S. Department of Labor, 2001).
4. We are aware of Gustavo Gutierrez's three-part definition of poverty—that is, material, spiritual, and biblical. Also, we are cognizant of his emphasizing the positive dimensions of spiritual poverty. We agree with these positive elements. However, for the purposes of our argument in this essay, we broaden Gutierrez's notion of spiritual poverty to include some deleterious effects. See his *A Theology of Liberation: History, Politics, and Salvation* (Maryknoll, N.Y.: Orbis Books, 1973), 288–99.
5. Hopkins first visited South Africa in the fall of 1982, and Thomas in 1985. Since those study trips, both continue to spend time in South Africa on a regular basis.
6. Katheryn A. Manzo, *Domination, Resistance, and Social Change in South Africa* (Westport, Conn.: Praeger, 1992), 31.
7. For the most comprehensive study of St. John's, see Linda E. Thomas, *Under the Canopy: Ritual Process and Spiritual Resilience in South Africa* (Columbia: University of South Carolina Press, 1999).
8. We would like to thank Madipoane Masenya, professor of Old Testament at the University of South Africa (Pretoria), for this translation and spelling. She is also a member of the Pan-African Seminar on Religion and Poverty.
9. Mamphela A. Ramphele, "The Politics of Space: Life in the Migrant Labour Hostels of the Western Cape," Ph.D. dissertation, University of Cape Town, 1991, 456.
10. The coauthors were part of the July 2003 immersion experience sponsored by the Pan-African Seminar, whose participants' observations comprise this volume. During this immersion, Hopkins also participated in a concurrent international Rastafari conference. We used the following texts for this analysis of Jamaica: Change from Within (an ongoing project at the University of the West Indies); *The Story of Four Schools* (Kingston: University of West Indies Press, 2003); Barry Chevannes, *Rastafari: Roots and Ideology* (Kingston: University of the West Indies Press, 1995); Barry Chevannes, ed., *Rastafari and Other African-Caribbean Worldviews* (New Brunswick, N.J.: Rutgers University Press, 1998); Barbara Makeda Blake Hannah, *Rastafari: The New Creation* (Kingston: Jamaican Media Productions, 2002); Patrick "Pops" Hylton, *The Role of Religion in Caribbean History: From Amerindian Shamanism to Rastafarianism* (Kearney, Nev.: Morris Publishing, 2002); Armando Lampe, ed., *Christianity*

in the Caribbean: Essays on Church History (Kingston: University of the West Indies Press, 2001); Winston Arthur Lawson, Religion and Race: African and European Roots in Conflict—A Jamaican Testament (New York: Peter Lang, 1998); Brian L. Moore, B. W. Higman, Carl Campbell, and Patrick Bryan, eds., Slavery, Freedom and Gender: The Dynamics of Caribbean Society (Kingston: University of West Indies Press, 2001); Verene Shepherd and Hilary McD. Beckles, eds., Caribbean Slavery in the Atlantic: A Student Reader (Kingston: Ian Randle Publishers, 2000); Philip Sherlock, The Story of the Jamaican People (Kingston: Ian Randle Publishers, 1998); and Maureen Warner-Lewis, Central Africa in the Caribbean: Transcending Time, Transforming Cultures (Kingston: University of the West Indies Press, 2003). The following papers are in the co-authors' possession and were presented at the July 2003 Jamaican seminar: Dr. Errol Miller, "The Prophet/Teacher and the Construction of Society: A Reflection"; Portia Simpson Miller, "Address by the Honorable Minister of Local Government, Community Development and Sport"; and Garnet Roper, "Public Expectation and Public Policy Versus Poverty and Insurgency."

11. David T. Adamo, Africa and the Africans in the Old Testament (Eugene, Or.: Wipf and Stock, 2001); Randall C. Bailey and Jacquelyn Grant, eds., The Recovery of Black Presence: An Interdisciplinary Exploration (Nashville, Tenn.: Abingdon Press, 1995); Charles B. Copher, Black Biblical Studies: An Anthology of Charles B. Copher (Chicago, Ill.: Black Light Fellowship, 1993); Cain Hope Felder, Troubling Biblical Waters: Race, Class, and Family (Maryknoll, N.Y.: Orbis Books, 1989); Cain Hope Felder, ed., Stony the Road We Trod: African American Biblical Interpretation (Minneapolis, Minn.: Fortress Press, 1991); and Jeremiah A. Wright Jr., Africans Who Shaped Our Faith (Chicago, Ill.: Urban Ministries, 1995).

12. Ennis Barrington Edmonds, Rastafari: From Outcasts to Culture Bearers (Oxford: Oxford University Press, 2003), 58.

13. Ibid., 59.

14. Ibid., 61.

15. Both coauthors have been participant observers at Trinity United Church of Christ in Chicago since 1998.

16. Frederick A. Davie Jr., "Poverty and Crime in America: One Faith-Based Response. Presentation to the Pan-Africa Seminar of Religious Scholars on Religion and Poverty, Princeton Theological Seminary, July 20, 2004." A copy of this paper is in the co-authors' possession.

17. See Dwight N. Hopkins, Heart and Head: Black Theology Past, Present, and Future (New York: Palgrave Macmillan, 2002), chap. 4, "A New Heterosexual Male."

18. On anthropological poverty, see Engelbert Mveng, "Third World Theology—What Theology? What Third World?: Evaluation by an African Delegate," in Irruption of the Third World: Challenge to Theology, ed. Virginia Fabella and Sergio Torres (Maryknoll, N.Y.: Orbis Books, 1983), 220.

19. For the most comprehensive study on African and African diasporic spiritualities, see Peter J. Paris, The Spirituality of African Peoples: The Search for a Common Moral Discourse (Minneapolis, Minn.: Fortress Press, 1995).

Madipoane Masenya | ## THE BIBLE AND POVERTY IN

AFRICAN PENTECOSTAL CHRISTIANITY

THE *BOSADI* (WOMANHOOD) APPROACH

A s the world becomes smaller and smaller through advances in technology that have enabled, among other things, globalization, the gap between the rich and the poor is becoming wider and wider. Globalization enables the rapid distribution of goods round the world, but with differing consequences: it leaves the poor much poorer and the rich much richer. Fatima Meer has captured this situation succinctly:

> The greatest challenge we face in the twenty-first century is that of poverty. Inherent in that challenge is our hope for an egalitarian world society, for democracy and for peace. The twentieth century has made phenomenal contributions to science and technology and abysmal contribution to ethics and morality. We have shrunk the earth, brought the continents within hours of each other and thoughts within seconds: *Yet the vast majority of humanity remains trapped in poverty—inarticulate, oppressed and powerless to influence their destinies.* Our social organisation negates our scientific and technological achievements by restricting their benefits to selected sectors of our people.[1]

The situation outlined by Meer is not foreign to South Africa. Rather, this country has an unfortunate history, characterized by an unequal distribution of wealth based on the race factor. Though we have moved beyond the first decade of democracy in South Africa, the socioeconomic situation of many African peoples in this country still leaves much to be desired. It is not surprising that the African National Congress as the ruling party promised during its election campaign to combat poverty by the creation of new jobs. Unfortunately, the promise is far from being realized.

Throughout Africa one's attention is arrested by the way ordinary people continue to cling to the Christian religion and its sacred scripture, the Christian Bible. My essay focuses on the Pentecostal churches in those settings and how their members use the Bible as a coping strategy for dealing with poverty. These churches, as Rev. Marjorie Lewis has noted, are Jeseocentric;[2] their sermons and teachings make Jesus their hermeneutical focus.

Lewis's claim is certainly true of the International Assemblies of God (IAG) church in South Africa, which is the main focus of this essay. A statement from the draft constitution of the Assemblies of God reads: "We of the Assemblies of God intend as citizens to make our influence felt where concrete social action is justified. . . . However, we reaffirm our deep conviction that the greatest need of man is for personal salvation through Jesus Christ, and we give this spiritual need its due priority."[3]

The central text for such salvation is, of course, the Bible. Particularly for Pentecostal believers, the Bible continues to play an important spiritual role in the daily lives of its adherents. However, the believers' everyday lives remain cut off from the church. This compartmentalization of life and religious practice results in the exclusion of many injustices like sexism and poverty from sermons and the church's teachings.

My thesis is as follows: The unwavering Jeseocentric faith of poor Pentecostal African believers enables them to survive the harsh conditions of poverty by focusing mainly on the spiritual condition of individual persons, but it also deprives believers of a holistic salvation because sexist, classist, and racist structures of domination are allowed to remain intact without any significant social critique.

Given the historical prominence of the Bible in both colonial and apartheid South Africa, it should not be surprising to discover that many Africans in South Africa have an ambivalent attitude toward that sacred text. The situation was aggravated by the way the apartheid government used Christianity and the Bible to perpetuate injustices against black people in the name of God. State/apartheid theology received sharp criticism from black liberation theologians (consider the Kairos Document, for example), who condemned a theology that provided no justice for the poor and powerless masses in South Africa.[4]

Those who are obsessed with the notion of being chosen by God to be a superior race can quote Psalms 132:13–14 to affirm the presence of God in the house of bondage. The same God who is portrayed by the Exodus narrator(s) as the deliverer of oppressed slaves in Egypt is understood to be on the side of the slave masters—an enslaving hermeneutic indeed! A hermeneutic that kept the fires of colonialism and apartheid burning for many years in South Africa.

Now, let us quickly remind ourselves that the history of the reception of

Christianity and its sacred texts by Africans in South Africa was not totally negative. Gradually, some black South Africans began to read the Bible, not in accordance with the reading strategies of the dominant white South African scholarship but through the lens of their own marginalized experiences.[5] This situation reminds us of African American slaves, who initially did not have the luxury of reading the Bible themselves. But, when afforded an opportunity to do so, they reread it, informed by their own experiences as slaves, and thus found within it a liberating message that released them from the shackles of the dominant reading strategies to embrace those life-giving traditions that had been concealed from them.[6]

In South Africa, the works of South African liberation theologians, ecumenical organizations like the South African Council of Churches, and the Institute for Contextual Theology bore witness to a similar venture. We may therefore argue that the same Bible used by the powerful to oppress, dispossess, impoverish, and denigrate was also used by the powerless to fight for their liberation and well-being.

This appropriation of the Bible by South African blacks was not only a scholarly endeavor but a grassroots venture by which Bible readers, most of whom were women, grasped its liberative message and appropriated the God proclaimed there as being on their side.

For the purpose of the present investigation, I will limit my analysis of the use of the Bible with regard to poverty to one African Pentecostal church in South Africa, the International Assemblies of God. Though this study is specific and localized, I hope that it will throw light on what the general pattern is in Pentecostal churches not only in South Africa but also in other African contexts, both on the continent and in the diaspora. As already noted, the Christian Bible continues to play an important role in African Pentecostal churches in addressing the overall lives of Christians, especially their spiritual lives. Yet, in these church settings, greater emphasis tends to be placed on the spiritual poverty of the members than on their material poverty.

Though the typical Pentecostalist approach to the Bible is not irrelevant, it is nonetheless not holistic. Moreover, it tends to leave systemic sins of injustices untouched. Those church members and leaders who become rich at the expense of the others fail to hear the prophetic voice challenging their greed and self-centeredness. In addressing these concerns, I will recommend the *bosadi* (womanhood) approach to reading the Bible. I hope that the bosadi approach will provide a more balanced hermeneutic to both African Pentecostal church contexts as well as the broader African Christian ecclesial context.

Let me now digress in order to reveal my personal relationship to the subject matter of this essay.

I grew up in a Christian family. As young children, my siblings and I were compelled to attend our family's church regularly. This should not give the impression that we always enjoyed what the church had to offer. We simply had no choice. In my teen years, I became attracted to Pentecostal spirituality. I then started attending two churches: the family church and my "newly found" church.

It is almost twenty years ago since I joined the International Assemblies of God Church in South Africa. Eight years later I was ordained as a minister in that church. My conversation with the Pentecostal churches in general, and the International Assemblies of God in particular, is informed by my long-standing experience as a member and a clergyperson in that context.

As a biblical scholar of Pentecostal orientation, I am now aware of the dilemma I sometimes face with regard to biblical hermeneutics. Some of the conservative views on the Bible strongly propagated by many Pentecostal Bible preachers and teachers are not always harmonious with my justice-seeking biblical hermeneutic. Often one has to struggle hard to do justice to the many different approaches to the same Bible. My rereading of the Book of Ruth in this essay will hopefully give a glimpse of some of these tensions.

History of Origins and Doctrinal Affirmations

The Assemblies of God originated as part of the great Pentecostal revival of the early twentieth century in the United States of America. The revival was born early in the twentieth century, during the years 1906–1908, in the historic movement of the Holy Spirit at the Azusa Street church in Los Angeles. The theological identity of the modern Pentecostal movement was established shortly afterward, in Charles E. Parham's Bethel Bible College in Topeka, Kansas, where Parham and his disciples taught that believers should expect a baptism in the Holy Spirit apart from their new birth as Christians. They believed that baptism should be accompanied by an initial physical sign of speaking in other tongues, in accordance with Acts 2:4.[7]

The churches and missions of the new Pentecostal movement grew virtually in isolation from one another, so a need arose to convene a general council of the different assemblies. Thus the Assemblies of God was instituted in the United States in 1914. Church planting and missions have been given high priority since its inception, and missionaries came to South Africa under their foreign mission program. Because of administrative challenges in South Africa, divisions arose in the black Assemblies of God

Church, which gave rise to the International Assemblies of God, which is the focus of my investigation. This denomination in fact still operates basically in the same way as its mother denomination does in the United States.

The Bible in an African–South African Pentecostal Context:
The International Assemblies of God

The Bible is used in this Pentecostal church setting mainly to facilitate the salvation of individuals.[8] Fallen persons (Rom. 3:22) are exhorted to repent from their sins and turn to God for salvation, which is made possible by God's gift to the world (John 3:16; 1 John 3:16). As the constitution of the International Assemblies of God states, "Salvation is received through repentance toward God and faith toward the Lord Jesus Christ. By the washing of regeneration and renewing of the Holy Ghost, being justified by grace through faith, man becomes an heir of God according to the Hope of Eternal Life. . . . The inward evidence of salvation is the direct witness of the Spirit (Romans 10:13–15). The outward evidence of all men is a life of righteousness and true holiness."[9] Individuals who have been saved by God or born again (see John 3:1–9) live with the hope of spending eternity with Jesus Christ in heaven. In my view, this hope in a better life in the hereafter is one of the important factors that sustain many Pentecostal Christians through adverse conditions of poverty, oppression, and illness, to name only a few.

Such a hope can be detrimental, however, when injustices are left intact, because the belief in a better home in the afterlife may help preserve the injustices. This way of using the Bible is in fact akin to its use in apartheid South Africa, when the Bible was generally used by the oppressors to keep the attention of blacks away from the atrocities done to them in the name of God.

Thus, I argue, a one-sided view of salvation that basically emphasizes salvation from individual sins cannot be helpful in tackling the issue of poverty. The fact that there are no treatises on poverty among the publications of the International Assemblies of God, or even a church statement on the topic, reveals something of this one-sidedness. This situation is an inheritance from the received tradition of the early American missionaries. Let me quote more fully the Assemblies of God statement cited above: "We of the assemblies of God intend as citizens to make our influence felt where concrete social action is justified in areas of domestic relations, education, law enforcement, employment, equal opportunity, and other worthwhile and beneficial matters. However, we reaffirm our deep conviction that the greatest need of man is for personal salvation through Jesus Christ, and we give this spiritual need its due priority."[10]

Pastor Maphori, the Limpopo District superintendent of the International Assemblies of God, has told me that he views poverty and the lack of education among the clergy as the main reasons for such one-sidedness. However, I agree more with the views held by the general secretary of the church, Pastor Lebelo, that this inattention to poverty-related matters is motivated by the church's primary doctrinal emphasis on the salvation of individual souls. My quotations from the church constitution underline that legacy.

In an attempt to address the one-sidedness through which the Christian Bible is approached by Pentecostal preachers and teachers, I will discuss briefly what I have called the bosadi approach to the reading of biblical texts, with a view to providing a holistic hermeneutic in our struggle against poverty.

The Bosadi Approach to the Reading of Biblical Texts

In my doctoral thesis, "Proverbs 31:10–31 in a South African Context: A *Bosadi* (Womanhood) Perspective," I developed this bosadi approach to the reading of biblical texts.[11]

The northern Sotho word *bosadi* is an abstract noun that comes from the word *mosadi*. David Ziervogel and Pontifus Mokgokong define *mosadi* as meaning "woman," "married woman," "wife." The word *mosadi* comes from the root *sadi*, which has to do with womanhood; *bosadi* for example may be translated as "womanhood" or "private parts of a woman."[12] The word *mosadi* also occurs, in different but related words, in other African–South African languages—*wansati* (Xitsonga), *umfazi* (Zulu/Xhosa), *musadzi* (Tshi/Venda), *mosadi* (Tswana)—a fact that reveals the resemblances between the different African ethnic groups in this country.[13]

The bosadi approach to the reading of the Bible grew out of my commitment to take seriously the unique experiences of African women in South Africa as they interact with the Bible. The contexts in which these women live, like those of women in the other parts of Africa, are typified by a variety of life-denying factors: classism (poverty), postapartheid racism/neoracism, gender inequalities (both in the African culture and in the broader South African society), ethnic-centrism, and HIV/AIDS, for example.

The bosadi approach acknowledges the significant role that the Bible continues to play as a spiritual resource in the lives of many South African women. They, and others, use the Bible as a weapon against life-denying forces, which they challenge and resist. The women also embrace the life-giving elements in the Bible, as they embrace life-giving elements in their own culture.

Unlike a typical Pentecostal biblical hermeneutic, whose main focus is on the Bible reader's spiritual life, the bosadi hermeneutic has a wide focus. It not only rereads the texts through the lens of the marginalized African–South African woman's experiences but also challenges ideologies of poverty/classism, sexism, ethnicity, and so on, as they appear in these texts.

Reading the Book of Ruth, the Bosadi Way

Let us begin by reimagining the social world in which the book of Ruth was produced. Such a reimagination is based on the belief that the Bible did not fall straight from heaven but that it reveals God's mind in human language. It emerged in particular cultures and historical contexts. The latter were, unfortunately, as patriarchal as many of the cultures in today's world, including those of Africa.

A PATRIARCHAL WORLD

The bosadi approach raises the conscience of concerned readers about the role of female characters in the text with the aim of affirming, where possible, contemporary women readers. In this approach, the Bible reader asks questions such as, What is the narrator's attitude towards women? How are female characters presented in the text? Do they appear as individuals in their own right? Or are they basically presented in the roles they were expected to play in patriarchal contexts? Are these characters helpful to African women who desire to be affirmed as free persons?[14]

As we ponder these questions while reimagining that ancient world that produced the book of Ruth, we see clearly that it is a patriarchal world. Though the book bears the name of a woman and relates the story of women who struggled with poverty in a male-dominated world, it appears that the book's principal agenda is about men and the perpetuation of the male line rather than the well-being of the women. Yet it must be acknowledged that women are portrayed as key stakeholders in bringing about their own well-being.

In this world, men were the chief providers for the needs of their families. Elimelech's decision to leave a hunger-stricken Bethlehem to settle in Moab makes sense in such a context. When he and his sons die, his wife, Naomi—an old woman who is conversant with marriage expectations in a patriarchal world—assures her daughters-in-law that their future cannot lie with her, for she is now a widow with no son. In her view, Ruth's and Orpah's futures would be secured if and when they got new husbands on returning to their mothers' houses (Ruth 1:11–14).

In that world, marriage seems to have been the main key to a prosperous future for a woman. Indeed, in ancient Israel as well as in traditional Africa, a woman or man could not be deemed a complete adult outside marriage. Normative womanhood (as in the African Pentecostal cultures) was and is viewed as exemplified in a married woman. Thus, the three women in this story are impoverished even further because their self-worth and self-identities are diminished by the absence of husbands in their lives. In the historical period in which this story is set, widows were doomed to an undesirable socioeconomic status because wives and daughters were not allowed to inherit from their husbands and fathers. The biblical situation reminds us of the high esteem still placed on marriage in many African Pentecostal church settings today, in which single women, irrespective of their strong socioeconomic positions, are still regarded by many as poor because they lack husbands.

An important question to ask is, can women struggle with poverty without men and succeed in such a setting? From the book of Ruth, it appears as though that could not have been the case: the two younger women emerge as winners in their struggle against poverty, but only because each succeeds in finding and marrying a man. Not only that: they also succeed in procreating another man, when each gives birth to a son. The narrator of this story clearly teaches us the lesson that in a male-oriented world, the struggle of women against poverty can only be won if women collaborate with the patriarchal system. Collaboration is made to happen at all costs, even at the risk of women making their bodies available for use by men (e.g., the activities at the threshing floor, Ruth 3:1ff.).[15] Do Pentecostal modern-day women readers of this story still subscribe to such a mentality?

If we evaluate the story in a bosadi way, we can assert that women are indeed capable of addressing life's challenges without being married to men. This does not, in fact, contradict the Pentecostal hermeneutic, for we could argue that no human being, including those who are closest to us (men or others), should take the place of Jesus Christ in our lives. What should make people (women and men) despair, as Christian believers, should not be the lack of a close friend, a spouse, a daughter, and so on. The cause of concern should rather be the absence of Jesus in our lives. It is Jesus whom we believe, who gives us the courage to challenge all the life-denying forces.

Though we understand and appreciate the efforts of Naomi and Ruth to struggle as they did, given the constraints of the patriarchal world of their time, we want to challenge structures in our day (governments, churches, religious organizations, business corporations) that continue to perpetuate patriarchy and refuse to legitimize female agency. We therefore challenge the churches and communities alike to "deidolize" marriage.[16] The latter should not be viewed as a gateway to women's success and particularly, to women's capability to achieve God's purposes for their lives as individuals. Thus, the churches should be enabled to affirm single women in their membership.

A World with Class and Ethnic Stratifications

The bosadi approach acknowledges socioeconomic and sociopolitical factors as important in shaping the identities of all Bible readers, including Pentecostal ones. Given the sociopolitical history that all South Africans have experienced, a history in which one's race also determined one's socioeconomic status, South African Bible readers from different racial and class backgrounds will naturally read the Bible differently.

The observation that the inhabitants of Judah have to leave their homes in order to look for greener pastures elsewhere reveals something of the class system of people living there at that time. Moab is depicted by the narrator as hosting the poor peoples of its neighbors. The reader cannot assume that Moab will remain a refuge for long, because sooner or later Naomi will return to her home country: "for she had heard that the Lord had considered his people and given them food" (Ruth 1:6). Given the book's presence in the Hebrew canon, and its being the product of the Hebrew narrators, it would make sense to its readers that Judah (where the city of Bethlehem lay—the place that was believed by the Israelites to be Yahweh's dwelling place) must not be portrayed as staying poor forever.[17]

The second chapter of Ruth reveals more clearly than the others the class stratifications that are notable in the book. Ruth, the poor, foreign widow (a woman without a man), is called Ruth the Moabite in this chapter. She is reduced to gleaning the fields of a rich man, a distant relative: "Now Naomi had a kinsman on her husband's side, a prominent rich man, of the family of Elimelech, whose name was Boaz. And Ruth the Moabite said to Naomi, 'Let me go to the field and glean among the ears of the grain, behind someone in whose sight I might find favour' " (Ruth 2:1–2).

In the Hebrew text, Boaz is referred to as the *gibbor hayil*. This Hebrew phrase literally means a mighty man of power (cf. its female counterpart *eshet hayil*, a woman of substance, the phrase consistently used by the sage to refer to the woman of Proverbs 31:10–31).[18] In this context, the phrase *gibbor hayil* also has the connotation of material wealth. Boaz is presented to the reader as the owner of a field and the employer of hired workers. Boaz is therefore a man of class.

Boaz is a Judahite. He is therefore an insider in terms of ethnicity. Boaz is not ordinary in terms of his relationship with Naomi—he is a kinsman on her husband's side. The bosadi reader will note that Boaz is not related to Naomi on her own family's side; she is related to him through Elimelech, her father-in-law, a man in Naomi's life. Once again, the possibility of a more permanent, "normative" relationship seems to loom. But the bosadi reader will note that, though these poor husbandless women seem not able to handle life without a man, Naomi's decision to return to Bethlehem was made independent of men.

In terms of class and ethnicity, Ruth stands in stark contrast to Boaz, the rich man of property. She is a woman who is manless, a widow, with few survival options. She is, moreover, from another ethnic group: Ruth, the Moabite. The Hebrew narrator of this story seems to take pleasure in reminding the readers that Ruth is a woman from an outside ethnic group (Ruth 1:22; 2:2, 21). This is the same woman, however, who through the help of another woman would make things happen: initiate a marriage and bear a son to the family, a son who would carry on the Davidic line. Her story will encourage women with many strikes against them that Yahweh (whom these women have also come to embrace as their God), unlike human beings, does not operate through the biases of race/ethnicity, class, gender, or age.[19]

A brief comment about the task of gleaning is in order at this point. Under Israelite law, gleaning was instituted as a primary means of support for those who were destitute (cf. Lev. 19:9–10, 23:22, and Deut. 24:19–22). The fields' edges were not to be harvested. The gleanings, or what was not picked up in the first pass of harvesting, were to be left behind for the alien, the poor, the orphans, and the widows. As a poor non-Israelite widow, Ruth can engage in this means of survival guaranteed by Israelite law.[20]

Clearly, patriarchal and class stratifications in the biblical context do not differ from those in contemporary African contexts. If the bosadi approach allows Bible readers to challenge negative class and ethnic ideologies in the text, it also allows us to challenge the "haves" in our churches to take cognizance of the situation of the "have-nots." The methodology's commitment to the believers' faith in God reminds poor Pentecostal women about the importance of remaining attached to their Maker even in the midst of life-denying forces like poverty, racism, and disease. But such a reminder to women to remain attached to their Maker through faith should not be mistaken for a call to remain silent in the face of such life-denying forces. The urgency of the prophetic voice against all forms of social injustices, including economic policies unfriendly to the poor, should be heard even now in the postapartheid South African context.

Holism as Religious

The bosadi methodology is committed to the Africanness of African women in South Africa by embracing the positive elements of the African culture while challenging the negative ones, just as the text of Ruth can be engaged along similar parallel lines. The discussion in this section will bring to light as far as it is possible the points of resemblance between the African and Israelite cultures.

In the African worldview, the whole is religious. One can discern a similar view in the lives of Ruth and Naomi in the book of Ruth. In this book—unlike in the Torah or the prophetic books of the Bible—Yahweh is not directly involved in the lives of the biblical characters. Notwithstanding this fact, in this book, just as in Africa, the whole seems to be religious. Actions that are either good or evil are attributed to Yahweh. Whatever emptiness Naomi has experienced, whether through death, famine, emotional turmoil, she attributes to God. Hence her response to the women of Bethlehem:

Call me no longer Naomi,
Call me Mara,
For the Almighty has dealt bitterly with me.
I went away full.
But the Lord has brought me
Back empty;
Why call me Naomi
When the Lord has dealt harshly with me,
And the Almighty has brought calamity on me? (Ruth 1:21)

In both the African and ancient Israelite cultures, any calamity that occurs in the community or in individual's lives is explained religiously. That is to say, it is attributed to the wrath of the ancestors or to God's wrath. Good deeds were believed to be rewarded, while bad deeds were punished (e.g., Boaz's blessing upon Ruth for the good she had done to her mother-in-law and for not going after younger men: Ruth 2:11–13; 3:10–11).

Both Israelite and African cultures attribute everything to God's agency (e.g., evil, emptiness, calamity). An important question to be asked is, if the poverty experienced by Ruth and Naomi were caused by unfair government structures, would it be fair to put the blame on Yahweh? Similarly, in an

African traditional setting, when calamity struck a particular family, it was not unusual for people to attribute the evil to the wrath of the ancestors. One of the main challenges of attributing all evil to the supernatural powers is the possibility of leaving all sorts of injustices intact and immune to criticism. Evil structures, exploitative preachers of the Word, and greedy people may continue to flourish with ease in such circumstances. In apartheid South Africa, the proclamations of apartheid theology succeeded in entrenching injustices against the black majority of the country in the name of God. In postapartheid South Africa, the demise of the prophetic voice and the continued silence of the church against social evils (patriarchy, classism, nepotism, xenophobia, governmental corruption, and so forth) helps to sustain the status quo. As justice-seeking, women-affirming readers of the story of Naomi and Ruth, we need to be conscious of this kind of mentality and, in our attempt to be faithful to the prophetic calling of the church, put the blame where it belongs.

Conclusion

Even in what some may designate a postmodern, post-Christian, postbiblical world, the Christian Bible continues to play a pivotal role not only in African Pentecostal church contexts but, more importantly, in the daily lives of Christian believers. What we find regrettable, however, is the compartmentalization that occurs in the lives of so many South African Pentecostal believers. We see it in the "spiritualist" biblical hermeneutics that continues to dominate the African Pentecostal interpretative landscape. Notwithstanding the possible strengths in such a hermeneutic, it does leave untouched the many injustices practiced against powerless poor believers, many of whom are African women. Thus, our search for a biblical hermeneutic that is holistic and African and that seeks justice; a hermeneutic that we find in a bosadi reading of biblical texts. Through this approach, the story of Naomi and Ruth is "smelled" anew, and the aroma that we detect is not the dominant one of those in power, but the fresh aroma of poor African women believers emerging from below.

Notes

1. Fatima Meer, "The Third World and the Debt Burden," *Bulletin for Contextual Theology in Southern Africa* 2.6 (1999): 6–9.
2. Marjorie Lewis, "It Must be a Duppy or a Gunman: Fear as Deterrent to Devel-

opment," paper read at the Pan-African Seminar on Religion and Poverty, Jamaica, 2003.

3. William W. Menzies, *Anointed to Serve: The Story of the Assemblies of God* (Springfield, Mo.: Gospel Publishing House, 1971), 394–95.

4. *The Kairos Document: From South Africa: A Challenge to the Church* (Johannesburg; Closter, N.J.: Theology in Global Context, 1985). This is a document in which South African black and liberation theologians, members of ecumenical organizations in South Africa, raised a prophetic voice against apartheid/state theology in South Africa, declaring the latter to be sin against God. This was done in an attempt to articulate a theology that would cater to the needs of the oppressed masses of South Africa.

5. See Itumeleng J. Mosala, *Biblical Hermeneutics and Black Theology in South Africa* (Grand Rapids, Mich.: William B. Eerdmans, 1989); Takatso A. Mofokeng, "Black Christians, the Bible and Liberation," *Journal of Black Theology in South Africa* 2.1 (1988): 34–42.

6. See Renita J. Weems, "Reading Her Way through the Struggle: African-American Women and the Bible," in *The Bible and Liberation: Political and Social Hermeneutics*, ed. Norman K. Gottwald and Richard A. Horsley (Maryknoll, N.Y.: Orbis, 1993), 31–50; also see Vincent L. Wimbush, "The Bible and African-Americans: An Outline of an Interpretative History," in *Stony the Way We Trod: African-American Biblical Interpretation*, ed. Cain H. Felder (Minneapolis: Fortress Press, 1991), 81–97.

7. Menzies, *Anointed to Serve*, 34–40.

8. In my conversation with Pastor M. T. Maphori, the Limpopo District superintendent of the International Assemblies of God Church in South Africa, I learned that only 3 percent of the sermons by pastors in that church have poverty as their focus. The general secretary of the IAG in South Africa, Pastor G. S. Lebelo, holds a similar view when he says that IAG churches involved in projects addressing the challenge of poverty could be fewer than ten in the whole of South Africa. When asked what the reasons were, he mentioned the following as key reasons: the historical legacy of emphasis being placed on the salvation of individuals, the lack of highly educated ministers who can write on such topics, and the challenge of poverty itself. Maphori argued along these lines: if the churches are unable to give their pastors a living wage, how can the leadership even think of projects that will cater to the needs of poor persons? A poor person, argues Maphori, is limited in his/her thinking. His main argument is that although the salvation offered by Jesus Christ is holistic, one's socioeconomic status will determine the nature of one's theory (sermons and teachings) and one's praxis. Drawing on the latter, it thus makes sense that those members who are actively involved in such projects, particularly on the relatively large scale, are American missionaries sent to do ministry in these churches. (Telephone conversations with Maphori and Lebelo, Pretoria, South Africa, 20 April 2007).

9. Constitution and By-Laws of the General Council of the International Assemblies of God: Draft, 2007–2008, quoted in Menzies, *Anointed to Serve*.

10. Quoted in ibid., 394–95.

11. Madipoane J. Masenya (ngwana' Mphahlele), "Proverbs 31:10–31 in the South African Context: A *Bosadi* (Womanhood) Approach," Ph.D. dissertation, University of South Africa, Pretoria, 1996, 156. See also Masenya (ngwana' Mphahlele), *How Worthy Is the Woman of Worth? Rereading Proverbs 31:10–31 in African–South Africa* (New York: Peter Lang, 2004).

12. David Ziervogel and Pontifus Mokgokong, *Comprehensive Northern Sotho Dictionary* (Pretoria: Van Schaik, 1975), 1154.

13. See Masenya (ngwana' Mphahlele), *How Worthy Is the Woman of Worth?*, 122.

14. Madipoane Masenya (ngwana' Mphahlele), "Their Hermeneutics Was Strange! Ours is a Necessity! Reading Vashti in Esther 1 as African Women in South Africa," in *Her Master's Tools? Feminist Challenges to Historical-Critical Interpretations: Global Perpsectives on Biblical Scholarship*, ed. Caroline van der Stichele and T Penner (Atlanta, Ga.: SBL, forthcoming).

15. For more details on Ruth's encounter with Boaz at the threshing floor, see my article "Surviving through Emptiness: Rereading the Naomi-Ruth Story in African South Africa," *Journal of Theology in Southern Africa* (November 2004, forthcoming).

16. I have argued in some of my writings that "marriage as norm," a mentality that has been inherited from the African cultures and continues to be propagated in our churches, cannot be helpful in our struggle against gender injustices. For as long as women are meant to feel that they cannot be complete human beings outside marriage, they will continue to seek marriage at all costs. If they happen to find it, they will persevere through abusive marriages at all costs. The negative consequences of such a perseverance cannot be overemphasized, particularly in the face of the deadly pandemic that is ravaging the African continent. See the following works for more details: my book *How Worthy Is the Woman of Worth?* and my essays "Trapped between Two 'Canons': African–South African Women in the HIV/AIDS Era," in *African Women, HIV/AIDS and Faith Communities*, ed. Isabel A. Phiri, Beverly Haddad, and Madipoane Masenya (ngwana' Mphahlele) (Pietermaritzburg: Cluster, 2003), 113–27; and "Polluting Your Ground? Woman as Pollutant in Yehud: A Reading from a Globalised Africa," in *Towards An Agenda for Contextual Theology: Essays in Honour of Albert Nolan*, ed. McGlory Speckman and Larry Kaufmann (Pietermaritzburg: Cluster, 2001), 185–202.

17. For more details on this argument, see Musa W. Dube, "Divining Ruth for International Relations," in *Other Ways of Reading: African Women and the Bible*, ed. Musa W. Dube (Atlanta, Ga.: SBL, 2001),179–95.

18. For more details on the *eshet hayil* of Proverbs 31:10–31, see Masenya (ngwana' Mphahlele), *How Worthy is the Woman of Worth?* 69–116.

19. See Madipoane Masenya (ngwana' Mphahlele), "A Commentary on the Book of Ruth," in *Global Bible Commentary*, ed. Daniel Patte et al. (Nashville, Tenn.: Abingdon Press, forthcoming).

20. See Katharine Sakenfeld, *Ruth: Interpretation: A Bible Commentary for Teaching and Preaching* (Louisville, Ky.: Westminster John Knox, 1999), 39.

Nyambura J. Njoroge | **THE STRUGGLE FOR FULL HUMANITY**

IN POVERTY-STRICKEN KENYA

> During the colonial period the people were called upon
> to fight against oppression; after national liberation,
> they were called upon to fight against poverty, illiteracy,
> and underdevelopment. The struggle, they say, goes
> on. The people realize that life is an unending contest.
>
> —Frantz Fanon, *The Wretched of the Earth*, translated by
> Constance Farrington

Berida's Narrative

We Only Come Here to Struggle is the title of a book that tells the story of Berida Ndambuki, a Kenyan businesswoman who deals in dried staples and whose dominant motif in her life is said to be *poverty*, with the critical submotif of *religion*.[1] In her own words, with the help of Claire C. Robertson, a white American Africanist and her junior coauthor, it is extreme poverty that drove Berida to become a businesswoman.[2]

> When I was growing up we were so poor; I decided my children would never wear rags like I did. The biggest problem for a parent, especially the mother because she feels most for her children, is to see her children not having food to eat, clothes to wear, or fees to go to school. My children weren't going to school and they had nothing to wear. I not only scrounged clothing from homes abandoned by their owners due to the famine, but I also had the problem of where the children would sleep. The little house where they used to sleep collapsed on them one night from the rain. I heard them screaming. I didn't even have a lamp to see. It was a square hut made with poles and mud and a thatched roof. The children had hidden under the table so they weren't hurt, but three goats that were asleep on the verandah died.[3]

Berida's life mirrors that of millions of Kenyan women and their families. She has powerfully demonstrated the "cyclic trap of poverty" presented at the Pan-African Seminar on Religion and Poverty in Kenya in July 2001 by Violet Nyambura Kimani.[4] For instance, despite being illiterate, Berida was a creative, courageous, and hard-working person; determined to fight poverty, she moved from drought- and famine-stricken Kathonzweni in Ukambani, a village east of Nairobi, to an urban setting (Gikomba, Nairobi) and established a business. She was able to rent only a room without electricity or toilet facilities because she could not afford better housing.[5]

Nevertheless, Berida not only helps the reader to grasp the meaning and dehumanizing impact of extreme poverty; she has also given deep meaning to the word "struggle." In her story we can see the ability of an African woman to resist systematic oppression, exploitation, and devaluation and to rediscover her God-given creativity and humanity. The struggle requires no less than a complete spiritual and psychological renewal from dispossession, victimization, stigmatization, presumed second-class citizenship, self-hatred, and exploitation due to patriarchy, sexism, colonialism, imperialism, racism, and religious captivity. Like the slave narratives of the United States of America, her narrative effectively gives voice and visibility to a much neglected story of millions of poor women and their families in Africa and people of African descent in other continents. A careful, critical reading of Berida's narrative reveals how religion and poverty are intricately related to bad governance, gender inequality, violence, corruption, and preventable and manageable diseases that lead to senseless suffering and death. The end product of extreme poverty and other social injustices is the assault on her humanity.[6]

The purpose of this essay is to argue that both religious scholars and the church in Kenya must play a critical role in transforming the political, cultural, spiritual, material, and psychological structures so that they might produce in the citizenry the type of social conscience needed to realize the fullness of humanity in a poverty-stricken society. Faith in God can make a major contribution in the lives of individuals, families, and communities as they struggle against bad governance, poverty, and other social injustices that have shattered the dreams and lives of so many Kenyans. The poor and the oppressed alone cannot transform this dehumanizing reality. Thus the church, its leadership, and scholars must participate in achieving this social change. We need to end the culture of dominance and dependence and nurture a new vision of positive governance, economic development, and life-giving theologies and ethics. According to Samuel Kobia, a Kenyan Methodist minister and secretary general of the World Council of Churches,

"Fundamental to a new vision for a better Africa is the struggle to eradicate poverty. Not merely to alleviate it, but to eradicate it. Others may be content with alleviation or reduction of poverty. For Africans, our goal should be to eradicate poverty because this goal is noble, and it is the right course to chart and pursue."[7]

My interest in the struggle for full humanity in poverty-stricken Kenya goes back to my parish ministry in the 1980s in the capital city of Nairobi, when I encountered many women like Berida and their families. This is when I woke up to the fact that the formal education system at all levels, including Christian education and ministerial training in the church, did not help us Kenyans to understand why we are so poor or how to confront the conditions that produce such destructive social, political, and economic systems. Unfortunately twenty-five years later the social, political, and economic conditions have steadily deteriorated—especially with the global HIV/AIDS epidemic—a reality that Berida keeps on repeating in her narrative to the point where she asks herself, "Why did I have my children?"[8]

Ironically, while this devastating reality is well acknowledged by many scholars, we are also reminded that Kenya is a very religious country, where people are free to declare their religious preference. In the case of Christians, many citizens aggressively go out to evangelize others on TV and open-air evangelistic crusades in the parks. Current statistics show that 66 percent of the population are Christians; among them 28 percent are Roman Catholic and 38 percent, other denominations. Among the remaining 34 percent of the population, 26 percent follow an indigenous African religion, 7 percent are Muslim, and 1 percent are "other."[9]

There is some official recognition of the problem. In July 2000, when we embarked on the series of Pan-African seminars, the Kenyan government issued its *Interim Poverty Reduction Strategy Paper, 2000–2003*, giving the most updated economic statistics.[10] It makes the statement, "The poor constitute slightly more than half the population of Kenya. Women constitute the majority of the poor and also the absolute majority of Kenyans. Three-quarters of the poor live in rural areas. . . . In 1997, rural food poverty was 51%, while overall poverty reached 53% of the rural population. In urban areas food poverty afflicted 38% and overall 49% of the population. The overall national incidence of poverty stood at 52%. Major characteristics of the poor include landlessness and lack of education. . . . The poor have larger families (6.4 members compared to 4.8 for non-poor) while in general rural households are larger than urban."[11] The report continues: "Empirical evidence shows that 13% of the urban poor have never attended school at all while the comparative rural figure is 29%. Of the poor, only 12%

of those in rural areas have reached secondary education while for the urban poor the figure rises to 28%. Dropout rates have risen, as have disparities in access, due to geographic location, gender and income. The main reason for not attending school is the high cost of education. Children are also required to help at home, while for girls socio-cultural factors and early marriage are significant factors."[12]

More than half of the population (15 million people) in Kenya live in poverty! But this report fails to portray the correct reality of demographics in Kenya. It neglects to mention that ours is a very young population and that the majority of the citizens need basic nurturing, guidance, and formal education. According to the 1999 census, the population was 28,808,658 (compared to 10,942,705 in 1969, when the first official census was conducted).[13] Out of this number, 43 percent were children 0–14 years and 54 percent were 15–64; those 65 years and over were 3 percent.[14] This means that more than 50 percent of the population not only live in poverty but are children,[15] and the same is true in all other African countries. Certainly such demographics should influence the way we go about addressing poverty in the country. Most tragically, however, the document says nothing about the impact of bad governance and poverty on human dignity, freedom, and self-determination to overcome these problems. Such an assessment came from Claire C. Robertson as she summarized Berida's narrative in 1999.

> Kenya's strengths are a creative, energetic, and hardworking peasantry with its urban counterpart, as well as the persistent idealism and honesty of those who work for constructive change. Its weaknesses are greed and dishonesty in pursuit of profit, the willingness at the highest levels to destroy the country's integrity and well-being for the purpose of self-enrichment, the victimization of those who at base keep the economy going, and the poverty caused by all of the above. In the last ten years there has been a seismic increase in pervasive lack of responsible social conscience throughout the society. The struggles of Berida and her family become ever more difficulty, materially worsened by a government that preys upon the people for whose benefit it should govern.[16]

Decolonize the Mind: Resisting Imperialism

The task ahead of us requires critical social-historical analysis even before we can begin to look for solutions. For instance, Chinua Achebe, a leading Nigerian creative writer, has brought to our attention the psychology of the dehumanized and dispossessed that resulted from the way Africans were declared inhuman and subsequently dispossessed of their ancestral land, culture, and dignity through slave trade, colonialism, imperialism, and, to some extent, the missionary enterprise. Using Kenya as an example in *Home and Exile*, Achebe revisits the story that Jomo Kenyatta wrote in the 1930s in *Facing Mount Kenya* of how the Europeans dispossessed the Gikuyu people (about 25 percent of Kenya's population) of their land. "It is the story of a dispossession that began with a little act of hospitality by the dispossessed."[17] Achebe concludes,

> What is both unfortunate and unjust is the pain the person dispossessed is forced to bear in the act of dispossession itself and subsequently in the trauma of a diminished existence. The range of aberrations and abnormalities fostered by this existence can be truly astounding. Take, for instance, those straitlaced Nigerian students in London in 1952 who felt so ashamed and embarrassed by Tutuola's story of their homeland, written, as they saw it, in incorrect English, that some of them went up in arms without reading the book! Their nervous confusion, the fragility of their awareness and self-esteem can only be imagined. Wasn't it part of that syndrome which told us while I was growing up that it was more civilized to fetch water in gallon tins from Europe than clay pots made by ourselves? And as we speak, have we grown wiser and put all that foolishness aside?[18]

After citing more examples in the area of literature, Achebe remarks, "The psychology of the dispossessed can be truly frightening," resulting in "a badly damaged sense of self. . . . An erosion of self-esteem is one of the commonest symptoms of dispossession."[19] As Achebe has attempted to demonstrate in the three lectures that make up *Home and Exile*, no doubt Africans have done much in the world of art and literature to engage in the process of "re-storying" or reclamation of the African story, despite the fact that these are "peoples who had been knocked silent by the trauma of all kinds of dispossession."[20] Unfortunately, the act of dispossession, and the resulting badly damaged sense of self, continues even in independent Kenya as we have seen with Berida, who declares: "I am a nobody."[21]

Consequently, in the 1970s, Ngugi wa Thiong'o, the leading Kenyan creative writer, called upon us to "decolonize the mind" from its Eurocentric captivity and to resist imperialism in all its forms.[22] Regrettably, among religious scholars little has been done to significantly reevaluate our colonial past, especially on the issues of landlessness, abuse of labor, and education, as well as the economic and political liberation motif that provoked the Mau Mau war in the 1950s. Here we stand to benefit from Noel Leo Erskine's book on *Decolonizing Theology: A Caribbean Perspective* (1981). Writing in the foreword for the revision of this book in 1998, Mercy Amba Oduyoye, the leading African (Ghanaian) woman theologian, says: "*Decolonizing Theology* has successfully woven this socio-historical theology through which we can find the Christian faith's vision for liberation and hope which inspires the struggle for freedom. It shows how in spite of appearing as the slave master's religion, Christianity was discovered to be an expression of the intentions of the God who struggles against oppression; a religion that affirms that oppression is not the final word and that freedom is to be found in the here-and-now because God is also in the here-and-now and freedom's will for humanity."[23]

Lewin L. Williams makes a similar point in his book *Caribbean Theology* (1994), especially the chapter titled "Missionary Theology as Theology of Domination," where he argues, "If a missionary believes in freedom for the home people under God but not the same freedom for the colonized under God, then missionary theology has to be a misrepresentation of Christian theology, to accommodate the contradictions."[24] The two books by Erskine and Williams are also very helpful in that, as Africans in diaspora, the authors have articulated the atrocities of both the slave trade and colonialism. Certainly, the experience of those who were sold into slavery and survived it in the new world is different from the experience of those left behind in Africa but colonized, but nevertheless there is a common heritage of being dispossessed and devalued. To underline that common heritage, it was important that we started our seminars in Ghana (in July 2000), where we had the opportunity, however painful it was, to revisit the history of transatlantic slave trade and to walk on the same grounds where our sisters and brothers were sold (by their own people) into slavery, in the Elmina and Cape Coast slave castles. Visiting the burial place of W. E. B. Du Bois, one of the leading scholars and advocates of Pan-Africanism, at Christianborg Castle in Accra, Ghana, was a powerful reminder of our common struggle for full humanity.

In the world of literature and art, Achebe recommends singers and writers to compose enabling stories of repossession. Likewise religious scholars need to create enabling theologies and ethics for healing painful memories. Analysis of dispossession and landlessness should not be limited to economic marginalization (material poverty); rather, we should reconsider their political, cultural, spiritual, and psychological (trauma) impacts over the decades from one generation to the other. Musa Dube, a leading global HIV/AIDS activist and New Testament feminist scholar, maintains, "As a Two-Thirds World woman of Botswana, I would insist that the contemporary Christian mission must concern itself with all issues that hinder the realization of God's kingdom on earth. It must focus on all that desacralizes life on earth. It must rally against all structural forces and institutions that militate against peace, equity and self-sufficiency for individuals and nations of various cultures. The Christian mission must identify as sinful those forces that hinder the blossoming of God's creation as a whole."[25]

In Search of a New Vision

Fortunately, Timothy Njoya, a Kenyan Presbyterian minister, scholar, and political activist, has taken on the task of defining a new vision in *The Divine Tag on Democracy* (2003).[26] In this book, he eloquently and convincingly demonstrates how a person of faith in God in pastoral ministry can mobilize the downtrodden and dispossessed to expose the failures of both the church (that is, Christianity) and the government in nurturing responsible social conscience, dignity, and fullness of life for all. Njoya narrates his own struggle for full humanity for a people who have not known positive governance since the days of colonialism to the present, despite the fact that Kenyans fought fiercely and bravely for land (economic justice) and freedom (self-governance) in what became known as the Mau Mau war.[27] Instead, Kenyans internalized Eurocentric dominance and their own dependence from the British government and Western Christianity, to the extent that in independent Kenya the regimes of Jomo Kenyatta (1963–1978) and Daniel Arap Moi (1978–2002), as well as the church, continued to practice the same policies. It is to be noted that in the 1960s and 1970s, there was significant resistance and struggle for justice and freedom by politicians and scholars who felt betrayed by Kenyatta's dictatorship when he turned Kenya into a de facto one-party system, only to be silenced with detentions without trial, torture, and even murder.[28] Some dissenters like Ngugi wa Thiong'o were forced to go into exile.[29] After the abortive coup on 1 August 1982, which led to more detentions, torture, and murders, in his unique style, Njoya used what was most readily available to him, his faith and the pulpit, to step up the struggle for positive governance:

> This book is the work of eyewitness testimony and original research: a borderland between theology and politics. It addresses faith as a context in which God sets the example of governance by being accessible and available to all for questions. It shows that when people fail to conduct their affairs responsibly, for their own good and for the glory of God, God assumes the responsibility of being the One who created them. The

fact that God's sovereignty operates by being accountable, fallible, finite and impotent, exemplifies how humanity should govern society. The whole purpose of incarnation was for God to change dominance into governance. . . . The joint accountability of God and humanity for both good and evil underpins the principles of democracy. This is the basis for God's grace, politics and economics. It provides the foundation on which every authority and government should be established.[30]

It is my submission that, just as the church in Kenya has failed to transform dominance and dependence to governance where participation, choice, and accountability are the hallmarks (Njoya's major argument throughout his book), so also Christian theology and ethics in Kenya have not come to terms with the pain the person dispossessed is forced to bear in the act of dispossession itself and subsequently in the trauma of a diminished existence. The church in Kenya and its Christian theology and ethics have been slow in recognizing and acknowledging the pain, trauma, and erosion of self-esteem that result from dominance and dependence, landlessness, abject poverty, violence, stigmatization and senseless death. It is no wonder that the church in Kenya and the rest of Africa south of Sahara has been very slow in facing the global HIV/AIDS epidemic, despite the fact that the disease spoke a religious and moral language from the beginning, when it was mainly associated with homosexuality, sin, and punishment.[31] In my view, this failure by the church (and government), despite all the gains from the protracted struggle for justice and freedom, has deepened the wounds and trauma of centuries of slave trade, colonialism, and imperialism. Kenyans have a long way to go in eradicating poverty and regaining their full humanity.

It should also be noted that the project of dispossession would not have been so successful without the divide-and-rule mind-set of the colonialists. Regrettably, since Christian missions founded a fragmented church along denominational and ethnic lines, we now need a united front with which to inspire a struggle for full humanity and a responsible social conscience. Despite great efforts in the last fifty years in nation building, ecumenism, and interreligious dialogue, the divide-and-rule mind-set has continued to thwart every effort to cultivate a common vision for a democratic society and economic development. Fortunately, figures like Berida Ndambuki, Timothy Njoya, Ngugi wa Thiong'o, and Chinua Achebe, despite their very diverse social locations, have given us food for thought as we seek a new vision that will enable us to address the destructive impact of bad governance and poverty in people's lives.

Needless to say, the task ahead is a daunting one. Even without looking elsewhere, Berida's and Njoya's narratives give us enough material for critical analysis and the courage to continue the search for full humanity through a theological and ethical framework that will sustain us in our struggle against many odds, challenges, and obstacles. Let us briefly explore some of these challenges and obstacles.

Challenges and Obstacles in the Struggle

To begin with, we need to remember that demographics in Kenya tell us that we are dealing with a very young population that demand a lot of attention and creative strategies to get them involved in constructive and self-empowering ways. Similarly, we must take note of the fact that more than half of the population are women, who comprise the majority of the poor and oppressed. The 1998 report of the task force for the review of laws relating to women in Kenya states, "The current state of gender relations treats male dominance as legitimate, natural, obvious and inevitable. The effect is to create a social-power hierarchy, in the context of which women are, by-and-large, reduced to powerlessness, economic marginalization, social vulnerability, and cultural inferiority, without any regard to their actual level of contribution to the processes of social production and development."[32] Tragically, some hard-working women like Berida believe that "the woman was created from the man's rib and therefore will always be lower."[33] Berida has resigned herself to having inferior social status despite her empowering leadership role among women both in the rural and urban setting as well as in her church. Addressing gender inequality and discrimination has become more urgent and critical than ever because in Africa, HIV/AIDS has the face of a woman and especially young women. The 2004 global HIV/AIDS epidemic report by the Joint United Nations Programme of HIV/AIDS (UNAIDS) is frightening on the female face of the epidemic: "Women are increasingly at great risk of infection. As of December 2003, women accounted for nearly 50% of all people living with HIV worldwide and for 57% in sub-Saharan Africa. Women and girls also bear the brunt of the impact of the epidemic; they are most likely to take care of sick people, to lose jobs, income and schooling as a result of illness, and to face stigma and discrimination. There is an urgent need to address the many factors that contribute to women's vulnerability and risk—gender and cultural inequalities, violence, ignorance."[34] It continues, "African women are at great risk, becoming infected at an earlier age than men. Today there are on average 13 infected women for every 10 infected men in sub-Saharan Africa—up from 12 for 10 in 2002. The difference is even more pronounced among 15 to 24 year olds. A review compared the ratio of young women living with HIV to young men living with HIV; this ranges from 20 women for every 10 men in South Africa to 45 women for every 10 men in Kenya and Mali."[35]

Moreover, two research documents by Human Rights Watch, *In the Shadow of Death: HIV/AIDS and Children's Rights in Kenya* (June 2001) and *Double Standards: Women's Property Rights Violations in Kenya* (March 2003), and one by Amnesty International, *Kenya: Rape-the Invisible Crime* (March 2002), clearly demonstrate the extreme powerlessness and vulnerability of children and women because of strongly entrenched gender and religiocultural inequalities in patriarchal, hierarchical, and sexist Kenyan society. The church in Kenya has not acknowledged its failure in promoting justice and equality between the genders and the protection of children, let alone addressing the prevalent dominance and dependence syndrome in our society. Of course, we did not have to wait for a terrible tragedy (global HIV/AIDS epidemic) to hit home for the church to acknowledge that the church's theology, ethics, liturgy, and practice of ministry have "fault lines."[36] But now that the church in Africa has acknowledged its ineffectiveness in dealing with the global HIV/AIDS epidemic, religious scholars should take the initiative and motivate the church to make it a safe site for the struggle against all forms of injustices and for creating life-giving theologies, ethics, and politics.

No doubt our failure to focus on the plight of children and women says a lot about education and politics in Kenya. Once again, Berida's experience in her efforts to provide education for her children and how they still ended up being unemployed speaks volumes about the obstacles faced by all those involved in the struggle. Above all, the high rate of violations of human rights, powerfully captured in both Berida's and Njoya's books, clearly demonstrates that even before we can begin to create life-giving theologies, ethics, and politics, we must as religious scholars investigate what is offered in both the secular and Christian educational systems. Let us not forget that the mission church in Kenya was instrumental in establishing the education system.[37] What this means is that, out of necessity and good practice, critical social historical analysis must occupy center stage in all that we do. According to the Kenyan historian William Robert Ochieng: "History, of course, is a very important subject in any developing country, for it is an important tool of socialization. History, more than any other discipline, helps one to understand clearer the public events, affairs and trends of one's time. Knowing what societies have been like in the past and the socio-economic dynamics of their evolution, will give clues to the factors that operate in them, the motives and conflicts that shape events. Knowledge of history is thus indispensable in the higher direction of society. We are arguing that if you cannot account for your whereabouts in time and space then you are not better than a rat trapped in a meat-safe."[38]

But any critical scholar must also ask, whose history or perspectives are taught in our schools, especially given our social historical background of being a colonized people? It is beyond the scope of this essay to delve into postcolonial theory that gives prominence to the history and literature written by "colonized subjects," but suffice it to say that regrettably, in Kenya, religious scholars have largely played deaf, dumb, and blind toward this body of literature.[39] For instance, the history of the slave trade is a much neglected area in the construction of African theology, ethics, and politics despite the fact that most of the first converts, evangelists, and ministerial formation students trained at the Divinity School at Freretown on the east coast of Kenya were freed slaves from Bombay, India.[40] Rarely do religious scholars make this historical connection with these pioneering Anglican Christian leaders who shaped the beginnings of the church in Kenya. Similarly, religious literature in Kenya has neglected to critically evaluate Christianity and church theology as it developed during the protracted struggle for land and freedom that culminated with the Mau Mau war, despite the fact that we have an abundance of literature by colonizers, settlers, Africanists, and Kenyans that tells a lot about colonialism and its impact in the society.

Furthermore, as Njoya has rightly claimed, Christian missions supported the colonial government even though there was a strong protest movement by Kenyan Christians who rejected the white man's Christianity and formed the African independent churches that comprise a large percentage of Christians in Kenya today. Thus, I contend that religious scholarship in Kenya today does not thoroughly assess the social, political, economic, and historical events that shaped Christianity in Kenya before independence and after independence. For instance, during the course of this research I encountered a very revealing document about the mind-set of church leaders with regards to the Mau Mau war. First, some background: the leaders of the freedom fighters (most of whom were Christians) failed to recruit most of the wealthy and literate Christians among the Gikuyu, whose families continued to support the Christian missions and the colonial government and to speak out against the so-called terrorists. On 22 August 1952, Gikuyu church elders, ministers, and priests from Roman Catholic, Anglican, and other Protestant churches met in Kiambu to announce that "God has a plan for

Kenya" and charged that the Mau Mau "thwarts God's wishes." They adopted the following six-point resolution:

1. We will fight this secret and violent organization to the end; we see the way to achieve this is for all men and women of good will to cooperate and work together for their just rights.
2. As true Christians and members of God's family we will have nothing to do with, nor cooperate with Mau Mau because its teachings are contrary to Christian teachings and our customs.
3. We are against it because it is against the Government, which maintains the law and order of the country and thus our safety and happiness.
4. We oppose Mau Mau because it is retarding the progress of Africans and also demoralizing them. It is also retarding the general progress of the country.
5. We will exclude its followers from our churches and also expel their children from schools, lest they infect the others.
6. We do not fear Mau Mau at all. If the Government does not succeed in stamping out the organization we are prepared to fight the Mau Mau adherents, even if it is with *pangas* [machetes].[41]

In my view, such a statement and the surrounding political circumstances should by now have created a whole series of theological and ethical research theses and books, because Mau Mau freedom fighters were not just a bunch of "terrorists" wishing to destabilize the country and the colonial government. Rather, they were fighting against dispossession and human indignity, as Kenyans suffered under a foreign occupation. The war had everything to do with the struggle against oppression, exploitation, and violence, yet religious scholars have not paid much attention to this period despite the fact that two churches, Bahati Martyrs Presbyterian Church in Nairobi and St. James Cathedral Anglican Church, in Murang'a town, were built in the 1950s in memory of Christians (including pastors) murdered during the Mau Mau war.[42] This statement says much about the theology of the day that deserves the attention of religious scholars, especially because of the continuum of violence in the society and the devastating effect of landlessness in Kenya today. Samuel Kobia has pointed to the reason why the church has not been effective on this score: "Ecumenical initiatives in advocating for justice and reconciliation can be difficult in situations where the church's prophetic ministry might have had a low priority in the past. The National Council of Churches in Kenya (NCCK) tried to create a forum for solving ethnic conflicts in Kenya in the early 1990s. However, because the church council had played a rather passive role in the 1960s and 1970s during the controversy surrounding the repossession of land, it was very difficult to create a neutral forum for solving disputes."[43]

Recreating Theologies, Ethics, and Politics

Given all this, it is vital that we critically evaluate the education system in Kenya and the quality of what is taught at every level to ensure that our youth are equipped with the right tools, ones that are self-empowering and self-affirming. The government must ensure that all kinds of education offered in the country serve to uphold justice, human dignity, and the fullness of life. At the same time we must engage in rigorous decolonizing and depatriarchalizing processes so that our theologies, ethics, and politics will be liberating.[44] Complicating these tasks is the fact that we are living in a globalized international trade system that does not seek equality and which is not driven by establishing justice in the world; it has become an instrument of death rather than life for millions of Africans.[45] Recreating African theologies, ethics, and politics in the era of globalization and the global HIV/AIDS epidemic therefore means engaging churches in resisting all death-dealing activities that erode our humanity. In Kenya and elsewhere in Africa, such poverty-related activities create a litany of woes in the daily newspapers and on radio, many of which concur with Berida's life story. Let me enumerate some of the problems facing the Kenyan society. The list is not exhaustive.

—High infant, child, and maternal mortality
—Poor reproductive health for girls and women, as well as breakdown of the overall health system
—Poor housing facilities, without privacy or hygienic environment
—High rates of teenage pregnancy (children having children) and deaths due to illegal unhygienic abortions; some girls and women survive but may never have other children or will have childbirth problems due to damage caused through the abortion
—Illiteracy, especially among rural women and girls who are forced to drop out from school and provide care for other siblings; this trend has become more prevalent with the HIV/AIDS epidemic, which has created a large number of orphans
—Increased violence in the society but especially gender-based violence, which also increases rapes, parental neglect of children (mostly by fathers), and sex and child abuse, including incest

—Acute shortage of food resulting in hunger, starvation, and malnutrition, stunting children and weakening the elderly

—High number of preventable injuries (road/boat/rail accidents, fires at home) and diseases (respiratory diseases among children, malaria, tuberculosis, and HIV/AIDS)

—Trauma among children and raped women

—Lack of facilities and education for people with disabilities

—High unemployment rate, ill-equipped professionals (including those in pastoral ministry)

—Lack of capacity building and poor leadership

—Hopelessness and despair, which increases lawlessness, anarchy, irresponsibility, and practices such as prostitution, all of which cause further problems

—Loss of creativity, freedom, self-esteem, and dignity

—Untimely and senseless death

This litany of problems facing Kenya means religious scholars must engage in political activism to the same extent as they are involved in academic responsibilities; in so doing they will be participating in the transformation of the dominance-and-dependence policy and theology that Timothy Njoya so vividly described in his book. Our poverty-stricken and death-dealing context demands that we take politics head on, because our governments have miserably failed to deliver.[46] Moreover, Christian ethics should guide Christian citizens, including children and youth, on how to hold religious and political leaders accountable for their failed responsibilities. For sure, the struggle against poverty and the global HIV/AIDS epidemic is such that we must hold our governments accountable, even as part of the church struggles to provide a continuum of care and compassion in the face of suffering and death.

Needless to say, whether it is the lessons learned from South Africa's struggle against apartheid, from the civil rights movement in the United States, or the Kenyan struggle for land and freedom, political activism does not come without a price. As Njoya has demonstrated, Christian political activism means mobilizing citizens and teaching them how to demand accountability from the religious and political leadership by using the space accorded to us in theological and ecumenical institutions as well as the churches. Certainly, this is a very challenging task in a context like Kenya, where Christians are taught to stay away from politics. To change this mindset, one has to go beyond religion and the institutional church and appeal to one's faith in God, as Njoya had to discover the hard way.

My salvation, education and ordination were not worth anything to my faith, and meant nothing for the society, until I abandoned following the all-powerful and triumphant Lord of the powerful Emperors, Kings, Presidents, Moderators, Generals, Bishops or Tycoons who formed impervious walls around themselves. They insulated corruption with religion and made it irrelevant to the issues affecting the oppressed, weak, marginal and poor. I started following the footsteps of the vulnerable Lamb of God who lived in Egypt as a refugee, was stripped naked, crucified, annihilated and deprived of beauty, honor and name. I saw Jesus as the one oppressed, weak, hungry and sick in my society. He was an infant but not infantile, child but not childish, young but not immature, man but not sexist and human but not inhuman.[47]

Njoya's argument and testimony reminds us that religious systems, institutions, and even theologies that claim to be the bearers of the gospel may fail to deliver the message, but faith in God as little as the mustard seed can transform the most horrific situation. In the same light, we are reminded that the struggle for full humanity in a poverty-stricken context is not an end in itself but the means to strive for the realization of God's reign in the world. Njoya explains, "Faith is penultimate concern for issues that concern God ultimately. This concern includes rights to participate in government in order to secure one's life, liberty and subsistence. This is what constitutes God's reign in the world. It makes democracy grounded on the gospel. There are some of the cardinal principles of democracy found in the gospel, participation, accountability and choice."[48]

Hence, the task of political, cultural, spiritual, material, and psychological transformation and renewal demands that religious scholars create biblical, theological, and ethical resources that will help people to cultivate and nurture their faith in God, in themselves, and with one another, so as to acquire meaningful living and to fully participate in society. Most important, however, we should not forego confronting church theologies and ethics that seem to be powerless in the face of bad governance, poverty, violence, and senseless death. Politics is the art of living together in a community, and we cannot escape being involved as citizens (and more so when we are leaders) unless we have abandoned our God-given responsibilities. Kobia implores scholars to take seriously the welfare of the community: "To guard the common welfare of the community is the responsibility, first of all, of the community leaders. . . . The academics in the community are challenged to be active members in the life of the community, allowing their intellectual resources to interact constructively with real situations on the ground. African intellectuals must strive to be organic intellectuals fully integrated into the life of the community and putting their gifts and talents at the disposal of the community."[49]

Making a U-Turn: Inevitable Paradigm Shift

In an overwhelming, poverty-stricken context like the one we find in Kenya, creating life-giving theologies and ethics and being involved in political activism should include income-generating activities that are community- or group-based. Some of these projects already exist, but they need to be nurtured and empowered so as to be more productive. For instance, Berida Ndambuki belongs to two women's groups, in the city as well as in the rural area. In Nairobi she belongs to Kyeni kya Gikomba (The Light of Gikomba), which she refers to as a "merry-go-round," and in the rural area of Kathonzweni, she belongs to a group of homemakers and small-scale farmers.[50] Much can be achieved through such organized groups, as long as there is commitment and common vision for a just society. In any poverty-stricken context religious scholars should get involved in political and economic advocacy together "with" (not "for") the poor in their struggle for full humanity. But much more is needed. There must be a paradigm shift in the way we read the Bible and do theology.

A religious scholar who has focused on already organized women's groups and conducted contextual Bible studies is Gerald West, a theological educator at the School of Theology and Religion, University of KwaZulu-Natal, in South Africa. West and his team have created a solidarity program for people living with HIV/AIDS in the Institute for the Study of the Bible and Worker Ministry Project (ISB&WM).[51] He writes, "The main goal [of the solidarity program] is to facilitate the development of sustainable community-based support groups, which would provide support and enhance motivation and encouragement to people living with HIV/AIDS as they struggle towards positive living, by enabling them to reach out to their communities, spreading the message of hope and life in spite of being HIV-positive."[52] He further explains, "The core purpose of the ISB&WM is to work with biblical and theological resources in collaboration and solidarity with the poor, the working class, and the marginalized, and so my interest is in how the Bible is a resource for social transformation among people living with HIV/AIDS. My focus on the Bible takes on added importance given the prevailing pejorative view within the church of people who are HIV-positive. In what ways, I ask, can the Bible be a resource for dignity, healing and wholeness when the church is clearly not (yet)?"[53]Even when the church ceases to be a resource for dignity, healing, and wholeness—in other words, a site for the struggle for full humanity—religious scholars should not give up their function of rediscovering the Bible and faith in God as resources. Both Njoya and West remind us that the church and Christianity do not have a monopoly on the Bible and faith in God. Since 1996, West has extended this question to women who have been raped and others who are subjected to other kinds of gender-based violence by doing contextual Bible studies; they focus principally on the Tamar rape narrative in 2 Samuel 13:1–22. From 2000 his team has used the text in what they call the Tamar Campaign to break the chains of silence and stop violence against women and children. West remarks, "A common understanding of abuse was that it was primarily physical. We felt it was important for women to be aware of the other dimensions of abuse, including sexual, economic, verbal, psychological and spiritual dimensions. Our cultures and religion clearly provide a setting for all these forms of abuse to take place without being reported or challenged. Most women have accepted this as their lot, believing this is how God has ordered the world. Some women believe the other kinds of abuse are not as bad as physical abuse!"[54] The Tamar Campaign has had great success and there is high demand to take it beyond KwaZulu-Natal province to other African countries. Socially engaged religious scholars can make a big difference when they are committed to work with the poor for social transformation and to restore their dignity. The ISB&WM project does not stop at creating critical awareness through contextual Bible studies. It also has other programs, like its economic justice program, which works for changes in the government's economic policy and with many other organizations to establish a basic income grant (BIG) of R100 a month for the poorest.[55] Advocacy takes many forms, and we should not shy away from tackling difficult subjects like rape and incest that form a continuum of suffering and disgrace for thousands of women and girls. Despite all the erosion of the African way of life, community-based life-giving activities remain a preferred option, especially among women, in the struggle for full humanity.

However, given the key role the Bible and culture play in fashioning our lives and activities in Africa, we must heed the insightful and powerful voices of African women theologians who have called for biblical and cultural hermeneutics in the business of creating life-giving theologies and ethics. For instance, in her book *Introducing Feminist Cultural Hermeneutics: An African Perspective*, Musimbi Kanyoro, a Kenyan Lutheran biblical feminist scholar and the secretary general of the World Young Women's Christian Association (YWCA), writes on the importance of cultural hermeneutics.

I suggest that a cultural hermeneutic is a first step towards a biblical hermeneutic. I argue that the culture of the reader in Africa has more influence on the way the biblical text is understood and used in communities than the historical culture of the text. By so stating, I suggest that not knowing the nuances of the culture into which the Bible is read or preached has far more wide-reaching repercussions for the exegesis of texts than is often acknowledged by biblical scholars and preachers alike. Cultural hermeneutics is a necessary tool for those who teach homiletics and pastoral work in seminaries and other clergy institutions, and a prerequisite to African women's liberation theology. I have discovered this by reading the bible with communities of African rural women. The lessons from such readings underscored for me the urgency of affirming the concepts of social and cultural hermeneutics so well dealt with by many authors.[56]

Another biblical scholar who combines doing feminist biblical hermeneutics, writing, storytelling, teaching, and activism on the global HIV/AIDS epidemic and on globalization is Musa Dube of Botswana, whose works I have already cited. Dube has targeted theological institutions and churches to train theological educators and church leaders and to produce biblical, liturgical, and theological resources.[57] In "Doing Theological/Religious Education: A Paradigm of Shattered Dreams & Cul de Sac/ed Roads," Dube narrates how she became engulfed by the global HIV/AIDS epidemic and its adverse impact in Africa south of the Sahara. As Dube became more involved in creating songs and biblical and theological literature addressing the epidemic, she realized (like Gerald West and Musimbi Kanyoro) that it was not enough to be socially engaged unless we also forge a paradigm shift in the way we do theology and read the Bible in Africa. Interestingly, what Dube says about the impact of the global HIV/AIDS epidemic can be said about the extreme poverty experienced by millions of Kenyans (Africans), if indeed we care about life in its fullness. Dube concludes, and I quote her at length:

> In short, HIV/AIDS has brought us into a particular context. To an eschatological moment, if I may. It has brought us to that *Cul de sac*, where we must stop, turn, go back and find another way around. For me what is tragic is not that we have been brought to a *Cul de sac* as such. It is not that HIV/AIDS has cruelly presented us with a picture frame of our shattered dreams; or raging rivers to be crossed without any bridge. Rather, what I find tragic is when we fail to see the "You [U] turn", when

we fail to turn right around to go back and to search for another way forward. Thus many of us have been frozen by the shocking picture of our broken dreams; by a future which is seemingly without a bridge. By hopelessness. By absolute despair. Fear has frozen many of us. It has bred amongst us the worst pandemic—HIV/AIDS stigma. As I argue elsewhere, the HIV/AIDS stigma is the worst pandemic to be brewed by HIV/AIDS disease, for it has infected more of us than the virus itself. While others have tragically come to a dead end, many have not even noticed that we are in a context of a *Cul de sac*. Such people are just shooting on, dangerously driving on—irrelevant for our HIV/AIDS plagued world. Such tragic and deadly accidents continue to plague our theological programs which have not responded [to] the paradigm shift demand[ed] by the HIV/AIDS context.[58]

A Holistic and Interdisciplinary Approach

The struggle for full humanity in a poverty-stricken and HIV/AIDS-infected and -affected context is very complex and urgent. In this essay, I have summoned religious scholars and the church in Kenya to play their role in the political, cultural, spiritual, material, and psychological transformation of this destructive reality of our time. To begin with, through Berida's narrative I have underlined how religion and poverty are intricately related to social injustices that lead to senseless suffering and death in Kenya. Second, I have called upon religious scholars and the church to decolonize the mind and to shun imperialism of all kinds in our search for a new vision. Third, I have highlighted some of the challenges and obstacles we face in the struggle. Fourth, I have counseled religious scholars to move away from theologies, ethics, and politics of domination and dependence that we inherited from our colonial past that was nurtured by a patriarchal, hierarchical, and sexist society and church. To do so, as Timothy Njoya has asserted, when religious systems, institutions, theologies, and leaders fail us we must turn to faith in God as a context and a resource for a new vision. Equally important, as Gerald West, Musimbi Kanyoro, and Musa Dube have demonstrated, we must pay particular attention to the way we read and interpret the Bible and the culture and methodologies of teaching theology. In other words, we need a paradigm shift in our theological curriculum and the way we form leadership, which takes into account all sectors of our lives, as the HIV/AIDS epidemic has demanded of us.

Simply put, we need to adopt a holistic approach in religious scholarship. In 1996, a group of theological educators and ecumenical leaders agreed on this holistic character of theological education and ministerial formation, "which is grounded in worship, and combines and inter-relates spirituality, academic excellence, mission and evangelism, justice and peace, pastoral sensitivity and competence, and the formation of character."[59] Put differently, a holistic theological education brings together

> the ear to hear God's word and the cry of God's people;
> the heart to heed and respond to the suffering;
> the tongue to speak to both the weary and the arrogant;
> the hands to work with the lowly;
> the mind to reflect on the good news of the gospel;
> the will to respond to God's call;
> the spirit to wait on God in prayer, to struggle and wrestle with God, to be silent in penitence and humility and to intercede for the church and the world;
> the body to be the temple of the Holy Spirit.[60]

Evidently such a theological curriculum demands engaging an interdisciplinary approach that reaches out to other academic disciplines, creates alliances with civil society, generates information sharing, and allows scholars to be socially engaged with the poor and all those afflicted by other social injustices; only in this way will social transformation take place. As I have argued in the essay, demographics must be taken seriously in this paradigm shift, so that the needs of children, youth, and women who comprise the majority of the church membership and the poor will be addressed. In order to create effective and fruitful theological curricula, religious scholars must work with these marginalized groups, which also include people with disabilities.

Consequently, in the first project toward eradication of poverty and other social injustices, the church must take a hard look at its theology and ethics and map out strategies on how it becomes an instrument of life rather than to participate in the destruction of God's creation. The church can transform its theologies and ethics with the help of religious scholars. Equally, religious scholars and the church must be involved in shaping the politics of the land in ensuring that democracy prevails not as an end in itself but as a means of creating and nurturing a new and just vision of God's reign. Making a paradigm shift or a U-turn in theological curricula is an act that calls for commitment, determination, boldness, and courage, for, as Samuel Kobia has insisted, "Eradication of poverty must be comprehensive and multifaceted, involving concerted efforts at all levels. While the primary responsibility lies with Africans themselves, external support and solidarity are expected to accompany African initiatives. This is the case especially for Europe which, after all, contributed immensely to the impoverishment of Africa. But the external contribution and involvement must be viewed critically. The paradigms, methodologies, and language used should not be taken at face value. The process must be evaluated at its different stages to ensure clarity at levels of concept, policy and implementation."

This is a tall order of expectations but one that is worth pursuing as we seek to create a new vision for a just society that will facilitate our claim for full humanity from centuries of dispossession and dehumanization. Berida's narrative should continue to be an inspiration, considering that the poor are not sitting passively waiting for handouts. Rather, the poor are overcoming systematic oppression, exploitation, and devaluation and working to rediscover their God-given creativity and humanity. While they are still oppressed, they are claiming their right to human dignity.

Notes

1. Berida Ndambuki and Claire C. Robertson, *We Only Come Here to Struggle: Stories from Berida's Life* (Bloomington: Indiana University Press, 2000), xi–xxxi.
2. I have decided to use Berida's first name to be consistent with the way she is referred to in the book.
3. Ndambuki and Robertson, *We Only Come Here to Struggle*, 53.
4. Violet Nyambura Kimani, "Poverty, Gender Inequity and HIV/AIDS: The Place of Religion in the Fight against Human Suffering and Death," paper presented at the Pan-African Seminar on Religion and Poverty, Loreto Mary Ward Centre, Langata, Kenya, 16–27 July 2001.
5. See Ndambuki and Robertson, *We Only Come Here to Struggle*, 68 and 99.
6. Ibid., chap. 4.
7. Samuel Kobia, *The Courage to Hope: The Roots for a New Vision and the Calling of the Church in Africa* (Geneva: WCC Publications 2003), 195.
8. Berida spends the whole last chapter, chap. 5 (99–114), agonizing on the deteriorating social, political, and economic life of independent Kenya.
9. Abacci Atlas, "Demographics of Kenya," available at http://www.abacci.com/atlas/demography.asp?countryID=239, consulted on 2 July 2004.
10. See http://www.imf.org/external/NP/prsp/2000/ken/01/INDEX.HTM.
11. Ibid., 4.
12. Ibid., 5.
13. In Kenya, a census has been conducted every ten years since 1969.
14. The population census is found in *The 1999 Population and Housing Census: Counting Our People for Development*, vol. 1 (Nairobi: Kenya Bureau of Statistics, 2001).
15. The designated age for children by the United Nations Children's Fund (UNICEF) is 0–18.
16. Ndambuki and Robertson, *We Only Come Here to Struggle*, 116.
17. Chinua Achebe, *Home and Exile* (2001; London: Canongate Books, 2003), 63. Achebe

is referring to Jomo Kenyatta's *Facing Mount Kenya: The Traditional Life of Gikuyu* (London: Martin Secker and Warburg, 1938). Kenya was colonized by the British for sixty-eight years (1895–1920 as a protectorate, and 1920–1963 as a crown colony), just as the slave trade was coming to an end.

18. Achebe, *Home and Exile*, 70.

19. Ibid., 72 and 81.

20. Ibid., 79.

21. Ndambuki and Robertson, *We Only Come Here to Struggle*, 76.

22. See Ngugi wa Thiong'o, *Decolonising the Mind: The Politics of Language in African Literature* (Nairobi: Heinemann Kenya, 1981).

23. Noel Leo Erskine, *Decolonizing Theology: A Caribbean Perspective* (1981; Trenton: Africa World Press, 1998), xiv.

24. Lewin L. Williams, *Caribbean Theology* (New York: Peter Lang, 1994), 33.

25. Musa W. Dube, "The Lord's Prayer in the Global Economic Era," in *The Bible in Africa: Transactions, Trajectories and Trends*, ed. Gerald O West and Musa W. Dube (Leiden: Brill, 2000), 611–30, quote at 628.

26. Timothy Njoya, *The Divine Tag on Democracy* (Yaounde, Cameroon: Edition Cle and CIPCRE, 2003).

27. Literature on the Mau Mau war and the protracted struggle for land and freedom in Kenya abounds: some by those who participated in the war and the struggle and some by Africanists. It includes Tabitha Kanogo, *Squatters and the Roots of Mau Mau, 1905–63* (Nairobi: Heinemann Kenya, 1987); James Mwangi Kariuki, 'Mau Mau' *Detainee* (London: Oxford University Press, 1963); Maina wa Kinyatti, *Mau Mau: A Revolution Betrayed* (New York: Mau Mau Research Center, 2000); Maina wa Kinyatti, ed., *Thunder from the Mountains: Poems and Songs from the Mau Mau* (1980; Trenton: Africa World Press, 1990); Maina wa Kinyatti, *Kenya's Freedom Struggle: The Dedan Kimathi Papers* (London: Zed Press, 1987); Donald L. Barnett and Karari Njama, *Mau Mau from Within* (New York: Modern Reader Paperbacks, 1966); Robert B. Edgerton, *Mau Mau: An African Crucible* (New York: Ballantine Books, 1989).

28. In 1969 Odinga Oginga, the first vice president of Kenyatta's regime, resigned and formed Kenya People's Union; he also published *Not Yet Uhuru* (freedom), which landed him in detention and caused the party to be banned. Others, like James Mwangi Kariuki and Jean Pinto, were assassinated. Daniel Arap Moi became the vice president and took over from Kenyatta upon his death in 1978 without elections after three months as required in the constitution. It is important to point out that in comparison with the extreme violent situation (civil wars and even genocide) experienced in neighboring countries after independence (e.g., Uganda, Rwanda, Burundi, Ethiopia, Sudan, Democratic Republic of Congo), Kenya has been described as a relatively peaceful country, and as a matter of fact it has been a home for many refugees from these countries. However, this should not be seen to mean that Kenyans have not had their share of bad governance and betrayal from those who took over from the British government; for many, Kenyatta—as Njoya has demonstrated—failed to deliver and to lay a strong foundation for democracy.

29. Ngugi wa Thiong'o was detained by Kenyatta's government in 1978, but since Kenyatta died the same year he was in detention, the new president Daniel Arap Moi was obliged by Kenya's detention law to release him. Ngugi, however, continued in the struggle for full humanity in his village Kamiirithu, so he was eventually forced to go into exile in 1982, since Moi continued the domination policy. Ngugi only

returned to Kenya on 30 July 2004. His struggle is mostly captured in Ngugi wa Thiong'o and Ngugi wa Mirii, *I Will Marry When I Want*, trans. from Gikuyu by the authors (Nairobi: Heinemann Kenya, 1982); and the following books, all by Ngugi wa Thiong'o: *Devil on the Cross*, trans. from Gikuyu by the author (Nairobi: Heinemann Kenya, 1982); *Decolonising the Mind: The Politics of Language in African Literature* (Nairobi: Heinemann Kenya, 1981); *Detained: A Writer's Prison Diary* (Nairobi: Heinemann Kenya, 1981).

30. Njoya, *The Divine Tag on Democracy*, 31. In this book Njoya tells the genesis of the current multiparty democracy in Kenya, which brought to an end the one-party system of Presidents Kenyatta and Moi (December 2002). That change was sparked by a live radio sermon that Njoya delivered on 5 October 1986 at the St. Andrews Presbyterian Church of East Africa. The sermon focused on detention without trial, worship of the presidency, and the lack of independent judiciary and academic freedom. Moi's government was infuriated and eventually forced the church to eject Njoya from the ministry; Njoya, however, was reinstated after a few years, and he continued using the pulpit for the struggle. He was subjected to police brutality more than once, but was lucky to survive to tell the story; many more that followed him met their death, while others were subjected to ethnic oppression. These ethnic conflicts are still under investigation, so it is hard to give the final count of all those who perished during this so-called second liberation struggle, the first being the Mau Mau war. Njoya credits his faith in God for having joined in the struggle.

31. It was this religious and moral language that prompted doctors at the World Health Organization to approach the general secretary of the World Council of Churches (WCC) to address the AIDS crisis in the mid-1980s. Subsequently, WCC organized the first consultation on AIDS in 1986 and since then it has struggled to respond to the challenge in a variety of ways. For a comprehensive overview of WCC's involvement see the CD-ROM *Resource Material for Churches and Communities* (Geneva: WCC, 2004).

32. Quoted in Human Rights Watch, *Double Standards: Women's Property Rights Violations in Kenya* 15.5 (A) (March 2003): 6.

33. Ndambuki and Robertson, *We Only Come Here to Struggle*, 25.

34. UNAIDS, *2004 Report on the Global AIDS Epidemic* (Executive Summary), 3.

35. Ibid., 6.

36. See World Council of Churches, *Plan of Action: The Ecumenical Response to HIV/AIDS in Africa; Global Consultation on the Ecumenical Response to the Challenge on HIV/AIDS in Africa* (Nairobi: WCC, November 2001).

37. For more discussion on the mission church and education system in Kenya, see my book *Kiama Kia Ngo: An African Christian Feminist Ethic of Resistance and Transformation* (Ghana: Legon Theological Studies Series Project, in collaboration with Asempa Publishers, 2000).

38. William Robert Ochieng, *The Third Word: More Essays on Kenya History* (Nairobi: Kenya Literature Bureau, 1984), 58.

39. Among religious scholars in Africa we have the pioneering, thought-provoking Musa W. Dube, a Botswana New Testament feminist scholar and HIV/AIDS activist; see especially her *Postcolonial Feminist Interpretation of the Bible* (St. Louis, Mo.: Chalice Press, 2000).

40. For more information see Provincial Unit of Research, *Rabai to Mumias: A Short History of Church of the Province of Kenya, 1844–1994* (Nairobi: Uzima Press, 1994), 15–

17. The Divinity School at Freretown was later moved to Limuru to become St. Paul's United Theological College, one of the places we visited in July 2001 during the Pan-African Seminar on Religion and Poverty. Freretown was named after Sir Bartle Frere, who wrote a report for the British government on the plight of freed slaves.

41. Robert B. Edgerton, *Mau Mau: An African Crucible* (New York: Ballantine Books, 1989), 84.

42. I learned about this history when I was posted as minister to Bahati Martyrs Church in 1980. I also discovered that this area of Nairobi, which was allocated to Africans (as opposed to better areas of Nairobi, which were reserved for whites and Indians), was the home of many survivors of the Mau Mau war who were freedom fighters or, in the case of women, informers and suppliers of food to the army in the forests. This was the beginning of my history lessons from freedom fighters on the Mau Mau war, which was noticeably missing in the school curriculum. All that I knew from my parents was the perspective of the mission church, as I had been born and reared in the manse.

43. Kobia, *The Courage to Hope*, 165.

44. A powerful example of this process is the writings of Dube, especially her *Postcolonial Feminist Interpretation of the Bible*. Also a must-read is Mercy Amba Oduyoye, *Daughters of Anowa: African Women and Patriarchy* (Maryknoll, N.Y.: Orbis Books, 1995).

45. Musa W. Dube, "Talitha Cum! Calling the Girl-Child and Women to Life in the HIV/AIDS and Globalization Era," in *African Women, HIV/AIDS and Faith Communities*, ed. Isabel Phiri et al. (Pietermaritzburg: Cluster, 2003), 71–93.

46. Nimi Wariboko and Jacob Olupona, both Nigerian speakers at the Pan-African Seminar on Religion and Poverty held in Princeton, N.J., 12–25 July 2004, acknowledged that it is politics in Africa that is responsible for the extreme poverty.

47. Njoya, *The Divine Tag on Democracy*, 249–50.

48. Ibid., 370. Kwame Bediako, a Ghanaian Presbyterian theologian, concurs with Njoya in his book *Christianity in Africa: The Renewal of Non-Western Religion* (1995; Maryknoll, N.Y.: Orbis Books, 1997), 247–49.

49. Kobia, *The Courage to Hope*, 96.

50. Ndambuki and Robertson, *We Only Come Here to Struggle*, 80.

51. The Institute for the Study of the Bible and Worker Ministry Project has been renamed Ujamma Centre for Biblical and Theological Community Development and Research.

52. Gerald O. West, "Reading the Bible in the Light of HIV/AIDS in South Africa," *Ecumenical Review* (Geneva: WCC Publications) (October 2003): 335. To appreciate the work of Gerald West and his efforts to be in solidarity with the poor and suffering as an academic scholar see his *Biblical Hermeneutics of Liberation: Modes of Reading the Bible in the South Africa Context*, 2nd ed. (Pietermaritzburg: Cluster Publications; Maryknoll, N.Y.: Orbis Books, 1995) and *The Academy of the Poor: Towards a Dialogical Reading of the Bible* (Pietermaritzburg: Cluster Publications, 2003).

53. West, "Reading the Bible in the Light of HIV/AIDS in South Africa," 336.

54. Gerald O. West and Phumzile Zondi-Mabizela, "The Bible Story that Became a Campaign: The Tamar Campaign in South Africa (and beyond)," *Ministerial Formation* (Geneva: WCC), no. 102 (July 2004): 10. Slowly African women are gaining the courage to tell their own stories of gender-based violence including incest. A good example is Thandeki Umlilo, *Little Girl, Arise!: New Life after Incest and Abuse* (Pietermaritzburg: Cluster Publications, 2002).

55. West, "Reading the Bible in the Light of HIV/AIDS in South Africa," 343.
56. Musimbi R. A. Kanyoro, *Introducing Feminist Cultural Hermeneutics: An African Perspective* (Sheffield, U.K.: Sheffield Academic Press, 2002), 19.
57. See Musa W. Dube, ed., *HIV/AIDS and the Curriculum: Methods of Integrating HIV/AIDS in Theological Programmes* (Geneva: WCC Publications, 2003).
58. Musa W. Dube, "Doing Theological/Religious Education: A Paradigm of Shattered Dreams and Cul de Sac/ed Roads," *Ministerial Formation* (Geneva: WCC), no. 102 (January 2004): 11–12.
59. John Pobee, ed., *Towards Viable Theological Education: Ecumenical Imperative, Catalyst of Renewal* (Geneva: WCC Publications, 1997), 1.
60. Ibid.

THE AMBIGUOUS RELATION OF RELIGION AND POVERTY

Kossi A. Ayedze | **POVERTY AMONG AFRICAN PEOPLE AND**

THE AMBIGUOUS ROLE OF CHRISTIAN THOUGHT

D espite its natural riches, Africa is known to the world as a poor continent. Although most people all over the world—especially children, women, racial minorities, or oppressed majorities—lack the sufficient material resources required for a decent life and "live in a state of weakness, dependency and humiliation," the phenomenon of poverty seems more blatant and offensively incongruous among African people.[1] Whether in Togo or Ghana in West Africa, Kenya or Tanzania in East Africa, or at Soweto and Alexandria in South Africa, poverty strikes more severely, and thousands of people are constantly at risk of hunger and social rejection, with children and persons with HIV/AIDS being especially vulnerable. Floods, drought, economic injustice and decline, regional political instability, and limited access to education and health services have contributed in all of these countries to a situation of poverty that only worsens year after year. The observable fact is heartbreaking and multifaceted, and a major question it raises is, who is to blame for this situation: the poor for their poverty, or the institutional structures that create poverty?[2] The end of the past millennium has produced international conferences dealing with the problem; and one could have expected that ways of uprooting poverty in Africa would have been largely discussed and effective methods of tackling the problem agreed upon. We still witness an increasing divide between rich and poor in this third millennium, and one wonders if the seemingly growing concern for Africa and its poor populations does not hide a form of hypocrisy on the part of the world's most powerful leaders.[3]

Within the many circles, conferences, and seminars that debate on the subject in our time, attempts are being made to explain and understand the causes of the phenomenon, as well as to consider and reflect on the remedies for it. Religious circles and ecclesiastical organizations are not outdone on the matter; and churches have been active for some time in development and charitable or welfare programs as well as in theological reflection on poverty.[4] Two conflicting views have emerged from the modern debate and reflection on poverty. One looks at structural social and economic systems as causes of the phenomenon and argues that "changes in the structural social and economic system will help preventing poverty as well as relieving misery."[5] The other view looks at each individual as responsible for his or her own situation and either blames the poor for their poverty, or tends to present poverty as "God's means of punishing and controlling the disobedient and heathen."[6]

As there is no clear teaching on wealth and poverty in religious circles, it is my opinion that there will be little chance for poverty to be eradicated in Africa—or to be alleviated, as one now terms it in international circles—as long as received thoughts and ideas on wealth and poverty do not change among African people themselves. Ideas have consequences. They have power to influence events and attitudes.[7] They have an impact on people's values and ethics. And it is my assumption, in this regard, that Africans' attitudes toward wealth and poverty—especially African Christians' attitudes—were strongly influenced by the received biblical and theological tradition of Christian thought. In other words, the Christian teachings Africans have received with regard to wealth and poverty have powerful bearings on their lives today.

As an African, I have seen firsthand the faces of poverty on the continent and witnessed how Christianity has ambiguously or hypocritically acted as response and cause to poverty. Churches, for example, raise money, but they very seldom raise questions about how wealth is acquired. Could it not be that people from whom churches get money are poor people's robbers? What are the Christian views on wealth possession and poverty alleviation?

In this essay, I aim at inquiring into Christianity's equivocal understanding of wealth and poverty and how it transmitted that understanding over the generations. I hope to argue that the way Christian missions in Africa understood and taught wealth and poverty continues to impact the lives of African people. If in the West the teachings of the church have helped people, strengthened them, and advanced the quality of their lives, in Africa, on the contrary, Christian teachings on wealth and poverty rather seem to have hurt people, weakened them, and failed to advance the quality of their lives.[8]

The Church and Poverty in Sub-Saharan Africa

Massive poverty is rampant in many African villages and city slums, especially among children, women, the illiterate, and unemployed youths. The situation is such that the aspects of poverty in Africa are often presented in terms like "African realities,"[9] as if no other realities constitute the world of and life in the old continent, cradle of civilizations. The media in the West could not describe Africa without referring to its severe food shortage, malnutrition, inadequate housing, inadequate clothing, inadequate medical care, disease, high infant mortality, illiteracy, or inadequate system of education.[10] The truth is that colonialism, postcolonialism, and the international financial institutions, as well as African leaders and intellectuals, share various degrees of responsibility for this gloomy situation of Africa. All of them are held responsible because of the "partisan, inhuman, incoherent, and generally unpopular remedy solutions"[11] they pretend to propose for the eradication of poverty in Africa, while they leave the continent excluded from the new economic trend of this third millennium; this they do by preventing its populations from having their share in the profits of globalization, which they advocate so highly. For their part, African leaders and intellectuals are to blame because of their malgovernance, undemocratic policies, and "lack of vision and responsibility."[12] Churches are not excluded. They also share some responsibilities in perpetuating poverty in Africa by failing to go beyond their charity missions and propose adequate solutions to tackle the problem of poverty in Africa.

Despite its material poverty, Africa as a continent is spiritually wealthy. It is a continent where Islam and Christianity are well established. While the northern third of Africa is overwhelmingly Islamic, the southern two-thirds of Africa is predominantly Christian and constitutes an area where Christianity is growing rapidly. In the 1900s, Christians in Africa were estimated at 10 million. The Bible then was translated in full or in part into 113 African languages. In 1984, the Christian population reached 234 million, with Bible translations into about 540 African languages. In 2000, the people who embraced the Christian faith were estimated at 394 million, with Bible translations into about 850 African languages.[13] Although the Western church still retained the lion's share of the church's material resources, dynamic faith, worship life, and missionary commitment blossom in Africa, where church members are largely poor and deprived of power and respect. Ironies like this constitute the relationship between the church and its members in Africa. This situation, in my opinion, has its source in the ambiguous teachings of the churches with regard to wealth and poverty, and the observable fallouts of these teachings in the living conditions of African church leaders compared to the living conditions of poor African Christians. In a recent publication, Alyward Shorter, principal of Tangaza College in the Catholic University of Eastern Africa (Kenya), has expressed how "it is a source of sadness and incomprehension to poor African Christians that their Church seems to have no relevance towards their struggle for survival."[14] This is true in the sense where church leaders and most of those who claim to have vowed themselves to a consecrated life, that is, a religious poverty, are very far from sharing in the material conditions of Africa's poor. It is a compromising situation that most pastors, bishops, priests, and nuns, especially when they are in a leading position, "are visibly seen to belong to the affluent section of the Church."[15] Their living conditions are far indeed from the degrading level in which most poor Africans live. They live in decent houses, built in wealthy neighborhoods, and they own possessions and have easy access to facilities by which wealth can be measured. "They know where their next meal is coming from. They have clean water and good sanitation. They do not have any insecurity about the future. When they fall sick, medical care is readily available for them."[16]

At the same time, most Christians from whom offerings are expected every Sunday live in a technically destitute and inhuman situation. They have difficulties affording meals, good clothing, and decent houses. They cannot afford to educate their children and may powerlessly watch their baby die of a disease that could easily be cured. Women suffer worst in these situations. For instance, mothers' lack of access to prenatal care leaves their babies to be born at much higher risk of premature birth; and their children are disadvantaged from the outset, with low birth weight, physical and mental impairment, and death before their first birthday.[17] It is women, rather than men, who constitute the majority of church members, and give to the church the sense of a community of faith. Outside the church, they are the ones "who ensure that their children go to school, who look after their children's health, and who have the interest of the family more at heart."[18] Yet they are the poorest and the most disadvantaged in the church and the society. And the male leadership of the church does not seem to care much about their degrading situation.

Churches of course have been active in charitable programs, working with and for the poor (women, sick, destitute, refugees, street children, unemployed youths, and so on), but most church leaders really "do not share in the lives of the poor. They belong to the ranks of the non-poor and have not really entered the world of the poor."[19] Generally speaking, though ecclesiastical efforts toward the poor appear laudable, churches have failed so far to get at the roots of the problem of poverty in Africa. Another irony is that if "poverty in the sense of deprivation has various causes which Christianity seeks to address . . . to some extent poverty is also seen as having a religious basis."[20] Indeed, though Christianity has "the ability to liberate, empower, and restore people's dignity, [it also] has been used as a tool to exploit, oppress, alienate and discriminate. . . . It can immobilize people and act as a palliative which tranquilizes people's aspirations."[21] This latter aspect appears to have been the case in many African churches, where believers have been exhorted to shun wealth in order to deserve heaven.

Teachings on Wealth and Poverty in African Churches

The glorification of poverty dominates exaltation of wealth in Christian tradition. This kind of glorification is evident in the New Testament as well as in the writings of such church fathers as Ambrose, John Chrysostom, and Prudentius.[22] Even Augustine, whose moderate view—we shall see—demarcates itself from others', seems occasionally to romanticize the poor.[23] Throughout its history, the church has tended to exhort believers to despise wealth. African Christians were not left out. During the missionary period, Africans have been introduced to a type of Christianity "which glorifies poverty to the point that African converts loathe profit."[24] This "poverty gospel" is unfortunately still prevalent in Africa, especially among mainline churches, though another brand of Christianity "which glorifies economic prosperity"[25] is being witnessed in every part of the continent. The problem this new trend of "prosperity gospel" poses is the difficulty in delineating "any observable difference between pastoral ministry and the entertainment industry."[26] And one wonders whether this prosperity gospel is not another tool for exploiting poor people and robbing them of whatever wealth and moral dignity they may still have.

Because they are extremely religious people and strongly believe that life continues after death, Africans appear more than other peoples ultimately concerned about salvation, and they take quite seriously biblical and theological teachings that condemn wealth, exhort them to give up everything to follow Jesus, and urge them to invest in heaven. From the beginning of the church in Africa, African converts have been taught that if they are poor on earth, compensation will come in heaven when they die. The command of Jesus Christ to his followers to take neither silver nor gold and his admonition to disciples to "sell all that [they] have and follow [him]" have been interpreted literally.[27] So while missionaries were becoming traders, Africans were expected to be passive and obedient observers of a Christian faith that tranquilizes their aspirations. Examples of this expectation from Africans abound in missionary practices. "When missionaries first arrived at the Cape in 1799," Roger B. Beck has observed, "they brought Bibles in their right hands, and beads and buttons in their left hands."[28] Beck nevertheless tempers his observation by the fact that early missionaries were poor, and they were liable to have to trade in order to survive. He justifies their actions thus: "The conditions under which they worked and the African societies among whom they lived obliged them to become traders upon their arrival in the Cape Colony. They did not always accept this commercial role willingly, but they often had little choice. The missionary societies responsible for their well-being did not always provide adequate funds, living allowances and supplies for these men (some of whom were accompanied by their wives and children) to exist in the isolated surroundings of the Cape interior."[29]

It will do justice to clarify that not all the missionaries became traders. The more devout understood their mission as a sacred calling, and they strenuously opposed the idea of trade with the African societies they had come to convert to Christianity. But these latter, who found it difficult to mingle secular activities with their evangelical calling, represent only a minority. "The majority traded and justified their actions either as necessary for their survival outside of the colony, or as a positive means of instilling European customs and beliefs. . . . A few felt more of a call to trade than to proselytize and abandoned forever the holy book for the account book."[30]

In their "civilizing mission," indeed, missionaries have been successful in instilling some European customs and beliefs in their mission field, but it is doubtful that they have ever encouraged any commercial effort among Africans. The then market of supply and demand was limited, and the right thing to do for any trade-minded person would be to put up some restrictions (moral or legal) that would help avoid any potential competition. Africans were thus discouraged from engaging in secular activities where they could make money or profits; making money had been presented to them as serving Mammon. It was the business of the traders or colonial settlers to make money and serve Mammon. The business of the African converts, according to the missionary teaching, was to serve God.[31] African Christians' attitudes toward wealth and the means to acquire it thus remained strongly influenced by this received missionary tradition on the matter. The question then arises whether these missionary teachings were part of a scheme to keep Africans out of the profits their natural resources might generate.

It was Peter Hinchliff's contention that there was "no evidence of missionary conspiracy to keep Africa in subjection to Europe."[32] This may seem true in consideration of the overall role missionaries have played in Africa in terms of education, health services, and other rescue missions. Many were sincere and believe in their civilizing mission. However, the blind collaboration between missionaries and colonial settlers witnessed in many mission fields suggests the existence of thoughts and ideas to keep Africans in subjection to Europeans. First of all, Africans were viewed as "savages," descendants of inferior species, never thought of as equals to Europeans, and it is hard to imagine that they were treated in a way different to the way they were viewed. Thoughts and ideas to subjugate them did exist; and these thoughts and ideas were generally expressed in informal discussions and table talk.

A Belgian document in *Avenir Colonial Belge*, dated 30 October 1921, supports the idea that a form of conspiracy existed between missionaries and colonial settlers in Congo to keep inhabitants of this region away from the riches of their soil and the advantages that these natural riches might generate. This should be no surprise to anyone who knows what happened in Congo, a region that King Leopold of Belgium considered his personal possession. The document is an excerpt of a discussion a certain Jules Renquin, minister of the colonies, had with the first Catholic missionaries in the Belgian Congo. According to the minister, he was asked to instruct missionaries to work hand in hand with the colonial administration.

In the style of a speech, the minister of the colonies starts by welcoming the missionaries as "Fellow Countrymen" to their "second fatherland," the Belgian Congo. He then proceeds to tell the missionaries that they had been sent to Congo not to serve the interests of Africans, but to work for the interests of Belgium. Therefore their interpretation of the Bible and their teachings must be done in the way that best serves Belgium's interests and smooths the progress of administrators, manufacturers, and traders in their contacts with Africans:

> The job you are invited to do here, is very delicate and requires a lot of tact. Priests, admittedly you have come to evangelize; but your evangelization must draw its inspiration from our great principle: "everything first and foremost for Belgium's interests." Therefore the main goal of your mission is not to teach Blacks to know God. They know God already. They talk about and submit themselves to a certain NZAMBE or a certain MVINDI-MUKULU, and so on. They know that killing, stealing, slandering, insulting, etc . . . is bad. Let's have the courage to confess that you have not come to teach Africans what they already know. Your role essentially consists in facilitating the job for administrators and manufacturers. This therefore is to say that you will interpret the gospel in the way that best serves our interests in this part of the world.[33]

The minister of the colonies then proposed to his audience a list of things that missionaries should see to in order to reach the goal that his administration had fixed. First, missionaries should not let Africans get interested in their natural riches by instilling in them the love of material resources.

Rather, they should find from the Bible teachings that recommend to believers the love of poverty, and try to keep Africans toward that inclination:

> Among other things, you will see to it to make our "savages" lose interest in the material wealth their soil and subsoil are brimming with, in order to avoid that being interested in, they bloody not compete with us, and dream of evicting us some day. Your knowledge of the Scriptures easily will help you find passages which recommend and get people to love poverty. For instance, passages like "Blessed are the poor, for the kingdom of heavens belongs to them"; and "it is easier for a camel to go through the eye of a needle than for a rich man to enter the kingdom of God." You will therefore do everything so that Blacks may be afraid of becoming rich in order to deserve Heaven.[34]

Thus the Beatitudes, which are meant to be an expression of Jesus' sympathy with those who are worse off in this world, an expression that their condition will not go uncompensated for, have been misinterpreted to condone poverty, adversity, and violence.

The audience was exhorted to help prevent any revolt or insurgence by teaching Africans to endure ill treatment, be passive in situations of conflicts and hostilities, and be forgiving when they are offended: "Contain them so that they may not rebel. From time to time, administrators and manufacturers will find themselves obliged to use violence (insults, beatings, etc . . .) to make themselves feared. Blacks would not retort or harbor feelings of revenge. For this, you will teach them to support everything. You will comment and invite them to follow the example of the saints who turned the other cheek, forgave their debtors, and received spits and insults without wincing."[35]

According to the minister of the colonies, Africans should be taught to be obedient and submissive. In missionary schools, no room should be left for youngsters being educated to develop critical thinking: "Insist particularly on blind obedience and submission. This virtue is better practiced when there is no room for criticizing. You should therefore avoid developing critical thoughts in your schools. Teach them to believe and not to think."[36] Most French-speaking countries in Africa unfortunately inherited this method of instruction, and this is still predominant in their system of education. The consequence of this is the observable difference in the social and economic development of these countries, worse in comparison to English-speaking countries in sub-Saharan Africa.

Further in the document that occupies us, the missionaries are instructed to use the sacrament of Confession as a means of detecting nationalists:

"Institute for them a system of confession which will make of you good detectives for denouncing all Black nurturing any self-awareness and claiming a National Independence."[37] Among his other recommendations, the minister of the colonies instructed missionaries to teach Africans to despise all that could give them the courage to affront Europeans, for example, the war fetishes that are said to make Africans invulnerable. The missionaries are promised protection from the administrators and financial support for their missionary work and trips, as well as free land and free labor for missionary constructions, because the king, Leopold, is said to attach great importance to their mission and their collaboration with the colonial administration.

Confronted with this Belgian document, historians could hardly deny that arrangements existed between some missionaries and colonial settlers to economically subjugate Africans to Europeans. Thus through their teachings Christian missionaries have encouraged faithful African Christians "to shun business and commerce, and be content with peasant economies."[38]

Apparently, the New Testament from which these missionaries in Africa culled so much of their teaching must have been the cause of their one-sided attitude toward wealth and poverty. Unlike the Old Testament, whose main premise is that all the world and its goods belong to God their creator, the New Testament describes the world as Satan's domain and portrays its inhabitants, especially Christians, as lost people "in the world," who are not "of the world." The natural human desire to acquire wealth is then regarded as evil or immoral—or worse, as worshipping Mammon, the god of wealth, and not as enjoyment of the goods God has created. Thus money changers will be thrown out of the temple on the charge that they are defiling a holy place. Possession of wealth will be presented not only as irrelevant to people whose kingdom and abode are not of this world but as an absolute barrier to salvation: do not store up for yourselves treasures on earth . . . store up for yourselves treasures in heaven, or blessed are the poor, for they shall inherit the kingdom of heaven, and cursed are the rich, for hell is their inheritance! Consequently in the parable of Lazarus and the rich man, it is the rich man who looks up from his torment to the poor man in Abraham's bosom. Could it be otherwise? Does not Christ himself bear the features of a poor man? New Testament writers portray him not only prohibiting his followers from using and pursuing wealth of all kinds but also demonstrating his own poverty: he was born in a manger because his parents could not afford a room in a motel; he had to borrow a coin to illustrate his teaching to "render unto Caesar" the taxes one owes; apart from his clothes, finally torn up by Roman soldiers when he was arrested, he apparently had no private property over which he could claim ownership. He and his disciples had a common purse carried by one of theirs, Judas. That is why this latter was the one to have gone astray, presumably because of his love of money. Similarly, Ananias and his wife, Sapphira, will die for having kept back some of the money from the sale of their property. Thus the need is established for the Christian to renounce the holding of private property as personal possession. This will be accepted by the members of the first community, either because of necessity (the money from the sales was distributed to each according to their needs)[39] or because of fear: "the church members were afraid," the author of the book of Acts has reported, "and so was everyone else who heard what had happened [to Ananias and Sapphira]."[40] Fear (of the unknown or of losing one's soul) is an element that cannot be neglected in the study of humans' attitude toward religious matters.

Manifestly in the New Testament writings, adulation of poverty (as the gateway to heaven) dominates approbation of wealth. In presenting wealth as an obstacle to heaven and the claim of private property as evil, New Testament writers have paved the way for an endorsement of poverty in subsequent Christians' teachings. It is not surprising that Christian missionaries in Africa have continued to interpret their writings to condone poverty, as if the church can only exist as a community of the poor.

Looking at the development of the church and its structure, "it is however undeniable that the post-Constantinian Church has been in many and various ways an immensely wealthy society, and that the acquisition of wealth has remained for most Christians and Christian societies an inescapable natural human desire."[41] Church historians know that "from an early stage in its development the Church became the largest landowner in Europe, creating its own princes, and from the proprietary churches of the medieval system to the lavish endowment of churches with treasures and monuments which has lasted into the modern period the Church has often seemed to be the outward and visible sign of an aristocracy at prayer."[42] Studies on religion, business, and wealth in modern Britain, for example, show that "even within the deliberate plainness of the Dissenting congregations there were those who took the lead in the industrial and commercial revolutions of the eighteenth and nineteenth centuries."[43] The great Quaker banking houses, the Methodists' and Congregationalists' business mentalités are cases in point.

Coming back to the Bible (which, should it be recalled, is the recorded history and experience of some peoples with God), it is clear that nobody can read it for long and fail to realize that "it is strewn with injunctions not to covet the neighbor's lands, houses, cattle . . . and other possessions; and that for much of their recorded history the Israelites were obsessed with the idea of *taking possession of the promised land and enjoying its overflows of milk and honey.*"[44]

In teaching African converts to "lay up for [themselves] treasures in heaven"[45] and discouraging them from enjoying their share of "milk and honey," Christian missionaries in Africa have obviously deviated from the traditional Christian teachings on the subject. They have chosen to limit themselves to poverty alone, and have taught it as if it represents the means necessary to deserve heaven. Augustine, the great doctor and theologian of the Church, characterized this one-sided understanding of the subject as heretical. In one of his many writings, *De Haeresibus*, Augustine informs us of a sect called the Apostolics, "who have arrogated this name to themselves because they do not receive into their communion those who . . . possess private property."[46] They are heretics, he describes them, "because they have separated themselves from the Church and think that there is no hope for those who make use of things that they themselves lack."[47] Augustine likewise attacks the Manicheans, who, because of their contempt of material reality, believe that the baptized should not own "fields or houses or any money."[48] Another group Augustine criticizes on this issue are the Pelagians, who taught that "a rich person, abiding in his wealth, is unable to enter the kingdom of God unless he sells all that he owns, nor will it be of any use to him should he observe the commandments by means of his wealth."[49] As the Apostolics, the Manicheans, and the Pelagians deviated from the mainstream of the patristic understanding of materiality and spirituality, so many Christian missionaries in Africa have departed from the right Christian teaching on the subject. A reading of this traditional teaching, from the early church via the Reformation period to the modern age, shows that neither the fathers of the church nor the reformers and subsequent teachers of the Christian faith limited themselves to poverty alone when they addressed issues of poverty, but they considered it in the context of wealth and private ownership. One may have noted a form of glorification of poverty here and there in the Christian tradition, but in their overall view on the subject, acknowledged spokespersons of the Church through the ages allowed, under certain circumstances, a legitimate place for wealth and the wealthy in the Christian scheme of things. In order for us to appreciate how much teachings on wealth and poverty in African churches have deviated from the right Christian teaching, I suggest that we now turn to look more closely at what has always been the teaching of the church on the subject.

Wealth and Poverty in the Traditional Teachings of the Church

Starting with the church fathers, the church's traditional approach to poverty was developed in conjunction with its approach to wealth. It was mainly how the wealthy were to treat the poor or how the rich were to use their wealth rightfully on behalf of God, rather than how the poor were to do away with their poverty, as if the poor had the duty to remain poor and be submissive to the rich. In other words, the church fathers' approach has rarely been a proposition on how the poor should go about acquiring wealth; it has rather been how the wealthy should *not* go about their task of accumulating riches. In addressing the issue the way they did, it becomes nevertheless unequivocal that the fathers of the church and all subsequent teachers of the Christian faith do not condemn wealth per se, but the attitudes of the rich and the ways by which their wealth is acquired. How could one fulfill the scriptural injunction to give to the poor if one was poor oneself? How could the Christian work ethic of the laborer being worthy of his hire be upheld if private property or personal possessions were to be denied? From the early church writings to recent papal encyclicals, wealth and private property have been acknowledged in one way or another in the Christian social teachings.

The patristic view on the matter may be characterized at best as moderate or neutral, at worse as ambiguous or ambivalent. The traditional line of argument for most church fathers starts with the admission that in reality all belongs to God. The world and its goods belong to God, their creator, and therefore the world's goods cannot justly be claimed as private property by any single individual or group of individuals. Humans really own nothing of their own. They are simply *stewards* of the divine wealth. Chrysostom asks, "Is not the earth God's and the fullness thereof?"[50] In Lactantius's words, God has put the world's goods at the disposal of all people "so that all may enjoy the goods [which the land produces] in common, and not in order that someone with grasping greed may claim everything to himself while [others are] deprived of the things the earth produces for all."[51] Accordingly, for anyone to claim ownership of what should be owned in common or be shared equitably among humans is, in the words of Gregory the Great, "an act of theft."[52] Augustine is more cautious: "Seeking wealth, like the pursuit of political power, for their own sakes," he says, "is theft: there is no true property right, because wealth cannot be rightful. Property in itself is a stolen property," because as he says elsewhere, "you cannot have more except at somebody else's expense: they must lose for you to gain; for you to inherit, someone must die. You cannot live without harming others, and trying to prevent them from doing to you what you are doing to them."[53]

This means that wealth and private ownership were not completely rejected by the church fathers. They were allowed under certain circumstances. Wealth, the fathers agree, is the root of all evil: it is always potentially dangerous and carries with it a permanent risk of corruption. But however evil it might become or to whichever sin it might lead, wealth remains, in the teaching of the fathers, a divine creation, and could be used to achieve good works and good deeds, and ultimately obtain salvation. As Augustine has asked, "Should the righteous shun such things [as] peace and quiet, order and abundance, plenty of all things in [his] houses and cities? Did not Abraham's house abound with gold and silver, children, servants, cattle?"[54] Even when Augustine considers these earthly possessions to "be happiness only on the left hand, the left hand of temporal, mortal, bodily things,"[55] he still acknowledges their importance for human sustenance and well-being. "I am not asking you to shun them," he exhorts, "but you must never make the mistake of thinking of them to be on the right hand, the right of God, of eternity, of years that fail not. Let us use the left hand for the time being, but ardently desire and long for the right hand to achieve eternity."[56]

In sum, for the fathers, the mere possession of wealth was not wrong, provided it was used for good ends—charitably or rightfully—and not desired for itself. Desiring wealth for its own sake, or falling into the pride and avarice that go with it, was that against which the fathers warned. Again, it is Augustine's words that summarize clearly and succinctly the mainstream position of the fathers of the church on the subject: "Gold and silver are bad for the bad and good for the good—not that gold and silver make people good, but that they are turned to good use when they are in hands of good people."[57] Teaching like Augustine's would have been beneficial to African believers, instead of teaching them to shun wealth. It would have influenced their manner of life and practices and helped them ameliorate the quality of their life. How could moneymaking continue to be regarded as serving Mammon while the banknote of the most blessed country of our time bears the motto "In God we trust"?[58] Since Constantine's interference in the church's affairs, a shift has occurred in the church's attitude to wealth and private property. The evangelical prohibitions on wealth have been defied and the capacity to hold wealth as private property acknowledged under certain circumstances to both clergy and laity. Even in the monastic orders, most of whose members came from the nobility, poverty was not material but rather spiritual in nature. Monasteries were frequently comfortable and occasionally magnificent. The medieval church was materially rich; and it was its material wealth—associated with the developing money economy of the eleventh century—that was at the origin of the mendicant movements with their emphasis on the abandonment of material wealth. This material wealth, and the avarice into which it could not prevent the ecclesial lords from falling, later played a certain role in the reformers' attacks on church authority, as well as in their continual calls for government control on unrestrained greed.[59]

But the church reformers, like the fathers, did not condemn wealth per se. They perceived wealth as a divine blessing. In Calvin's words, "Riches and poverty, contempt and honor, are dispensed by [God's] will."[60] Recent studies done by historians on the Reformation and social change give hints on the reformers' attitude to wealth and poverty.[61] Indeed, as Lindberg has well stated, "in attacking the theological idea that poverty is a virtue as well as an opportunity for the rich to do good works of almsgiving, Luther and other Reformers such as Zwingli and Calvin exposed the social roots of poverty and contributed to the development of social welfare programs directed to systemic, and not merely individual change."[62] But how could the Reformation enact legislation that instituted a "common chest" to support social welfare, subsidize education, give low-interest loans to poor workers and tradesmen, and train people for jobs, and how could that legislation be effective, if one had no money or goods to offer and endow? Reformers did acknowledge the legitimacy for individuals to own wealth and do business. Anyway, with their new ethos of vocation, they undercut the medieval dualism of the sacred and the secular. In other terms, in emphasizing that all mundane tasks hold religious value, the reformers instituted a change in the understanding of spirituality and materiality. This normally meant that money could no longer be associated with Mammon.

Likewise, because they are a divine blessing, material riches should not be understood as the result of a personal achievement of the individual. Material wealth is a blessing to be shared with the whole human community. Conversely, poverty is an expression of the divine wrath not toward the individual but toward the sin of humankind. Accordingly, the whole human community should work to alleviate the plight of the poor and eventually eradicate poverty. Among theologians and preachers that succeeded the reformers, John Wesley appeared to be the one who understood this more clearly. He regarded poverty as an evil that had to be fought by every possible means, and did even better in terms of having possessions and gaining wealth.[63] He has given modern Europe the best approach to the question of "religion, business and wealth" when he recommended that Christians are to "gain all they can, save all they can, and give all they can."[64] Wesley echoes Augustine when he acknowledges that "money is the root of all evil," but affirms that the fault is not with the money itself, but with the person who uses it. Used well, it has many advantages, particularly for the hungry, the thirsty, the naked, and the stranger, as well as for the widow and orphan. It can be used in stewardship to provide for their needs. Using it well will make us faithful stewards in the cause against the "Mammon of unrighteousness."[65]

In sum, if we are to be logically faithful to the teachings of the reformers and their succeeding generation of Nonconformists—teachings whose point of reference is the teachings of the church fathers—we should take every association of money with Mammon, every fostering of the belief that poor or subjugated people bear the curse of God, every "blame the victim, praise the achiever" ideology in our modern times, to be nothing but false teachings, individualist and inhuman theologies.

Conclusion

Because they are "symbols which act to establish powerful, persuasive, and long-lasting moods and motivations" in human beings, religious teachings have human consequences. They help or hurt people, strengthen or weaken them, advance or diminish the quality of their life. In late nineteenth- and early twentieth-century Europe, the teachings of the Christian religion to some extent served to advance the quality of life of many Europeans. In Great Britain for instance, where churchmen among business leaders were numerous, it was claimed that a religious worldview could serve to stimulate a valorization of economic activity. It is reported that "in some denominations business failure among members had been regarded as likely evidence of moral failure which therefore required investigation by church deacons and elders."[66] This way of linking religious beliefs with economic life paved the way for the association of Christianity with commerce during the missionary era. Echoes of the facility with which commerce and Christianity were coupled together are found with committed advocates of such thought like Bishop Samuel Wilberforce and David Livingstone.

Speaking in May 1860 at Leeds on behalf of the Universities' Mission to Central Africa, Bishop Samuel Wilberforce championed the view that there is a strong connection between Gospel and commerce: "There is a great connection between them, he argued. In the first place, there is little hope of promoting commerce in Africa, unless Christianity is planted in it; and, in the next place, there is very little ground for hoping that Christianity will be able to make its proper way unless we can establish a lawful commerce in the country."[67] Indeed, inside the church, it was largely believed that commerce was a providential gift to ease the way of mission and evangelism. As it was believed and proclaimed, "Commerce is a mighty machinery laid down in the wants of man by the Almighty Creator of all things, to promote the intercourse and communion of one race with another, and especially of the more civilized races of the earth with the less civilized."[68] Or in other words, "The providence of God . . . has ordained that when Christianity is placed in any great center, it should be borne everywhere by the natural power of commerce itself. . . . Commerce . . . is intended to carry, even to all the world, the blessed message of salvation."[69] Likewise, for Bishop Wilberforce's fellow countryman David Livingstone, "Christianity and commerce are two pioneers of civilization and should ever be inseparable."[70] This "providentialist" belief, expressed on numerous occasions, became the pattern of thinking very common in nineteenth-century Britain. Thus, Christian people were regarded as "a wealth producing people, an exporting people, and so, a commercial people."[71] This pattern of thinking served to increase widespread interest for Christian mission to the point where it became difficult to say which of commerce and Christian mission brought the most support or contribution to the other.

Another religious worldview that appears to have served to stimulate a valorization of economic activity is Calvinism, as developed by Max Weber.[72] Whatever Weber may have said or intended, and whichever controversy his theory and methodology may have provoked, agreements have emerged that Calvinist theology did provide a certain tonic that fostered economic virtues. Thus, in Wilberforce's Britain or in Weber's Germany, some teachings of the Christian religion appear to have encouraged an economic spirit. This seems not to be the case when the same religion was exported abroad to supposed uncivilized heathens.

In the mission fields, the pattern of thinking instilled into "the less civilized" was to frown upon trade and despise wealth. Though the necessity of money was admitted, and new exportable agricultural products were introduced into Africa (primarily for the benefit of the introducers), the making of money for its own sake had been condemned as sin and concupiscence. Moneymaking was regarded as morally and religiously dangerous. The notion that the rich person could only with difficulty please God thus found its way into consciences and continues to impact the lives of many Christians in Africa.

The importance of a religion, however, lies in its capacity to serve humans and make them blossom, spiritually as well as materially. Taken either as divine institution or as social organization, the purposes of religion cannot exclude its concern for the full development of humans, in their souls as well as in their bodies. When religion does not reach such a goal or fails to fulfill such a purpose, it becomes a bad religion. With regard to the subject that occupies us, the Christian religion in Africa runs the risk of being declared a "bad religion" if the churches fail in their special obligation to the poor and the vulnerable, or in their moral responsibility to protect and enhance the dignity of the human person. As they are dealing with embodied souls, African churches should not ignore the basic questions of existence of their members, nor think about any aspect of the Christian faith without reassessing its impact on the life of the human person. Christian education in Africa should rethink its teachings on wealth and poverty. This would unequivocally be the starting point in our efforts to alleviate poverty among African people, and eventually eradicate it from the earth.

Notes

1. The concept of poverty itself is very complex, and there is a considerable debate about the most suitable description and definition of the phenomenon. It can be described and defined in many different ways, depending on the historical, social, and economic setting. The description I quote is the one proposed by Mollat in "The Poor in the Middle Ages," quoted by Carter Lindberg in *Beyond Charity: Reformation Initiatives for the Poor* (Minneapolis: Fortress Press, 1993).
2. See Auguste Marcon, "Les Faiseurs de pauvres," in *L'Eglise et les pauvres: Journal d'un travailleur manuel* (Paris: Harmattan, 2002), 11–12.
3. For example, during his 2000 presidential campaign, the forty-third president of the United States, George W. Bush, clearly stated that though Africa was important, it did not fit into the American national and strategic interest. (See *New York Times*, 5 July 2003.) The world's most powerful leader having openly said this, his own visit to Africa three years later, and the one of his predecessor Bill Clinton five years before, rather appear to present Africans as people at the mercy of Western generous people whose interests and goals are elsewhere, but who have decided to silence the voice of their conscience by giving to Africa aid and charity that hardly reach the poor populations or meet their expectations.
4. As a member of the Pan-African Seminar Group on Religion and Poverty, I had the privilege to visit some of these development, charitable, and welfare programs in the countries we visited; for instance, in Kenya, I saw Nyumbani, the Children of God Relief Institute in Nairobi, which cares for HIV-positive orphans; Nyumba ya Wazee, the hospice for poor and very destitute elderly run by the Little Sisters of the Poor; also at Athi River, the Seventh Day Adventist Church's program of primary education for Masai girls, customarily married off as children. The Catholic Relief Services run agriculture, community health, and education programs in other African countries as well. On a strictly academic level, see, for example, the initiatives of the World Council of Churches and the Lutheran World Federation described in the three volumes written and edited by Julio de Santa Ana: *Good News to the Poor: The Challenge of the Poor in the History of the Church* (Geneva: World Council of Churches, 1977); *Separation without Hope? Essays on the Relation between the Church and the Poor during the Industrial Revolution and the Western Colonial Expansion* (Geneva: World Council of Churches, 1978); and *Towards a Church of the Poor* (Geneva: World Council of

Churches, 1979); see also Béla Harmati, ed., *Christian Ethics: Property and Poverty* (Geneva: Lutheran World Federation, 1985). There is also the Latin American Roman Catholic Church's liberation theology, with its "preferential option for the poor," and its method of theological reflection from "the underside of history."

5. Carter Lindberg, *Beyond Charity: Reformation Initiatives for the Poor* (Minneapolis: Fortress Press, 1993), 2.
6. Ibid.
7. David Steinmetz, *Luther in Context* (Bloomington: Indiana University Press, 1986), ix.
8. The topic, as proposed, is essentially intellectual and theological, and the approach will be from the standpoint of *mentalités*, or the social history of ideas. My essay will deal with how a particular religious idea has evolved in time and space and raise the question of its social consequences. It is not my intent to indict Christian missions in the era of colonialism. Rather, I aim at obtaining light from the past on problems and ideas which are still with us. Western scholars have investigated the influences of religious teachings and enthusiasm on their people. It is important in our collaborative scholarship, and in the new venture of globalization, to look at the way the apparently same religious teachings and enthusiasm have evolved in other contexts. Moreover, whenever an inquiry is made into the influences of colonialism and Christian mission on the "well-being" of Africans, such research seldom takes into account the impact of Christian teachings on the existential struggles of Africans. As we are nowadays more than ever aware of the fact that interpretations and evaluations of facts and events always are made from a certain perspective or point of view, it is important for scholarship to evaluate such investigation also from the point of view of an African.
9. Abdoul Hamidou Sy, "African Realities," *The Great Challenges of Africa, The Train of Urban and Rural Mission* 1 (January–December 2002): 6–9.
10. Education is the sector that suffers the most in Africa. Out of 854 million adult illiterates in the world (United Nations estimation of 2002), more than one-third are in Africa. And of the continent's population of 778.5 million individuals, about 41 percent over fifteen years of age are illiterates. The percentage of young girls under eighteen in full-time education is less than 35 percent, and their insertion becomes a serious problem for the whole of Africa.
11. Sy, "African Realities," 8.
12. Ibid.
13. Statistics adapted from *World Christian Encyclopedia*, ed. D. B. Barrett (Nairobi: Oxford University Press, 1982) and John S. Mbiti, *Bible and Theology in African Christianity* (Nairobi: Oxford University Press, 1986).
14. Alyward Shorter, *Religious Poverty in Africa* (Nairobi: Paulines Publications Africa, 1999), 8.
15. Ibid.
16. Ibid.
17. Cf. the Mustard Seed Program of the Catholic Church in the Spanish Town section of Kingston, Jamaica.
18. Shorter, *Religious Poverty in Africa*, 7.
19. Ibid.
20. Philomena N. Mwaura, "Religion, Poverty, and the African Instituted Churches," paper presented at the Pan-African Seminar on Religion and Poverty, in Nairobi, Lorento Mary Ward Center, 23 July 2001, 2.

21. Ibid.
22. For Ambrose, see *Exameron* 6.8.52; for John Chrysostom, see *Homily on Matthew* 53.6, *Homily on John* 22.3, and *On Poverty and Almsgiving*; for Prudentius, see *Peristephanon* 2.186ff.
23. See *Enarratio in Psalmo* 127.16.
24. J. N. K. Mugambi, "Christianity and Poverty in Contemporary Africa," paper presented at the Seminar on Religion and Poverty, Nairobi, 16–27 July 2001, 3.
25. Ibid.
26. Ibid.
27. On not accepting silver and gold, see Matthew 10:9; compare Luke 9:3, Acts 3:6, 1 Peter 1:18. On selling all and following Jesus, see Matthew 19:21, Mark 10:21, Luke 12:33 and 18:22.
28. Roger B. Beck, "Bibles and Beads: Missionaries as Traders in Southern Africa in the Early Nineteenth Century," *Journal of African History* 30, no. 2 (1989): 211.
29. Ibid. For a brief discussion of the monetary and material support received by missionaries from the London Missionary Society, see Richard Lovett, *The History of the London Missionary Society, 1795–1895*, vol. 1 (London, 1899), 507–8, 529, 540.
30. Ibid.
31. Mugambi, "Christianity and Poverty in Contemporary Africa," 3.
32. Peter Hinchliff, "Africa," in *Oxford History of Christianity*, ed. John McManners (Oxford: Oxford University Press, 1993), 502.
33. "Les Devoirs des missionnaires dans notre colonie," *Avenir colonial belge*, Brussels, 30 October 1921.
34. Ibid.
35. Ibid.
36. Ibid.
37. Ibid.
38. Ibid., 4.
39. Acts 2:44–45; 4:32–35.
40. Acts 5:11.
41. M. Wilks, "Thesaurus Ecclesiae (Presidential Address)," in *The Church and Wealth, Studies in Church History* 24, ed. W. J. Sheils and Diana Wood (Oxford: Basil Blackwell, 1987), xv.
42. Ibid.
43. Ibid.
44. Ibid., xvi. See further, W. D. Davies, *The Gospel and the Land: Early Christianity and Jewish Territorial Doctrine* (Berkeley: University of California Press, 1974).
45. Matt. 6:20.
46. *De Haeresibus* 40. See also Boniface Ramsey in *Augustine through the Ages: An Encyclopedia*, ed. A. D. Fitzgerald (Grand Rapids, Mich.: Wm. B. Eerdmanns, 1999), 877.
47. Ibid.
48. *De moribus ecclesiae* 1.34.75–1.35.77, and its twin text, *The Catholic and Manichaean Ways of Life* 1.34.75–1.35.77.
49. *Epistula* 157.23.
50. See P. C. Phan, ed., *Social Thought: Message of the Fathers of the Church* (Wilmington, Del.: Glazier, 1984), 159.
51. Ibid., 95.
52. *Homiliarum in evangelia* 2.40, 3 (*PL* 76, cols. 1304–5). See also "The Problem of

Private Ownership in Patristic Thought," *Studia Patristica* 6, Tubingen 81 (1962): 533–42.

53. *De civitate Dei* 19.12; *Enarratio in Psalmos* 64.9. See also Michael Wilks, "Thesarus Ecclesiae," *The Church and Wealth: Studies in Church History* 24 (1987): 38.

54. *Enarratio in Psalmos* 143.18.

55. Ibid.

56. Ibid.

57. *Sermons* 72.4; cf. 48.8; 61.3; 311.9.

58. Note that almost all the presidents of the United States of America end their speeches with the words "God bless America."

59. See further Carter Lindberg's *Beyond Charity*; also his articles in *Christianity: A Social and Cultural History*, ed. Howard Kee et al. (Upper Saddle River, N.J.: Prentice Hall, 1998), 207ff.

60. R. C. Gamble, ed., *Calvin's Thought on Economic and Social Issues and the Relationship of Church and State*, vol. 2, *Articles on Calvin and Calvinism* (New York: Garland, 1992), 128.

61. See for instance Lindberg, *Beyond Charity*; also his articles in Kee et al., *Christianity*.

62. Kee et al., *Christianity*, 268.

63. M. T. Marquardt, ed., *John Wesley's Social Ethic: Praxis and Principles* (Nashville, Tenn.: Abingdon, 1992), 43.

64. Ibid., 37. See also W. R. Ward, "Methodism and Wealth," in *Religion, Business and Wealth in Modern Britain*, ed. David J. Jeremy (London: Routledge, 1998), 63–70.

65. See George W. Forell, *Christian Social Teachings: A Reader* (Minneapolis: Augsburg, 1966), 275–76.

66. David J. Jeremy, *Capitalists and Christians* (Oxford: Clarendon, 1990), 53.

67. Quoted by Andrew Porter, "Commerce and Christianity: The Rise and Fall of a Nineteenth-Century Mission Slogan," *Historical Journal* 28.3 (1985): 597.

68. Henry Rowley, ed., *Speeches on Missions* (London: Wm. Wells Gardner, 1874), 176–77.

69. Ibid., 212.

70. William Monk, ed., *Dr Livingstone's Cambridge Lectures* (Cambridge: Deighton, Bell, 1858); Porter, "Commerce and Christianity," 598.

71. Ibid.

72. See Max Weber, *The Protestant Ethic and the Spirit of Capitalism* (London: Routledge, 1992).

Esther M. Mombo | **RELIGION AND MATERIALITY**

THE CASE OF POVERTY ALLEVIATION

It is generally accepted these days that Africa is caught up in a trap created by the global culture of power vested in the private institutions of the market. As the Arusha Charter states, "We are united in our conviction that the crisis currently engulfing Africa is not only an economic crisis but also a human, legal and social crisis. It is a crisis of unprecedented and unacceptable proportions manifested not only in abysmal declines in economic indicators and trends, but more tragically and glaringly in the suffering, hardship and impoverishment of the vast majority of African people."[1] Those who advocate for poverty reduction programs would argue that the way out of this is through reparation, debt relief, and/or fair trade. Although this is a familiar argument, it is too simplistic when applied to the African situation. Indications are that Africa's marginalization and poverty have continued to worsen. This is true among Africans in the diaspora too. The situation is viewed as an entanglement of complex systems that results in a poverty trap. You cannot disentangle yourself from one system without dealing with the other. In that complex, you have material poverty, physical weakness, isolation, vulnerability, powerlessness, and spiritual poverty all working to reinforce the chains of poverty that are so hard to escape.

In the cities of Accra, Nairobi, Johannesburg, and Kingston, where I visited as part of this Pan-African religion and poverty project, it was clear that the majority of people in those cities were poor, particularly those living in areas that were slums. A visit to Mathare, Kenya, and to one of the churches there was a case in point. It is in this connection that Carol Mandi observes that "there is a grinding poverty humorously referred to as Kenya's only growth industry at the moment—that is now becoming a cliché as the government continues with the Poverty Reduction Strategy Paper talks in various provinces."[2]

The contemporary basic concern of people worldwide seems to be with economic matters. This is evident from a simple content analysis of any randomly selected issue of a newspaper anywhere in the world. One can always find a newspaper filled with consumer advertisements and references to banks, globalization, debt relief for poor nations, and poverty alleviation programs. In the same newspaper one also finds ads from religious circles dealing with the issues of poverty alleviation in various ways, including prayers of deliverance from poverty. The interaction between spirituality and materiality has manifested itself, particularly, in the emergence of a new phenomenon of religious commercialization. There is a visible mushrooming of seemingly "Christian" religious groups, which interpret salvation in terms of material relief and the quick-fix solution of material poverty of individuals. The theological content of their preaching is popularly known as "prosperity gospel."[3]

From a secular perspective, methods for poverty alleviation include (as noted above) reparation, debt relief, and/or fair trade. And indeed, movements such as Jubilee 2000 emerged from discussions among the World Bank, the Anglican provinces in Africa, and the Anglican Lambeth conference of 1998.[4] Jubilee's goal was later adopted by Protestants, Catholics, and others round the world. This essay seeks to investigate the historical developments of such poverty alleviation specifically by the church and the involvement of the church in debt relief.

I argue that if the church is going to be involved with poverty alleviation, it needs to seek a more permanent strategy than merely putting food into people's mouths or coins in their wallets. Such a strategy would transcend the bounds of mere religion and theology and would seek to integrate the best of other disciplines such as economics, science, and ethics, to name but a few.

The Beginnings of the Church and Poverty Alleviation in Africa

Material poverty is a relative concept. People in precolonial Africa may have been poor by contemporary Western standards, but they did not necessarily regard themselves as poor.[5] In fact by their own criteria, some of them might have been extremely rich. But the interaction between Africa and the West through the European voyages of world discovery, the transatlantic slave trade, and colonial and missionary expansion was motivated by the impulses of religion, commerce, and politics.[6] The effects of the three motives cannot be rubbed out or swept aside easily. The way Europe viewed Africa helped formulate their policies and mission programs.

The Christian mission in particular had a conviction to convert the people to Christianity, through which they would improve the living standards of the African peoples whom they saw as poor in comparison to themselves. The Africans were depicted as people who were both poor and living in deplorable situations.

David Livingstone, who came to Africa with the London Missionary Society, said in a lecture at the University of Cambridge on 4 December 1857, "I beg to direct your attention to Africa. I know that in a few years I shall be cut off in that country, which is now open. Do not let it be shut again! I go back to Africa to try and make an open path for Commerce and Christianity; do you carry out the work which I have begun. I LEAVE IT WITH YOU!"[7]

It is in this context that most mission societies developed ways to alleviate poverty. The first way was to introduce Christianity through evangelism; this was meant to deal with the spiritual life of the person. The second way was through health and or medical work to deal with health issues. The third way was through formal education, so that people would be employed to earn a living. Formal education was gendered, so men got more education, which equipped them with knowledge and skills to participate fully in society and have more central and secure positions in society. Women, on the other hand, received education to help them become evangelists and Christian mothers. In terms of poverty this led them to be among the poorest and most vulnerable people in society. The fourth way was through industrial training in order for people to learn skills to improve their living. It was the responsibility of God to change the inside of the human beings while the missionary improved the outside with what were seen as adequate skills.

Across Africa these were ways that the mission societies used to help people alleviate poverty, as it was seen then.[8] During this period of mission establishment, there was a strong link between spirituality and materiality. Those who managed to join the mission schools or stations at the time were the ones who benefited from material prosperity. They changed their lifestyles and modeled them on the missionary styles, even in simple things like housing.

The missionary experience as a modernizing experience was supported by the colonial enterprise. This type of modernization did not fit into the indigenous legacy. Instead, the colonial and missionary projects took their stand from the assumption that useful history in Africa was that which started with them taking over. Anything that had existed before was considered valueless to the needs of the African society at the time. Africans, unlike other human beings, were prevented from modernizing from a basis of their own culture. Instead, modernization was within the framework of existing

economic, political, and military domination and racist attitudes and behavior. These behaviors and attitudes undoubtedly infected mission societies and their personnel.[9]

During the colonial administration some mission societies in some African countries received financial assistance through what were called grants-
in-aid to run health care and education services under their management.
Most contemporary mainline churches inherited the mission structures
without the necessary resources to run them, and they were thus not able to
deal with the situations of poverty.

The people who were able to pass through the colonial economic and
social systems managed to gain material things, which moved them from
one class to the other. But even within this class there were those who did
not make it and remained an underclass. The mission societies, together
with colonial systems, helped create cities, and it is in the cities that one now
finds people living in abject poverty; examples are Mathare and Kibera Valley
in Nairobi, Kenya.[10] These places, where the majority of poor people live, are
also places where there is too much religion. There are more churches than
toilets, and one wonders how the people cope with the call of nature. One
may ask what the connection is between religion and toilets. There is a
connection, in that the role of religion is seeing the development of the
whole person. And if cleanliness is next to godliness, then a religion that
ignores the living conditions of its members is deficient.

Although the mission societies acted to alleviate poverty from the African
people during the colonial period, Africans who fought for their independence viewed them as linked up with the colonial forces. Consequently, most
of those who sought independence founded their own churches rather than
stay in the churches that preached equality but did not practice it. These
churches were known as African independent churches and later as African
instituted churches. In Kenya, for example, some of the adherents of the
original independent churches are those whose families physically fought in
the war of independence. After the war of independence, most of these
people were pushed to the periphery of society because they did not have
resources that could help them in the independent states. Most of their
churches are on the periphery of the cities, especially in the slums.

Poverty Alleviation during the Independence Era

When most African countries gained independence from colonial rule in the
1960s, the feeling of well-being that swept across the continent was infectious. Leaders such as Dr. Kwame Nkrumah of Ghana counseled Africans to

seek first the political kingdom and the rest would be added later; his advice captures not only the naiveté at the heart of this choice but also brings out the ironic commitment of Africans to the inheritance of the colonial state structures, which have remained almost unchanged in most African countries. This is despite the fact that the leaders could see the problems of poverty, disease, and ignorance and called on people to work hard.[11]

For a while there was a marked economic growth in the world, which was extended in a marginal way to Africa as well. But this prosperity was short-lived because of the leadership wrangles among the leaders, leading to coups-d'état in a good number of governments. What followed was a rapid increase in poverty levels as the economies that had been thriving began to collapse. Infrastructure became dilapidated; school buildings and the quality of education deteriorated. Real income per capita dropped by 14.6 percent from its levels at independence. Several reasons account for this decline. Some of them are external, while others are internal. Africa became a testing ground for developmental policies by foreign agencies.

In the meantime, African leaders became obsessively preoccupied with the issue of their own survival, so much so that they had no time to improve the lives of the poor in their respective countries. As a result, the ideals that were embodied in the people's wars of independence were abandoned and the nationalistic cause ultimately betrayed. The result of this was that political independence did not lead to economic autonomy as had been predicted with the coming of independence.

As this was happening, the churches that had become independent from mission societies began to look at the issue of poverty alleviation to help their members. In Kenya, for example, the national Council of Churches established village polytechnics from 1966 to provide youth with marketable skills.[12] The village polytechnic scheme was a challenge to the elite education given in schools, which led to many school dropouts, who joined the vicious circle of poverty. After the polytechnics, the church developed colleges of technology to help give people skills that they could use to earn a good living and thus move away from being poor. In order to alleviate poverty the church had to invest in people skills so that they could be self-employed. The sector of self-employment later to be known as jua kali has continued to be a major aspect in resisting or alleviating poverty.[13]

As well as the development of village polytechnics, the National Council of Churches and its member churches embarked on large development projects that had to do with basic health, agriculture, gender issues, animal husbandry, and small-scale businesses. The church's aim was to alleviate poverty by empowering people rather than giving them handouts.[14] Develop-

ment in terms of small-scale business was one way the church was responding to poverty and taking note of economic issues.

One church leader who took seriously the notion of poverty alleviation
was the late Rt. Rev. Bishop John Henry Okullu. He served in a rural region,
which was riddled with poverty, unemployment, degraded social services
(schools, hospitals), and other shortcomings. Bishop Okullu noted that if
people had access to credit facilities they could improve their lifestyles. He,
together with others, started a micro-lending program. Since the banks in
this area did not offer poor people credit, the poor were not able to participate in economic development because they lacked access to loans.[15]

The situation of people in the poor nations got worse in the 1980s with
the introduction of structural adjustment programs (SAPs). This was a policy encouraged by the International Monetary Fund as a way to economic
recovery for poorer nations that were struggling. The loans given to a country were granted or rescheduled on conditional principles of austerity, reduction in government spending, and devaluation of the currency.[16] As a result,
funding for education, health, and agriculture was cut. These were, however, the most important sectors for the poor nations because they dealt with
issues of life. Thus the poor were denied a chance to live even modestly well.

The eighties and the nineties saw such deterioration of the poor nations
that they were worse off than they had been during the colonial and independent periods. By the end of the century, one in five of the world's people lived
on less than one dollar a day.[17]

The alleviation of poverty was high on the agenda of most churches and
nongovernmental organizations (NGOs). Some of the NGOs were faith-
based; others were not. Several reasons account for the proliferation of
NGOs in poorer countries, the most salient of which was "a broad public
concern in the west with poverty, coupled with the emergence of a popular
form of third worldism among young people. NGOs were able to connect
with this public sentiment, either in its more conservative apolitical humanitarian form, as was important with the big NGOs or in its more radical
politicised form in which it challenged the West."[18] The NGOs worked with
communities on projects to help alleviate poverty. The churches in Kenya for
example began the Christian Community Services (CCS) to develop their
people and help them move out of the trap of poverty. The CCS were to do
this through income-generating projects for groups. The NGOs and the CCS
were taking over the roles the mission agencies had played in the preinde-
pendence era in Africa, when they provided services in all sectors of the
community life.[19] The two groups were to nurture "holistic development,"
which would contribute to poverty alleviation. However, development that is

based on income-generating projects seems not to have had much effect on the alleviation of poverty, as observed by S. I. Oladeji. "Targeting the poor by means of social programmes is the most direct approach, followed by the adoption of specific programmes to enhance the earning capacity of the poor. Both of these select the particular groups to be reached and therefore, presumably, reduce poverty immediately within these groups. The problem with these strategies in practice is the possibility of leakages of benefits to unintended groups. Administratively, they can be expensive to implement, inefficient in operation and outcome and lack sustainability."[20]

The reason why poverty alleviation by the NGOs, the religious institutions, and the government appears not to be taking root lies in the development models of modernization. These models go back to the Second World War, when the concept of development was synonymous with economic reconstruction and growth. In its classical sense, development theory referred to the level or mode of production of a given society's economy.

According to this model, African countries are somewhere between second and third stage, and depending on the policies they adopt, they can either stagnate or fast-track their development processes. While this version of development is no longer mainstream, it continues to linger in the models of some theorists.[21] The funding of the development programs run by the church was through donor agencies of the West, which saw themselves bringing progress to a "backward" world. The philosophy that informed such thinking was a linear historic process that links all nations' histories and experiences on a single plane, putting some ahead while others lag behind. Development thus became an alienating and humiliating process for the people who helplessly remain undeveloped.

This model of development was criticized by liberation theologians because it implied that the solution to poverty alleviation in the poor countries did not lie in mimicking the rich countries. At the same time the advantages that the rich countries enjoyed were a consequence, directly or indirectly, of their historic relationship with the poor countries.[22] This historic relationship includes slave trade and colonialism, which exploited Africa's wealth and sowed the seeds of poverty. The crucial issue here is that alleviation of poverty must of necessity be related to a particular context and that it must be comprehensively construed in relation to the diversity of factors that impact on the totality of human existence.

Alleviation of poverty through SAPs, NGOs, and CCs seems to have failed. This is because none of them worked toward making policies that the governments would adopt and implement for the sake of the poor. Policy implementation on poverty alleviation remains a matter of discussion.[23] The next move for the churches was the Jubilee 2000 proposal, which called for a cancellation of debt that the poor countries were paying to the World Bank and the International Monetary Fund.

The models of the so-called Bretton Woods institutions (i.e., the World Bank, the International Monetary Fund) applied to Africa were wrong prescriptions, mainly because the principal governing themes were devised after the Second World War and need revision in order to be relevant to third world countries in our time. The models and policies have produced few socioeconomic benefits but eroded a great many of the traditional strengths of the African society. Africa has been trying to develop herself out of wrong and inappropriate experience of Europe, rather than drawing on her own history and culture to benefit her people.

Break the Chains: The Jubilee 2000 Campaign for Debt Relief

"Must we starve our children to pay our debt?" Julius Nyerere once asked.[24] His remarks on that occasion were made in a wider move to relieve the third world of the yoke of debt through a campaign called Jubilee 2000. The history of Jubilee 2000 goes back to 1990, when Martin Dent, a fellow of Keele University, together with staff and students at Keele, founded the campaign. It was based on two incompatible requirements that had to be reconciled: on one hand, the need to uphold the general principle on which all banking and commerce depend, that is, that debts must be honored, and on the other, the need to remove the monstrous imbalance whereby poorer parts of the human family owe unpayable debt to the richer part.

The only way Dent and others considered to reconcile these two requirements was to have a special time (a jubilee) leading to a moment at the end of which there could be a new beginning. The idea was to seek for a period of time to forgive all debt, as in the old jubilee in ancient Israel. Such remission would break the continuous chain of special measures to reduce debt, an immensely tedious and time-consuming rescheduling process that was hobbling the poorer countries.

The religious basis of the jubilee concept is found in the Bible, and especially the books of Leviticus, Deuteronomy, Nehemiah, Isaiah 58 and 61, and Luke 4:18–19 (where Jesus speaks of a time of deliverance and liberty, the "acceptable year of the Lord"). The proximity of the year 2000 offered great potential to associate debt remission with the ideas of jubilee. According to Jonathan Sacks, "The Bible is candid in its appeal to lenders. Not only is debt relief a moral duty, it is in the long run a key to collective prosperity."[25]

The Christian Aid organization in Britain took up the Jubilee 2000 campaign as a move to help alleviate the poverty of the poor nations. The campaign for debt cancellation of the poorer nations was necessary because debt had brought untold miseries to many innocent people. First, paying off debt meant that the governments had less money to spend on education and other essentials like safe water and sanitation. It meant that the poor continued to suffer when money was diverted to rich countries and to the International Monetary Fund and World Bank. In many of the poor countries debt servicing had been the largest expenditure.

Second, when a country builds up debts that are too large for it to have a reasonable chance ever to pay off, it is said to have debt overhang. The problem with debt overhang is that it puts off investors, making it even more difficult for a country to get the resources it needs to develop.

Third, foreign debt has to be repaid in hard currency. So debtor countries had to find hard currency. This is why they had problems servicing their debts, as their sources were aid money and export earnings. But most poor countries did not earn enough through exports to manage their debts easily, and of course they also needed to import items like oil simply to keep going at all. So there is also an immediate cash flow problem. Poor countries are currently being pushed hard to export as much as possible, without much regard to the environmental or social consequences. The problem underlying the debt issue is that of trade and development.[26]

It is in this connection that Sacks notes, "Nothing is more effective in alleviating poverty than giving individuals the chance to create small business. But to allow debt to accumulate is also wrong. The economic system must encourage freedom, not financial slavery. That is why periodic debt release is necessary. It enables people to begin again freed of burdens of the past."[27]

In view of this the Jubilee 2000 campaign was twofold. First, it was aimed at asking the governments of the North to cancel bad, unpayable, and odious debts; and second, it was to make proper plans to avoid the further buildup of unpayable debt after the millennium. As much as there were good reasons why the third world debt should be cancelled, there were also reasons from the rich countries why the matter was not that simple.

The reasons against cancellation of debt put forward were, first, the moral hazard of debt cancellation. That is to say, if debt is cancelled it will encourage reckless future borrowing. The immorality of this argument came from allowing "children to starve to pay debt," in the words of Nyerere. The idea of moral hazard also wrongly placed all blame for debts on the borrower, but not the lender, who may have acted irresponsibly.

The second reason against debt cancellation was that of future creditworthiness. Would debt cancellation undermine the credit worthiness of poorer countries? While countries remained heavily indebted, they found it hard to attract credit; yet opponents of relief said cancellation would further undermine credit worthiness. Even the World Bank recognized that the vast majority of the highly indebted poor countries would never be able to pay off their crushing debt.

The third reason against cancellation of debt was corruption, through which aid was being lost. While this may have been a valid claim, corruption was not only an issue in the poor nations; it is a human issue. Both the poor and the rich were involved in corruption; both the lender and the receiver survived through networks that supported corruption in one way or another. In many ways it was in the interest of the rich nations to bolster the position of corrupt administrators because they were, and still remain, good markets for the export of arms and military equipment.

The fourth reason against debt cancellation was military spending. Why should the North cancel the debt of countries that spend money on arms? Arms spending is not the issue of one continent but of most countries. In fact the North spends more on arms than the South or the poor countries. The arms industries based in the North encourage the manufacture and sale of arms, while the South consumes them.

The Anglican Conference of Bishops, held every ten years at Lambeth, England, met in 1998 and addressed the issue of debt cancellation. James Wolfensohn, then president of the World Bank, addressed the gathering. In his address on the debt cancellation, he acknowledged the fact that "in many countries the payment of debt is a principal reason that social services could not be provided," but he argued that debt cancellation was not an easy thing to do. In reality, he said, "debt is part of life and there is a level where you can live with debt. That is both on an individual level and also as a country. . . . If the World Bank has to forgive debt then how will it survive?"[28]

In the Lambeth Conference, the church called for an economy that enhanced full humanity, arguing that the church can make the poor present and their voices heard. The church condemned the double standards of the debtor nations and the fact that money had more powerful rights than human rights.

Both the Lambeth Conference and the Jubilee 2000 campaign succeeded more in sensitizing the masses to the plight of poor countries than in making the rich governments cancel the debts of the poorer nations in order to alleviate poverty. This was yet another attempt to alleviate poverty—yet all these economic, political, social, and religious arguments about debt failed.

Conference of Anglican Provinces in Africa and the World Bank

From what I have recounted, there seem not to have been much collaboration between church and governments for poverty alleviation. With the Jubilee 2000 campaign the churches were in solidarity with one another in challenging the governments on debt cancellation. The Lambeth Conference also issued its challenge to the World Bank, without engaging the bank in the deliberations. From the Lambeth Conference of 1998, it was agreed that since Africa is adversely affected by poverty, a conference on poverty alleviation should be held. The aim of the conference would be to provide a forum for dialogue between the church and the World Bank on the issues of poverty alleviation on the continent.

In January 2000 the World Bank held a consultation in Johannesburg, where the major focus of debate was the issues of poverty. It was revealed that, among economists, cultural anthropologists, and sociologists alike, there was agreement that any measurement and definition that did not include the religious dimension would be inadequate.[29]

In March 2000, there was a conference on alleviating poverty specifically in Africa, sponsored by the Council of Anglican Provinces of Africa (CAPA) and the World Bank. It was held in Mbagathi, Nairobi, partly as a follow-up to the Lambeth 1998 conference, where poverty and debt cancellation had featured. The conference brought together bishops of the Anglican Church and other church people drawn from the National Council of Churches with World Bank officials from both Africa and abroad.

Through the presentation of papers, the conference considered various areas of poverty, especially among women and children; the HIV/AIDS pandemic in the midst of abject poverty; the crisis in education; and debt repayments as a burden on the economies of many poor countries. The conference resolved that in order to alleviate poverty there was a need to put people at the heart of development, to prioritize women, children and youth, and to address education and health issues, especially HIV/AIDS. At the same time it was important to deal with conflict prevention and to pursue postcolonial conflict reconstruction.

For the first time, the religious sphere and the World Bank had come together to talk about poverty alleviation; not only that, but the two groups had resolved to work together on poverty alleviation by targeting the most vulnerable groups in society. Women in the rural communities are the most vulnerable group affected by gender inequality, by a lack of access to education, and by poor health services. The agreement between the World Bank and the Anglican Church stated that "the World Bank can work with the church to assess the impact of programmes of both institutions that are targeted to this group and to enable men and women to work together in mutually supportive partnership in the home and the community."[30]

This paradigm shift was significant for the religious groups because it justifies the role of religious groups in poverty alleviation in discussing economics with the authorities. The church was to bring into the discussions the human face to development, in which development is a mission of God, as noted by Carl E. Braaten: "As long as Christian faith is oriented by the history of promise and eschatological significance of Christ, there will be a Christian mission in world history—the universal scope of the history of promise posits the whole world as the horizon of mission—the world is not something that can be added on. The world stands within the horizon from the beginning or simply comes too late to prevent evangelistic backlash or ecclesiastical retrenchment . . . The doctrine of the Church needs to be reconceived within the horizon of the eschatologial mission of the God in world history."[31]

The involvement of the church in poverty alleviation is not optional; it is the extension of God's mission on earth. The mission societies began doing this when they set up the fourfold strategy of mission work, but they seem only to have created a new form of poverty. The many policies and models that have been tried in the continent have produced few social and economic benefits.

The move by the Christian churches to be involved in poverty alleviation is wonderful, but it is superficial and does not go to the root causes of why Africa is in the current state. One cannot ignore the fact that burgeoning technological advancements and profound geopolitical realignments are presently shaping and directing our world, and the two together are inexorably leading to an alarming marginalization of Africa. At the same time Africa at the present moment has neither the technological power nor the kind of political muscle that would make her respected in the global forums. It appears then that Africa has no choice other than to use all available opportunities to transform herself while resisting the pressure and influence of the very powerful neighbors with whom she shares the planet.

So how does Africa meld the worthwhile societal systems and elements of the present and those elements of the "global civilization" that are impinging on the entire continent? This constitutes the enduring challenge with which Africa is faced. Although the major forces of poverty alleviation programs continue to come from outside the continent, it is true that it is ultimately only those who live in the continent that will transform Africa. But the chances that they can carry it out alone without the help of the outside are slim. It is no service to the African cause to ignore the problems involved or make them look lighter that they actually are. There is the indomitable will of African peoples, coupled with their faith in the future of Africa, that provides us with a basis of thinking and believing that African leaders will, in time, put aside their parochial visions for a more inclusive one that would weaken the hold of the myth of national sovereignty and personal power.

Conclusion

In this essay I have sought to look at the church's involvement in poverty alleviation in historical context. I have tried to show that the route taken to develop Africa created a poverty trap. So how does Africa break out of the vicious circle of poverty in which she is trapped? This is a worrying situation, which cannot be dealt with in simplistic ways but needs to be looked at in a wider context. The fundamental problem in the poverty reduction debate is the link between the widening unequal distribution of income or wealth in general and poverty. As a structural phenomenon, poverty cannot be erased by providing the poor with welfare and opportunities; we need also to transform larger underlying structures like the nation-state apparatus and income and asset distribution mechanisms that are today in operation in many countries in Africa. Such a strategy would transcend the bounds of mere religion and theology by integrating the best of other disciplines— economics, politics, science, ethics, and sociology, to name but a few.

Notes

1. African Charter for Popular Participation in Development and Transformation (Arusha, 1990), 17. During the week when Nelson Mandela was released from prison, the International Conference on Popular Participation in the Recovery and Development Process in Africa was held in Arusha, United Republic of Tanzania, 12 to 16 February 1990. The conference comprised a large assembly of peoples' organizations, government and nongovernmental representatives, and United States agencies, all searching for the role of the populace in Africa's transformation. It was the third such conference organized by the United Nations Program of Action for African Economic Recovery and Development (UN-PAAERD) and crafted what would be known as the Arusha Charter.
2. Carol Mandi, "The Poor Die Everyday, Everywhere, Anyway," Daily Nation, 10 May 2001.
3. Kenneth Copeland, The Laws of Prosperity (Fort Worth, Tex.: Kenneth Copeland Ministries, 1978); Kenneth Hagin, How God Taught Me about Prosperity (Tulsa, Okla.: Kenneth Hagin Ministries, 1978); Otabil Mensa, Enjoying the Blessings of Abraham

(Accra: Altar International, 1992); Otabil Mensa, *Four Laws of Productivity: God's Foundation for Living* (Accra: Altar International, 1992).

4. Jubilee 2000 was an international campaign in over forty countries that sought the cancelation of third world debt by the year 2000. It later split into an array of organizations round the world driven by the same aim. The concept derives from the biblical idea of the year of the Jubilee in Leviticus when all the people were set free from their debts to begin anew on an equal footing rather than remaining hindered by the debts of the past.

5. Africa cannot be treated as a homogenous cultural set, nor can Africans be treated as members of a homogenous cultural system. At best, Africa is merely the name of a geographical continent and Africans are natives of that continent.

6. Roland Oliver, *The Missionary Factor in Africa* (London: Longman, 1952); Brian Stanley, *The Bible and the Flag* (Leicester, U.K.: Apollo's, 1990).

7. Quoted in Stanley, *The Bible and the Flag*, 70.

8. W. B. Anderson, *The Church in East Africa* (Nairobi: Uzima, 1977); John Karanja, *Founding an Anglican Faith: Kikuyu Anglican Christianity* (Nairobi: Uzima, 1999); Carl-Erik Sahlberg, *From Krapf to Rugambwa: A Church History of Tanzania* (Nairobi: Evangel Publishing, 1986); Zablon John Nthamburi, *A History of the Methodist Church* (Nairobi: Uzima, 1982).

9. Margaret Crouch, *A Vision of Christian Mission: Reflections on the Great Commission in Kenya, 1943–1993* (Nairobi: NCCK, 1993), 5.

10. J. O. Oucho, *Urban Migration and Rural Development* (Nairobi: Nairobi University Press, 1996), 16.

11. Felix Kiruthu, *Voices of Freedom: Great African Independence Speeches* (Nairobi: Cana Publishers, 2001), 75.

12. Crouch, *A Vision of Christian Mission*, 39.

13. Kenneth King, *Jua Kali Kenya: Change and Development in an Informal Economy, 1970–1995* (London: James Currey, 1996).

14. Mutava Musyimi, "Building God's Kingdom through Microenterprise Development," *Transformation: An International Dialogue on Mission and Ethics* 20.3 (July 2003): 152–53.

15. Henry Okullu, *Quest for Justice: An Autobiography of Bishop Henry Okullu* (Nairobi: Shalom Publishers, 1997), 173.

16. Graham Bird, *IMF Lending to Developing Countries: Issues and Evidence* (London: Routledge, 1995).

17. Jessica Willams, *Facts That Should Change the World* (London: Icon Books, 2004), 56.

18. Juliee Hearn, " 'The Invisible' NGO: U.S. Evangelical Missions in Kenya," *Journal of Religion in Africa* 32.1 (2002): 45.

19. Agnes Chepkwony, *The Role of Non-Governmental Organisations in Development: A Study of the National Council of Churches of Kenya (NCCK), 1963–1978* (Uppsala: University of Uppsala, 1987).

20. S. I. Oladeji and A. G. Abiola, "Poverty Alleviation with Economic Growth Strategy: Prospects and Challenges in Contemporary Nigeria," *Journal of Social Development in Africa* 2 (July 2000): 45.

21. Tim Allen and Alan Thomas, *Poverty and Development in the 1990s* (Oxford: Oxford University Press, 1992).

22. Gustavo Gutierrez, *A Theology of Liberation* (Maryknoll, NY.: Orbis Books, 1973).

23. Government of Kenya, *Kenya Interim Poverty Reduction Strategy Paper, 2000–2003* (Nairobi: Government of Kenya, 13 July 2003).
24. E. Wayne Natziger, *Economic Development*, 4th ed. (Cambridge: Cambridge University Press, 2006), 561.
25. Jonathan Sacks, *The Dignity of Difference: How to Avoid the Clash of Civilisation* (London: Continuum, 2003), 115.
26. Ann Pettifor, *The Coming First World Debt Crisis* (New York: Palgrave, 2006), 26.
27. Sacks, *The Dignity of Difference*, 117.
28. James Wolfensohn, "International Debt I," speech given at the Lambeth 1998 conference, in *Report of the Lambeth Conference, 1998* (London: Morehouse, 1999), 345–52.
29. Molefe Tsele, "The Role of Religion in Development," *Transformation* 17.4 (2000): 136.
30. Conference paper on poverty alleviation in Africa, for a conference hosted by the Council of Anglican Provinces in Africa (CAPA) and the World Bank, 6–10 March 2000, Nairobi, Kenya.
31. Carl Braaten, *The Flaming Centre: A Theology of the Christian Mission* (Philadelphia: Fortress Press, 1977), 54.

Anthony B. Pinn | **WARM BODIES, COLD CURRENCY**

| A STUDY OF RELIGION'S RESPONSE TO POVERTY

Is there a relationship between religion and poverty? If so, what is the nature of this relationship?

I argue for a strong link between religion and poverty, a link in the form of an epistemological and aesthetic (a "fullness" of being) tension, a negative relationship. Various modalities of poverty exist, including intellectual poverty, emotional poverty, and so on, but I limit this discussion to economically oriented poverty.

Whereas many religious communities seek to address issues of poverty through food programs and other activities reminiscent of the social gospel movement of the mid-twentieth century, these activities are dependent on economic resources. However, churches and other religious communities, irrespective of resources, demonstrate a resistance to the dehumanizing consequences of poverty through theological and ritual formulations. It is this second modality of resistance that frames this essay, giving shape to the thesis guiding the following pages.

My effort here is to extend my previous theoretical work on the nature of religion and on the meaning of religiously inspired praxis, particularly as found in *Terror and Triumph: The Nature of Black Religion* (2003). I seek to accomplish this through a more focused discussion of religion within the context of poverty, based on a simple assertion regarding the nature of religion. Black religion in the context of Africa and the African diaspora seeks to push against the dehumanizing consequences of poverty. It does so through praxis as housed in institutional formations and ritualized performance of resistance perhaps most highly dramatized in healing rituals and spirit possession. Both praxis and ritual in this context point to a general and theologically formatted aesthetic recovery of black bodies as the "hallmark" of religious resistance. I present these religious mechanisms of "transformation" vis-à-vis two representative geographic areas—the United States and Kenya. In shaping this discussion, I give attention to two areas:

(1) churches and social activism, and (2) body aesthetics as critique of poverty's attack on quality of "being," and the body in movement vis-à-vis worship as antipoverty activism.

Poverty: A Brief Profile

Poverty characterized life for the vast majority, roughly 90 percent, of African Americans before the end of World War II.[1] While the years after this war marked a major shift in the status of both white Americans and African Americans in the United States, the former climbed out of poverty in a more marked manner. By 1970, because of the G.I. Bill and other governmental policies, roughly 70 percent of the white American population could be classified economically as middle-class.[2] African Americans, however, did not experience the same level of prosperity, with more than 40 percent of them living in poverty throughout the years of available statistical information. Tied to this, the number with economic means—extreme wealth—increased, but the percentage of African Americans living in poverty remained high. Their economic status improved in the 1990s, with a poverty rate of roughly 27 percent representing a decrease in impoverishment. Yet, the African American middle class did not increase in substantive ways, and most in African American communities remained close to the poverty line. What one finds, then, is a polarization—an increase in the number of wealthy African Americans, a small middle class, and large numbers of African Americans flirting with poverty.[3]

The changing nature of the U.S. economy as of the 1970s—a shift away from industry—advanced wealth in certain ways while leaving behind a segment of society called the chronically "poor" or, in some cases, the (multi-layered) "underclass." For those living in the inner cities, the shift of industry to suburban areas and other countries meant limitations on job options. Growth in high-technology jobs does not mean much to the poor who do not possess the necessary skills and educational background to secure high-paying jobs. African Americans do not account for most of the underclass, but according to sociologist Orlando Patterson, "the impressive growth of the Afro-American middle class should not be used to mask the fact that, in comparative ethnic terms, the economic record is decidedly mixed. In 1995, the median income of all Afro-American families was $25,970, which was 60.8 percent of the Euro-American median family income of $42,646. This was only a 1.6 percent improvement on the ratio of 59.2 percent in 1967."[4] Taken in terms of African Americans, by some accounts, by the late twentieth century, 7.5 million black Americans had incomes below the poverty line, resulting in roughly three out of ten living below the poverty line as opposed to one out of ten white Americans.[5]

The statistics over the course of the past three decades leave room for disagreement among scholars. But as the range of interpretations of the economic condition of African Americans attests, it is reasonable to say that some have done well. Nonetheless, even more continue to struggle with economic hardship. As a recent study indicates, there has been increased income for African Americans but with respect to the "black-white gap," African Americans still lag behind and will through the twenty-first century without radical intervention.[6] The best way of describing or categorizing this group—the poor—has changed over the past four decades, but certain factors remain consistent.

The economic problems faced by African Americans in the United States have wide-ranging implications with respect to overall quality of life. One of the most telling areas involves health and health care.

The gains made over the course of the past four decades have not necessarily translated into better quality of life with respect to health and resources for effectively managing health issues. Health care has become an industry, viewed as an enterprise with primary concern for profit as opposed to treatment. And those without financial resources receive limited care. According to social ethicist Emilie Townes, the highest death rate and the deepest concentration of those suffering from hypertension, upper respiratory illnesses, and eye disease, for example, have an annual income under $9,000.[7] It is true that the official desegregation of health care held benefits for African Americans in that it, in theory, increased access to the nation's health care infrastructure, but the benefits were in reality limited. With respect to one pressing issue in particular, although African Americans do not constitute, in actual numbers, the bulk of those suffering with HIV/AIDS, the rate of infection is frightening. African Americans are at risk in that African American men are almost three times as likely as white men to contract AIDS, and African American women are twelve times as likely as white women. In terms of current statistics, "blacks constitute 37 percent of all those who contracted AIDS through needles and 48 percent of those who contracted AIDS through partners who used dirty needles. These patterns of transmission largely explain why blacks are 27 percent of all people with AIDS, and black women are 52 percent of all women with AIDS."[8]

Furthermore, from global warming to nuclear waste, the development of complex human societies with relatively unchecked and shortsighted approaches to the natural environment has taken a toll on the health of many within the context of the United States. Although all peoples face environmental crisis on some level, environmental crises have stronger effects in some communities than in others. For example, roughly 60 percent of all African Americans live dangerously close to toxic waste.[9] And there is nothing random about the placement of hazardous materials. Rather, this situation points to environmental racism, by which it is understood that socioeconomic conditions premised on racism are a factor in a community's exposure to environmental problems.[10] The racialized and class-based nature of exposure to environmental hazards accounts for large numbers of African Americans living within the context of health-threatening environmental situations. For example, for much of the city of Houston's history, processing plants related to waste disposal have been placed in areas with high concentrations of African Americans.[11] This practice is repeated across the country for African Americans who live in areas with low tax bases and limited political visibility.[12]

The situation for Africans, taking Kenya as our example, is no better.[13] Beginning with the project of colonization, Kenya's resources were collected and processed for the benefit of others. Though their country's conditions were not as graphically brutal as, say, the arrangements that characterized Congo under King Leopold, Kenyans nonetheless experienced economic and social disorientation that David Gordon describes as being similar to the forced labor, pass laws, and other racial caste–centered tensions experienced in South Africa.[14] Colonization ripped resources away and altered Kenya and what it meant to be Kenyan in profound ways, and with devastating economic consequences. Trade deficits, international debt, and governmental mismanagement of funds all took their toll. As of the 1990s, this troubled economic situation resulted in Kenya depending more on foreign aid than all but two countries in Africa (Tanzania and Egypt).

Kenya's economic picture was not always so grim. In fact, until the 1980s, mixed free enterprise managed by the government sparked an annual growth rate of 6.8 percent when 4.5 percent was the rate of growth for all African countries taken together.[15] Yet, as the economic prosperity of Africa declined in general terms during the 1980s, Kenya faced declining revenue from coffee and tea production and increased expenditures for oil and other imports. The production of food items such as pineapples actually increased during the 1980s. However, the profit generated by export sales decreased because of a decrease in world prices.[16] The available workforce continued to grow, with 250,000 persons added in 1981 alone, but employment opportunities decreased. And so, for example, of the 250,000 new members of the potential workforce in 1981, only 50,000 found employment. Roughly one-fifth of all those entering the job market find wage-producing opportunities because the private sector accounts for only 90,000 new jobs each year. Of those suffering economically, perhaps the hardest hit are uneducated rural women, who have few economic outlets and quite limited rights to land, while urban women as of the 1980s accounted for a small percentage of the urban workforce.

Some outside Kenya might think such an expansive country must be able to provide environmental resources to sustain even its rapidly increasing population. Regardless of such assumptions, the following statement made in 1986 by the Land Development Resources Centre points to a different reality: "Everywhere there is competition for limited land and water resources, the potential for further gains in production being limited in many areas to yield increases derived from more intensive use of farm inputs and improved management. As the population increases . . . [h]ighland farms are increasingly fragmented and people are forced into the semi-arid margins, where cropping is precarious and where successful pastoralism depends on maintaining livestock numbers in equilibrium with range potential."[17] Kenya is increasingly dependent on urban areas that are unable to provide necessary jobs and cannot begin to meet the nation's needs with respect to basic foods. In addition, there are issues related to maintenance of wildlife areas, sufficient water, energy, and so on that suggest long-term problems.

I do not want to suggest that the problems described above are being ignored. To the contrary, attention has been directed to these areas. Kenya has more public and private, national and foreign organizations concerned with economic growth and maintenance of resources than any other country in Africa.[18] Yet the likelihood that the economic situation in Kenya will improve in the near future is dismal when one considers that Kenya's public debt increased by over $4.4 billion between 1970 and 1990.[19]

Finally, as is the case in the United States, the lack of economic stability results in levels of poverty exposing people to a variety of problems, including but not limited to issues of health and health care. Perhaps one of the major issues of concern related to health in Kenya is HIV/AIDS. While this crisis grew, many were reluctant to aggressively deal with it for fear of lost tourism and denied international assistance. Without aggressive measures, however, it is possible that "health-care systems will be overwhelmed, and heavy losses of life within the country's most productive age-groups will leave an unmanageable number of younger and older dependents."[20]

The Effects of Poverty

In the United States the "War on Poverty" and the "Great Society" frame-work had as their mission improving the condition of those in poverty through direct assistance in the form of jobs. They were also concerned with greater economic support for health care through the "mainstreaming" of the poor and elderly into the medical establishment. The idea was to pro-mote an increase in community-based mechanisms for care, such as health centers and also governmental financing of private mechanisms through Medicaid and Medicare. Initial plans for more than 1,000 health centers in 1967 did not materialize because the subsidies needed by these centers were not approved. While the number of centers did grow from 125 to over 800 during the Carter administration, their impact remained limited.[21] Medicaid and Medicare proved too costly from the perspective of many governmental officials, resulting in states cutting Medicaid and Medicare budgets and restricted access to the programs. Under Ronald Reagan, federal support for Medicaid was compromised and states were given greater freedom with respect to the operation of such programs. For example, the 1981 Omnibus Budget Reconciliation Act reduced assistance for the working poor and restricted eligibility for participation, rendering some 500,000 people dis-qualified for health coverage. Therefore, a smaller percentage of the poor is covered, and this results in limited attention to preventive health care mea-sures and an increase in resulting chronic illnesses. Class-based and racial differences in the United States can result in poor communication with patients and assumptions that compromise the type and quality of service.[22] What Anselm L. Strauss said in 1967 still rings far too true today:

> Health professionals themselves complain that the poor come to the clinic or hospital only with advanced symptoms, that parents don't pay attention to children's symptoms early enough, that they don't follow up treatments or regimens, and delay too long in returning. But is it really the fault of whole sections of the American population if they don't follow what professionals expect of them? . . . To them a careful concern about health is unreal—they face more pressing troubles daily, just get-ting by. Bad health is just one more condition they must try to cope—or live—with.[23]

Even efforts to invest in proper health care point to the manner in which "reform" of the existing system does not allow for the full integration of the poor. That is to say, the health care complex is not designed with sensitivity to the manner in which the socioeconomic and political landscape affects attitudes toward and approaches to issues of health.[24]

The connection between poverty and health is real and mutually dependent.[25] Poverty and its accompanying health-related challenges result in the poor having a higher death rate. In fact, African Americans have a higher death rate than white Americans in almost every age group. Concerning infant mortality, a good measure of impoverishment, African American babies born in the United States are less likely to live through the first year than babies born in areas such as Cuba and Chile.[26] In general terms, African Americans have a degree of illness and shorter life span among the worse in the United States. They have a higher mortality rate (adjusted for age) than white Americans for the ten leading causes of death—including heart disease, cancer, stroke, HIV/AIDS, and diabetes.[27]

In Kenya and other parts of Africa, international aid and loans in theory were meant to alleviate similar dimensions of poverty. However, such assistance has not had profoundly positive consequences, in that debt increased and healthy life options decreased. Black Kenyan bodies continue to bear the marks of economic need such as dysentery and malnutrition. As Esther Mombo's essay in this volume notes, crowded conditions in impoverished areas, combined with a lack of clean water and basic food items, fester and foster a cycle of illness. The "natural" environment cannot bear the conditions of population growth and technology. So, "carbon monoxide, nitrogen oxide, and sulfur oxide emitted by cars, trucks, and buses have been found to be very high," particularly during peak periods of the day and this results in health problems that go untreated. A prime example of those exposed to this dilemma in the context of Kenya must be the street children.[28]

Comprising a population in the thousands, these young children leave rural areas for cities such as Nairobi in search of economic opportunities.[29] Often they are forced to seek nutrition from refuse, which results in a high rate of diarrhea and stomach ailments. In addition, skin infections, damaged feet (due to a lack of shoes), and cuts are frequent. Many of these children seek to escape their suffering through substance abuse, with glue being a favored product. One ethnographic study of street children in Kenya speaks to this dilemma: "Children report a number of recurring reasons for imbibing glue. The most common reasons given are that it suppresses depression, shyness in begging, hunger, and cold. One boy called glue 'his blanket.' Another boy of about fourteen years made this statement concerning his use of glue: 'when I sniff glue I forget my sufferings.' "[30] In addition, some of these children turn to "survival sex," selling their bodies to earn money. The result for many of the children involved in this sex trade is HIV/AIDS.

Some conservative thinkers assume the poor refuse to adhere to the standard principles that allow for economic success. In opposition to this many liberals point to structural factors that shape a certain defeatist mentality. In either case, and in both the United States and Kenya, economic and health-related concerns faced by the poor often result in issues of motivation —a series of behaviors and activities resulting from the circumstances of poverty while also contributing to their perpetuation.

Poverty is continually played out through heart disease, high blood pressure, diabetes, and so on. That is to say, poverty and its health-related offshoots are borne on and through the body. Essays in this volume by Barbara Bailey and others give more attention to the full weight of the connection between religion and poverty within the life situation of women. Yet, it must be at least noted that this situation is only intensified when one considers the manner in which women in Kenya and in black America face not only the poverty-related ramifications of race, but also class and gender.

The socioeconomic, political, and environmental ramifications of poverty shape the physical body in both literal and figurative ways. With respect to the latter, poverty encourages its victims to think of themselves as of limited worth, their bodies of limited value and beauty. Regarding the literal wearing of poverty, the physical health and carriage of the body are harmed as poverty-related illnesses destroy its integrity. In a sense, poverty "erases" the physical body through progressive deterioration caused by poor diet and inadequate health care. In other words, wealth renders the body invisible to some extent because the wealthy person is understood to be more than the body. However, poverty has an odd effect in that it renders bodies visible yet invisible (with respect to issues of importance, worth, and—as Simeon Ilesanmi notes in his essay—rights, as they are highlighted, but "deformed" and of no grand or exalted value. Economic means proclaims one a subject of history. Poverty renders one strictly a body, a gross object.[31]

Poverty does not simply involve a compromise of mundane realities. It also connotes an attack on the psyche, the deeper elements and modes of existence through which poverty's ensuing social isolation and stress are felt in nonphysical ways. But is this situation inevitable and beyond remedy? Is Michael Harrington to be proven prophetic in arguing the circular nature of poverty in the United States (and I would add Kenya)—moving from generation through generation?[32] Pessimism may be grounded in historical realities and socioeconomic structures, but according to the religiously inclined poverty is not insurmountable and inevitable. Such optimism raises a question: What are the ways in which those of African descent within the religious community attempt to address poverty?

Religion as a Response to Poverty

Situating bodies by fixing their meaning and placement is of essential importance, if poverty is to be maintained. However, religious action and thought are attempts to rupture or break this abusive arrangement through the assertion and securing of a full range of rights and privileges. In other words, the religious is historically situated and culturally bound, dealing with "the material world of outer nature" and "the human world of social life."[33] For example, there is a deep and central concern behind historical expressions such as the black church in the United States and African instituted churches in Kenya.

In various writings I have referred to this elemental impulse as the quest for complex subjectivity.[34] This quest is concerned with a push toward the fullness of being, the further unfolding of the individual self within the context of healthy community. Religion's elemental nature, this impulse for complex subjectivity, is historically manifest through rituals and doctrines, institutions, and practices. By means of these historically conditioned materials, black religion, as the inner quest, manifests itself through a platform of liberation by which identity is reconstituted socioeconomically, politically, culturally, and spiritually.

Black religion so conceived does not equate poverty with sin and inherent inadequacies.[35] Oppressive manipulations of John Calvin's theological response to economic success, or the Protestant work ethic, do not substitute for hard critique of the conditions and causes of poverty. This inner impulse, the elemental nature of black religion, fosters an urgent recognition that those suffering are meant for better. And the historical manifestations of religion are meant to provide historically conditioned ways of moving toward this something better. In the remaining pages two examples of this process are discussed.

LIBERATION WALK AND SOCIAL ACTIVISM

More progressive black churches in the United States have developed forms of praxis geared toward addressing the terror and dread of objectification. The primary focus of their concern revolves around nurturing sociopolitically and economically vital and vibrant Americans, who enjoy all the rights and responsibilities endemic to full citizenship. From initial activities during the nineteenth century, through social gospel activism, to more recent modes of community engagement, black churches have grown to provide schooling, jobs, recreational and social outlets, and political influence.[36] While one might think this praxis is limited to larger and heavily endowed churches, recent sociological studies point to work done by churches of varying size and means.[37] Hence, most churches maintain some type of outreach emphasis and thereby address pressing needs of particular communities. The number of outreach programs sponsored is proportionate to the size (and one can assume resource base) of the congregation.[38]

Even when many black churches became "deradicalized," to borrow a term from historian Gayraud Wilmore, during the late nineteenth century and first five decades of the twentieth century, the otherworldly orientation did not lose sight of dehumanization or poverty as evil. A sympathetic read would suggest that some churches approached transformation through sociopolitical and economic activism, while churches holding to an otherworldly perspective addressed it in more passive ways through a preoccupation with the spiritual condition of African American communities. For the latter, the underlying rationale is simple. Spiritual growth entails closeness to God that must imply the full humanity of the practitioner. I want to be clear that I am not advocating this more passive approach. Rather, I am merely noting its existence.

An otherworldly versus a this-worldly orientation as suggested here should not be pushed too strongly, in that what occurs is not a complete displacement of one for the other. Instead, it is a matter of both orientations being present in tension, with one given priority over the other at any particular moment. The difference, then, involves an effort to secure liberation through spiritual means over against liberation through forms of societal engagement.[39] Liberation from the vantage point of black churches revolves around a transformation of existing relationships, both physical and spiritual, through which the chosen of God—the impoverished and oppressed— have their existence transformed.[40]

Scholars remind us that a commitment to social transformation is not limited to black churches in the North American context. One must also be mindful of the processes by which Africans, like their North American counterparts, interpret the Christian tradition through a "dialectical process" and in light of their existential situation. All this takes place for the improvement of life circumstances by investing life with meaning, in keeping with the quest for a fuller sense of being.[41] This religious stance was given institutional form in Kenya and elsewhere through the development of congregations that are commonly called African instituted churches (or African initiated churches, or African independent churches).

These are Christian communions that take as their starting point the application of scripture as a liberative text. Their transformative tone is evident to some extent in their facing proscription prior to 1964, when Kenya gained freedom from colonial authorities. This new political and social reality marked a new freedom that allowed these churches to extend their concern to issues of race, education, and health over against the onslaught of poverty as a destructive force.[42] As one scholar notes, these churches "enriched not only African Christianity, but Christendom as a whole by the richness and creativity of their liturgies, and by their exploration of an insight that the West has often lost sight of but is now rediscovering: the unity of health of mind and body."[43]

The African Brotherhood Church, composed of roughly 100,000 members within several hundred churches as of 1966, developed in part as a response to efforts on the part of African Inland Missions (AIM) to restrict educational opportunities to evangelism-based activities in local languages. The African Brotherhood Church argued for full educational opportunities in English, including proper training for pastors such as was available at St. Paul's United Theological College (Limuru, Kenya). Education, this church argued, was meant to provide for new opportunities for full expression of African life. It had to provide the means by which Africans could do for themselves. Such an attitude often resulted in what some considered a nationalist and antigovernment perspective. Many of these African instituted or organic churches were initially viewed as heterodox, but by the 1960s, with changing political realities, they expressed a sense of agency that spoke in powerful ways to the concerns of Africans seeking to shake off colonial control.

BLACK BODIES ON DISPLAY AND IN MOTION

For some time now I have used Mary Douglas's theory of the body to inform my understanding of black bodies as symbol and as lived, as being a physiological and biochemical reality set in historical experience.[44] More important for this study is an extension of this definition to reveal the black body's religious importance, borne out through the historical record of dehumanization experienced by those of African descent, and continued through "cycles" of poverty.

Socioeconomic need forces a restriction on the importance of the body by limiting its value and the spaces in which it is recognized. In addition, poverty—and the social systems supporting the cycle of poverty—mutates the physical body, taking away its strength and vitality. It is this attack on the body that religion seeks to address through a reconsideration of aesthetics.

Demonic mechanisms were put in place to guarantee social control over "marked" or black bodies, and much of the history of Africans in the United States and Kenya involves recognition of this process and efforts to subvert it.

A liberative agenda emerges not only through protest, but also through the very act of worship or celebration, particularly within the Pentecostal-influenced communities present in large numbers in both the United States and Kenya.[45]

The call to be in the world but not of it, generated particularly by more evangelical and/or fundamentalist churches, has often played out as a need to bring the body under control, to "discipline" it as a safeguard against the outrages of an impoverished society. Others, usually less evangelical or fundamentalist in nature, have expressed a rejection of poverty and its social consequences through an embrace of bodies hated by the dominant society and awkwardly "handled" by many black churches in the United States. Religious attention to the body (e.g., concerning the placement of these bodies in space and a type of aesthetic reconfiguration through various modes of decoration) retards the social system's ability to exercise traditional power relationships over the short term. Issues of poverty are at least temporarily suspended.

The altering of the body's presentation in time and space also serves as a strike against the ramifications of poverty within the Kenyan context. Holy Spirit churches, one of the African instituted churches in that country, make the body a primary indication of the divine's presence in human history in that the body is acknowledged and respected within the context of energetic worship as the site of transformation. Think about this in terms of the following depiction of conversion ritual and the display of the body as critique of colonialism and poverty: "New converts were required to wash the whole body in order to cleanse them of the perceived impurities . . . and purify them for the community of the Arathi. After washing, converts were endowed with a new set of white clothes, symbolizing their new state, and given extensive instructions in the laws of purity and impurity that Arathi observed."[46] The theological implication is clear. The body has beauty and importance in that it maintains a profound relationship to the divine. Such an elaborate and ritualized presentation of the body in community speaks to the manner in which the body is "converted" or "resurrected" from the socioeconomic death brought on by poverty and the racism that supports it. And through this process of resurrection it is recognized and celebrated as having spiritual and aesthetic (through the process of purification) meaning and significance.

Black churches in the United States and churches such as the Holy Spirit churches of Kenya respond to the dehumanizing effects of poverty by seeking to establish blacks as agents of will—with all the accompanying benefits and responsibilities. Christian gatherings orchestrated by these churches serve as a ritual of exorcism, so to speak, in that they foster a break with status as will-less objects—impoverished forms—and encourage new forms of relationship and interaction premised on black intentionality and worth.

Poverty and its resulting conditions push on the poor a sense of worthlessness, of nihilism, by which life is rendered of little value and their bodies —as the mechanism of this life—are seen as having little importance. Based on this, it becomes normal for young people within the context of the United States, for example, who are confined to areas of poverty to think more quickly of their funerals than their futures. A similar imposed shortsightedness, I would argue, is also present in Kenya within the community of street children. In other words, I would suggest that poverty encourages impoverished children both in the United States and in Kenya to "not uphold the sacredness of their persons."[47] Yet the black body, within the context of ritual process, becomes the primary indicator of divine presence and movement. This is certainly the case with regard to spirit possession by positive spiritual forces through which the body becomes a source of healing, divine communication, and a certain type of erotic encounter.

Here I refer to a Tillichian understanding of the erotic as a complex modality of relationship that allows for a better appreciation of *agape* and *philio* forms of love.[48] Through the more ecstatic modes of black worship, the black body is rescued temporarily from the physical ramifications of poverty in that the body becomes a vessel for cosmic energy. In this capacity, the potential for healing and "reworking" the body increases in that the person so possessed can provide important messages, be the source of healing, and can spark an ecstatic response from others.

It must be noted that there is also recognition in various religious traditions that possession by negative forces or demons can also occur. Yet even this can point to the significance of the body in that it becomes the vehicle through which the age-old battle between the forces of God and the forces of evil takes place. In this regard, belief in spirit possession by both positive and negative forces alludes to the place of physical bodies in the cosmic drama.

In terms of possession by positive forces such as the Holy Spirit, expression of this action can involve shouting or other movements influenced by the spirit. This activity, in both the United States and Kenya, exposes the beauty and value of black bodies as flesh that can bring people into proper relationship with God and can channel the spirit of God. Through this process black bodies are redeemed in ways that fight efforts to terrorize and impoverish them. When spiritual awareness is increased by means of fasting or other rituals, the individual is open to more intimate connection with the divine in the form, for example, of shouting and possession.[49] Relationship with God is manifest through possession by the Holy Spirit, evidenced by speaking in tongues (glossolalia) as well as dancing in the spirit.[50] Specifically with the development of Pentecostalism in the late nineteenth century, being "filled" with the Holy Spirit or "baptized" in the Spirit became an increasingly important mode of redress against the connotations of economic poverty. The terror of poverty and its consequences are attacked through the body's role as instrument of God's presence in the world. The physical consequences of poverty felt through the body are of limited effect when God has manifested God's power, beauty, and purpose through black bodies. At the very least, this situation provides a theological argument for regarding the body as vital and vibrant.

Truth is no longer defined by the ability of a group to enforce its will, its desires, and its recollection of things. Now, through increased spiritual vitality, the truth about Africans and African Americans, about existence, is tied only to the power of God to manifest in the flesh of believers. The Holy Spirit's presence and establishment of *communitas*—a space in which external dilemmas are held at bay—momentarily mitigate the rules and tortures of this hostile land and harmony is the rule.[51]

Furthermore, reformation with respect to health concerns is addressed through the "healing" potential of the divine. What were once considered bodies of limited value in the larger social setting are given great worth. Would the divine manifest in anything less than an important and useful vessel? Possession by the "holy" gives the poverty-stricken body new value, a new level of spiritual beauty that overrides—at least during the period of communitas—the physical realities of life under the status quo.

Is Religion's Attack on Poverty Enough?

The above discussion highlights the subtle and less aggressively "political" or "public" ways in which religion seeks to counter the destructive processes of poverty. One can assume even these subtle methods have merit and importance. Yet, as the title for this final section brings to the fore, a pressing question remains. Is the work done by the various forms of black religion noted in this essay enough; does it connote a sustained response to poverty with "felt" merit? No.

There is no doubt that this answer, a cautionary note concerning the need for modest enthusiasm concerning religion's response to poverty, requires explanation, particularly in light of the rather positive assessment of religion given above.

Religiously inspired work is somewhat useful in that it brings attention to the difficulties faced by Africans and African Americans. Nonetheless, theologically informed attention to poverty typically involves a framework by which poverty is understood in terms of dis-ease as opposed to disease. The "soft" benefits of ritual activity, for example, are embroiled in a paradox regarding the body. That is to say, black church practice and rituals in general terms are typically premised on an old theological dilemma—tension between body and spirit. This, I believe, hampers attention to the needs of the body because priority remains on a subduing of the body in order to secure spiritual development. In other words, the body is still approached with suspicion in that some within religious community might still consider it a hindrance to union with the divine through proper living and spiritual focus. It does not always move through the world as we would like. Regarding this, keep in mind the Apostle Paul's lament: Those things I don't want to do are the very things I do. And those things I want to do are the things I fail to accomplish.

I am not suggesting that black Christianity in Africa and the United States is the only manifestation of religion to suffer from this problem. Nor am I suggesting that it is more intense within the context of black Christianity over against the practice of Christianity in white communities. The body/spirit tension is an inherent dimension of Christianity regardless of the community in which it is practiced. Yet, with that said, there are ways in which this tension's negative ramifications are intensified for Africans and African Americans in that their bodies become not only sociopolitically and economically suspect, but also spiritually problematic. There is, then, a doubly damaging discomfort with the body.

Furthermore, the gospel of prosperity popular in both contexts appears to maintain a "truce" of sorts between the body and the spirit, recognizing that the former can be tamed and trained. Even so, the gospel of prosperity provides an impediment to a sustained attack on the root causes of poverty. This is because it highlights success and poverty with regard to spiritual fitness. The theosocial platform suggested involves a spiritualization of historical dilemmas, whether this involves an improper relationship with God as the cause of poverty or, in the case of some prophecy-centered African instituted churches, suffering as a result of spiritual warfare (e.g., witchcraft).

Economic hardship is commonly associated with an improper interpretation or application of scriptural principles. The corrective involves life in accordance with an accurate application of scriptural lessons and principles. Such a blueprint for "happiness" does not bring into question the economic structures of capitalism—combined with issues of race and gender—that promote economic inequality. In other words, although there are exceptions to this rule, the critique of troubling socioeconomic and political structures receives scant attention and a less than robust challenge. Megachurches and more modest churches may provide job training, housing opportunities, and so on, but these efforts serve only to treat the symptoms of poverty. They do not pose a strong threat to the inner logic and mechanisms supporting poverty. A theologically informed reevaluation of the body through ritual as discussed above provides even less of a notable challenge to poverty and its felt ramifications.

In spite of such shortcomings there is something of merit, however limited, to this critique of poverty. At its best, religion, I believe, might serve to promote an ethos of assumed subjectivity and historical worth that, in turn, might serve as the theological backdrop—the religious impetus—for a more forceful and deeply public struggle against poverty.[52] The "critiques" of poverty highlighted in this essay are important in that they promote "soft" forms of discontent with and reaction against poverty. Yet, their appeal is rather limited. Institutional and aesthetic dimensions of black religious experience are useful, but restricted for the most part to the area of worship within the context of the like-minded. Hence, while it promotes an individual (and communal, that is, community of believers) struggle against poverty and its consequences, this corrective is really a matter of signification, a signifying of the economic status quo. Important as this is, its potential for fostering sustained systemic change is questionable, while its potential for fostering a new sense of being and importance on the level of the individual is noteworthy.

Notes

1. Some of the ideas presented here draw from and are extensions of attention to the impact of poverty on religious sensibilities and activities in my book *The Black Church in the Post–Civil Rights Era* (Maryknoll, N.Y.: Orbis Books, 2002) and in my article "Religio-Theological Formations and the (Re)Making of Black Kenyan Bodies: An African American's Perspective," forthcoming in *Africana Studies: A Review of Social Science Research*.

2. The G.I. Bill, or the Servicemen's Readjustment Act of 1944, was put in place by President Franklin D. Roosevelt to provide education and training for those who have been in the armed forces. For more information, see, for example, http:// www.gibill.va.gov.

3. Reynolds Farley, "Demographic, Economic, and Social Trends in a Multicultural America," in *New Directions: African Americans in a Diversifying Nation*, ed. James S. Jackson (Washington, D.C.: National Policy Association, 2000), 28–29. Middle-class status is defined by Farley as an income two or three times that of the poverty level ($17,184.00 in 1999).

4. Orlando Patterson, *The Ordeal of Integration: Progress and Resentment in America's "Racial" Crisis* (Washington, D.C.: Civitas/Counterpoint, 1997), 25.

5. Donna L. Franklin, *Ensuring Inequality: The Structural Transformation of the African-American Family* (New York: Oxford University Press, 1997), 182.

6. James S. Jackson, introduction to *New Directions: African Americans in a Diversifying Nation*, ed. James S. Jackson (Washington, D.C.: National Policy Association, 2000), 5.

7. Emilie M. Townes, *Breaking the Fine Rain of Death: African American Health Issues and a Womanist Ethic of Care* (New York: Continuum, 1998), 39.

8. *Third Triennial Report* (Rockville, Md.: U.S. Department of Health and Human Services, 1991), 114; Clarence Lusane, *Pipe Dream Blues: Racism and the War on Drugs* (Boston: South End Press, 1991), 50; Angela Davis, *Women, Culture and Politics* (New York: Vintage, 1990), 58–59.

9. Townes, *Breaking the Fine Rain of Death*, 72.

10. Robert D. Bullard, introduction to *Confronting Environmental Racism: Voices from the Grassroots*, ed. Robert D. Bullard (Boston: South End Press, 1993), 10–11.

11. Charles Lee, "Beyond Toxic Wastes and Race," in *Confronting Environmental Racism: Voices from the Grassroots*, ed. Robert D. Bullard (Boston: South End Press, 1993), 49; Robert D. Bullard, "Environmental Justice for All," in *Unequal Protection: Environmental Justice and Communities of Color*, ed. Robert D. Bullard (San Francisco: Sierra Club Books, 1994), 3–4, 14–15; and Karl Grossman, "The People of Color Environmental Summit," ibid., 280.

12. For additional information on why communities of color have such high concentrations of hazardous industry, etc., see Regina Austin and Michael Schill, "Black, Brown, Red, and Poisoned," in Bullard, *Unequal Protection*.

13. Some of this information on poverty in Kenya is drawn from my essay "Religio-Theological Formations and the (Re)Making of Black Kenyan Bodies: An African American's Perspective," *Africana Studies: A Review of Social Science Research* (forthcoming). I also give some attention to the subtle revolt against poverty expressed through African Christianity in that essay as well. This essay extends those comments and places them in a different context.

14. David F. Gordon, *Decolonization and the State in Kenya* (Boulder, Colo.: Westview Press, 1986), 31.

15. Norman Miller and Rodger Yeager, *Kenya: The Quest for Prosperity*, 2nd ed. (Boulder, Colo.: Westview Press, 1994), 127.

16. Ibid.

17. Land Development Resources Centre, *Kenya: Profile of Agricultural Potential* (Surbiton, U.K.: British Overseas Development Administration, 1986), 1. Quoted in Miller and Yeager, *Kenya*, 66.

18. Miller and Yeager, *Kenya*, 68.

19. Ibid., 154–55.

20. Ibid., 72.

21. Paul Starr, "Health Care for the Poor: The Past Twenty Years," in *Fighting Poverty:*

What Works and What Doesn't, ed. Sheldon H. Danziger and Daniel H. Weinberg (Cambridge, Mass.: Harvard University Press, 1986), 110–13.

22. Ibid., 113–14.

23. Anselm L. Strauss, "Medical Ghettos," in *The Sociology of American Poverty*, ed. Joan Huber and Peter Chalfant (Cambridge, Mass.: Schenkman Publishing, 1974), 240.

24. Ibid., 235.

25. Bradley R. Schiller, *The Economics of Poverty and Discrimination* (Englewood Cliffs, N.J.: Prentice Hall, 1976), 86.

26. Jackson, *New Directions*, 6, 7.

27. Thomas A. LaVeist, "African Americans and Health Policy: Strategies for a Multi-ethnic Society," in Jackson, *New Directions*, 144–46.

28. I recognize that some are offended by the term "street children." However, I use it not because I approve of it, but rather because it is the term that dominates the literature. My use is not meant to bring into question the humanity of these children, but simply to point out their economic and social predicament.

29. Octavian N. Gakuru, Priscilla W. Kariubi, and Kennedy M. Bikuri, "Children in Debt: The Experience of Street Children in Nairobi," in *Poverty, AIDS, and Street Children in East Africa*, ed. Joe L. P. Lugalla and Colleta G. Kibassa (Lewiston, Pa.: Edwin Mellen, 2002), 39.

30. Philip Kilbride, Collette Suda, and Enos Njeru, *Street Children in Kenya: Voices of Children in Search of a Childhood* (Westport, Conn.: Bergin and Garvey, 2000), 123.

31. Radhika Mohanram, *Black Body: Women, Colonialism, and Space* (Minneapolis: University of Minnesota Press, 1999), 37.

32. See Michael Harrington, *The New American Poverty* (New York: Holt, Rinehart, and Winston, 1984).

33. Paget Henry, "African and Afro-Caribbean Existential Philosophies," in *Existence in Black: An Anthology of Black Existential Philosophy*, ed. Lewis R. Gordon (New York: Routledge, 1997), 15.

34. This theory of religion is drawn from the more fully developed theory of religion found in my book *Terror and Triumph: The Nature of Black Religion* (Minneapolis: Fortress Press, 2003).

35. Bradley R. Schiller, *The Economics of Poverty and Discrimination* (Englewood Cliffs, N.J.: Prentice-Hall, Inc., 1976), 4.

36. For additional information on black Church activism, see Frederick C. Harris, *Something Within: Religion in African-American Political Activism* (New York: Oxford University Press, 1999); Peter Paris, *The Social Teaching of the Black Churches* (Philadelphia: Fortress Press, 1985); Stephen W. Angell and Anthony B. Pinn, eds., *Social Protest Thought in the African Methodist Episcopal Church, 1862–1939* (Knoxville: University of Tennessee Press, 2000).

37. C. Eric Lincoln and Lawrence H. Mamiya, *The Black Church in the African American Experience* (Durham: Duke University Press, 1990); Andrew Billingsley, *Mighty Like A River: The Black Church and Social Reform* (New York: Oxford University Press, 1999); Hans A. Baer and Merrill Singer, *African-American Religion in the Twentieth Century: Varieties of Protest and Accommodation* (Knoxville: University of Tennessee Press, 1992); Gayraud S. Wilmore, *Black Religion and Black Radicalism* (Maryknoll, N.Y.: Orbis Books, 1983); Harris, *Something Within*.

38. Billingsley, *Mighty Like a River*, 198–206.

39. Paris, *The Social Teaching of the Black Churches*, 2.

40. While I acknowledge the important role the black church has played in the development of black Americans, I find much of its theological framework faulty. This is particularly the case with respect to its theodicy. For information on this see my books *Why, Lord?: Suffering and Evil in Black Theology* (New York: Continuum, 1995); *Moral Evil and Suffering in African American Religious Thought* (Gainesville: University Press of Florida, 2002). Also see *By These Hands: A Documentary History of African American Humanism* (New York: New York University Press, 2001).

41. Thomas Spear and Isaira N. Kimambo, eds., *East African Expressions of Christianity* (Athens: Ohio University Press, 1999), 3.

42. J. N. K. Mugambi, *African Christian Theology: An Introduction* (Nairobi: Heinemann, 1989), 36.

43. Elizabeth Isichei, *A History of Christianity in Africa: From Antiquity to the Present* (Grand Rapids, Mich.: Wm. B. Eerdmans, 1995), 253.

44. See Mary Douglas, *Natural Symbols: Explorations in Cosmology* (New York: Routledge, 1996). In more recent work, I have extended my thinking on the nature and meaning of the body through attention to the work of scholars such as Chris Shilling and Bryan Turner. See, for example, Chris Shilling, *The Body and Social Theory*, 2nd ed. (Thousand Oaks, Calif.: Sage Publications, 2003), and Bryan Turner, *The Body and Society* (Oxford: Basil Blackwell, 1984).

45. For an interesting introductory and comparative approach to worship see Pedrito U. Maynard-Reid's *Diverse Worship: African-American, Caribbean and Hispanic Perspectives* (Downers Grove, Ill.: InterVarsity Press, 2000). This text should be read in the context of Joseph Murphy's more substantive treatment (yet meant as an introduction), *Working the Spirit: Ceremonies of the African Diaspora* (Boston: Beacon Press, 1994). See also J. N. K. Mugambi, *From Liberation to Reconstruction: African Christian Theology after the Cold War* (Nairobi: East African Educational Publishers, 1995).

46. Maynard-Reid, *Diverse Worship*, 234.

47. Anselm L. Strauss, "Medical Ghettos," in Huber and Chalfant, *The Sociology of American Poverty*, 240.

48. See, for example, Paul Tillich, *Love, Power, Justice: Ontological Analyses and Ethical Applications* (New York: Oxford University Press, 1954); Alexander Irwin, *E.R.O.S toward the World: Paul Tillich and the Theology of the Erotic* (Minneapolis: Augsburg Fortress Press, 1991).

49. For a comparative study of possession as well as a discussion of the African influence on black religion, see Walter F. Pitts Jr., *Old Ship of Zion: The Afro-Baptist Ritual in the African Diaspora* (New York: Oxford University Press, 1993).

50. Some churches also accept as evidence of the indwelling of the spirit dancing, emotional release through tears, or being "slain by the spirit," which entails passing out in response to the overwhelming power of the spirit.

51. See Sheila S. Walker, *Ceremonial Spirit Possession in Africa and Afro-America: Forms, Meanings, and Functional Significance for Individuals and Social Groups* (Leiden, Netherlands: E. J. Brill, 1972), 97–103. Readers will find the analysis of ritual activities such as the ring shout an important addition to the discussion presented here. See Sterling Stuckey, *Slave Culture: Nationalist Theory and the Foundations of Black America* (New York: Oxford University Press, 1987).

52. I discuss such programs in *The Black Church in the Post–Civil Rights Era*.

PRACTICAL THEORIES FOR COMBATING POVERTY

Laurenti Magesa | **NYERERE ON *UJAMAA* AND CHRISTIANITY**

AS TRANSFORMING FORCES IN SOCIETY

There are two conspicuous and persistent social phenomena in the contemporary world, and particularly in societies of the global South—religion and poverty. Facing these realities, the question that seems to present
itself to anyone's mind is whether there is any relationship between them.
If so, what is it? And, is this connection, if indeed it exists, intrinsic or
accidental?

It would not be too difficult to demonstrate how religion has been used by
some nations, groups, or even individuals as an instrument in the expropriation of the human and natural resources of others, thus becoming a reason
or justification for their exploitation and oppression. If we take the African
continent as a case, we can point to the slave trade and colonialism as just
two examples, both of which went hand in hand with Christian missionary
evangelizing activity. In either case, as is well known, the Christian religion
was often used to support the mercantile and political endeavors, and thus
acted as an important agent in the pacification of the slaves and the colonized. Not infrequently it urged them to accept their situation as God's will.[1]

But in discussing this subject, balance is important. For it is also possible and necessary to cite cases where religion—or more precisely religious
groups, organizations, and institutions—has acted as a liberating force,
variously empowering people through belief to recognize themselves as
worthwhile before God. Religion has therefore in this way acted as an instrument promoting human equity and dignity.[2]

So then, the question is, how has religion factored in the dynamics of
oppression, exploitation, and consequent poverty among people, on the one
hand, or of liberation, justice, and equity on the other?[3] This is the issue that
the Pan-African Seminar on Religion and Poverty set out to study in a series
of meetings held in Accra, Ghana (2000); Nairobi, Kenya (2001); Johannesburg, South Africa (2003); Kingston and Ocho Rios, Jamaica (2003); and
Princeton, New Jersey, United States (2004). The seminar's inquiry concen-

trated on both the theoretical and practical relationships between poverty and religion among peoples of African origin in Africa and in the diaspora, specifically, the Caribbean islands and the Americas.

Approaching the Issue

At one level the relationship between religion and poverty is a theoretical-philosophical question that may be considered in terms of how religious principles may and do inform and inspire political, economic, and social action. But it is as well a pragmatic-ethical issue at another level, and it can be studied from the perspective of what concrete political, economic, and social action certain professed religious principles have practically inspired in any given situation.

The theoretical-philosophical concern of the seminar was dealt with during the predominantly academic part of the gatherings, constituting various presentations by academics, religious leaders, and social activists. To deal with the practical aspect of the question, the seminar participants toured various places in each of the regions mentioned to observe for themselves the facts on the ground. Thus although some ideas for an answer to the intricacies of the relationship between religion and poverty were suggested during the formal presentations, each participant had to form his or her own opinion on the issue through assessment of the evidence observed during the tours. Often very powerful, this evidence provided the context within which to situate reflection and necessitated looking for a relevant theory or theories from which to construct an approach to the issue.

Nyerere's Philosophy of Ujamaa as a Viable Method

Consequently, I have chosen for this essay to take as basis of analysis the thought and policies of Julius K. Nyerere, statesman, political and social theorist, and former president of the United Republic of Tanzania for more than two decades between 1962 and 1985.[4] The purpose of the essay is to show that Nyerere has bequeathed to the world a legacy in his conviction that Christianity has the moral responsibility to join forces with his political, economic, and social theory and policy of ujamaa in the struggle against poverty because it dehumanizes people who, as Christianity itself believes, are the images of God.[5]

My choice of Nyerere's ujamaa theory narrows down significantly enough the spectrum of the discussion and engagement of this essay for us to have a clearer perception of the issues than would otherwise be possible. This is because Nyerere's thought provides us with clear parameters for thought because his socioeconomic theory is based on several important considerations. First, Nyerere looks at the issue of poverty and religion mainly from within the African situation based on African cultural assumptions and social-ethical conditions. Second, himself a devout Catholic Christian, Nyerere looks at the social question from a Christian, and specifically Catholic, viewpoint. Thus, without ignoring the wider Pan-African situation considered during the seminar, the basis of the discussion here with ujamaa as context will be the African situation. The wider concepts of "Christianity" (in the title of the essay) and "religion" (in the theme of the seminar) will be used by implication as an extension of, and inference from, Nyerere's specific perspectives of Tanzania and Catholicism.[6]

The nature of the seminar, I believe, warrants this approach. The categories of Tanzania or Africa on the one hand, and Catholicism on the other, are directly linked to the theme of religion and poverty. Further, Nyerere's thought is important as a specifically black *African* attempt to provide an alternative approach to the social question, distinct from the Euro-American, white, proletariat- or middle-class-originated ideologies of actual Bolshevism (that is, atheistic socialism/communism) in the Soviet Union and Eastern Europe and liberal capitalism in Western Europe and North America.[7]

Necessity of an African Approach

Why, however, a specifically African approach to the social question?

An African approach, such as Nyerere's ujamaa, is not only important in itself for its seriousness as an alternative systematic perception on human dignity, justice, and rational material consumption; for ethical and ecological reasons, the world needs it. Yet it is also important because of the African identity and pride it can promote. The latter is not an insignificant issue. For a long time now, African contributions on the issues of the day—health, education, economic or political organization, to mention only a few—have not received a fair hearing in the court of international discourse. They are usually dismissed out of hand as without value, largely because of lack of avenues of exposure to the world through academic study and mass communication. This becomes increasingly the case as the process of globalization gathers strength. It is therefore crucially important for the African continent and the African diaspora to disabuse themselves and the world of this complex situation of inferiority and superiority so prevalent even in the contemporary world. The seminar showed how self-deceiving it would be for anyone to think that this situation is dead.

But another justification for adopting ujamaa as a basis of analysis is internal to the system itself, as J. S. Lee has shown.[8] Lee's thesis is that Nyerere's thought and work are a legacy or "testament" to humanity. Citing Jacques Derrida, Lee observes that humanity may receive a great legacy in several ways. Two, however, are prominent and frequent. On the one hand, humanity may relegate a legacy to the past, to become a relic of things done and gone by. But there is another mode or "inflection," as Derrida calls it, to approach and appropriate a legacy, if it "is always made in front of witnesses, a witness in front of witnesses . . . to open and enjoin, . . . to confide in others the responsibility of a future."[9] It is Lee's conviction that Nyerere intended his work to be a legacy for the future. "There can be no question," he writes, "that Nyerere himself sees his philosophical legacy in . . . [the] second sense [above] of opening up a vision of the future and asking others to be answerable for this future."

But to be of any use, this legacy or testament must be applied by us, in our present circumstances. And so, as Lee phrases it, the question today is "whether or not Nyerere's testament opens up a viable future *for us*, a future for which we might be willing to accept responsibility."[10] Nyerere himself realized this, and as he put it referring to the ujamaa system: "It may be that we shall create a new synthesis of individual liberty and the needs of man in society. . . . There is need for a new synthesis; . . . we have the lessons of the East and the West before us and we have our own traditions to contribute to Mankind's pool of knowledge. If we can integrate these things into a new pattern of society then the world will have reason to be grateful that we have gained our independence."[11]

"A new pattern of society" is the intent of Nyerere's ujamaa, a moral contribution to ethical thought with reference to the contemporary economic, political, and social conditions, and in view of political and Christian religious responsibility.[12] Nyerere's thought can also form a basis for African cultural and economic renaissance whereby global issues affecting Africa must be considered with the situation of Africa in mind, especially with regard to what contribution African culture and traditions can bring to attempts to find answers to African and global issues and questions.[13]

The Issues in Focus: Religion and Poverty

The economist J. K. Galbraith distinguishes between two kinds of poverty. There is, he says, "individual" or "family" poverty afflicting "the few" or "the minority" in a generally well-off society, on the one hand, and "mass poverty," afflicting all but a few or a minority in a generally poor society, on the other. While the first form of poverty is understandable and defensible, or at least explainable, Galbraith argues that the second can have no justification; injustice, oppression, and exploitation, resulting in this kind of poverty, are failures of human civilization.[14]

This is the point Nyerere underlines in ujamaa and, according to him, mass poverty is also a sign of failure in the practice of religion, and specifically the Christian religion. Nyerere considers it one of the primary roles of the Christian faith, religion, and church to struggle to minimize or if possible eliminate this "condition" of injustice and oppression in the world, a condition he describes as both unchristian and ungodly. For Nyerere, the Christian religion has as its reason for existence the moral responsibility of creating or supporting attitudes and structures in society that aim to change or minimize mass poverty. This is necessary, he argues, "in order to fulfil its own purpose of bringing men to God." For him, "the Church must seek to ensure that men can have dignity in their lives and in their work. It must itself become a source of social justice and it must work with other forces of social justice wherever they are, and whatever they are called."[15]

According to Nyerere, this obligation is imbedded in, or is a constitutive part of, the Christian faith itself, not to do which amounts to its betrayal. "We say," he reminds Christians, "that man was created in the image of God. I refuse to imagine a God who is poor, ignorant, superstitious, fearful, oppressed, wretched—which is the lot of the majority of those He created in his own image."[16]

Based on what I saw in touring different places of the regions we visited and what was said by different scholars during the seminar, Nyerere deplores what is certainly today still the lot of the vast majority of Africans and peoples of African descent in the diaspora. Nyerere hoped that his struggle in Tanzania under the African-inspired ujamaa system would be joined by the church and would become an inspiration for justice and human dignity to other parts of the world as well, to create ethical sociopolitical and economic systems respecting principles of justice and equity.

The seminars' academic presentations and our observations in the field in Kenya, Jamaica, and the United States underline the central concern of Nyerere's ujamaa. For Nyerere, the problem confronting the world is not poverty. His contention is that the world today has the technical know-how and the material wherewithal to do away with mass poverty. The "real problem" of the world as he sees it, "the thing which creates misery, wars and hatred among men—is the division of mankind into rich and poor."[17] This is not a problem inherent in creation or nature. Nyerere believes that it is, rather, a sociopolitical and structural problem, created by human systems. It can be and needs to be faced and corrected or transformed. For Nyerere, the church's role in this task is crucial.

Nyerere's contention is that it is the role of the church to protest and support those who protest against any ideology and system that in any way takes away the dignity of the human person. Poverty and ignorance must be fought by the church because they "demoralize" those who are bound by them. A central tenet of Christian belief is that the human person images God on earth, and this for Nyerere is contradicted by the existence in society of mass poverty and its consequences.[18] This entails for Nyerere the church's actual involvement into a "revolutionary" process: "The Church must help men to rebel against their slums; it has to help them to do this in the most effective way it can be done. But most of all the Church must be obviously and openly fighting all those institutions, and power groups, which contribute to the existence and maintenance of the physical and spiritual slums— regardless of the consequences to itself and its members."[19]

Nyerere is clear in his expectation that "whenever and however circumstances make it possible, the Church must work with the people in the positive tasks of building a future based on social justice. It must participate actively in initiating, securing, and creating the changes which are necessary and which will inevitably take place."[20] What Nyerere foresees and incorporates in his vision is a constructive revolution intended to create solidarity and community, for solidarity and community as "familyhood" on the national and international levels is what ujamaa means.

Although Nyerere does not mention it explicitly, he is familiar with the social teaching of the Catholic Church, which is very developed with regard to the question of justice, human rights, and the distribution of wealth. The similarity between ujamaa's charter (the Arusha Declaration) and Pope Paul VI's letter "On the Development of Peoples" (*Populorum Progressio*), both issued in 1967, cannot be missed. The only open question is which influenced which. Very early in the letter, for example, the pope echoes directly Nyerere's concerns about the "violence" of mass poverty when he writes: "Freedom from misery; the greater assurance of finding subsistence, health, and fixed employment; an increased share of responsibility without oppression of any kind and in security from situations that do violence to their dignity as men; better education—in brief, to seek to do more, know more and have more in order to be more: that is what men aspire to now when a greater number of them are condemned to live in conditions that make this lawful desire illusory."[21]

Specifically about conditions in the South, the pope identifies the "need" of "peoples who have recently gained national independence . . . to add to . . . political freedom a fitting autonomous growth, social as well as economic, in order to assure their citizens of a full human enhancement and to take their rightful place with other nations."[22]

The Situation in Nairobi, Kingston, and Ocho Rios

Touring Nairobi and the environs of Athi River in 2001 made it painfully clear how far behind the world is from realizing the church's vision of a human civilization as articulated by Pope Paul VI and encapsulated in the philosophy and policies of ujamaa. It demonstrated how grotesque the situation of poverty in that city is, side by side with evidence of immense wealth in terms of living facilities (buildings) and social services (sanitation, roads, schools, and shopping centers). In the Mathare and Kibera slums of Nairobi, living conditions there could only be described as unfit for any human being in the twenty-first century.

In Mathare and Kibera, there were conditions that typified material poverty itself: there were open sewers everywhere, and whole families shared single-roomed corrugated iron, earthen, or cardboard structures. There were simply none of the modern conveniences here that some would take for granted, such as running water or electricity; nor were there playgrounds for the children or recreational facilities for adults. We were informed that prostitution, crime, and violence were rampant because of the ready presence of alcohol and other substances harmful to health. Observing living conditions in Kibera and Mathare, it became crystal clear that economic poverty breeds sociological and ethical problems, which in turn breed economic poverty. No one observing this situation could avoid the question, how could and would this vicious cycle of dehumanization be broken?

In contrast, the affluence of Lang'ata and Karen, Lavington and Westlands, constituting some of the wealthy suburbs of Nairobi, was like night and day in comparison to Mathare and Kibera. This showed itself not only in the size and style of buildings, some of which looked like mansions, but also in the condition of roads and other facilities found in these places. It is relevant to this discussion to note that in the Lang'ata-Karen area, there are numerous, extremely large Christian church institutions, one of which, though of moderate size compared to the others, was the venue of the seminar.

This situation repeated itself even more starkly in Jamaica, when contrasting the conditions in the section of the city of Kingston where we stayed, and especially the maroon Accompong village in the interior of the island, to the hotel resort town of Ocho Rios. In its history and political situation, Jamaica shares most of the conditions of any "two-thirds world" country, except that, being so geographically close to the United States, and depending for its survival almost entirely on tourism, its political and economic independence—worse, for example, than Kenya—is more easily manipulated by U.S. power politics and wealth. At Ocho Rios this was very clear. Observing the patrons of the hotel at the time, except for the servants at the reception desk and the maids cleaning the rooms and making up the beds, there were practically no black Jamaicans as vacationers there, despite the fact that the vast majority of Jamaicans are black. Needless to say, this is because they are poor.

In the United States, what was the situation?

The Role the Churches Have Played

Visiting churches and church-related institutions in Nairobi and in Kingston one came away with one overriding impression: the Christian churches have not as yet instituted pedagogical structures and programs that go to the root of the problem of mass poverty. But one can even go further and ask: What precisely is presented as the Christian gospel in these places, both to the materially well-to-do and the poor?

As examples, in Athi River a school run by the Seventh Day Adventist Church offers primary education to young Masai girls who had been married off by their parents or guardians while they were still children. In the Karen area of the city of Nairobi, a Roman Catholic priest runs a place called Nyumbani (meaning "at home"), which takes in and cares for orphaned and HIV-infected children. We visited a similar institution just outside of Kingston, also established by another Catholic priest, catering for severely disabled children. At another place in Jamaica the community, perhaps not directly inspired by religious but by humanitarian principles, runs a technical training program for young people.

While all of these initiatives are important and laudable, and form an intimate part of the responsibility of the Christian church as witness of the love of God for all humanity, one cannot but wonder whether they do not remain at the level of charity; whether, that is, they are not only caritative efforts that do not do much to address the root causes of the problem of mass poverty and alienation of the poor. Is this all the church sees itself doing as its mission "to proclaim the Lord's year of favour" as Jesus in Luke

4:19 describes his own mission? This is the most fundamental question that Nyerere's thinking addresses.

"The Purpose [of ujamaa]," as Nyerere entitled one of his speeches explaining the meaning of his program, "Is Man," "the practical acceptance of human equality. That is to say, every man's equal right to a decent life before any individual has a surplus above his needs; his equal right to participate in Government; and his equal responsibility to work to contribute to the society to the limit of his ability."[23] But as Nyerere sees it, the same human person is also the purpose of the Christian faith and the church, making, therefore, the promotion on earth of the equality and dignity, justice and peace, democracy and freedom of all human beings a fundamental mandate. These tenets constitute ujamaa's closest link with the Christian faith, according to Nyerere. For him, "The equality of man may or may not be susceptible to scientific [in the sense of concrete, tangible] proof. But its acceptance as a basic assumption of life in society is the core and essence of socialism,"[24] as it is for the church.

This assumption that is essentially a belief or, in religious terms, an approach of faith for things not seen but hoped for, is the basic attitude of mind that makes a person or a society socialist, more precisely a mjamaa, according to Nyerere. "No one who qualifies his belief in the equality of man is really a socialist," he avers.[25] All genuine socialist organization anywhere, though concretely it may differ and must differ in form according to various factors on the ground, must flow from this basic attitude of mind or belief. "A society in which all men are of equal account will probably be socialist [even without the label], because socialist organization is really the means by which the diversity of mankind is harnessed to the common benefit of all men. Socialism, as a system, is in fact the organization of men's inequalities to serve their equality."[26]

Taking the sense of his entire corpus of writings into account, Nyerere implies that this is basically the foundation and meaning of Christianity as well. For, as he says, the church exists to create and demonstrate visibly the dignity that is in every person as a creature and reflection of God. He believes in the revolutionary power of religion, and specifically Christianity, as a transforming agent of society based on equality, justice, human rights, and dignity. He does not fear but welcomes this power. In Nyerere's view, the socialist who is a Christian is more to be welcomed than the socialist who is an atheist. The Christian socialist seems, to Nyerere's mind, to have an advantage over other socialists with respect to the attitude of mind toward human dignity and equality that is necessary for a true socialist.

Fyodor Dostoevsky's novel *The Brothers Karamazov* may serve to illustrate this position. At one point in the novel a tsarist police official declares about socialists: "We are not particularly afraid of all these socialists, anarchists, infidels and revolutionaries. We keep watch on them and know all their doings. But there are a few peculiar ones among them who believe in God and are Christians, but at the same time are socialists. These are the people we are most afraid of. They are dreadful people. The socialist who is a Christian is more to be dreaded than the socialist who is an atheist."[27]

Nyerere's conviction about the role of religion in social change is well expressed here, that religion, and specifically Christianity, adds or rather *must* add a peculiar and fundamental dimension to the project of social change. In other words, the practice of authentic Christianity, according to Nyerere, must reorient society in a certain concrete direction, the direction of "rebellion" against systems and structures that dehumanize people, and toward justice, human dignity, and peace. Otherwise, as he puts it in graphic terms, the church will become in these fundamental issues of life and salvation "irrelevant to man and the Christian religion will degenerate into a set of superstitions accepted by the fearful,"[28] or worse, "it will become identified with injustice and persecution."[29] Uncompromisingly, he states: "Unless the Church, its members and its organizations, express God's love for man by involvement and leadership in constructive protest against the present [unjust and oppressive] conditions of man, then it will become identified with injustice and persecution. If this happens, it will die—and, humanly speaking, deserve to die—because it will then serve no purpose comprehensible to modern man."[30]

What should make Christians more revolutionary in matters of justice and human dignity than anyone else—and therefore turn them into people to be feared by those not interested in, or particularly opposed to, systems and structures of justice and human dignity—is, therefore, according to Nyerere, the very foundation or source of Christian behavior, namely, the Christian faith-in-practice. Because Christians are motivated in their actions by belief in the equality of the person as "a unique creation of a living God" created in God's image, the God of Jesus Christ, a God of justice and human dignity,[31] they have a program and commitment different from all others. This is what makes them in some people's eyes particularly "dangerous" people.[32]

Injustice and Poverty: Root Causes of Violence

In the academic part of the seminar, most of the guest speakers in Kenya and Jamaica—while of course approaching the issue from different perspectives according to their disciplines—concurred that poverty, even more than "terrorism," is the great problem of the twenty-first century. Poverty and inequality are at the root of violence, only one—and comparatively small—aspect of which is terrorism. The gap between the wealthy regions of the northern hemisphere and the poor regions generally in the southern hemisphere is seen to be increasing even as the wealth of the world in general increases.[33] The violence and sources of global violence in and from the South (and even from the South in the North) also seem to be increasing exponentially, showing the necessary link that exists between poverty and violence. When individuals, groups, or societies are alienated by poverty amidst obvious opulence surrounding but withheld from them in ways that they find to be unjust, they become fertile grounds for deep dissatisfaction, simmering resentment, anger, and violence. This is the case for Africa and among people of African descent everywhere.[34]

Whatever area of life or form of discourse one may choose to look at or use (e.g., social, political or economic, or emotional, rational, or religious), we note one sad fact. Contact between Africa and the outside world has predominantly been a story of unequal relations of oppression and exploitation against the African continent and its peoples. When we speak about people of African origin in the diaspora—specifically in Europe and the United States—we cannot avoid thinking about the phenomena of slavery and racism, forms of blatant exploitation and human degradation that contributed in a major way to the unequal relationship between the white and black peoples. They also affected negatively the growth of the African economies, the consequences of which are still evident today.[35]

Necessity of Comprehensive Democratization

Nowadays, as Horace Campbell has pointed out, "discussion on globalization seeks to assert a political agenda which depoliticises those with an objective interest in developing the ideas, organisation and leadership to transform the present lopsided division of the product of human labour."[36] However, "A thrust to democratise access to the new technologies so that the reconstruction of the global economy and the rehabilitation of the natural environment would call on the skills, knowledge and experience of the African peoples and other oppressed peoples to reverse the destruction which now proceeds unchecked in the name of market forces is urgent."[37] Nyerere recognized this and during his leadership in Tanzania refused to allow unrestrained "liberalization," recognizing that the developed countries were unwilling to "democratize" technologies. He realized that in the prevailing system Tanzania and the South would continue to be sucked inexorably into neocolonialist situations under the leadership of economic multi- or transnational economic organizations that are also representatives, in Nyerere's perception, of political ideological systems of exploitation and human degradation. He was convinced that the last thing they would do is to undercut their economic, and therefore social and political hegemony by "calling on the skills, knowledge and experience of the African peoples," as Campbell puts it, except to enhance their power and profits.

As chairman and member of the Group of 77, the largest political forum of the South, Nyerere relentlessly warned against the economic policies of the Bretton Woods institutions (i.e., the World Bank, the International Monetary Fund), which were in the forefront of pushing this on to the South. Under them, the new international economic order proposed by the South—which called for a change in systems of trade so that there would be equity of value between the raw materials from the South and the manufactured goods from the North—would not be possible. These northern-initiated institutions were pushing for more "aid,"[38] but what Nyerere was asking for the South, as the key to break the cycle of exploitation through and under the guise of the global market, was fair trade.

In Nairobi, Jude Ongonga, for example, pointed out in his presentation how the economies of Africa continue to crumble today, largely because of the built-in inequalities in the systems of the movement of globalization.[39] As evidence of this he cited the high rates there of malnutrition, illiteracy, disease, and infant mortality, and the unimaginably squalid living conditions such as were witnessed in Kibera and Mathare during our tours around the city—and this as we enter the twenty-first century. According to Ongonga, this is because Africa does not control the enormous material and human resources it possesses. In this sense, globalization has become a process of removing these resources from Africa (and other parts of the two-thirds world) to and for the benefit of the industrially developed parts of the North.[40] Obviously, the "trickle down" economic theory advanced by so many capitalist economists, which maintains that the wealth of the rich inevitably trickles down to satisfy the needs of the poor, has not worked for Kenya. Another presenter in Nairobi, J. N. K. Mugambi, put it pithily this way: "Africa produces what it does not consume and consumes what it does not produce."[41] As far as African societies are concerned, that is the tragedy, a cause and consequence of poverty.

The implications of this situation on the economic development of the continent and on its people's sense of freedom, dignity, and respect for their human rights are immense, and they are completely negative. Agnes Aboum in Nairobi offered specific examples.[42] She mentioned how global institutions such as GATT (the General Agreement on Tariffs and Trade), one of the institutions set up at Bretton Woods, in the United States, by the West after the Second World War to regulate global economic transactions, has over the years ensured the recolonization of Africa through structures that entrench indebtedness in the continent's economies. The World Bank continues to function in the same way, according to Aboum. As she explained, the bank's structural adjustment programs imposed on African countries in return for bi- or multilateral loans or aid fundamentally turn every aspect of human life in Africa into a commodity. So also do the conditionalities for loans and grants set up by the IMF. "Development," in the view of these institutions, becomes purely technocratic, with little room for the insights that indigenous culture, knowledge, or religion can offer. This Nyerere rejected.

The only effective antidote against this is, in the mind of Nyerere, the process of democratization, and not only political but also, and especially, *economic* democratization. This is what ujamaa sought to do for Tanzania. Nyerere's conviction was that there cannot be political independence where economic independence is lacking. For him, the principle of democracy and participation derives from the foundation of equality and human dignity. As Lee concludes from studying Derrida and in line with Nyerere's thinking, "The spirit of democracy . . . is to be found in the promise of an encounter with the unique and absolute otherness of the other. To do justice to this spirit . . . would be to nurture a cultural imagination in which it will be possible for the infinite alterity of others to be recognized as such and, thus, to be fully encountered."[43] Continuing, Lee writes: "The moral for democracy is clear: for the spirit of democracy to be realized, we each must develop and nourish the paradoxical ability to give what we do not have. In particular, we must, in some sense, give the other the other's infinite alterity. That is, we must imagine and try to construct a society in which the other's alterity can be fully recognized and realized, not reduced to some finite characteristics already found in ourselves."[44] The economic North has, however, persistently found it hard to recognize this otherness of the African other. It found it difficult to understand Nyerere when he planned for Tanzania and the South to develop "out of our own roots . . . by emphasizing certain characteristics of our own traditional organization, and extending them so that they can embrace the possibilities of modern technology and enable us to meet the challenge of life . . . [today]."[45] What the North seeks to do is to "globalize" radically, which simply means turning the other into its own image and likeness, economically, politically, and culturally.

Anne Nasimiyu at Nairobi, though critical of some oppressive aspects of

African culture, expressed her conviction that African culture and religion can help in the process of eradicating anthropological poverty in terms of affirming the Africanness of Africans and the self-acceptance of people of African origin anywhere in the world.[46] It can also provide practical orientations on the moral obligation to share wealth. Nasimiyu's most profound observation was that without self-acceptance and esteem, an aspect of the process of recognizing the otherness of the other, economic development for this other will inevitably be hampered.

The process of recognizing and accepting the other's alterity, which Lee calls the "democratic imagination," is for Nyerere the "attitude of mind" that, in his view, should be the driving principle of "socialism" or ujamaa—understood as economic and social systems and processes based on justice and equity—within and among nations. For Nyerere, "In a socialist society it is the socialist attitude of mind, and not the rigid adherence to a standard political pattern, which is needed to ensure that the people care for each other's welfare."[47]

Lee explains this in terms of intellectual and moral orientations, "the creative products of culture—institutions, works of art, bodies of knowledge —that serve as the 'third thing' mediating between one person and another, one community and another," and facilitating "a mode of exchange that goes 'beyond the law.' "[48] The entire political, social, and economic project of Nyerere and ujamaa lies in this effort.

Further Dimensions of Poverty

Although the phenomenon of poverty is immediately perceived as material deprivation—which is of course true—the presentations in Nairobi and Ocho Rios showed that it has a psychological dimension on the human person as well, since the person is constituted of somatic, pneumatic, and psychic dimensions. Eric Asseka at the Nairobi seminar session mentioned these dimensions as entry points of religion in economic considerations, and that they provide the possibility of discussing economics ethically.[49] With examples taken from various African initiated churches whose ethical foundations are African, Philomena Mwaura illustrated for the conference in Nairobi how these churches approach this situation more successfully than the mainline Christian churches.[50]

For Asseka, it is an essential element of religion to work with the poor toward justice and social empowerment. In his view, material poverty, according to the Bible, affects the body, the temple of the Holy Spirit; it dampens the human spirit, tending it toward evil in contradiction to God's intent for the human person; it dulls the mind, which, because of its creative potential, makes the human being the closest creature to God.[51] Because corruption is a form of injustice and causes poverty, it is an ethical issue. Asseka finds that the church has consequently a fundamental duty to attack it on the individual, institutional, and systemic levels. But this is precisely Nyerere's point with ujamaa.

The Dominant Discourse of Homogenization

The tensions and conflicts typifying much of the world today are a logical consequence of the dominant discourse currently controlling the social, economic, and political life of groups and nations. Since the last two decades of the twentieth century, international discourse is marked by extreme homogenizing theories, tendencies, and practices. In its essence and basic form, this is not new; it is characteristic of and basic to brute human relations. The tribal shared psychic feeling of exclusion, of "we," different from "them," and therefore against "them," has existed, as far as we can tell, since primitive times.

But the logic of exclusion leads inevitably to the logic of oppression, imperialism, and assimilation, and ultimately genocide. It is a form of reasoning and behavior that ultimately does not acknowledge the other as other. Yet, it is even more radical in destructive consequences. Because the others are different from us, they do not deserve to exist. Hence, their existence may legitimately be wiped out or, at the very least, must be pegged to ours. This was precisely the innermost objective of slavery and imperialism, the latter most clearly expressed in the form of classical colonialism.[52] It is also the logic of all kinds of discrimination and oppression, overt or covert, and ultimately genocide, as was the case with the encounter between the colonialists and conquistadors from Europe and the native peoples of North and South America and Australia. Classism (that is, the notion and ideology of class distinctions based on a priori established socioeconomic and often political value judgments), racism, and sexism also find their foundation and justification here.

Obviously, this was the basic and controlling element of the theoretical discourse and practical confrontations during the cold war between the communist and capitalist ideologies, often expressed in very crude ways of open struggle for dominance of the universe. The development and subsequent use of weapons of mass destruction (used for the first time on the Japanese cities of Hiroshima and Nagasaki) and the arms race in general since then were direct consequences of this. Even apparently the benign scientific advances in space exploration that followed were motivated by militaristic competition between the then Soviet Union and the United States, the leaders of the Eastern and Western blocs of nations. In the countries of the southern hemisphere, the competition between these two powers played itself out by proxy. Until the collapse of Soviet communism in the late 1980s, African, Asian, and Latin American nations were continually being divided into two camps, economically and politically, to advance the respective ideologies of the two powers.

Because of changed circumstances in awareness throughout the world, classical imperialism has been rendered politically odious, socially impractical, and often economically unprofitable or unviable. This is not to say, however, that the logic of assimilation among humans has been thereby somehow miraculously eliminated. Something else has taken its place—the sophisticated assimilation of globalization. Its purpose and consequences are the same as the original: it negates the identity of the other; it denies the dignity of the other and the other's right to exist except as an appendage of the dominator; it causes destruction of cultures and identities and thrives on expropriation of resources from the dominated regions. Whatever language it is couched in, these are its practical and intended results. It is not a civilizing process, as evidenced by the conflicts it has and is engendering. Nyerere intended ujamaa as a movement to counter this unchristian spirit.

As Nyerere saw things, "civilization," in the true sense of the notion, involves taming and directing the primitive human instincts of domination and assimilation in interpersonal relations, but particularly in intergroup and international relations. Civilization allows the process of sociocultural and politico-economic cross-fertilization indeed to take place, but to do so symbiotically, as it were, each element benefiting from the other without necessarily eliminating it. This is also in essence the meaning of radical democracy, including, as has been stated, not only political representation, but most basically economic empowerment. The reasoning here is that there cannot be authentic recognition of the other's identity on the basis of political democracy alone. There must also exist economic equity, in the sense that essential needs of every human person in the social entity are fulfilled.[53]

Concluding Remarks

By way of conclusion on ujamaa as Nyerere's testament or legacy to humanity, I need to address some important points. There are two major objections frequently advanced against ujamaa. Because, as we have seen, ujamaa claimed to be a "socialist" program at a time when real existing communism was exerting a considerable (and, in the view of many, negative) influence in many parts of the world, the leaders of the Christian church—particularly in Tanzania itself—and the noncommunist world in general, accused it of being an atheistic ideology. It has already been noted how Nyerere debunks the notion that ujamaa was a clone of communism. We have also noted how he insists that although ujamaa as a system was not allied to any religious persuasion, and could not do so and remain democratic, it was nevertheless not antireligion. Nyerere is clear in his expositions of this position that the freedom of religious assembly and worship cannot be infringed without jeopardizing ujamaa's principle of democracy.[54]

But perhaps a more serious criticism against ujamaa is that it was not realistic in its principles and that it failed to take into account the facts of—in Christian terms—"fallen" human nature. In other words, Nyerere and ujamaa are seen by these critics as too utopian and therefore too naive to be practical. Although love and sharing may be good religious aspirations, it is argued, they cannot be made principles upon which to construct a political system for a nation.

From very early on, Nyerere was acutely conscious of this criticism and objection. But he rejects it as "nonsensical." Explaining, he argues that all "social principles are, by definition, ideals towards which to strive and by which to exercise self-criticism. The question to ask is not whether they are capable of achievement, which is absurd, but whether a society of free men can do without them. Like democracy, they are easier to approximate in smaller societies than in large ones. But like democracy, they remain equally valid for both small and large societies—for both traditional and modern Africa."[55]

Derrida puts this claim of Nyerere more philosophically. For him, authentic democracy in this contemporary situation of globalization implies

the opening of . . . [the] gap between an infinite promise (always untenable at least for the reason that it calls for the infinite respect of the singularity and infinite alterity of the other as much as for the respect of the countable, calculable, subjectal equality between anonymous singularities) and the determined, necessary, but also necessarily inadequate forms of what has to be measured against this promise. To this extent, the effect, or actuality of the democratic promise, like that of the communist promise, will always keep within it, and it must do so, this absolutely undermined messianic hope at its heart, this eschatological relation to the to-come of an event and of a singularity, of an alterity that cannot be anticipated.[56]

But how are we to know whether or not Nyerere's work is a testament of significance for our future, that of the Christian faith, and of the church in the contemporary world?

The only way to do so is to begin by getting familiar with the testament itself, or at least the principles that make it viable from our perspective as Christians. Christians, to be sure, see, experience, and are affected by the same reality as anybody else. But they are mandated to see something more in reality. The Christian faith and orientation are believed to give that edge in perception that might elude the nonbeliever.

Concretely, then, what do Christians see in the present reality of poverty in Africa and elsewhere, and what are the ways to deal with it, which would be a unique contribution to the contemporary world that is now character-ized above all by economic, cultural, and even political globalization? If we revert to Lee again, he sees the underlying principle of Nyerere's philosophy to be transformation or what in technical theological terminology we would refer to as conversion, *metanoia*. For Nyerere, the necessary and basic foun-dation of his ujamaa system is not primarily a certain particular ideology or social structure. Yes, these are important to him and have to be devised, because they are needed to make ujamaa sociologically concrete and ef-fective. But what is most important of all is the transformation of the mind and heart toward human unity and equality, the civilization of mutual care, formed by the human conscience for society in its political, social, and economic manifestations.

There is no need to belabor the point here that Nyerere therefore opposed universal uniformity in the socialist economic and political forms and prac-tices then existing. This civilization has to be created depending on the concrete circumstances presenting themselves at every particular time and place. He scoffed at the attempts then prevailing to collapse all forms of socialism worldwide into one so-called "scientific socialism." This to him amounted to making a dogmatic religious belief out of socialism, something that he utterly rejected, saying:

> This attempt to create a new religion out of socialism is absurd. It is not scientific, and it is almost certainly not Marxist—for however combatant and quarrelsome Marx was, he never claimed to be an infallible divinity! Marx was a great thinker. He gave a brilliant analysis of the industrial capitalist society in which he lived; he diagnosed its ills and advocated certain remedies which he believed would lead to the development of a healthy society. But he was not God. The years have proved him wrong in certain respects just as they have proved him right in others. Marx did not

write revealed truth; his books are a result of hard thinking and hard work, not a revelation from God. It is therefore unscientific to appeal to his writings as Christians appeal to the Bible, or Muslims to the Koran.[57]

For Nyerere in the context of Tanzania (as for everywhere else), this means that "our social change will be determined by our own needs as we see them, and in the direction that we feel to be appropriate for us at any particular time. We shall draw sustenance from universal human ideas and from the practical experiences of other peoples; but we start from a full acceptance of our African-ness and a belief that in our own past there is very much which is useful for our future."[58]

Today, liberal capitalism remains the strongest ideology in the world. It is undergirded and spread by the wings of globalization, and operates under an attitude of mind almost as rigid as that of last century's communism. What is the place of Nyerere's testament in this turn of events? We can agree with Lee that if ujamaa remains for Christians a beacon into the future, and not merely a relic of the past, "this is because his [Nyerere's] call for transformation of attitudes of mind has a new relevance in the cultural context of informational capitalism."[59]

Notes

1. On this, see, for example, the discussion by Kossi A. Ayedze elsewhere in this volume on the ambiguous role of Christianity with regard to poverty in sub-Saharan Africa.

2. This came about through the reading of the Bible, catechesis, and civil education, and even though such teaching was not directly intended to be liberating in the sense that we are pointing out, this was nevertheless the result.

3. The significance of this question is for Christianity as old as the Christian religion itself. Jesus was very conscious of the poor to the extent of defining his mission, as in Luke 4:18–19 and Matt. 25:31–46, in terms of their liberation. But of course, in Christian self-perception, the link between religion and poverty is even much older, as can be seen in the demands for the Jubilee Year in the Hebrew Scriptures (the Old Testament) in Lev. 25. Similar attitudes seem to be evident in Islam in the Koran, as well as in other religions, to the extent that it can be said that all religions are in practice ethical systems or systems of ethics.

4. Of all the African statesmen of the twentieth century—the century of Africa's political independence from colonial rule—Ghana's Kwame Nkrumah, South Africa's Nelson Mandela, and Julius K. Nyerere must surely be counted among the most significant. But, arguably, of all African leaders of the twentieth century, it is Nyerere who gave the clearest and most concrete articulation to Africa's commitment to freedom, human rights, dignity, and unity—Africa's "otherness"—in his sociopolitical-economic philosophy and expression in the policy of ujamaa, a form of socialism founded on African culture. For the achievements of Nyerere and his leadership, see,

for instance, Haroub Othman, ed., *Reflections on Leadership in Africa: Forty Years after Independence (Essays in Honour of Mwalimu Julius K. Nyerere, on the Occasion of His 75th Birthday)* (Waversesteenweg-Brussels: VUB University Press, 2000); Y. N. Vinokurov, ed., *Julius Nyerere: Humanist, Politician, Thinker* (Peramiho, Tanzania: Benedictine Publications Ndanda, 2003); and Godfrey Mwakikagile, *Nyerere and Africa: End of an Era. Biography of Julius Kambarage Nyerere (1922–1999)* (Colchester, U.K.: Protea Publishing, 2002).

5. Nyerere left behind a fuller record than many of his fellow contemporary African leaders of his thought and political program on behalf of the dignity and humanity of the poor in his writings and speeches, poems, translated works, and other written reflections. The ujamaa "experiment" in Tanzania has generated much academic thought and discussion all over the world.

6. According to Horst Sing, "Since the beginning of industrialisation Christianity has, more than any other religion, dealt with the social question. In this context it is particularly the Catholic Church that has developed a social doctrine that is not only to be understood in a theological sense but also corresponds to non-theological-philosophical understanding." See his "Emerging Alternatives to Globalization and Transformative Action," in *Globalization and Its Victims As Seen by the Victims*, ed. Michael Amaladoss (Delhi: Vidyajyoti Education and Welfare Society/ISPCK, 1999), 202.

7. Since the late 1980s socialism/communism has generally been discredited by many around the world as a failed ideology, with the consequent split in the former Soviet bloc of countries. Capitalism, on the other hand, has since then largely been celebrated as having "triumphed" over all other socioeconomic ideologies to become the only viable universal socioeconomic system, with the accompanying spread of capitalist globalization. These may be statements of fact; they do not, as far as Nyerere was concerned, necessarily confer ethical or moral value upon these systems.

8. See J. S. Lee, "The Testament of Julius Nyerere," in J. M. Bahemuka and J. L. Brockington, *East Africa in Transition* (Nairobi: Acton Publishers, 2001), 212.

9. Lee, "The Testament," 212.

10. Ibid. Italics are his.

11. Quoted in J. van Bergen, *Development and Religion in Tanzania: Sociological Soundings on Christian Participation in Rural Transformation* (Madras: Christian Literature Society, 1981), 234.

12. "Ujamaa" is often loosely interpreted as "socialism." But the correct interpretation of the concept, according to Nyerere, would be "familyhood," the sum total of institutions and attitudes that made possible the existence and survival of the African family, clan, and society, whose major requirements were cooperation and sharing, adapted to modern requirements and needs. Above all, and contrary to Marxist socialism, ujamaa was not atheistic. As Nyerere explained it, "Always socialism [or ujamaa] will try to enlarge freedom, and religious freedom is an essential part of man's liberty." See Julius K. Nyerere, *Freedom and Socialism/Uhuru na Ujamaa: A Selection from Writings and Speeches, 1965–1967* (Dar es Salaam: Oxford University Press, 1968), 14.

13. The idea of an "African Renaissance," broached a few years ago by South African president Thabo Mbeki, is gaining strength in the discourse on African development in African academic and political circles, as well as in popular thought, as

evidenced by the popular press. The idea is crucial for the identity and development of the African continent and for peoples of African origin in general, wherever they may be, especially at this time when, more than ever before, African peoples are being exploited in overt and covert ways economically, culturally, religiously, and intellectually. This is an insidious situation because, as a result, African peoples and people of African descent are being impoverished "anthropologically," that is, thoroughly in every way. Their human dignity is subtly being progressively degraded at every level of their existence. Nyerere's perspective on combating this situation of absolute impoverishment, and the role of the Christian religion in the effort and struggle to change it, provides a useful and relevant approach to the social question, one that the community of nations in the twenty-first century cannot afford to ignore.

14. J. K. Galbraith, *The Nature of Mass Poverty* (London: Penguin Books, 1979), 13–14.

15. Julius K. Nyerere, *Freedom and Development/Uhuru na Mendeleo: A Selection from Writings and Speeches, 1968–1973* (Dar es Salaam: Oxford University Press, 1973), 219. Nyerere's use of what is now gender-insensitive language was at the time innocent. In all references and quotations from his writings, I have left it as it appears in the original sources.

16. Ibid., 216.

17. Ibid., 213.

18. See ibid., 216.

19. Ibid., 220.

20. Ibid.

21. Paul VI, *Populorum Progressio*, no. 6. The text of the letter can be found in, among others, David J. O'Brien and Thomas A. Shannon, eds., *Catholic Social Thought: The Documentary Heritage* (Maryknoll, N.Y.: Orbis Books, 1982), 240–62; or Michael Walsh and Brian Davies, eds., *Proclaiming Justice and Peace: Papal Documents from Rerum Novarum through Centesimus Annus* (Mystic, Conn.: Twenty-Third Publications, 1991), 223–44.

22. Paul VI, *Populorum Progressio*.

23. Nyerere, *Freedom and Socialism*, 324–25.

24. Ibid.

25. Nyerere, *Freedom and Socialism*, 4.

26. Ibid.

27. Quoted by J. C. Cort, *Dreadful Conversions: The Making of a Catholic Socialist* (New York: Fordham University Press, 2003), vi.

28. Nyerere, *Freedom and Development*, 215–16.

29. Ibid., 216.

30. Ibid.

31. Ibid.

32. See also Acts 16:20–21. Because of Paul's action of restoring a slave girl to wholeness, the people who have turned her into an instrument of profit become angry and accuse him and his companion Silas of sedition: "These people . . . are disturbing our city and are advocating customs that are not lawful for us . . . to adopt or practice." Similar accusations for similar reasons of liberating goodness are to be seen throughout the book of the Acts of the Apostles.

33. Wayne Ellwood in *No-Nonsense Guide to Globalization* (Oxford: New Internationalist Publications; London: Verso, 2001), 23, points out that many people now refer to the

South, mainly with demographics in mind, as "the Two-Thirds World," "the Majority World," or geographically simply as "the South." But it should also be kept in mind that the situation of poverty found in the global South can also be found in sections of the northern hemisphere: thus the designation the "South in the North."

34. See Garnet Roper, "Materiality and Spirituality: Religion and Poverty in Africa and Its Diaspora. Public Expectations and Public Policy vs. Poverty and Insurgency," address to the members of the Pan-African Seminar on Religion and Poverty, United Theological College of the West Indies, July 2003. Also Takatso Mofokeng, "The Informal Economy: The Religion of Global Capital," and J. N. K. Mugambi, "Christianity and Poverty in Contemporary Africa," lectures delivered at the Seminar on Religion and Poverty, Nairobi, July 2001. All of these papers are in unpublished form in the ownership of this author.

35. See Denis Benn and Kenneth Hall, eds., *Globalisation: A Calculus of Inequality. Perspectives from the South* (Kingston: Ian Randle Publishers, 2000). Also Katie G. Cannon, "An Ethical Mapping of the Transatlantic Slave Trade," this volume.

36. Horace Campbell, "Visions of Leaders in the 21st Century: The Nyerere Legacy," in Othman, *Reflections on Leadership in Africa*, 73. His entire article, 67–92, is worth reading for the insight it provides on Nyerere's vision or testament. See also S. M. Wangwe, "Globalisation and Marginalisation: Africa's Economic Challenges in the 21st Century," in Othman, *Reflections on Leadership in Africa*, 179–94.

37. Campbell, "Visions," 73.

38. Even where "aid" is concerned, very few wealthy countries give to the South in bilateral or multilateral economic assistance the very small percentage of the GNP proposed by the United Nations. Moreover, "assistance" is offered in such a way that all of it and more is repatriated in other forms, for example, by insisting that experts and machinery to actuate the projects for which assistance is given be from the donor country, even though it would have been cheaper and more efficient to use local resources or those from a third country.

39. Jude Ogonga's ideas are recalled from my notes on his lecture to the seminar in its meeting in Nairobi. I do not have his paper at hand.

40. See Ellwood, *No-Nonsense Guide*, chart on 33, and also for the South in general, charts on 47, 48, 50, and 101. See also L. Wallach and M. Sforza, *The WTO: Five Years of Reasons to Resist Corporate Globalization* (New York: Seven Stories Press, 1999), 55–58.

41. Recalled from notes on his presentation to the seminar in Nairobi.

42. Her ideas are recalled here from my notes on her presentation to the seminar.

43. Lee, "The Testament," 219.

44. Ibid.

45. Nyerere, *Freedom and Socialism*, 2.

46. Ideas recalled from personal notes on her presentation.

47. Nyerere, *Freedom and Unity*, 162.

48. Lee, "The Testament," 221.

49. His ideas are recalled from personal notes on his presentation.

50. See Philomena Njeri Mwaura, "Religion, Poverty and the African Instituted Churches," paper presented at the Pan-African Seminar on Religion and Poverty, Loreto Mary Ward Centre, Langata, Kenya, 23 July 2001. The paper is in the possession of this author.

51. See Psalm 8.

52. In relation to sexism in the Christian religion, for example, through its inter-

pretation of the Bible, see the penetrating feminist theological-biblical critique of biblical hermeneutics by Musa W. Dube, *Postcolonial Feminist Interpretation of the Bible* (St. Louis, Mo.: Chalice Press, 2000).

53. See Reginald Herbold Green, "Vision of Human-Centred Development: A Study In Moral Economy," in *Mwalimu: The Influence of Nyerere*, ed. Colin Legum and Geoffrey Mmari (London: James Currey; Dar-es-Salaam: Mkuki na Nyota; Trenton, N.J.: Africa World Press, 1995), 80–107. Other contributions in the volume are also useful to read on this issue.

54. See Nyerere, *Freedom and Socialism*, 12–14.

55. Nyerere, *Freedom and Unity*, 13.

56. Quoted by Lee, "The Testament," 219.

57. Nyerere, *Freedom and Socialism*, 15.

58. Ibid., 316.

59. Lee, "The Testament," 216.

Noel Leo Erskine | **CARIBBEAN ISSUES**

THE CARIBBEAN AND AFRICAN AMERICAN

CHURCHES' RESPONSE

The Caribbean islands are among the better known countries in our world. Yet their importance is marginal. Like many other third world countries they emerged from centuries of colonialism, mismanagement, and the struggle to eke out an existence. In spite of this history it is difficult to find a people who are more inventive, creative, and committed to struggle to make their world a better place.

The history of the region is one in which the colonial overlords imposed their will on indigenous populations, resulting in their extermination and the enslavement of millions torn from their homes in Africa and forced to work on plantations. The history of the Caribbean then is a history of a people who struggled against colonial empires that sought to expropriate their lands. It is the history of a people who sought to free themselves from the control of their imperialistic masters. Because of this common history the word "Caribbean" points to a people with a common legacy, similar problems, and a vocabulary that includes such words as "colonialism," "neocolonialism," "racism," "underdevelopment," "plantations," "slaves," "sugar cane," and "bananas." The history is one, and the problems are similar. There are also similar patterns in our culture. Sergio Arce Martínez and Dora Valentín of Cuba capture this for us:

> Of course, there are instances where the syncretism does not produce exactly the same results but they are never very different. Jamaican *pocomania* (like Haitian "voodoo") is the equivalent of Cuban *Santeria*. Does a Cuban or a Dominican, a Puerto Rican or a Haitian need an explanation of Trinidad's calypso? Do not the deeply rooted Cuban *soneros*, Dominician *merengueros*, or Puerto Rican *plenarios* find their counterpart in that country's deep rooted "calypsonians"? Origins, pains, problems, mixtures,

creations, struggles, hopes, religions: above and beyond the futile differences—linguistic and otherwise—we are all joined not only by a common geography, but, more importantly, by a common history.[1]

Martínez and Valentín, while correct concerning many similarities among several islands, do not sufficiently call attention to differences such as languages and religions. For example, in several islands Spanish, French, Dutch, and English are spoken and along with the difference in languages are cultural differences. In Guyana and Trinidad Hinduism is a major religion, which also points to ethnic tensions in these populations. Many Christians in Jamaica would not be able to make sense of Hindu ritual. While we affirm the commonalities among Caribbean people, we must also be aware that there are many differences.

Martínez and Valentín further characterize the Caribbean culture as one of resistance. This resistance took various forms as Caribbean people resisted the colonizers, often without weapons as the colonizers sought to steal their lands, gold, and women. Although the natives virtually disappeared, they bequeathed to us a culture of resistance. It should also be noted that enslaved Africans outnumbered Europeans in most Caribbean islands during the eighteenth and nineteenth centuries.

In many of the colonies they organized uprisings, burned plantations, and killed slave masters. Some of the leaders are still remembered: Nanny and Sam Sharp in Jamaica, Cuffy in Guyana, and Morales in Cuba.[2] The culture of resistance was dramatized in the island of Haiti in 1789, the largest sugar plantation in the Caribbean. This resistance was led by Toussaint L'Ouverture, a slave, under the slogan of the French revolution, "Liberty, Equality, and Fraternity." Haitians rebelled for freedom and turned Haiti into an independent republic in 1803.[3]

The Haitian revolution kindled the imaginations of African peoples in the diaspora when enslaved persons in North Carolina under the leadership of Denmark Vesey and Nat Turner in Virginia rebelled for change. "The Haitian revolution gave courage to enslaved persons all over the Caribbean. In Guadeloupe and St. Lucia the slaves helped repel British invasion and sustained French revolutionary control. In Grenada and Dominica the slaves joined free mulattoes and resident French. There was a major slave revolt in Dutch Curaco."[4]

The culture of resistance, characteristic of Caribbean people for over five hundred years, provided a key that unlocked the doors of freedom in many island states. In this essay I will investigate the way Caribbean scholars and ecclesiastical leaders talk about the crises afflicting the Caribbean and inquire concerning the responses Caribbean and African American churches make. I inquire concerning the role of the church, Caribbean and African-American, in the formation of a culture of resistance for a number of reasons.

First, as brothers and sisters of the African diaspora, we share a common history of slavery and seek the common goal of freedom. Further, the basic fact of our existence is poverty. What is especially hurtful for our brothers and sisters in the United States of America is the reality that they live in the midst of an economy of abundance. Martin Luther King Jr. describes the plight of the African Americans as constituting "an island of poverty in an ocean of plenty." Far too many African Americans continue to live on the margins of society, still hoping to make the American dream their own. In a profound sense the black person in America also needs the formation of a culture of resistance to tackle the plethora of crises that demean the spirit and harm the community. Much of black existence in the United States is tantamount to life in the colony in which the white man gives the orders, makes the rules, and occasionally allows blacks into the white world as long as they are willing to play by white rules. Failure to play by white rules results in becoming devalued. What is needed here are strategies and practices that mirror a culture of resistance. In the Caribbean we dream of the day when we will move from the status of developing nations to become self-sufficient. In the United States of America the black person still dreams of the day when he/she will be treated with fairness and justice, of the day when the playing fields will be leveled. Some speak of this day as integration, others of liberation into the world of economic well-being. The black person in the United States of America has discovered, as we in the Caribbean learned long ago, that our poverty is not due to our laziness or indolence; the truth is, our poverty is contrived. We have both discovered that there is a history of colonialism, of exploitation, and domination. We have been made poor. Our poverty is a consequence of the relationship of the "colonizer and the colonized." Colonialism was not merely an aspect of the history of slavery and the struggle for political independence and adult suffrage; it was a relationship in which white people controlled the lives of black people.

When we look at the plight of the black male, whether in the Caribbean or in the United States of America, we see a history in which the oppressor provided for the black man's family, protected his family, and found ways too numerous to mention to emasculate him. The black man was reduced to being a boy as he internalized the negative self-image of his oppressor. The protracted oppression made black people impotent. The situation was even worse for the black woman. She was an object of frequent rape, violence, and abuse of the master. Often her family was sold away from her and she had to work in the fields from sunup until sundown. She too was brutally flogged by the master, sometimes while pregnant. Thus, our consciousness is a dominated consciousness. In a context in which we are still not allowed to raise critical questions, we dare to require an answer from the oppressor.

I find much help in an article by Emmanuel Katongole of East Africa, "Liberalization Is Not the Only Solution: Pastor Reflects on Poverty in Africa." He contends that the most important theological problem in Africa is the widening gap between rich and poor and the increasing impoverishment and pauperization of the great majority of the African population. He presses for a church in Africa that will adopt strategies and a theology of salvation that will make a material difference in the living conditions of people. There is a danger that the church will just go along with the status quo and refuse to question why so many Africans are poor and what may be done to change their lot. "The church just faithfully walks alongside those condemned by the harsh realities of poverty, helping them carry the cross by offering spiritual encouragement and promise of a good reward in heaven."[5] Katongole presses for a prophetic church that is committed to practical solutions to Africa's problems. A similar point was made in a visit to the All Africa Conference of Churches in Nairobi in July 2001, where the conference insisted that Africa needs a prophetic church that will translate the gospel of Christ into social praxis as a way to lead people out of economic and social maladies. I found a theology of faith and hope in Ghana and South Africa in recent visits. In these countries I found churches that were proactive in providing answers for poor people, whether in fighting AIDS among children or in care for the elderly.

It is precisely at this point I believe that African and African American churches have much to teach us in the Caribbean. As the Caribbean learns from these churches, it must access the riches of its own experience and speak in its own voice. We must pray, "Lord lead us not into imitation." Caribbean people must break the stranglehold of our oppressor and begin to fashion a language that will open up a new future for us, a future of our own making. We must begin to break the chains that control our minds. We must cease asking for permission; rather, we must seize the opportunity to create a future for ourselves and our children. As we fashion a culture of resistance to help us deal with issues of identity, gender, sexual orientation, class, and race, we must begin to raise critical questions concerning the ordering of society. We must ask why power is concentrated in the hands of a few people while the majority are powerless to determine their own destinies. We must affirm that the image of God is rooted in all of us and as such we are all sons and daughters of God. It was this discovery in the civil rights movement in America that became the turning point of the movement, the discovery that the central issue was not access to white establishments, whether these were restaurants or churches; the issue was power. And so when Rap Brown and Stokely Carmichael (who was both African American and Caribbean) cried black power, the walls of segregation were shaken to their very foundations. As Martin Luther King Jr. taught us, love without power is anemic and power without love is calculated. Love coupled with power leads to the creation of the just society—a society in which we do not only press for equality of opportunities but for equality of conditions as we create space for the enhancement of justice in all dimensions of our common life.

Bob Marley reminds us in his "Redemption Song" that God empowers the oppressed as they seek to fashion a culture of resistance:

Old pirates, yes
They rob I
Sold I to the merchants ships
Minutes after they took I
From the bottomless pit
But my hand was made strong
By the hand of the Almighty
We forward in this generation
Triumphantly.
Won't you help to sing
These songs of freedom?
Cause all I ever have
Redemption songs.[6]

The African American Witness in Jamaica and Haiti

I would like now to look at the African American contribution to Jamaica and Haiti at the turn of the eighteen and nineteenth centuries and see what lessons we may learn as we press for cooperation between Christian churches in the United States and the Caribbean. I have chosen Jamaica and Haiti as points of departure for talk about cooperation between African Americans and Caribbean peoples for a number of reasons.

First, the African American connection goes back to the period of slavery, when several hundred British loyalists migrated to Jamaica in 1783 with about five thousand of their slaves. The sheer number of Africans from the United States ensured that their contributions on the island would be significant. In more recent years the traffic has been from the Caribbean to the United States, and we are in danger of forgetting that in earlier times Africans traveled from the United States to the Caribbean. This traffic of Africans from the mainland continued in the nineteenth century, as we learn from Bishop R. R. Wright: "Because the Wesleyans refused to ordain native Haitians, the Free Methodists was formed in Haiti. The Episcopalians started under Reverend, later Bishop, J. C. Holly, who led III persons from New Haven, Connecticut, in May 1871; they were given lands about 3 miles from Port-au-Prince at Drouilland."[7] Bishop Wright points out that as early as 1823 African Americans, including Baptists, Seventh Day Adventists, Pentecostals, and members of the Church of God in Christ churches, traveled to the Caribbean to participate in the development of that region.

It should not be surprising then that President Boyer of Haiti "sought to induce a large number of African-Americans to come to Haiti, especially to work on farms. He promised to each a certain allotment of land, and encouraged them to make Haiti their permanent home, and to become citizens."[8] President Boyer sought the cooperation of the African American church and wrote to the founder of the African Methodist Episcopal Church, Bishop Richard Allen, with his request. In reply Bishop Allen stated:

To his Excellency Jean Pierre Boyer, President of the Republic of Haiti
Port-au-Prince, Haiti
August 23rd 1823
Sir
It is with deep sentiments and the most ardent respect of gratitude that I am addressing you the following lines. My heart burns affectionately in acknowledging the kind offer you have made to these poor oppressed people here in the United States, by offering them an asylum where they can enjoy liberty and equality. In spite of great opposition, I invited the people to assemble in my church (Bethel) and explained to them your propositions. I found that they were willing to accept them. I then prepared a book to inscribe the names of those who were willing to embark for your island. I have on my list over 500 names ready to embark as soon as the necessary provisions can be made, plus those who have already embarked. . . . I have no doubt that soon there will be thousands who are willing to come to your country in spite of the efforts of the white inhabitants who are trying to stop them. . . .
With sentiments of the greatest respect
Very truly yours
Richard Allen[9]

Native Baptists and the Formation of a Culture of Resistance

The energy and passion of African Americans working for change in Haiti was also very visible in Jamaica. Africans who had settled in Jamaica, among them George Liele, Moses Baker, Brother Gibb, George Lewis, and Nicholas Swiegle, were foremost among the leaders of the Native Baptist movement, which organized for political and social change. These Africans from the United States provided the basis for the emergence of Native Baptist "Daddy" Sharp, who provided leadership for the Baptist war of 1831 in Jamaica. The Baptist war, as the 1831 rebellion in and around Montego Bay is referred to, brought to a climax the long struggle of Afro-Jamaicans for freedom from colonial rule. The struggle over the years took the form of slaves running away, many—as in the case of the maroons of Jamaica— fleeing to the hills, from which they would organize attacks on the British from time to time. The focus of the Baptist war was Afro-Jamaicans organizing to withdraw their labor and because of this the brunt of their attack was on institutions of the plantation. A total of 120 buildings on the sugar estates were torched as Afro-Jamaicans insisted that they were human beings who had a right to freedom and a right to withdraw their labor from institutions that kept them in slavery. The Baptist war "differed from earlier uprisings, such as that of Tacky's Coromantis recently arrived from Africa and that of King of the Ebos with his small band of plantation slaves, in that more than 20,000 African-Jamaicans were involved. The call went out to slaves everywhere, not a call to arms but a call to withdraw labor, and it was issued to people who were determined to win their freedom."[10] The leader of the revolt, Daddy Sharp, was a man of great sincerity, rhetorical powers, and captivating magnetism. Edward Hylton, one of Daddy Sharp's followers, tells of an evening in the hills when he received a message from Daddy Sharp to attend a meeting at William Johnson's house at the Retrieve Estate in the parish of St. James. The gathering took the form of a prayer meeting. After the meeting Daddy Sharp, Johnson (who became one of the leaders of the Baptist war), Hylton, and a few others remained behind. "After a while Sharp spoke to them in a low, soft tone so that his voice would not be heard outside. According to Hylton he kept them spellbound while he spoke of the evils and injustice of slavery, asserted the right of all human beings to freedom and declared on the authority of the Bible, that the white man had no more right to hold blacks in bondage than blacks had to enslave whites."[11]

The meeting went on late into the night while they agreed on a strategy to overturn slavery. They covenanted not to work after the Christmas holidays but to seize their right to freedom in faithfulness to each other. "If backra would pay them, they would work as before. If any attempt was made to force them to work as slaves, they would fight for their freedom. They took the oath and kissed the Bible."[12] It seems as if what Daddy Sharp intended was a nonviolent protest that would be expressed as a labor strike. The plan was that on the day after the Christmas holiday an overseer or driver would go to the "busha" on each estate and inform him that slaves would not work until they agreed to pay wages. The bushas were to be kept on the estates until they agreed to pay wages for work. The leadership of the Native Baptists had organized themselves into a trade union arm of the Native Baptist Church, advocating and negotiating wages for slaves. Philip Curtin suggests that what happened was that the Native Baptists had skillfully detached the Baptist missionary organization from white missionaries and were using the Baptist organization as a European trade union uses the bargaining powers of the workers.[13] "On 27 December William Knibb [the Baptist missionary], visiting Moses Baker's chapel at Crooked Spring, now Salter's Hill, tried to persuade the slaves that rumors about freedom having been granted were untrue, but his words were received with evident dissatisfaction by many slaves present, several of whom left the chapel offended.. Others remarked: 'the man must be mad to tell us such things.' "[14] Further, Knibb stated: "I am pained—pained to the soul, at being told that many of you have agreed not to work any more for your owners, and I fear this too is true. I learned that some wicked person has persuaded you that the king of England has made you free. Hear me! I love your souls and I would not tell you a lie for the world; I assure you that this is false, false as hell can make it. I entreat you not to believe it, but to go to your work as formerly. If you have any love for Jesus Christ, to religion, to your ministers, or to those kind friends in England who have helped you to build this chapel, and who are sending a minister for you, do not be led astray. God commands you to be obedient."[15] Fired by the spirit of the Native Baptists, Daddy Sharp responded:

We have worked enough already, and will work no more.
The life we live is too bad, it is the life of a dog.
We won't be slaves no more.
We won't lift hoe no more.
We won't take flogging anymore.[16]

It is reported that when Daddy Sharp was apprehended he said that "he had rather die than be a slave." The price exacted for this stand for freedom by Daddy Sharp and his compatriots was very high. In the parish of St. James eighty-four persons were sentenced to death; in the parish of Hanover, ninety-six, and in Westmoreland, thirty-three. Daddy Sharp learned of the executions while in prison. Daddy Sharp was publicly hanged on 23 May 1832. In the aftermath of the Baptist war six hundred Afro-Jamaicans were killed. In their defense they killed fourteen whites. But the seeds for the destruction of slavery were sown by the Native Baptists. On 1 August 1834 the people of Jamaica received a partial emancipation, with a more complete freedom following on 1 August 1838.

Contemporary Expressions of African American and Caribbean Churches

Throughout the nineteenth and twentieth centuries the African Methodist Episcopal and several Baptist churches were quite active throughout the Caribbean islands, founding congregations and in many cases planting schools that were related to those churches. As a son of the Native Baptist Church and one who later served as pastor of several of these churches in Jamaica, I can attest to the role of the church in founding villages and building schools and hospitals for the masses of people in Jamaica. The church was very instrumental in placing the liberative agenda of the gospel in conversation with a society that was harsh for most of its citizens. And this was not unique to Jamaica. The church throughout the Caribbean has been proactive in alleviating the grinding poverty that has been the lot of the vast majority of its citizens.

One of my first encounters with an educated clergyperson was with the African Methodist Episcopal pastor Rev. Charles Isaac Higgins. Rev. Higgins, who was born in Jamaica in 1890, received his B.A. from the University of London in 1923 and his B.Th. from Howard University in 1926. Returning to Jamaica, he served as headmaster for several schools and later established a preparatory and commercial school for young people in Jamaica. He embodied for us the coming together of two traditions, the Caribbean and African American, working for transformation in the Caribbean.

I would like to highlight another instance of the African American and Caribbean churches working for the transformation of the Caribbean person, namely, the collaboration between the Caribbean/African American Dialogue and the Caribbean Conference of Churches. These two organizations brought together representatives from throughout the Caribbean, North America, and the United Kingdom in a consultation held at Marian Retreat Center, in Verdum, Barbados, 1–3 May 1992. It represented the first Caribbean activity in the implementation of decisions taken at the First Inter-Continental Consultation of Indigenous, African/American, and African/Caribbean peoples on racism in the Americas, convened by the World Council of Churches in Rio de Janeiro in September 1990.[17]

The consultation focused on dominant factors in the historical condition of the Caribbean. Among the issues considered were racism and economic domination. It was noted that one way Caribbean people fought back in the face of these forms of oppression was in creating cultural systems of religion, worldview, and language to help deal with the central question, how may Caribbean people escape the throes of helplessness, hopelessness, alienation, and dehumanization? In an attempt to get a handle on this central question we will look at three issues that were important for the consultation: racism, Caribbean cultural identity, and economic democracy.

Racism

Participants at the consultation noted that, although people have always feared or resisted the presence of or the intrusion of other people or groups because they were different, it was only in the sixteenth century that the mercantile system gave birth to capitalism and this xenophobia developed into full-blown racism. For it was also in the sixteenth century that racism took on a new face as a reality in which one race (namely black Africans) were labeled genetically inferior on the basis of their different origins and color of skin. Within the decade that followed the intrusion of Columbus into this part of the world, most of the indigenous populations were exterminated by European conquistadors in their quest for gold. It was in the attempt to capitalize on cheap labor that Africans were brought to the Caribbean, with the blessing of the church.

Europeans classified black Africans as subhuman, just above the animal, and devoid of intellect and soul; thus they could be sold as cattle. The color of the African skin was interpreted by religious authorities as living proof that Africans were cursed by God. Neither the intellectual capacity nor the spiritual life of Africans was recognized. As a consequence of this way of relating to each other, both the so-called superior race and the so-called inferior race came to internalize these beliefs about themselves.

The conference observed that, although we are some five centuries removed from the intrusion into the Caribbean world by Europeans, racism is still never far away. Racism takes many forms among us: we keep repeating the same self-debasing sayings and proverbs about ourselves and our skin color; often we encourage the same self-destructive attitudes toward ourselves and our people, persistently seeking European approval before we accept recognition of ourselves as an able, talented people, and endorsing and perpetuating the same evils against other minorities; our women are overworked and underpaid in the workplace; our Haitian brothers and sisters endure endless suffering; worst of all, we make ourselves guilty of initiating among or against our oppressed fellow human beings the same patterns of racial hostility from which we have so directly suffered. The conference affirmed that it is high time peoples of the Caribbean break away from Eurocentric frames of reference and move into a human design in which Caribbean people take responsibility for their own destiny, with pride in our past and in celebration of the contributions we have made to humanity.

Caribbean Cultural Identity

The Caribbean culture was formed in the mix between African and European patterns: "Born of displacement, resistance, and survival, it is a cultural identity attested to in the creolization of both the languages and life styles adopted from Europe and our ready adaptability to their models; attested to also in the significantly open-air aspects of our lifestyle, in the percussive character and notable folk-rhythm of our music, in the catching sensuality of our dancing, in our pervasive religiosity."[18] Although Caribbean people live in the cultural tension between Europe and Africa, there is an African ethos that spreads across all the Euro-determined national and linguistic boundaries of the Caribbean with an identifiable Caribbean identity and unity. There is also a heritage forged in the fires of adversity, which makes recognizable certain skills and values. For example, there are ways of harnessing the environment, of preserving foods, of making medicines from the bush; additionally there are values and responsibility to the family. Caribbean culture has emerged as an identifiable reality out of a society and way of life that are often very harsh for the majority of its citizens. Whether it's watching a game of cricket, dancing to calypso music, or attending worship service in the open air, Caribbean culture has a way of bringing together and binding Caribbean peoples.

This places us on notice to guard against the ways of outside cultures, especially through tourism and the mass media, which seek to penetrate and damage our culture. In order to renew and preserve our culture there are aspects of our way of life that need to be discarded. There is a negative valuing of self that must be transcended. One expression of this negative view of the Caribbean self is the tendency toward self-effacement before Euro-American ways of being, a tendency to believe that the foreign is better than what is indigenous to our way of life. This is one reason why, for many Caribbean people, God is a foreigner and we address God through prayers, hymns, and liturgies that are imported from Europe or the United States of America. Other flaws in our culture which must be addressed are the tendency to value more highly persons with lighter skin and to find ways of justifying racism. There is also, in many places, an unwillingness to put structures of accountability in place for those whom we entrust with leadership and responsibility.

Economic Democracy

Economic democracy is a question of justice. While it is clear that many islands have made tremendous progress in the area of political democracy, it is also quite clear we have not made much progress in the area of economic democracy. There is an unwillingness to relate the political and the economic spheres. This is one area in which a reliance on an African cosmology would be most helpful to Caribbean people. In African cosmology all of life is related. There is no arbitrary separation between secular and sacred or the political and the economic. This is one area in which the Euro-American model of separation between the political, economic, and spiritual spheres has not served us well.

We have not been able to identify values that tend toward the common good in ways that spell security, dignity, a better standard of living, and fairness for the majority of our people. The historical condition, which has its roots in slavery, is one in which the contradiction between the economic and the political spheres is accepted. The majority of people are content to live with shantytowns and widespread economic inequality without any sense of outrage. And one reason for this is the arbitrary separation between the economic and the political, which engenders the injustice of hunger, want, deprivation, and economic insecurity. Greed is also a major problem for us in the Caribbean as we watch the widening gap between rich and poor, a rabid individualism that seeks to satisfy the wants of a few and devalue the needs of the collective community.

The 1992 conference in Verdum, Barbados, discussed in previous sections, affirmed that economic democracy rests on the notion of reordering the priorities of the state and society. It was affirmed there that space should be created in which the poor are allowed to participate in the creation of institutions that have their best interest at heart. For example, the largest landowners in the Caribbean are churches. The membership, who are predominantly poor people, should insist on land reform, which should include the church making its vast resources of land available for economic development. The church should view the lands it has as a trust for the people. The conference also called for gender equality, which would include giving women access to economic and political power through the abolition of patriarchal structures. Economic democracy is impossible with discrimination of any kind.

Toward a Partnership: African Americans and Afro-Caribbeans

Growing up in the Caribbean during the 1950s and the 1960s I was keenly aware of the role of the civil rights movement in the United States of America and its fight against racial discrimination. The struggle for civil rights in the United States of America, led as it was by the pastor of an African American church, kindled the imaginations of Caribbean people: several Caribbean countries agitated for self-rule from colonial powers and received political independence in the 1960s and 1970s. There was an added incentive for Jamaica, as Martin Luther King Jr. was often in that country. Whenever the struggle for civil rights in the United States became overly stressful, King would steal away to Jamaica and find renewal among the people.[19] King's legacy in the Caribbean endured in many ways. In 1984, for example, I served as a member of a delegation to a conference in Cuba titled "Theological Homage in Memory of Martin Luther King, Jr." The conference was called by the Ecumenical Council of Cuba, which represents the Baptist Student Council and the Methodist, Baptist, Presbyterian, Episcopalian, and Pentecostal churches. Although the archbishop of the Roman Catholic Church in Cuba attended a worship service at the conference in which he was publicly embraced by Fidel Castro, the Roman Catholic Church did not participate in the conference. Attending from the United States were pastors, laity, and theologians from the African American church.

> Dr. Paul Fernandez, the President of the Ecumenical Council of Cuba, pointed out during the opening session of the conference, that it was the hope of the Council that the conference would aid in the renewal of the church in Cuba. He felt the presence of Christians from the United States of America would facilitate the process of church renewal in Cuba. The economic blockade which was imposed by the government of the United States against the Cuban government had the effect of severing communications between the church in Cuba and the Church in the United States. According to Fernandez, the people of Cuba have not only suffered from an economic blockade for twenty-four years from the most powerful country in the world just ninety miles away, but the Cuban Church has suffered from the blockade of ideas concerning God and his work in the world. The lifting of the blockade would also mean the opening of dialogue between the churches in both countries.[20]

Representatives from the African American church met with members of Fidel Castro's government and received reports on initiatives concerning health care policy, the eradication of illiteracy, the government's policy regarding care for the disabled particularly children, and the country's intolerance for discrimination based on race, gender, and national or ethnic origin. It was providential that, while delegates from the African American church were in conversation with church and governmental leaders in Cuba, Rev. Jesse Jackson, one of the torchbearers of the civil rights movement in the United States of America, arrived in Cuba to free prisoners, both American and Cuban. Jackson claimed he had come to Cuba to launch a moral offensive aimed at the removal of the blockade between the peoples of the United States and Cuba. He held extensive meetings with Fidel Castro and members of his government and in the end secured the release of several American and Cuban prisoners.

At the end of the negotiations between Jesse Jackson and the Cuban government, Jackson, along with members of the delegation from the African American church, was invited by Fidel Castro to the private library at his residence for fellowship and conversation. As we fellowshipped with the Cuban leader, Rev. Jackson called for prayer. We sang several Negro spirituals. "We joined hands together in a circle, church leaders, Fidel Castro and leaders of the revolution, as Rev. Jackson called on God to bring peace in that part of the hemisphere."[21] In the years following that conference, in 1986, 1988, and 1990, many other theologians, pastors, denominational executives, community activists, and young people from the African American church have visited Cuba through the agency of the black theology project. Each dialogue focused on a theme taken from the life and ministry of Dr. Martin Luther King Jr. "The Black theology project . . . sought to engage its Cuban partners in an examination of King's work and its implications in light of the situation of African American Christians in the United States today and of Christians in their post-revolutionary situation in Cuba. . . . The result has been a deeper understanding and appreciation of each other's suffering and struggle, of the challenges of racism, sexism, classism in each place, and the richness of the two cultures so deeply penetrated by the philosophy and religion, aesthetics and spirituality of Africa."[22]

Perhaps there is no group of Christians from the United States of America that has worked more assiduously to affect public policy issues in the Caribbean than the Pastors for Peace Project sponsored by the Inter-religious Foundation for Community Organization (IFCO). They have sought to affect the quality of life of the people of Haiti, Nicaragua, El Salvador, and Cuba. A listing of activities of IFCO in these islands during 1999 is instructive:

March 7–17: Nicaragua Construction Brigade
March 27–April 6: Health care trip to Cuba
May 27–June 26: U.S.-Cuba Friendship Caravan
July 29–August 7: URACCAN Construction Brigade
August 29–September 7: Minnesota Sustainable Agriculture Trip
September 15–October 8: Haiti Caravan
November 12–December 18: Central American Caravan
December: Music and Art Delegation.[23]

The Pastors for Peace have been active in Cuba, seeking to alleviate the hurricane of poverty that has ravaged that country. In 1992, one hundred caravanists brought into Cuba fifteen tons of humanitarian aid: powdered milk, medicines, Bibles, bicycles, and school buses. In 1993, they took in school buses, computers, and medical equipment. They have sponsored these missions to Cuba every year since 1992. In 1997 and 1998 aid was targeted to children and the elderly. IFCO indicates that its participation in the struggle with Cuba is not limited to supplies, whether medical or educational, but that they are proactive in encouraging dialogue between the United States and Cuba to end the economic blockade.

The Church and Poverty: The Cuban Model

In a conversation with the liberation theologian and priest Frei Betto, the Cuban president Fidel Castro—after informing Betto that he was baptized in the Roman Catholic Church in Cuba—pointed out that it was critical for the church in Latin America and the Caribbean to tackle poverty, which he regards as the overarching problem of this century. Castro indicated that he had come to this conclusion after discussions with members of the World Council of Churches, churches in Jamaica, El Salvador, Nircaragua, and Chile.

Castro had this to say: "You know of my meetings with the Christians for Socialism in Chile. . . . When I visited that country during the Allende administration and had a very pleasant, extremely interesting meeting with priests and other Christians—there were around 200 of them. . . . Later during a visit to Jamaica, I also met with representatives from various Christian communities there. I was very impressed by what you said concerning the difference between European reality and that of our hemisphere, where the massive nature of poverty is the basic, determining factor."[24]

Castro observed that in the Caribbean, where nation-states are poor economically, the church will have to join with the state in providing leadership to guide people out of poverty. This identification of the church with the oppressed is in stark contradiction with the history of the church over the centuries in the region. "Nobody can deny that the church—was on the side of the conquerors, oppressors, and exploiters. It never categorically denounced slavery, an institution that is so repugnant to our consciences now."[25] Castro posits that the church in the Caribbean today has the opportunity of rejecting that negative past as it affirms a new identity: that of the liberation church, a church in solidarity with the poor. "I think that the enormous historic importance of liberation theology, or the liberation Church . . . lies precisely in its profound impact on the political views of its followers. It constitutes a point of contact between today's believers and those of the past—that distant past of the first few centuries after the emergence of Christianity, after Christ. I could define the liberation Church . . . as Christianity's going back to its roots, its most beautiful, attractive, heroic, and glorious history."[26] Castro encouraged the liberation church to recall the words of Acts 4:32, 34–35:

> And the congregation of those who believed were of one heart and soul;
>
> And not one of them claimed that anything belonging to him was his own; but all things were common property to them. . . .
>
> For there was not a needy person among them, for all who were owners of land or houses would sell them and bring the proceeds of the sales,
>
> And lay them at the apostles' feet; and they would be distributed to each, as any had need.[27]

Frei Betto further articulates the theological basis for the church's tackling the stubborn reality of poverty in the region. " 'For I was hungry and you gave me food: I was thirsty and you gave me drink.' And today we can add, I was ignorant and you gave me schools; I was sick and you gave me health; I was homeless and you gave me shelter. Then Jesus concluded, 'Truly I say to you, as you did it to one of the least of my brethren, you did it to me.' "[28]

Castro's invitation to the church to join forces with the state is encouraging and offers the prospect of a united assault on poverty in the region. The truth is that Castro's invitation to the church is really a description of a relationship that has existed on a more limited scale over several decades in the Caribbean, where the church and state have had to cooperate for the creation of a more just society in which economic well-being is a gift available to all persons. Throughout the Caribbean, the church has often been in the forefront of change in building educational institutions and staffing them with teachers. The churches have also been active in building hospitals and in some cases have provided lands for farming. And this has had the good effect of pushing beyond the separation of the tasks of church and state. The church is often viewed as being concerned with the soul, and the state with the body; the state is often seen as being concerned with matters of material well-being, and the church as invested in salvation as a task that occurs in the church. The Cuban model seeks to join salvation and material well-being. It is in this context that Castro pointed out that in a country in which church and state unite for the creation of a just society, there would be an advance in the quality of life. "In my talks with the bishops, I even added that just as they sent missionaries to the Amazon, for example, to live in the Indian communities or to work with lepers or the sick in many parts of the world, we have our internationalist workers. . . . I mentioned the example of our teachers who went to Nicaragua: 2,000 teachers, who shared the very difficult living conditions of the Nicaraguan farmers."[29] Castro felt it was important that the teachers who went to Nicaragua lived in the mountains with their students in thatched-roof huts and ate what the students ate. "Sometimes the family—the married couple and their children—the teacher and the animals all lived under the same roof."[30]

The church knows something about solidarity with those who are locked out of opportunity for justice making. An important key in dismantling structures of poverty in the Caribbean is the commitment to be with victims and together to imagine a new future. The way forward is solidarity with others, which has as its goal the creation of an alternative reality.

The significance of the Cuban model is that Christians are invited to participate in the "politics of solidarity." The church, when it ignores economic violence, ceases to be the church of Jesus Christ. This means that churches themselves must be willing to change as they become agents of change, insisting that violence against the poor must stop. Castro raised the question of what a state in which the church was active as a transforming agent would look like for poor people:

> I told them [the bishops] that, if they organized a state in accord with Christian precepts, they'd create one similar to ours. . . . You surely wouldn't permit and would do every thing possible to prevent gambling in a state governed by Christian principles; we've eradicated gambling. You wouldn't have beggars; Cuba is the only country in Latin America where there are no beggars. You wouldn't allow a little child to remain abandoned or to go hungry; not a single child in our country is forsaken or goes hungry. You wouldn't leave the elderly without help or assistance; in Cuba all old people have help and assistance. You wouldn't have a

country with a high unemployment rate; there is no unemployment in Cuba. You wouldn't permit drugs; in our country drug addiction has been eradicated. . . . All those things we have fought against, all those problems we've solved, are the same ones the Church would try to solve if it were to organize a civil state in keeping with Christian precepts.[31]

The church, as it tackles Caribbean issues, must aim at the creation of a just and compassionate society in which poverty loosens its grip on the oppressed. This would become a society in which children, the elderly, and the infirm would be valued and celebrated as sons and daughters of God.

For What May We Hope?

The Caribbean theologian Kortright Davis speaks of emancipatory connections between Caribbean and African American peoples as the way forward. I have noted throughout this essay some of the crises confronting the Caribbean: persistent poverty; cultural and economic dependence; alienation from race, language, and belief systems; and imitation in religious, theological, and social issues. I have argued throughout the essay that one way in which we can fashion a culture of resistance to assist in tackling these problems is to join forces with our brothers and sisters in the African American churches. We value these emancipatory connections because they are a part of our heritage, as illustrated by the African Americans who migrated to Jamaica in the eighteenth century and to Haiti in the nineteenth century. I have also noted the value in consultations and in the important work done by the Pastors for Peace in Cuba. But we must guard against this relationship becoming a new kind of dependence, even if we stress the reciprocal nature of the exchange by recalling that Marcus Garvey, Malcolm X, and Frantz Fanon represent the movement from the Caribbean to the United States to empower African Americans. The partnership with our African American brothers and sisters does not mean that we in the Caribbean wait on them in order to tackle the crises confronting us but that we strike out against the evils assailing us in confidence that the church is one and we are not divided brethren. Kortright Davis places the issue before us:

The official policy of divide and rule was relentlessly pursued by the colonial overlords and rigidly woven into the fabric of colonial social life. It encouraged Caribbean people to become mutually contemptuous and to accept patterns of self-contempt, sometimes as a means of social progress or acceptance by others. That which was foreign was good; that which was local was not good. So people were alienated from each other by inducement. They were also alienated from their natural cultural endowment (race, color, language, belief systems, relationships, preferences, entertainment and leisure, work schedules, family mores, personal aspirations) and from their rightful corridors of power influence, opportunity, and social access. . . . Unmarried fathers were regarded as social outcasts by self-righteous priests and pastors; so that mothers would sometimes present their own brothers as fathers of their babies to unsuspecting priests.[32]

There is much that we will have to do for ourselves as Caribbean people. We must break the chains that bind us. We must be proactive in acknowledging that economic poverty must be confronted with genuine economic growth. Collective self-reliance must become the antidote to political independence, and cultural alienation must be confronted with an urgency in the Caribbean church and community. Imitation must give way to indigeneity. But each step of the way the Caribbean church is encouraged to value emancipatory connections with the African American church. "Because their God has been a help in ages past, Caribbean and African-American people hold unflinchingly to the assurance that, in prosperity or poverty, God is the hope for years to come."[33] The church itself must become the site of resistance. This means the church must be willing to speak from the cross, from the hurts and despair of God's people. As Christ's body was broken for us, so must the church, as it identifies with those who suffer, be willing to be broken for the sake of all who are marginalized and abused. The church must refuse to be satisfied with a partial liberation and act from the conditions of the real world, where the spirits of our people are colonized and their lives are crippled. The situation in the Caribbean has been one in which the real misery and pain of the people is hidden behind the partial liberation of salvation of the soul. And the church, especially the missionary church from Europe and North America, has been guilty of preaching and advocating the salvation of the soul while it fails to make connections with real life issues that confront the body. The church for too long has been preoccupied with the question, what must I do to become a believer? and ignored the other question, what must I do to have my humanity restored? The problem with the church's preoccupation with the first question is it has turned inward in an attempt to maintain and preserve its identity. The church's fear of losing its faith makes it defensive and self-protective, and allows it to ignore the structures of oppression. The Native Baptists showed us the way forward, for they took on both questions and related personal faith to social justice. The attempt to conjoin these questions allows the church to affirm its commitment for the transformation of the world and the affirmation of the church's faith. It affirms that good news is for the poor. The mission of the church becomes solidarity with those who are excluded and oppressed. Faith becomes activity with and on behalf of those who are weak and heavy laden. It is as the church enters into solidarity with the victims of oppression that it points to what "God is up to in the world."

This means the Caribbean and African American churches would be engaged with real-life situations, where people are stripped of their dignity and struggle not so much with the issue of being nonbelievers as with the issue of being nonpersons. The church must seek to bring to consciousness a new identity and a new spirituality as the values of family, work, pride, worship, and play are affirmed. The church becomes an "Exodus church": a church committed to leading oppressed people out of traditions of bondage into the emancipation and deliverance that belong to all God's children.

Notes

1. Sergio Arce Martínez and Dora Valentín, "The Caribbean: An Overview," in *The Caribbean: Culture of Resistance, Spirit and Hope*, ed. Oscar L. Bolioli (New York: Friendship Press, 1993), 2–3.
2. Ibid., 6. See also chap. 2, "Black People and Their World," in Noel Leo Erskine's *Decolonizing Theology* (Trenton, N.J.: Africa World Press, 1998).
3. Martínez and Valentín, "The Caribbean," 6.
4. Ibid., 6.
5. Emmanuel Katongole, "Liberalization Is Not the Only Solution: Pastor Reflects on Poverty in Africa," *Dossier* (Comboni Missionaries, Uganda), no. 395 (May 2001): 24.
6. Carolyn Cooper, *Noises in the Blood* (London: Macmillan Education, 1994), 123–24.
7. See R. R. Wright Jr., comp., *History of the Sixteenth Episcopal District of the African Methodist Church* (Philadelphia: Bethel A.M.E Archives, 1964), 15.
8. Ibid.
9. Ibid., 16.
10. Philip Sherlock and Hazel Bennett, *The Story of the Jamaican People* (Kingston: Ian Randle Publishers, 1998), 212.
11. Ibid., 214.
12. Ibid.
13. Philip D. Curtin, *Two Jamaicas* (New York: Atheneum Press, 1970), 86.
14. Sherlock and Bennett, *The Story of the Jamaican People*, 216.
15. John Howard Hinton, *Memoir of William Knibb* (London: Houlston and Stoneman, 1847), 118.
16. Trevor Munroe and Don Robotham, *Struggles of the Jamaican People* (Kingston: E. P. Printery, 1977), 16.
17. "Reclaiming Identity: T. Verdun Proclamation," in *The Caribbean: Culture of Resistance*, ed. Oscar L. Bolioli, 49.
18. Ibid., 53.

19. The United States' ambassador to the United Nations, Andrew Young, in conversation with me, pointed out that Martin Luther King Jr. had access to a home in Ocho Rios, Jamaica, to which he would often retreat and from which he wrote most of his books. Ambassador Young was a guest lecturer for my class "The Theology of Martin Luther King Jr.," Emory University, 24 April 2001.

20. Noel Leo Erskine, "A Theologian's Reflection: The Church and the Cuban Revolution," *Journal of the Interdenominational Theological Center* 9.1–2 (Fall 1983–Spring 1984): 115.

21. Ibid., 117.

22. Jualynne E. Dodson and Gayraud Wilmore, "Black Theology Project Papers in Dialogue with Cubans," *Journal of the Interdenominational Theological Center* 15.1–2 (Fall 1987–Spring 1988): 172–73.

23. Gail Walker, ed., "What's Happening at IFCO/Pastors for Peace in 1999?" *IFCO News* (Winter 1999): 16.

24. Frei Betto, *Fidel and Religion* (Sydney, Australia: Pathfinder Press, 1985), 194, 210.

25. Ibid., 204.

26. Ibid., 205.

27. *New American Standard Bible.*

28. Betto, *Fidel and Religion*, 185. Betto quotes from Matthew 25:35, 25:40.

29. Ibid., 186.

30. Ibid.

31. Ibid., 187.

32. Kortright Davis, *Emancipation Still Comin'* (Maryknoll, N.Y.: Orbis Books, 1990), 83.

33. Ibid., 117.

Simeon O. Ilesanmi | **AFRICA'S POVERTY, HUMAN RIGHTS,**

AND A JUST SOCIETY

S ince the European scramble for and partition of Africa in the late nineteenth century, the continent has been experimenting with various modalities of social, political, economic, religious, and cultural existence. Save
in the religious sphere, where Africans seem to rank above the rest of the
world in their depth of religious commitments, the other experiments have
been anything but successful. Even our assessment of religion in Africa must
take full cognizance of its checkered career.[1] But generally, most scholars
agree that Africa's performance on politics, and economics in particular, has
been abysmal. And it has not mattered much whether the agents of these
experiments were Africans or outsiders; the human impact of their failures
is the same. This much is clear from the observations of the participants
in the multiyear Pan-African Seminar on Religion and Poverty. In Ghana,
Kenya, and South Africa we had a firsthand encounter with the complexity of
Africa's predicament, and a mystifying awareness of the radical differences
between the existential condition of peoples of African descent and those of
other races. In an era characterized by fierce competition for supremacy in,
and distributional benefits of, science and technology, Africa visibly remains
the "other" continent, eking out a precarious existence at what, to me, is not
just the margin but the margin of the margins. For the past two decades, the
continent has been "the scene not only of the third great genocide of the
twentieth century, but also of many of the world's most intractable wars, of
immense and deepening poverty, of an AIDS epidemic that seems likely to
undo the economic gains of the few countries that are not almost beyond
economic help."[2] Even countries that maintain a semblance of order have
been reduced to pathetic caricatures of true nation-states due to their crushing debt, collapsing infrastructure, and their grave inability to accumulate
and valorize capital.

This situation poses immense intellectual and ethical challenges to all who
are concerned about the fate of Africa and its peoples. To start with, scholars

have raised the issue of whether or not the African situation, given its magnitude, is amenable to human solutions, and if so, how the solutions are to be articulated. There are pessimists who declare Africa exceptionally irredeemable, in part because of what they perceive to be the cyclical nature of the continent's crises, and the belief, albeit flawed, that Africa's "social groupings are in the simplest descriptive sense backward, largely preliterate, with low productivity, weak overarching social solidarities and slight abilities to organize themselves for the better."[3] To this group of thinkers, Africa's problems transcend the universal dilemmas of institutional stewardship, but reflect an existential condition that almost guarantees in perpetuity what T. S. Eliot has called, commenting on the perversities of the modern age, "an immense panorama of futility and anarchy."[4] The problem with this view is that it exaggerates Africa's exceptionalism in the worldwide experience of failed social and political arrangements, and represents a reversal of the buoyant spirit displayed by generations of scholars, Africans and Westerners alike, whose conviction about the continent's potential for positive development has been unflagging. The issue, then, is not whether Africa's condition of poverty is reversible, but what would be required to accomplish the task.

The central argument of this essay is that a full implementation of *fundamental* human rights is pivotal to any efforts to address poverty in Africa. As forcefully argued by Mandla Seleoane, a South African scholar and guest lecturer at our seminar held in Johannesburg, "It is not a forced notion that rights ought to help eliminate or, at the very least, mitigate poverty," where poverty is understood as "the deprivation of the things that human beings need in order to survive *as such*."[5] Of course, evidence of professed commitment to human rights is not lacking in Africa, but the commitment is beleaguered by theoretical confusion and governmental lukewarmness. The confusion exists at two levels. The first has to do with the extent to which the idea of human rights is compatible with African religious and cultural worldviews. A similar concern has also been raised with respect to other non-Western societies and traditions. This question dominated earlier contributions of African scholars and leaders to the human rights debate, and the pervasive predilection then was to invoke the image of a naive and simple Africa whose cultural uniqueness warranted a hermeneutical distancing from the moral and political impulses of modernity, of which the idea of human rights was an archetype. But invoking this image as a statement of African collective disposition has lost its erstwhile appeal; many now find it to be not merely self-indulgent and even in a very real sense demeaning, but ultimately disabling for the requirements of today. An image of Africa that is insouciant to the instrumentalities of human rights cannot be part of a serious project of liberating the continent from the plague of poverty.

However, even those who defend the cultural intelligibility of human rights in Africa disagree about the kinds of rights that society and government should promote. My focus in this essay will be on the disagreements at this level. I will delineate the issues that define the key camps, explore their strengths and weaknesses, and suggest a framework for normative rapprochement between them. The first part of the essay proceeds from a perception that what is unique about African human rights stances, distinguishing them from forms of Western political and moral thought, is that Africa's deprivations and deformities in the economic realm make any concern for civil and political liberties a luxury.[6] This claim, which revolves around three principal concerns, is succinctly stated in the African Charter on Human and People's Rights, otherwise known as the Banjul Charter.[7] Given the causal relationship between civil-political rights and the stability of advanced democracies, coupled with their instrumental potential to foster competitive economic growth, other analysts see the theory of the lexical priority of social, economic, and development rights over their moral counterparts as nothing more than a squint-eyed ideological orthodoxy.

The second part of my essay thus examines the contrasting argument that what give rights their distinctive cutting edge are the conceptual connections between the notion of a right and the cognate notions of duty and justice.[8] Such connections are only attributable to rights whose primary function is to impose constraints upon the action of others, whether individuals or the state, and only civil-political rights qualify in this respect because they protect values such as basic liberties, due process of law, and participation in the political system.[9] Their denial to anyone, special circumstances aside, will count as injustice. Thus, to say that I have a right to some good or service is not to say that it would be nice or generous or noble of others to give it to me; it is, rather, to say that they are obliged to do so, that it would be unfair or unjust of them not to, that I am entitled to expect or demand it of them. This idea of a strict correlation between notions of duty and justice on the one hand, and that of civil and political rights on the other, is denied to what we have come to regard as social and economic rights. These latter rights, it is contended, only establish ideals or objectives, not assignable duties.

In the final section of the essay, I offer a critique of the dichotomous mindset in the African human rights debate, and propose in its stead an interdependent theory of rights that accommodates concerns in the two contested areas of political and economic relations. I argue that nothing short of this integral vision of rights is needed in a continent where the popularity of human rights is evident more in their breach than in their protection and preservation. A proposal for an interdependent theory of rights for Africa is thus a tactical and pragmatic move designed to disarm those who might want to invoke the exclusionary paradigm to justify the trivialization and violation of those human rights they do not accept. A bifurcated notion of human rights furnishes boundless opportunities for equivocation. Africa has known enough of these excuses; a religiously and ethically informed theory of rights might be one useful way to stem their tide.

A final preliminary remark about the rationale for a human rights approach to poverty resolution is pertinent. This calls for a conceptual clarification of rights. As understood by members of the international community, the language of rights serves the important function of enabling us to articulate those basic conditions that human beings need in order to flourish in society. Human rights are moral (and some would say legally enforceable) claims that individuals have on each other and on society for certain minimum conditions without which the value of human life would be harmed in some crucial and fundamental way. Some traditions ground rights in the dignity vested in each person by God, while other thinkers see them as moral consequences of what is most basically involved in being human.[10] To be deprived of rights is to endanger the normal functioning of human being. For this reason, the moral validity of human rights is independent of and prior to their acknowledgment by particular societies. While no human right is absolute in the sense of being indefeasible, every legitimate moral claim has both a presumption of priority, which requires that infringements be justified by morally acceptable reasons, and a graduated urgency corresponding to the varying importance and necessity of the values they protect.

Poverty As an Economic Problem:
Three Proposals in the Banjul Charter

The most fundamental aspect of postindependence Africa has been the elusiveness of economic and material prosperity. For many Africans independence had created high expectations, especially regarding the restoration of human dignity, which had been suppressed and brutalized during the colonial period. However, in many cases, the hopes ended in disappointment. The change of guards at government houses from white to black had not meant much in content.[11] Edward Jaycox, former vice president, Africa Region, for the World Bank, summarized the African situation after the second 1979 oil shock thus: "The region had no industrial base to speak of, its human resource and management skills were extremely thin, its infrastructure was sparse and often run down, its technological options were limited, and it was rapidly losing its competitiveness to other developing regions. Wrong-headed policies fed into and exacerbated these basic problems."[12]

IN DEFENSE OF THE RIGHT TO DEVELOPMENT

On 20 January 1981 the African heads of states and governments adopted the Banjul Charter, which came into force in October 1986, and the observance of which hopefully would arrest the escalation of those factors that had impeded the realization of independence from material indigence. Although the charter was not expected to replace the existing national constitutions of member states, its ability to exercise corrective and transformative influence on them was taken for granted.[13] The document was also intended to be a specifically African contribution to the global human rights discourse, one in which philosophical ideals combined with empirical realities to articulate a normative vision that would be responsive to concrete human needs. In anticipation of charges that a regional document on human rights has the potential to encourage xenophobic behavior,[14] several African jurists have invoked cultural reasons to justify the necessity of supplementing the universalist vision of the United Nations rights documents with a less vacuous, more focused regional experiment in moral and political innovation. At the early stages in the formation of the charter, the African philosopher of *négritude* and former president of Senegal, Leopold Senghor, advised the experts working on it to avoid the temptation of mirroring other peoples' ideas in their conception of human rights, keeping in focus Africa's "beautiful and positive traditions," and using the values derived from them, together with the continent's divergent political and material needs, as the only yardstick for determining an acceptable human rights document.[15] To divorce human rights ideas from the continent's immediate experiences would merely recycle the Western view of African beliefs as a parody of Western precepts.

The preamble to the charter stipulates that it is "*henceforth essential* to pay particular attention to the right to development and that civil and political rights *cannot be dissociated* from economic, social and cultural rights in conception as well as universality and that the satisfaction of social and cultural rights is a guarantee for the enjoyment of civil and political rights."[16] Among the cluster of interpretations associated with this preambular statement, a prominent one is the explicit affirmation of the right to development, understood to be a new category of rights that is distinct from the first two generations of rights associated with the ideological blinkers of the Western and former socialist countries.[17] This is a right that Africa and the rest of the third world believe they genuinely have against the secure and prosperous nations of the world. The policy framework for the realization of this right was spelled out in the final report of the Monrovia Symposium on the future of the continent organized by the Organization of African Unity in early 1979. This includes, among other things: "(1) The creation of a material and cultural environment that is conducive to self fulfillment and creative participation; (2) [The formation of] policies for the rational use and exploitation of natural resources, entailing above all self-sufficiency in food and local processing of raw materials; (3) [A fresh look at] the whole educational and training set-up . . . and [the removal] of barriers . . . between education and employment, education and society, education and culture—in other words, between education and life; (4) [Understanding fully] that the issues of freedom and justice can no longer be left in abeyance."[18]

To appreciate the significance of the developmental right, its proponents emphasize the historicity of the postcolonial African states, analyzing them in terms of their genesis, "the strategies of the actors, the procedures of accumulation and the world of political make-believe which have all been vehicles for the production of social inequality."[19] They condemned and demanded atonement for the real debilitations suffered by Africans as a result of European imperialism. The colonialist expeditions in Africa culminated in an array of contradictions: cultural distortion, economic underdevelopment, and the incorporation of the continent "into the capitalist-dominated structured division of labor."[20] These interlinked predicaments were dictated by the logic of colonialism. Being exploitative and extractive in its operations, it was primarily concerned with how much it could remove and transport to metropolitan industry in terms of material (and initially human) resources.[21] Africa's contemporary problems, therefore, are peculiar to that new phase inaugurated by the end of the colonial rule; they form part of its legacy, and constitute the rough path that Africans have to tread as they grope in its aftermath toward a new order of life and awareness. Moreover, and sadly too, political independence has been too feeble to alter the tributary status of African states, as many of them still look up to London or Paris or Washington for the structure and direction of their local economies. Because of the manner in which it is integrated into the global economy, Africa is the most overburdened among the regions classified by the international financial institutions—the World Bank and the International Monetary Fund—as highly indebted.[22] Unlike other members of this unenviable group, Africa is conditioned to never-ending impoverishment. For instance, Africa's external debt burden since the 1980s has grown more onerous and increasingly unmanageable.

According to the 1998 *African Economic Report*, the burden of the debt overhang remains one of the most critical hindrances to the economic recovery of the continent. It argues that debt strongly and negatively affects economic growth, threatens the sustainability of reforms and prevents the development of a capable and functioning state due to the fiscal crisis that it engenders.[23] In 1996 alone, for example, the $12 billion spent by sub-Saharan African governments on debt servicing was equivalent to more than 5 percent of the region's gross domestic product for the same year. Expressed differently, this amount of resources represented more than the subregion's combined expenditure on primary health and basic education for that year. These relatively huge transfers from the world's poorest region are slowly but inexorably consigning African citizens to a future of deepening poverty and helplessness. In fact, the African continent is the only developing region in the world whose human welfare indicators are worsening and whose proportion of people living below the poverty line is increasing.[24] Life expectancy is below sixty years in twenty-eight countries. Life expectancy is below fifty years in eighteen countries. Life expectancy in Sierra Leone is just thirty-seven years; about half of the adult populations of at least thirteen countries are illiterate. Half or more of women are illiterate in at least eighteen countries. Children under five die at rates in excess of 100 per 1,000 in at least twenty-eight countries. In Sierra Leone, the rate is 335 per 1,000.[25] In short, "the plight of the African continent remains the most serious challenge for the emerging world order."[26]

On the basis of this historical and empirical analysis, advocates of development rights conclude that the countries of the North, which have been the primary beneficiaries of unfair global structures, do have moral obligations to assist African countries in overcoming their burden of poverty and dependency. In the opinion of one African jurist, the developed nations are the powerful agents of global events:

> Since they bring about these events in their interests alone, it is proper, considering that they benefit from the advantages, that they share the disadvantages. They decide on peace and war, the international monetary system, the conditions governing business relations; they impose ideologies, and so on. What could be more natural than that they should assume responsibility for the consequences of events and circumstances that are their own doing? What other justification could there be for the right of veto held by only five States out of the whole family of the United Nations? . . . The responsibility for the harm inflicted should be shouldered by those who caused it; it is a matter of elementary justice.[27]

Keba M'Baye's view is consistent with the position of the All Africa Conference of Churches, which accused the West of unjust trade and debt repayment policies that "create fertile ground for the exploitation of labor, the plundering of Africa's material resources and broadening the gap between rich and poor, urban and rural communities."[28] The conference also criticized the process that allow African dictators to obtain loans from banks in the West, which are invariably siphoned out of the countries in whose behalf they are borrowed, and then squandered on luxuries or to acquire mansions in Western cities. Africa cannot realistically develop, the conference warns, unless Western nations are willing to, at the maximum, cancel Africa's huge and asphyxiating debt, or at the minimum, allow "dictator wealth and loot in international banks" to be used in repaying debts.[29] Additionally, they must be willing to offer better financial assistance, price indexing, and better trade agreement terms for stabilization of commodity and raw material prices.

The African Catholic bishops expressed a similar view in a communiqué entitled "Forgive Us Our Debts: Open Letter to Our Brother Bishops in Europe and North America," issued at the conclusion of their 1994 synod, in which they explain the plight of the continent in reference to the harshness of the international environment, rising debt services, frequent increases in the cost of imports, direct military violation of the territorial integrity of African states, Western support for dictatorial and oppressive regimes, and the declining foreign assistance. Invoking the authority of the 1986 statement of the Pontifical Commission for Justice and Peace entitled *An Ethical Approach to the International Debt Question*, which calls on both creditors and debtors to undertake a joint sharing of the consequences of the debt crisis, the African episcopates suggest that "the burden should not fall disproportionately on poor countries . . . [for] it is morally wrong to deprive a nation of the means to meet the basic needs of its people in order to repay debt." They went further to argue that "the needs of the poor take precedence over the wants of the rich."[30]

Reactions to the case for developmental rights, both from African scholars and their Western counterparts, have been mixed, but before looking at these it is necessary to examine the second major solution to poverty prescribed by the Banjul Charter.

ARGUMENTS FOR SOCIAL AND ECONOMIC RIGHTS

It is widely agreed that a special case for social and economic rights in Africa is necessary in light of the fact that developmental rights, especially as conceived by the African states, do not address the wide spectrum of people's material needs. Reflecting on the political and legal culture in South Africa, Mandla Seleoane suggests that social and economic rights are intended to protect "the rock-bottom of human existence," by which he means the constitutional guarantees for protecting the necessities of life and providing for the foundations of an adequate quality of life.[31] The necessities of life at a minimum encompass rights to adequate nutrition, housing, health, and education, all of which "provide foundations upon which human development can occur and human freedom can flourish," and they require conceptualizations "in terms of an entitlement both to be equal as humans and to be equal as members of society."[32]

The inspiration for the inclusion of this category of rights in the Banjul Charter partly derives from the International Covenant on Economic, Social, and Cultural Rights, which was intended to enhance local and global social justice. Unlike the 1948 U.N. Declaration on Human Rights, this covenant, together with the one on civil/political rights, was a legally binding treaty especially for those nations that voted for its ratification.[33] Recent studies indicate that as of 2001, 142 states including 42 African nations have ratified or acceded to the covenant.[34] Accordingly, social-economic rights are distinguishable from developmental rights in that they are held by people against their national governments rather than against the international community. Another major difference between the two is that one (i.e., developmental rights) is concerned with the growth of a nation's physical and economic infrastructures, while the objective of socioeconomic rights is "distributional equity, that is, the increasing diffusion of the benefits of growth to the mass of the population."[35] The norm of distributive justice recognizes the right of all persons to have access to those public goods which are essential for the protection of their dignity in the actual conditions of social life. Its cardinal objective is to prevent one group of people from monopolizing social goods so as to dominate their fellows.[36] Distributive justice thus calls for "equality of opportunity for entry into the social, economic, cultural and political relationships which constitute the common good."[37]

In postcolonial Africa, the continuing suffocation of civil society, massive human rights abuses, waste and mismanagement, political corruption and irresponsibility, the manipulation of primordial loyalties and differences, and lack of leadership accountability are some of the factors that have negated even the most resilient conditions for the realization of distributive justice. In a statement that amounts to self-indictment, the Nigerian president, Olusegun Obasanjo, admits the complicity of his colleagues to "indulge in 'colonialist-bashing' and West-bashing,' " by blaming external actors for their woes.[38] This blaming propensity on the part of African leaders hides what Richard Joseph refers to as their "prebendalist" habit of competing for public offices and then utilizing them for their personal benefit as well as that of their sectional constituents—misdeeds that are often defended on the grounds that they reflect the participation of the appointed or elected representatives of groups sharing in public power and largesse. The consequence, of course, is that "the official public purpose of the office often becomes a secondary concern, however much that purpose might have been originally cited in its creation or during the periodic competition to fill it."[39]

By making social and economic rights the ethical cornerstone of the Banjul Charter, the proponents hope to resuscitate the value orientations of traditional African culture as a moral counterpoise to the nepotism and greed that currently predominate. In fact, a few of the early postindependence rulers fashioned their domestic policies after their interpretive version of indigenous morality. "African socialism" in Kenya, *ujamaa* in Tanzania, and "humanism" in Zambia were all espoused as prescriptive responses to the deleterious and embarrassing gap between the haves and the have-nots, the men of power and those they govern.[40] Julius Nyerere, the chief exponent of ujamaa, declared that there are more important things in life than the amassing of riches, and that "if the pursuit of wealth clashes with things like human dignity and social equality, then the latter will be given priority."[41] His philosophy of wealth and social justice has an African pedigree in the political culture of the Anuak people, who live on the border of the Sudan and Ethiopia, and whose practice of political appointment has been well documented by Asmarom Legesse. It was customary within each community to elect a chief on the basis of his wealth and leadership qualities. On assumption of office, the chief is expected to feast his subjects so often that his resources are soon depleted and he becomes impoverished. He then returns to his original status of common citizen and another wealthy candidate is put in his place. This practice of periodic rotation of offices, together with the obligatory sharing of fortunes, prevents an undue concentration of wealth in a few hands and guarantees everyone's access to those conditions of social life without which no person can seek, in general, to be himself at his best.[42] It also eliminates the hackneyed charge of the indeterminateness of the objects against whom to make the claims for social and economic opportunities.[43]

THE LEXICAL PRIORITY OF SOCIAL AND ECONOMIC RIGHTS
OVER CIVIL-POLITICAL RIGHTS

The Banjul Charter suggests that in the context of Africa social and economic rights should be given priority over their conceptual contenders. This proposal is usually attributed to communitarian practices like the one just cited, which many African theorists believe underscore a fundamental opposition between the Western approach and African value systems. The late Nigerian political economist Claude Ake believed that the Western approach "lacks concreteness; it ascribes abstract rights to abstract beings."[44] The values it celebrates are neither interesting nor communicable in the African context. Proceeding from a consequentialist standpoint, he argued that rights are only justifiable if they promote the best kind of society, by which he means not one that maximizes aggregate happiness or well-being, but one that leads to the greatest amount of economic development and liberation for the members of society. Especially in Africa, economic considerations outweigh civil and political considerations. The two problems facing the continent are starvation and fascism, and combating them would lead to quite a different way of ranking human rights than is typical in liberal Western political theories, where "there is much concern with the right to peaceful assembly, free speech and thought, fair trial, etc. The appeal of these rights is sociologically specific. They appeal to people with a full stomach who can now afford to pursue the more esoteric aspects of self-fulfillment. The vast majority of our people are not in this position. They are facing the struggle for existence in its brutal immediacy. Theirs is a totally consuming struggle. They have little or no time for reflection and hardly any use for free speech. They have little interest in choice for there is no choice in ignorance. There is no freedom for hungry people, or those eternally oppressed by disease."[45]

The end of apartheid in South Africa and the country's establishment of constitutional democracy have rekindled interest in the moral legitimacy of social-economic rights and their presumed parity with or superiority to civil-political liberties. Russel Botman of the University of Stellenbosch sees the inclusion of social rights in a bill of rights as the only way to redress the entrenched economic imbalance among the South African population.[46] However, in contrast to those who call for the suspension of civil-political liberties until there is a full and optimal realization of social justice in the economic spheres, advocates of social-economic rights in South Africa have insisted on the constitutionalization of both categories of rights in the nation's political culture.[47] The debate in South Africa also coincides with the emergence of an array of prodemocracy movements in other African countries, whose objective is not just to challenge military and one-party oligarchies but also to significantly redefine the meaning of democratic engagement.[48] These democratic currents reflect a theoretical outlook that challenges the primacy of social and economic rights, and it is to this that I now turn.

Poverty as a Political Problem: A Case for Civil-Political Rights

Advocacy for social-economic and development rights is by no means confined to Africa; neither is the challenge to their moral status as vehicles for human flourishing and societal advancement. There are three pertinent reasons, helpfully identified by Darryl M. Trimiew, why the idea of economic rights is so controversial in the West. The first is "whether rights discourse is the appropriate mode of discourse to use in connection with human material needs"; the second is "whether the protections intended under the umbrella of economic rights would foster or degrade human dignity," and the third has to do with the "precise protections and guarantees [that] are implied and encompassed in the notion of economic rights."[49] My intention in this section is to discuss the objections to social-economic and development rights in Africa against the background of these concerns.

Jack Donnelly and Rhoda Howard are the two notable critics of the notion that African countries need to channel their political and moral energies to the implementation of economic and development rights at the expense or total neglect of civil political liberties. There are three lines of criticism here. To begin with, Donnelly contends that "the right to development is both conceptually and practically misguided, at best a legally and morally confused notion that is likely to be positively detrimental to the realization of human rights."[50] Since the Banjul Charter locates the subject of this right in the nation-state, euphemistically understood as the people, it seems absurd to claim that a state possesses intrinsic dignity on the basis of which it can make a justifiable claim to development against other states.[51] Ordinarily, development is construed both as a process—that is, "a right to participate in a process of growth, to strive after self-actualization in conditions of dignity"—and an end—that is, "a right to be developed." A right to development in the first sense is redundant because that is also the chief object of civil-political rights, and rarely attainable in the second because that "is an overarching moral goal" to which no one is ordinarily entitled simply by virtue of being a human being: "There is no more a right to be developed than there is a right to be just or to be holy."[52] The central problem, then, in the African conception of rights is its failure to distinguish aspirational statements or goals from human rights, in the strict sense of titles and claims.

Second, proponents of the right to development have been criticized for self-interestedly exploiting the causal links between colonialism and Africa's problems. While no one disputes the role that imperialism, transnational corporations, unequal exchange, and foreign domination and exploitation have played and continue to play in the generation, consolidation, and reproduction of the African predicament, these facts should not be exploited to justify and rationalize the deficiencies and shortcomings of the ruling elite, nor to obscure "indigenous class accumulation of national wealth, and indigenous use of coercive state power to ensure that wealth stays in the hands of those who control the government."[53] Other observers, including Africans, agree. Moeletsi Mbeki, the brother of South Africa's president Thabo Mbeki recently expressed an opinion that many would consider abominable: that the average African is worse off now than during the colonial era. In his address to a meeting of the South African Institute of International Affairs, he compared the differing modes of governance between the two eras: while current African elites steal money and keep it abroad, "colonial rulers planted crops and built roads and cities."[54] Regardless of the unorthodoxy of this view, it cannot be denied that many African rulers have converted their countries to personal fiefdoms, extorting and exploiting their fellow citizens rather than developing and empowering them.[55]

Third, critics contend that the very nature of social, economic, and development rights make them unjusticiable, with justiciability defined as "the ability to judicially determine whether or not a person's right has been violated or whether the state has failed to meet a constitutionally recognized obligation to respect, protect, or fulfill a person's right."[56] This objection rests on the familiar distinction between positive rights and negative rights. The former are said to require governmental action; to be resource-intensive and therefore expensive to protect, progressive and therefore requiring time to realize, and vague in terms of the obligations they mandate; and to involve complex, polycentric, and diffuse interests in collective goods.[57] These characterizations lead to the conclusion that it would be foolhardy for African countries, most of which are chronically poor, to impose upon themselves the obligation to protect these rights.[58] Other theorists agree. Joel Feinberg suggests that "rights to be given certain essentials—food, shelter, security, education—clearly depend upon the existence of an adequate supply, something that cannot be guaranteed categorically and universally."[59] On the other hand, civil and political rights are justiciable because they are, paradigmatically, negative rights and therefore cost-free; immediately satisfiable; precise in the obligations they generate; and comprehensible because they involve discrete clashes of identifiable individual interests.[60] All that is required to satisfy negative rights is "the omission of activities that infringe them," an obligation not beyond the power of both individuals and government to meet.[61] This of course assumes the existence of propitious social conditions, especially "a set of institutional arrangements for securing legally binding guarantees beneficial to the individual" and "a secure and procedurally regularized legal system."[62]

THE PRIORITY OF CIVIL AND POLITICAL RIGHTS

It is this minimalist thrust of negative rights that their proponents believe should commend them to transitional societies still in search of a stable and enduring culture of constitutionalism. Challenging the likes of Nyerere and other "culture embracers" for whom the legitimacy of any human rights documents lies in their compatibility with local culture and mores, Cass Sunstein contends that it would be more fruitful to construe such documents as "*precommitment strategies*, in which nations use a founding document to protect against the most common problems in their usual political processes."[63] Only then can these societies hope to undo their most threatening tendencies, such as corruption of the elite, political repression, and the debilitating culture of dependency. Elevating positive dispensations from the state to the level of individual entitlement will have corrosive effects on individual enterprise and initiative, and thereby stigmatize their God-given productive capacities. No less than the right to development, social and economic rights are to be understood as good things that are worth having in a decent society, but if a human rights document "tries to specify everything to which a decent society commits itself, it threatens to become a mere piece of paper, worth nothing in the real world."[64]

Arguments like this provide the background for understanding the paradigm shift in the attitudes of Western countries to the domestic excesses of their cold war allies in Africa. The perception during the cold war that Africa had a strategic significance had lured the superpowers to reward compliant regimes with economic support and military hardware even if those regimes chose to unleash those ammunitions against their own citizens. The end of the cold war in the 1980s transformed the external environment in which African political systems operated. Increasingly convinced that the absence of democratic government and political accountability was a significant factor contributing to Africa's pervasive poverty, a number of Western governments and international financial agencies such as the World Bank and the International Monetary Fund began to insist that aid and investment be linked to political reform in Africa. The reform was seen as a touchstone of the structural adjustment programs that African countries were required to undertake, whose components would include the emergence of more effective governing institutions, respect for the rule of law, the curbing of corruption, the transparent management of public finances, and executive agencies being held accountable horizontally (by parliaments and judiciaries) and vertically (by civil society and periodic national elections).

Reactions to the design and implementation of the structural adjustment programs (SAPs) decreed by these international financial and development institutions were mixed,[65] but relevant to our discussion here is the contention that they have actually prompted widespread impoverishment and pauperization, spurring riots and protests,[66] and a vicious cycle of political authoritarianism:

> Structural adjustment affects working conditions and the right to work through retrenchment as a result of deindigenization,[67] privatization, and liberalization of trade controls. The extent of available health care and its cost is severely affected by the introduction (as in Zimbabwe) of user fees, which is an additional burden on people who are already impoverished and exist largely in a subsistence economy. The nature of educational services and their accessibility is affected by the increase in fees for tuition. . . . Finally, the ability to provide food and combat overall poverty is affected by the overall concentration on export crops and the removal of subsidies for market staples.[68]

These observations notwithstanding, scholars like Mandla Seleoane defend the priority of civil-political rights, arguing that the way a society is politically organized determines whether or not it will succeed in overcoming poverty. Thus, it is important to "tame the power of those who have control over the things that others need in order to survive, since their ability to allocate these resources gives them the power of life and death over other people."[69] South Africa's Center for Policy Studies expressed the same view when it observed that poverty reduction programs in the country have failed or been ineffective because their design "fails to reflect the concerns of the poor" or grossly misconstrues "what people require to address their poverty."[70] We can infer two important theoretical points from these observations about the structural priority of civil-political rights. First, they perform the instrumental function of "providing incentives and information toward the solution of economic privation."[71] In a well-researched study on food shortage in selected Asian and African countries, Amartya Sen proposes that government response to intense needs and sufferings almost always depends "on how much pressure is put on it, and whether or not pressure is put on it will depend on the exercise of political rights (such as voting, criticizing, protesting and so on)."[72] Thus, while no substantial famine has ever occurred in a country with a democratic form of government and a relatively free press, they have occurred in ancient kingdoms and in contemporary authoritarian societies, in primitive tribal communities and in modern technocratic dictatorships, in colonial economies governed by imperialists from the North and in newly independent countries of the South run by despotic leaders or by intolerant single parties. The reasons he offers are persuasive: "Famines kill millions of people in different countries in the world, but they do not kill the rulers. The kings and the presidents, the bureaucrats and the bosses, the military leaders and the commanders never starve. And if there are no elections, no opposition parties, no forums for uncensored public criticism, then those in authority do not have to suffer the political consequences of their failure to prevent famine. Democracy, by contrast, would spread the penalty of famine to the ruling groups and the political leadership."[73]

In addition to the instrumental power of civil and political rights to advance significant human purpose, they also have a *constitutive* and *asymmetrical* connection to economic need, and a procedural priority perforce follows from this asymmetry. Their moral weight far exceeds the personal advantage that holders of these rights may derive from them, for it is their existence that makes the comprehension and conceptualization of need possible. In order, therefore, to avoid the horrors of a closed and regimented society, we must have more than an instrumental appreciation for civil and political rights. The Nigerian Nobel laureate, Wole Soyinka, makes this point forcefully in his book *The Open Sore of a Continent*, where he denounces as spurious the proposition to give up civil and political rights for the sake of any national ideology, be it of development or something else. This is too much a price to pay, he says, for "wherever the nation ideal becomes a notion beyond the centrality of its human composition, where the nation ideal becomes, for instance, conflated with notions of racial [or gender] purity or other forms of extreme nationalism, we know only too well what the guaranteed consequences have been. We encounter immediately exclusivist policies that go beyond expelling other human units beyond a specific national space; the new imperative demands that they be totally excluded from the category of humanity, and thus from the physical world altogether."[74] Ultimately, the exigency of promoting civil and political rights in a society like Africa is a matter of existential imperative, grounded in the moral "respect we owe each other as fellow human beings"; as "people with rights to exercise, not as parts of a 'stock' or a 'population' that passively exists and must be looked after."[75] An appeal to these rights implies "a respect which places one within the referential range of self and others, which elevates one's status from human body to social being."[76]

Poverty as a Negation of Justice:
Toward an Interdependent Theory of Rights

The weakness of the foregoing perspectives on human rights is a double disjunction of elements of justice that need to be interpreted in their interplay: a disjoining of social and economic transformation from political empowerment; and of civil and political liberties from meaningful and comprehensive liberation from material indigence. To be truly just, any human rights solution to Africa's poverty must have a unitary perception of economic and political life. Without civil-political rights, Eric Masinde Aseka of Kenyatta University explained, people will have little or no chance of effective political participation in their societies, besides the fact that these rights are also functionally necessary for advancing human and communal socioeconomic and developmental interests.[77] Conversely, the provision of minimum economic conditions is required to render any notion of political participation meaningful. Inspiration for this unitary vision of empowerment can already be gleaned from the competing views discussed above. Relevant is the conviction on both aisles of the issue that human rights are pertinent to the advancement of human flourishing; as well as their common perception of the postcolonial state as the greatest obstacle to the realization of human rights objectives on the continent. This unintended consensus provides a normative framework for developing a holistic theory of rights that affirms the interdependence and hermeneutical interactiveness of civil-political liberties and social-economic goods.

Interdependence is both a strategic and normative principle, the objective of which is to capture the idea that "values seen as directly related to the full development of personhood cannot be protected and nurtured in isolation."[78] It advocates within human rights discourse "a full conception of human freedom and a full and integrated conception of the self,"[79] thereby rejecting a related series of fundamental oppositions or dichotomies that can serve to privilege certain conceptions of the self, and to reinforce marginalization. It is informed by the religious vision of the "fullness of life" as the organizing framework of moral discourse, and grounded in the all-encompassing Divine Reality that is related to all realms of life.[80] So conceived, it enables us to see and address problems preventing the continuation of life, whether political, social, or economic. By affirming the normative unity of all rights, the principle of interdependence furnishes us with critical tools to arrest the dangerous trend of reckless human rights violations in Africa, which are often excused on grounds of public order or inadequate material resources. The pertinence of this principle to combating poverty in Africa through the instrumentality of rights is discernable at three principal levels.

First, it posits a philosophical challenge to the tendency to rank human rights along the lines of ideological preference. Such ranking, in the African context, has served as a pretext for sacrificing both categories of rights. Perhaps no other African country illustrates this dismaying reality better than the Democratic Republic of Congo (formerly Zaire), where its late dictator, Mobutu Sese Seko, amassed a fortune far in excess of the country's national debt, thereby bankrupting what must be one of the richest nations on the continent. Like many of his African colleagues, he emerged in the early 1960s as an apostle of development, a task that supposedly required his fellow citizens to sacrifice their civil and political rights. In reality, African leaders have exploited the ideology of development "as a means for reproducing political hegemony."[81] Affirming the mutual interdependence of rights may help to prevent this situation of turning the state to an institutional appendix of a clique. It may also help put a brake on the new myth of globalization with its neoliberal and neocolonial message of unaided market forces as an engine of economic development and material prosperity. For people who "lack the resources needed to become involved in the markets" and "are also marginalized from genuinely active involvement in the democratic process because of their economic plight,"[82] arming them with civil-political rights may be the only way to wrest the control of the political process from the hands of the already existing elites.

Second, the principle of interdependence bridges the gap between the so-called negative rights and positive rights, thereby refuting the attendant claim that only the former are genuinely enforceable. This distinction rests on a flawed assumption that for every human right there is only one correlative obligation, rather than seeing all human rights as entailing a complex, multilayered structure of obligations.[83] Henry Shue invokes the dynamic character of rights (the fact that a right is not only a ground for different duties, but also that the duties it generates may change over time) to argue that economic rights are no less justiciable than civil/political rights. Using the right to food as an example, he explains that there are four duties corresponding to it: the obligation to respect, the obligation to protect, the obligation to ensure, and the obligation to promote. The first is a classic negative obligation of noninterference, while the other three require varying degrees of positive action or state policy.[84] This moral overlap underscores the need to promote in tandem both categories of rights. As one philosopher rightly puts it, "The effective distribution of civil liberties, far from being a passive effect of the proper distribution of food, housing, and health care, can strongly facilitate the latter distribution."[85]

Finally, the principle of interdependence takes into account the social realities of the people; its primary focus is to promote what it means to be human or what the capacity to be human means. According to Peter Paris, an understanding of the intrinsic sociality of the human status is informed by the distinctively personalist character of African religious ethics, which focus on the human person, the *subject* of rights, whose full development is inextricably linked to his or her material and political empowerment.[86] By shifting the argument from the *content* of rights per se and locating it at the center of the quest for an understanding of what it means to be human, the interdependence principle brings a dynamic and sense of urgency to human rights and poverty crises in Africa. The social realities of the African person are affected by a vicious circle of existential woes: civil wars, cultural oppression, political autocracy, economic stagnation, natural disasters, population explosion, precarious health conditions, and refugee crises, all of which contribute to, and are symptoms of, poverty. Without a moral strategy that combines both the aspirations for political liberation with the imperatives of economic sustenance and empowerment, life in Africa will continue to be brutish and alienating. While the scale, number, and content of economic and social rights may be contested, their legitimacy should not. Similarly, there is a need to develop new instrumentalities for the control of governmental excess, and to protect the essential parameters of a decent human existence. A society that promotes only one category of rights—for example, civil-political rights—projects an image of truncated humanity. Symbolically, but still brutally, it excludes those segments of society for whom autonomy means little without the necessities of life.

Notes

1. See Reuben Abati, "Religion As Obstacle," *Guardian* (Nigeria), 16 May 2004, remarking that religion in Nigeria has become an obstacle not only to rational discourse but also to political and economic progress.
2. David Rieff, "Hell and Humanitarianism," review of Philip Gourevitch, *We Wish to Inform You That Tomorrow We Will Be Killed with Our Families*, in *New Republic*, no. 4377, 7 December 1998, 39.
3. John Dunn, *Western Political Theory in the Face of the Future* (Cambridge: Cambridge University Press, 1999), 75.
4. T. S. Eliot, "Ulysses, Order, and Myth," *Dial* 75 (November 1923): 483.

5. Mandla Seleoane, "Socio-Economic Rights: An Instrument to Mitigate Poverty?" paper presented at the Pan-African Seminar on Religion and Poverty, 14–28 July 2002, Johannesburg, South Africa, 2, 6.

6. An illuminating summary of this view can be found in Rhoda E. Howard, "The Full-Belly Thesis: Should Economic Rights Take Priority over Civil and Political Rights? Evidence from Sub-Saharan Africa," *Human Rights Quarterly* 5.4 (1983): 467–90.

7. Banjul, the city after which the charter is named, is the capital of Gambia.

8. Steven Lukes, "Five Fables about Human Rights," in *On Human Rights: The Oxford Amnesty Lectures 1993*, ed. Stephen Shute and Susan Hurley (New York: Basic Books, 1993), 19–40.

9. Ronald Dworkin, "Rights as Trumps," in *Theories of Rights*, ed. Jeremy Waldron (Oxford: Oxford University Press, 1984), 153–67.

10. For a religious account of human rights, see John Onaiyekan, "Evangelization and Human Rights Issues in Africa Today: Some Pastoral Reflections," *West African Journal of Ecclesial Studies* 3 (1991): 1–8. For a contrasting view suggesting the possibility of developing an understanding of the meaning and implications of human rights claims without explicit reliance on the authority of specific religious traditions, see Kwame Gyekye, *An Essay on African Philosophical Thought: The Akan Conceptual Scheme* (Cambridge: Cambridge University Press, 1987), 207–8.

11. J. F. Ade Ajayi, "Expectations of Independence," *Daedalus* 111.2 (1982): 1–9.

12. Edward P. Jaycox, *The Challenges of African Development* (Washington, D.C.: World Bank, 1992), 15.

13. The regulative influence of the Banjul Charter is most vividly seen when the document is contrasted with an earlier O.A.U. Charter, adopted by the first leaders of independent Africa in May 1963. Article 3(ii) of the earlier charter provides that member states must adhere to, among other things, the principle of noninterference in the internal affairs of other states. The article turned out to be a Frankenstein's monster, as many states invoked it at various times to justify their mishandling, torturing, and even butchering of their own citizens while the rest of Africa watched helplessly. Thus, the adoption of the Banjul Charter may be seen as a blow to regimes that hide under the noninterference clause in the O.A.U. Charter to callously violate their citizens' rights. For analyses of the evolving interaction between the Banjul Charter and various national constitutions in Africa, see Olusola Ojo and Amadu Sesay, "The O.A.U. and Human Rights: Prospects for the 1980s and Beyond," *Human Rights Quarterly* 8 (1986): 89–103; Jack Donnelly and Rhoda E. Howard, "Assessing National Human Rights Performance: A Theoretical Framework," *Human Rights Quarterly* 10 (1988): 214–48; and Sakah S. Mahmud, "The State and Human Rights in Africa in the 1990s: Perspectives and Prospects," *Human Rights Quarterly* 15 (1993): 485–98. For a full text of the Banjul Charter, see Chris Maina Peter, *Human Rights in Africa: A Comparative Study of the African Human and People's Rights Charter and the New Tanzanian Bill of Rights* (New York: Greenwood Press, 1990), 103–16.

14. Charles Villa-Vicencio, *A Theology of Reconstruction: Nation-Building and Human Rights* (Cambridge: Cambridge University Press, 1992), 174–75.

15. Philip Kunig, Wolfgang Benedek, and Costa Ricky Mahalu, eds., *Regional Protection of Human Rights by International Law: The Emerging African Systems* (Baden-Baden: Nomos Verlagsgesellschaft, 1985), 121. Also subscribing to this view is a Nigerian political and legal theorist, G. O. Olusanya, who contends that "for any law to grow and be

productive it must be rooted in the culture and tradition as well as the realities of the people for whom it is made." His view was quoted in Olusola Ojo, "Understanding Human Rights in Africa," in *Human Rights in a Pluralistic World: Individuals and Collectivities*, ed. Jan Berting et al. (Westport, Conn.: Meckler, 1990), 119.

16. Peter, *Human Rights in Africa*, 104 (emphasis mine).

17. For a good account of the evolution of human rights on the international scene, see David Hollenbach, *Claims in Conflict: Retrieving and Renewing the Catholic Human Rights Tradition* (New York: Paulist Press, 1979), 7–38.

18. *What Kind of Africa by the Year 2000? Final Report of the Monrovia Symposium on the Future Development Prospects of Africa towards the Year 2000* (Geneva: OAU/International Institute of Labour Studies, 1979), 14–16.

19. Jean-François Bayart, *The State in Africa: The Politics of the Belly*, trans. Mary Harper (London: Longman, 1993), ix.

20. Julius O. Ihonvbere, "The State, Human Rights, and Democratization in Africa," *Current World Leaders* 37.4 (1994): 63.

21. George W. Shepherd Jr., "The Tributary State and 'Peoples' Rights' in Africa: The Banjul Charter and Self-Reliance," *Africa Today* (1st and 2nd quarter 1985): 41.

22. These are societies whose citizens are severely deprived and "struggling to survive in a set of squalid and degraded circumstances almost beyond the power of our sophisticated imaginations and privileged circumstances to conceive." See Peter Singer, *Practical Ethics* (Cambridge: Cambridge University Press, 1993), 219.

23. Economic Commission for Africa (ECA), *African Economic Report—1998* (Addis Ababa: UNECA, 1998), 8–9.

24. United Nations Development Program, *Human Development Report 1994* (New York: Oxford University Press, 1994), 165.

25. World Bank, *World Development Report 1998–99* (Washington, D.C.: World Bank, 2000).

26. World Bank, *World Development Report 1995* (Washington, D.C.: World Bank, 1995), 122. For a fuller account of the correlation between globalization and Africa's poverty, see Simeon O. Ilesanmi, "Leave No Poor Behind: Globalization and the Imperative of Socio-Economic and Development Rights from an African Perspective," *Journal of Religious Ethics* 32.1 (2004): 71–92.

27. Keba M'Baye, "Emergence of the 'Right to Development' as a Human Right in the Context of New International Economic Order," paper presented to the UNESCO Meeting of Experts on Human Rights, Human Needs and the Establishment of a New Economic Order, Paris, 19–23 June 1978, Doc. SS-78/CONF.630/8.

28. All Africa Conference of Churches (AACC), "AACC Jubilee Convocation Message: Time to Rediscover the Gospel," *Tam Tam: A Publication of AACC* (January–June 2001), 29.

29. Ibid.

30. African Faith and Justice Network, *African Synod: Documents, Reflections, Perspectives* (Maryknoll, N.Y.: Orbis Books, 1996), 114–15.

31. Seleoane, "Socio-Economic Rights: An Instrument to Mitigate Poverty?" 4.

32. Craig Scott and Patrick Macklem, "Constitutional Ropes of Sand or Justiciable Guarantees? Social Rights in a New South African Constitution," *University of Pennsylvania Law Review* 141.1 (1992): 9–10.

33. Hollenbach, *Claims in Conflict*, 9. The act of ratification makes the treaty *jus cogens*, i.e., "peremptory norms of international relations which states cannot derogate

from." See Nana Kusi Appea Busia and Bibiane G. Mbaye, "Economic and Social Rights: The Debate Continues," *African Topics* 1 (1993): 12.

34. J. Oloka-Onyango, "Beyond the Rhetoric: Reinvigorating the Struggle for Economic and Social Rights in Africa," *California Western International Law Journal* 26.1 (1995): 13.

35. Jack Donnelly, "Repression and Development: The Political Contingency of Human Rights Trade Offs," in *Human Rights and Development: International Views*, ed. David Forsythe (New York: St. Martin's Press, 1989), 307.

36. Michael Walzer, *Spheres of Justice: A Defense of Pluralism and Equality* (New York: Basic Books, 1983), xii–xiii.

37. Hollenbach, *Claims in Conflict*, 149.

38. Olusegun Obasanjo, *African Perspective: Myths and Realities* (New York: Council on Foreign Relations, 1987), 1.

39. Richard Joseph, *Democracy and Prebendal Politics in Nigeria: The Rise and Fall of the Second Republic* (Cambridge: Cambridge University Press, 1987), 8.

40. Asmarom Legesse, "Human Rights in African Political Culture," in *The Moral Imperatives of Human Rights: A World Survey* (Washington, D.C.: University Press of America, 1980), 125–28.

41. Julius Nyerere, *Uhuru na Ujamaa: Freedom and Socialism* (London: Oxford University Press, 1968), 325.

42. Legesse, "Human Rights in African Political Culture," 125–26.

43. L. W. Sumner defines "the *objects* of a right" as "those against whom it is held." See his *The Moral Foundation of Rights* (Oxford: Clarendon Press, 1987), 11.

44. Claude Ake, "The African Context of Human Rights," *Africa Today* (1st and 2nd Quarters 1987): 6.

45. Ibid., 5–6.

46. H. Russel Botman, "The Terror of Poverty: A Fundamentalist Assault on Human Dignity," paper presented at the Pan-African Seminar on Religion and Poverty, 14–28 July 2002, Johannesburg, South Africa, 1.

47. See Puleng LenkaBula, "Poverty and Inequality in South Africa: A Mosotho Woman's Perspective," paper presented at the Pan-African Seminar on Religion and Poverty, 14–28 July 2002, Johannesburg, South Africa.

48. Julius Ihonvbere and Olufemi Vaughan, "Democracy and Civil Society: The Nigerian Transition Programme, 1985–1993," in *Democracy and Political Change in Sub-Saharan Africa*, ed. John A. Wiseman (London: Routledge, 1995), 71–91.

49. Darryl M. Trimiew, "The Economic Rights Debate: The End of One Argument, the Beginning of Another," *Annual of the Society of Christian Ethics* (1991): 85–86.

50. Jack Donnelly, "The 'Right to Development': How Not to Link Human Rights and Development," in *Human Rights and Development in Africa*, ed. Claude E. Welch Jr. and Ronald I. Meltzer (Albany: State University of New York Press, 1984), 261.

51. Ibid., 268.

52. Ibid., 273.

53. Rhoda E. Howard, "Economic Rights and Foreign Policy," in *Human Rights and Development: International Views*, ed. David P. Forsythe (New York: St. Martin's Press, 1989), 217.

54. "Africa 'better in colonial times' " at http://news.bbc.co.uk/2/hi/africa/3679706.stm.

55. The Banjul Charter itself is partly responsible for this dismaying reality. See articles 2(3), 3(3), 4(1), and 8(1)—all of which ascribe to the state an expansive role not only

in the formulation and execution of development policies, but also in the overall definition of public life.

56. Scott and Macklem, "Constitutional Ropes of Sand or Justiciable Guarantees?" 17.
57. Ibid., 24.
58. Busia and Mbaye, "Economic and Social Rights," 11.
59. Joel Feinberg, *Social Philosophy* (Englewood Cliffs, N.J.: Prentice-Hall, 1973), 88.
60. Robert Nozick is the doyen of this school of thought. For him, rights are to be thought of as *side constraints*: limits on the kinds of action individuals are entitled to perform. Rights can never require an agent to perform a certain act. See his *Anarchy, State and Utopia* (New York: Basic Books, 1974), chap. 3.
61. John Langan, "Defining Human Rights: A Revision of the Liberal Tradition," in *Human Rights in the Americas*, ed. Alfred Hennelly and John Langan (Washington, D.C.: Georgetown University Press, 1982), 76.
62. Richard Pierre Claude, "The Western Tradition of Human Rights in Comparative Perspective," *Comparative Judicial Review* 14 (1977): 8, 10.
63. Cass Sunstein, "Against Positive Rights," *East European Constitutional Review* 2.1 (1993): 36.
64. Ibid.
65. The SAP (structural adjustment program) was a form of economic reform program prescribed for most African countries in the early 1980s, and closely supervised by the World Bank and the International Monetary Fund. The programs were prompted by the conviction that African governments were unable to manage economic resources efficiently and that the private sector discipline of making a profit would ensure a more efficient use of resources. The main elements of these reform programs included, inter alia, the reduction of the size of the African state and its controls over the economy, the establishment of incentive prices for agriculture, the freeing-up of prices and the reduction of state subsidies and public employment rolls, the privatization of trade and exchange controls, and the revising of investment codes to encourage private (foreign and domestic) investment. See Paul J. Kaiser, "Structural Adjustment and the Fragile Nation: The Demise of Social Unity in Tanzania," *Journal of Modern African Studies* 34.2 (1996): 227–37.
66. The ironic result of political conditionalities imposed by the West is that they undermine the very civil and political rights they were designed to promote. African governments typically respond to popular discontent against their austerity measures through crackdown and brutal repression. Thus, the West can "rightly be accused of complicity in the human rights abuses of regimes that it supports for narrow economic principles." See Earl Conteh-Morgan, "The Military and Human Rights in a Post–Cold War Africa," *Armed Forces and Society* 21.1 (1994): 78.
67. Adebayo Adedeji explains that "deindigenization" is the converse of "indigenization," which was the term coined for programs established in the early years of African independence that sought to involve indigenous entrepreneurs more intimately in business. It was a type of postcolonial affirmative action instituted to counteract the domination of business, trade, industry, and government either by the colonial master, or by nonindigenous communities (e.g., South Asians in East Africa, and Lebanese in the West). Deindigenization thus reverses the programs of conferring such privileges on the local populace. See his *Indigenization of African Economies* (New York: Africana Publishing, 1981).
68. Oloka-Onyango, "Beyond the Rhetoric," 23.

69. Seleoane, "Socio-Economic Rights," 7.
70. Civil Society and Poverty Reduction in Southern Africa (Centre for Policy Studies: Johannesburg, 2002), 2.
71. Amartya Sen, "Liberty and Poverty: Political Rights and Economics," Current 362 (May 1994): 22.
72. Ibid., 24.
73. Ibid., 25.
74. Wole Soyinka, The Open Sore of a Continent: A Personal Narrative of the Nigerian Crisis (New York: Oxford University Press, 1996), 116–17.
75. Sen, "Liberty and Poverty," 28.
76. Patricia J. Williams, "Alchemical Notes: Reconstructing Ideals from Deconstructed Rights," Harvard Civil Rights–Civil Liberties Law Review 22 (1987): 416.
77. Eric Masinde Aseka, "Religion and Poverty: A Socio-Economic and Political Perspective," paper presented at the Pan-African Seminar on Religion and Poverty at Loreto Mary Ward Centre, Langata, Kenya, 19 July 2001. See also Sumner B. Twiss, "Religion and Human Rights: A Comparative Perspective," in Explorations in Global Ethics: Comparative Religious Ethics and Interreligious Dialogue, ed. Sumner B. Twiss and Bruce Grelle (Boulder, Colo.: Westview, 1998), 155–75.
78. Craig Scott, "The Interdependence and Permeability of Human Rights Norms: Towards a Partial Fusion of the International Covenants on Human Rights," Osgoode Hall Law Journal 27.4 (1989): 786.
79. Ibid., 804.
80. This vision is captured by the concept of moyo among the Chewa of Malawi and the concept of okra among the Akan of Ghana. See Harvey Sindima, "Community of Life," Ecumenical Review 41.4 (1989): 543–49; and Kwasi Wiredu, "An Akan Perspective on Human Rights," in Human Rights in Africa: Cross-Cultural Perspectives, ed. Abdullahi Ahmed An-Na'im and Francis M. Deng (Washington, D.C.: Brookings Institution, 1990), 243–60. See also Laurenti Magesia, African Religion: The Moral Traditions of Abundant Life (Maryknoll, N.Y.: Orbis Books, 1997), 75–114.
81. Claude Ake, Democracy and Development in Africa (Washington, D.C.: Brookings Institution, 1996), 9.
82. David Hollenbach, "Solidarity, Development, and Human Rights," Journal of Religious Ethics 26.2 (1998): 314.
83. J. Raz, "On the Nature of Rights," Mind 3 (1978): 197–99.
84. Henry Shue, "The Interdependence of Duties," in The Right to Food, ed. P. Alston and K. Tomasevski (The Hague: Martinus Nijhoff, 1984), 83.
85. Alan Gewirth, Human Rights: Essays on Justifications and Applications (Chicago: University of Chicago Press, 1982), 66.
86. See Peter J. Paris, The Spirituality of African Peoples: The Search for a Common Moral Discourse (Minneapolis: Fortress Press, 1995), 101–27.

Peter J. Paris | **SELF-INITIATION**

A NECESSARY PRINCIPLE IN THE AFRICAN

STRUGGLE TO ABOLISH POVERTY

The purpose of this essay is to explore the moral and religious strivings of African peoples in their struggle to abolish poverty. My interest in this subject was heightened when I listened to one of Africa's preeminent theologians, Mercy Amba Oduyoye, deliver the keynote address at the 1997 meeting of the All Africa Conference of Churches in Addis Ababa. She began her speech with a statement of fact, namely, "Africa is rich," and followed it immediately with a provocative question: "Why then are Africans poor?" Those words clearly expressed Africa's enduring dilemma of being both rich and poor at the same time.

It is well known that for many centuries countless traders from both the western and eastern worlds plundered the continent of Africa and removed from its shores immeasurable amounts of material and human resources for the purpose of developing and enriching their respective nations. Three centuries of the African slave trade, one century of colonialism, and a half century of postcolonial dictatorships and widespread corruption have greatly weakened that continent's capacity for any adequate recovery. In fact, that infamous history has had a deleterious effect on the development of African peoples both on the continent and throughout the diaspora.

It is important at the outset to define three major terms in this essay. First, the term "morality" refers to the qualitative dimension of human action and, more specifically, action that preserves and enhances the lives of persons and groups. Second, the term "religion" refers to particular practices of specific groups that express their relation to the source of what they consider to be ultimate reality for them. Third, the term "poverty" refers to the denial of and exclusion from the necessary material, societal, and spiritual conditions for a good life.

"The material dimension of life" refers to such necessary conditions of life as adequate food, clean water, and viable shelter. "The societal dimension" refers to such conditions as quality education, affordable health care, meaningful work, a livable wage, personal security, and the opportunity to participate in the making of public policies that affect one's life and destiny. "The spiritual dimension" of life refers to the capacity of the human spirit to initiate and create novel responses to oppressive societal conditions. That capacity is nurtured and protected by an ethos of human and civil rights, communal identity, political participation, and religious practice.

Given the enormous lack of material resources among African peoples throughout the world and most peoples in the southern hemisphere, I conclude that the global condition of poverty constitutes the major moral problem of the twenty-first century. Tragically, poverty objectifies people by denying them the means to actualize their potentialities. In doing so, it greatly diminishes life by severely limiting its quality, growth, and preservation. Further and most important, the structural conditions of poverty guarantee its cyclical nature from generation to generation.

Presuppositions

This essay presupposes that the conditions of poverty are not freely chosen by the people but are inflicted on them by some natural or human causes. In either case, the poor are not the cause of their poverty. Further, I assume that certain habitual practices of the poor are consequences of poverty, while others serve to perpetuate it. For example, illiteracy, disease, and the depletion of natural resources are the results of poverty but the willful acquiescence of the poor to their social condition contributes to their own degradation as self-respecting human beings. Yet, since the poor do not control the means needed for eradicating the conditions of poverty, they require the assistance of external allies to help them realize the desired social change.

I also assume that a certain amount of material substance is a necessary condition for the moral well-being of persons and communities. Apart from some basic level of materiality the people become creatures of necessity and deficient of any freedom of choice. Since the latter constitutes their humanity, they must strive to sustain the potentiality to become free agents by struggling to liberate themselves from the conditions that threaten to diminish and destroy their lives.

Finally, I assume that since most human beings are incapable of altruist practices, and since poverty undermines the capacity of people to make choices and initiate action for the promotion of their communal well-being, it is necessary for African peoples themselves to initiate the processes for their own empowerment and liberation.[1] In other words, they should not expect their empowerment to come from others. Rather, they, alone, must initiate practices aimed at preserving and enhancing justice both for themselves as persons and their respective communities. That alone will enable them to gain control over their destiny. But, if they fail to do so, they will become permanent victims to the unjust practices of others in virtually every sphere of life. Of course, they will need to form coalitions with all others of goodwill who desire to join them in their struggle.

The Conquest of Africa by Both the Slave Trade and Colonialism

Between the sixteenth and nineteenth centuries, the African continent was hit hard by the devastating impact of the western and eastern slave trade. Thereafter the collaborative enterprises of European colonialism and the Christian missionary movement constituted a further wave of conquest. Though most Africans persistently and valiantly resisted those forces of cultural oppression and destruction, they were defeated nonetheless by the superiority of European military technology.

Clearly, the eventual abolition of the slave trade merely prepared the way for the birth of colonialism under the guise of "legitimate" commerce and Christian expansionism. Soon the integrated philosophy of so-called civilization, commerce, and Christianity was born. The missionary work of building and operating schools and hospitals contributed immensely to the denigration of many indigenous African cultural beliefs and practices. Yet, African resistance to that process preserved many cherished traditions and values.

Now, it is important to note that in most traditional African villages before the European conquest, virtually everybody had the same amount of material possessions. The absence of an economic hierarchy implied that there was no competition for scarce resources. Such a condition of economic equality easily facilitated the development and preservation of a communal ethos of sharing and belonging. That ethos was greatly ruptured, however, by the impact of the African slave trade, Western colonialism, and the Christian missionary movement.

Chinua Achebe's classic novel Things Fall Apart vividly portrayed that enormous social upheaval that pervaded the African continent. In that novel, he dramatized life in an Ibo village prior to the coming of the Western colonialists and the Christian missionaries. The emergent conflict between the strong man, Okonkwo, and his son, Nwoye, who became a Christian convert, is representative of the cataclysmic cultural conflict that eventually permeated the continent and wrought havoc on the various traditional African cultures. The conflict occurred between those bent on preserving the cultural traditions and those who embraced the cultural ways of their conquerors.

Okonkwo symbolizes the tradition of great Ibo leaders who uncritically honored and obeyed their ancestral customs, beliefs, and practices by dedicating themselves fully to the pursuit of the community's well-being, which the people had long viewed as the ground and source of all religious, political, moral, and personal value. All of this was undermined and thwarted by the conquering ethos of Western civilization, commerce, and Christianity. Further, the coercive transplantation of Africans outside of the continent had devastating consequences for African peoples everywhere, the implications of which continue up to the present day.

Self-Initiation in Sub-Saharan African Struggles for Political Justice

Throughout those centuries, African peoples were not mere victims of the external forces of conquest. Rather, they devised various creative responses of survival and resistance. These involved cultural retentions and hybridizations, political reinventions, religious, moral and aesthetic syncretism, clandestine practices through secret societies, religious associations, literary and cultural organizations, public protest, mass demonstrations, boycotts, speeches, sermons, prayers, literature, drama, music, and song. All of these activities manifested the power of new initiatives that emerged in the midst of astounding odds—initiatives that evidenced their enduring devotion to the goal of communal well-being in the form of religious organization.

African cultural traditions reveal the primacy of the community as the ground and source of all religious, political, moral, and personal value. In traditional societies, personal identity necessitated a community of belonging that, in turn, implied various social obligations. In fact, the Bantu peoples of southern Africa demonstrate the relation of the person and the community in their use of the word *ubuntu*, a Zulu word for "person" as grounded in and constituted by the community. In the words of Bishop Sigqibo Dwane, "*Ubuntu* broadly speaking is the idea that other people's humanity and its claims upon one must be taken seriously."[2] Thus, many contemporary scholars and others view ubuntu as the foundation of African personality.

Contrary to its desired goal of cultural conquest, the colonial educational system unwittingly produced a bicultural people whose indigenous languages and cultural practices were retained alongside the colonial linguistic inheritance. In fact, according to the noted historian Lamin Sanneh, the translation of the Bible, sermons, and songs into indigenous languages greatly enhanced the value of traditional beliefs and practices in the minds of the people.[3] Obviously, such a process was neither understood nor appreciated by the early Christian missionaries.

Further, Western education in Christian mission schools also served a different purpose from what the missionaries had intended. Lamin Sanneh argues that the art of translating the Christian message was not only a stimulus for cultural pride among indigenous peoples; it also constituted a primary condition for the birth of the nationalist spirit, which invariably fueled the growth of independence movements both in religion and politics. Thus, he concludes, the art of translation was a primary agency in the empowerment and liberation of indigenous African cultures. The translation of the message into the mother tongue of the indigenous peoples provided them with a tool of immense hermeneutical and psychological advantage. Regardless of the attitudes and intentions of the Christian missionaries, biblical translation per se virtually implied the surrender of the Western cultural linguistic hegemonies to indigenous linguistic systems. By preserving their languages and worldviews, Africans were able to seize the opportunity to liberate themselves from the clutches of cultural and religious domination.

In brief, the Christian missionary attempt to change the African's religious consciousness failed. Its aim had been to replace traditional African understandings with Christian understandings. Africans did the unexpected by mediating the Christian gospel through their own linguistic and religious contexts. Thus, the art of translation served the function of ennobling the peoples and their cultures rather than demoralizing them. Most important, the art of translation coupled with the quality of education gained in the mission schools provided African students with an excellent introduction to the basic values and norms of Western culture.[4] Ironically, that included the historical and literary study of such values as human and civil rights, equality, liberty, freedom, democracy, independence, to mention only a few; eventually, bright young students (indeed an elite in themselves, since illiteracy was more the norm than not) would soon begin applying those understandings to their own situation. Those endeavors gave birth to the political independence movements that emerged everywhere following the Second World War.

Now, one of the principal aims of colonial education was to prepare a limited number of men and even fewer women for employment in the junior levels of the colonial administration, where they were expected to function willingly as managers of the system. By definition, however, no African civil servant would ever be viewed by colonialists as the equal of a European expatriate. The colonial privileges of residential and social segregation, a higher pay scale, so-called home-leave policies of six-month stays in the colonial capital every eighteen months, and hardship allowances, constituted structural barriers to any such presumption. Though many Africans in the colonial civil service assumed condescending attitudes toward their own peoples, most of them did not do so, in large part because of their many and varied familial obligations that they were obligated to honor. Those who spent many years living abroad, however, experienced a measure of relief from such duties even though they also felt the need to honor their familial obligations at least minimally. Upon returning to the homeland, however, they would reassume their familial responsibilities. Both social and psychological pressures would guarantee their compliance.

Ironically, most of the fathers of African independence had been trained either by the colonialists in so-called government schools or by missionaries in mission schools. In either case, they received an education equal to that of their peers in the colonial countries. Before 1948 such secondary school graduates attended universities either in the colonial country or in one of the two oldest universities on the continent, Fourah Bay College in Sierra Leone and Fort Hare University in South Africa. Both of these were started by missionary societies and offered an education equivalent to that of the universities in Great Britain. Since those universities served the continent as a whole, they provided the students an excellent environment for the development of a Pan-African consciousness of mutual respect for and a general education about their respective countries.

Early Initiatives of African Independent Leaders

Though time and space do not permit any detailed outline of the historical development of the consciousness that led to the independence of Africa, suffice it to say that it was very much under way in various circles by the turn of the twentieth century. Gradually, that consciousness grew steadily on the continent and in the diaspora following World War I. In fact the first Pan-African Congress that took place in Paris in 1919 consisted mostly of Africans who were living there at the time. African Americans could not procure passports, and few Africans came to the conference directly from Africa. W. E. B. Du Bois reported, "Of the fifty-seven delegates from fifteen countries, nine were African countries with twelve delegates. Of the remaining delegates, sixteen were from the United States and twenty-four from the West Indies."[5]

Between 1919 and 1927 four Pan-African Conferences were held. At that point travel became prohibitive during the Great Depression and the Second World War. But, immediately following the war, the fifth and final Pan-African Congress was held in Manchester, England, 15–21 October 1945. Over two hundred delegates took a bold step by calling for the united force of all African peoples for democracy for black folk everywhere. Those present at the conference included Kwame Nkrumah, destined to be the first president of the first country in Africa to overthrow colonialism; Kenya's Jomo Kenyatta, who would become the first president of Kenya; the trade union leaders I. T. A. Wallace-Johnson from Sierra Leone and Chief A. Soyemi Coker from Nigeria; and George Padmore from Trinidad, who came as a representative of Southern Rhodesia (now Zimbabwe). This fifth Pan-African Congress was united in its call for political independence for all African peoples. Most important, the report of that final congress conjoined the issues of political independence and economic democracy.[6]

Several of those who attended the last Pan-African Congress, and many who were not able to do so, had either served prison sentences or were destined to do so within the next decade. At any rate, I claim that these leaders represented the true models of traditional African leadership. Their cause was the freedom and empowerment of their respective peoples. Instead of seeking their own selfish gain, they were ready to suffer and even die for the freedom of their people. Though their names were legion between 1945 and the 1960s, the most prominent of them were Nnamdi Azikiwe and Abubakar Tafawa Balewa of Nigeria, Kwame Nkrumah of Ghana, Milton Obote of Uganda, Jomo Kenyatta of Kenya, Ahmed Sekou Toure of Guinea, Felix Houphouet-Boigny of Ivory Coast, Hastings Kamuzu Banda of Malawi, Samora Machel of Mozambique, Leopold Senghor of Senegal, Julius Nyerere of Tanzania, Kenneth Kaunda of Zambia, and Albert Luthuli and Nelson Mandela of South Africa.[7]

Most though not all of these leaders eventually gained the trust of other ethnic groups in addition to their own. Few of them could ever be accused of promoting tribalism or being motivated by his own self-interest. Consequently, they are immortalized among Africans everywhere as paradigmatic leaders because they remained faithful to their ancestral traditions. Each in his own way sought to expand human community rather than limit it. Each uplifted the spirits of his people by inspiring them to dream about new possibilities of freedom and justice for all. Kwame Nkrumah longed for a United States of all Africa. Accordingly, Nigeria became the locus for the founding meeting of the All Africa Conference of Churches and the Organization of African Unity, organizations that were supported by virtually all the leaders mentioned above. The paramount figure of suffering and triumph in the liberation struggle is Nelson Mandela, who gained worldwide acclaim for his astounding leadership qualities.

Shortly after the dawn of independence, however, those who represented Achebe's Okonkwo type of great leader were succeeded by a wave of "little men," whose ruthless use of military power showered their peoples with decades of political oppression, economic exploitation, colossal corruption, moral abuse, cultural deprivation, and personal suffering in abundance. Achebe later fictionalized such leaders in his book *Anthills of Savannah*. In reality, this new breed of tyrants appeared on the pages of postcolonial history as Siaka Stevens of Sierra Leone, Charles Taylor of Liberia, Idi Amin of Uganda, Mobutu Sese Seko of Zaire, Flight Lieutenant Jerry Rawlings of Ghana, and many others who terrorized their people and added greater misery to their bitter sufferings.[8] Contrary to expectations, the moral quality of these indigenous leaders failed to surpass that of their former colonial rulers. In fact, some of their practices were even worse because their widespread corruption oppressed their own people.

Unfortunately, in most countries in Africa, so-called independence from colonial rule meant a transfer of European political hegemony to various African despotic rulers most of whom continued to enjoy reciprocal relationships with their former colonial governments. The consequence was a steady increase in the suffering of the masses. Yet, none of this in any way constitutes justification either for the continuation of colonial rule or the argument that Africans were not prepared for independence. Rather, colonialism was the antithesis of democracy and hence could not have prepared the people adequately either for its emergence or its preservation. In fact, colonial rulers were exemplars of unregulated capital markets that enriched the few and impoverished the many by their passion for profiteering, greed, corruption, and hedonistic individualism. Many of their African successors did likewise.

Yet, in every stage of African history both on the continent and in the diaspora various initiatives were undertaken to resist domination and exploitation of every type. Those strategies included (a) clandestine practices in secret societies, religious associations, literary and cultural organizations; (b) direct public protest via peaceful mass demonstrations, boycotts, underground publications, speeches, sermons, prayers, literature, drama, music, song, and similar; (c) the cultivation of morally supportive groups among peoples of goodwill everywhere; and (d) limited armed insurrections.

Now, it is a curious fact that the dawn of independence did not result in significant retaliations against the former colonial rulers. Rather, those who had been oppressed by the latter for so many generations extended the grace of forgiveness and friendship to their former oppressors. This was clearly illustrated time and again at numerous official ceremonies where the colonial flag was lowered by a former colonial representative as the newly independent nation's flag was raised, signifying the dawn of a new sovereign nation. That same spirit of generosity was also manifested in such recent events as the 1999 presidential election in Ghana, which marked the termination of rule by Flight Lieutenant Jerry Rawlings, a once ruthless military ruler who had transformed himself into an elected autocrat as a way to soften his image in the final years of his presidency. But, nowhere could one possibly imagine a greater display of a nation's goodwill than the 1994 election of Nelson Mandela to the presidency of South Africa. Their adoption of one of the most progressive constitutions in the world manifested black South Africa's grace and forgiveness, as did their proposed Truth and Reconciliation Commission, which was intended to heal the wounds of the past through the unfinished practices of granting amnesty to those who were willing to confess their crimes in public, and which promised reparations to those who had suffered so greatly.

Self-Initiation in African American Struggles for Racial Justice

In much of the literature concerning poverty among African Americans, racism continues to be viewed as a significant causative factor.[9] The impact of the Atlantic slave trade and its aftermath of racial segregation have resulted in the growth of an enormous literature in African studies in both Africa and the diaspora. No attempt will be made in this essay to review that literature, apart from assuming that the plight of the African poor everywhere is, to some extent, related to those eras when the Western world plundered Africa with impunity. Under such conditions, African peoples, territories, and cultures were either wasted or seriously impaired by the hegemonic powers of military technology, economic exploitation, political control, Christian imperialism, educational conquest, and white supremacy.

As I mentioned above, the key to deliverance from poverty is rooted in the capacity of the poor for self-initiation. That principle implies freedom that must be asserted, affirmed, and grasped by the poor themselves. In the following sections of this essay I will demonstrate how Africans in the diaspora have striven to liberate themselves in the past from racial oppression and are continuing to do so in our day.

Antebellum Initiatives

Africans in the diaspora have a long history of seizing the initiative in launching their liberation struggles. During the antebellum period the ubiquity of racism in every dimension of American life greatly hindered and invariably threatened all forms of social justice for freed African slaves who sought a modicum of liberty, economic well-being, and social development in various northern and southern cities. In his book *The Free Black in Urban America, 1800–1850*, the historian Leonard Curry describes the quality of life for freed blacks in American cities during that period. The title of his fifth chapter, "A Wholly-Distinct and an Outcast Class: Discrimination, Subordination, Segregation, Oppression, and Exclusion," aptly describes the issue. It begins with the following assertions: "White superiority—and, hence, the 'innate' inferiority of Negroes—was, in antebellum America, a concept requiring neither scientific, nor theological justification, nor documentation by evidence. It was a given."[10]

As a consequence freed blacks in antebellum cities were constantly harassed, insulted, assaulted, and resented in every conceivable way. Both law and social custom prevented them from either selling or using alcoholic beverages, and from obtaining licenses to operate any type of business, or to work in the building and trades industries.[11] The small number of black teachers, ministers, doctors, lawyers, musicians, and clerks were not listed in the city directories. Severe restrictions and limitations in employment prevented most free Africans from developing the capacity to become property owners. This lack of employment opportunities also meant that the majority of free blacks lived in abject squalor, where they were habitually exploited by greedy, ruthless landlords.[12] They were discriminated against at the polls and even their migration from state to state was hindered by their being forced to register at the mayor's office, post a bond, and receive a residence license with a one-year expiration date.[13] In short, free Africans were excluded from participation in any social practice that might imply equality with whites. Racial exclusion and discrimination were practiced everywhere, including the almshouses for the destitute, schools, hospitals, public accommodations, churches, and cemeteries. Thus Curry writes: "But not one sentient black in antebellum America could escape the knowledge that he lived in a white land under a white government that administered white law for the benefit of a white population, and that in the eyes of all these he was a being inferior to all but the most base and degraded of the whites. And that no amount of conformity to white mores and customs or acceptance of white values could change that reality."[14]

The breadth of racial segregation especially in southern life was astounding throughout the first half of the twentieth century. Robert Weisbrot vividly provides a taste of its impact in public affairs:

In 1905 Georgia prohibited Negroes and whites from using the same park facilities; donors of land for playgrounds had to specify which race could use them. Until 1940 Negroes and whites in Atlanta, Georgia, were not able to visit the municipal zoo at the same time. In 1915 Oklahoma authorized separate telephone booths for white and Negro callers. A Mississippi ordinance of 1922 barred members of different races from sharing a taxi cab unless the vehicle held more than seven passengers and was traveling from one city to another. New Orleans struck a quaint blow for morality by separating Negro and white prostitutes. . . . Separate bibles for oath taking in courts, separate doors for white and Negroes, separate elevators and stairways, separate drinking fountains, and separate toilets existed even where not required by law.[15]

Thus, free Africans could not merely stand by and wait for whites to acknowledge their humanity by granting them civil justice. Rather, they had to seize the initiative and struggle to build a surrogate world alongside that of hostile whites as an interim arrangement until such time as their full citizenship rights could be attained. This was a dangerous activity in which to engage since whites could and often did assault the black community with impunity. Yet free Africans persisted in their endeavors to demonstrate their humanity by constructing their own civil society while not losing sight of the aim of challenging the white society to practice racial justice.

Postbellum Initiatives

When the conditions were ripe, free Africans formed churches and mutual aid societies for the purpose of improving the condition of their people. Most important, those societies expressed a communal ethos that was distinctively African and that had survived centuries of enslavement. As the paramount social reality among African peoples, communal belonging has always implied a corresponding set of obligations, duties, and responsibilities for each of its members. Such mutual, reciprocal actions constituted the chief indicators of one's communal affirmation. In other words, communal belonging required habitual actions to preserve and enhance mutuality and reciprocity.

The rapid spread of independent African churches and other religious institutions, along with the organization of Freemasonry societies, fraternities, sororities, schools, colleges, hospitals, businesses, mutual aid societies, newspapers, and civil rights organizations, evidenced the desire of African peoples to express their humanity in the formation of an African community. Near the end of the nineteenth century, the black women's club movement came into existence. All of these organizational ventures resulted from initiatives devoted to the creation, maintenance, and enhancement of social justice in the midst of countless obstacles.

As we have seen above, those initiatives were in harmony with similar ventures designed and executed by twentieth-century independence movements both on the continent and in the Caribbean. Most important, the struggle against apartheid in South Africa, the civil rights struggle in the United States, the black nationalist movements, and the African women's movements both on the continent and in the diaspora owe their origins to the initiatives of the people themselves. And, of course, the creative and improvisational genius of African peoples also expressed itself in various genres of art, double entendre, humor, music, song, dance, religion, and theater. Athletics and sports represented yet another initiative that contributed to the development of an African community in the midst of powerful hostile forces.

Many works in contemporary African American studies support the claim that the initiatives of African peoples have been governed by the principle of communal solidarity, which has been the bedrock for the development of African communities everywhere. After centuries of communal destruction by North American slave holders, it is virtually miraculous that the spirit of communal solidarity was reborn. Evidence for that rebirth is provided in W. E. B. Du Bois's 1899 study *The Philadelphia Negro: A Social Study*, and such subsequent studies as James Weldon Johnson's *Black Manhattan* and St. Clair Drake's and Horace Cayton's *Black Metropolis: A Study of Negro Life in a Northern City*, to mention only two. In each of those works the authors demonstrated how blacks had taken the initiative in developing cities within cities as their response to the ubiquity of racial hostility.

Self-Initiative as Racial Uplift

The historian Kevin Gaines has provided a thoroughgoing analysis of this principle of initiative, as it presented itself, in the ubiquitous term "uplift," which dominated the social thought of African leadership in both the antebellum and postbellum periods. He shows how the term had a variety of mixed meanings. For example, many free Africans both before and after the Civil War used it to refer to the moral and spiritual transcendence over oppression and suffering that they sought both in this world and in the world to come. Following the Civil War, most of the community's leaders understood uplift as a symbol of the struggle for political freedom and social advancement.

In every case, however, the concept of uplift pointed to the initiatives of free Africans to make their contribution to civil society. Needless to say, perhaps, the concept implied an optimistic view of the future. In 1900 that optimism was immortalized by James Weldon Johnson's poem, "Lift Every Voice and Sing," which was put to music by his brother Rosamond and continues to be widely considered the African American national anthem. Thus, Gaines writes: "the optimism of this secular hymn . . . was rooted in the memory of past horrors, 'Sing a song full of the faith that the dark past has taught us / Sing a song full of the hope that the present has brought us.' "[16]

Gaines's book painstakingly clarifies the complexity of the word "uplift" as it came to be understood over the period of a century. Since Booker T. Washington's 1895 Atlanta Exposition speech, which catapulted him into national and international fame, the term has often been associated with the process of cultural assimilation and political accommodation. In fact, it gradually became associated primarily with Washington's act of forging a compromise with the practices of racial discrimination and segregation in the South. In his judgment, the aim of that compromise was to bring about a measure of harmony between the races in which the southern planters would agree to support his self-help program of industrial education in return for his continued commitment to the political and social separation of the races.

Yet, it is important to say that the concept of uplift occasioned a conflict of enormous proportions among post-Reconstruction African American leaders: a conflict that was represented by the Washington–Du Bois debate over the primacy of industrial or classical education for African Americans. Despite their differences, each advocated a social policy that was deeply rooted in alternative views of African anthropology and social progress. The Washington side of the debate was based on a model of cultural assimilation wherein elite blacks would be seen as embracing the values of class differentiation and self-help programs.[17] This appeal implied a process of social evolution that dismissed the issue of racism in favor of classism with the hope that whites would gradually view middle-class black elites as worthy of equal citizenship. Washington's compromise also implied that black elites were not interested in advocating social equality with whites.[18]

In addition to the cultural assimilationists, Gaines demonstrates how civil rights advocates, nationalists, back-to-Africa advocates, and the black women's club movement all adapted the idea of "racial uplift" to fit their respective ideologies, societal initiatives, and political strivings. He also shows the ambiguous nature of a concept that rendered all who embraced it vulnerable to the charge of complicity with the racist ideology that he claims they had internalized unconsciously.[19]

Clearly, the diversity of legitimate African American leaders shared one common value throughout the eighteenth and nineteenth centuries, namely, that of serving the communal interest of their people. Insofar as their people viewed them as sensitive to their needs, they were praised as "race leaders." Not all of them, however, had the capacity to represent those needs to the white community while maintaining their integrity as black leaders. Those who were able to do so were highly praised and gained a measure of immortality since their speeches, actions, and deeds were recorded in various organizational and institutional documents that later became the primary source material for various academic histories.

Twentieth-Century Changes in African American Leadership

After the First World War, there was the beginning of a class divide, or more precisely, a social divide emerging within the African American community. Yet, since racial segregation forced all blacks to live in the same residential area, and since the wider black community comprised the clientele for all black skilled and professional workers, it would seem there was little opportunity for the development of a high degree of alienation between the black social elites and the masses. Nevertheless their differing social lifestyles did manifest a high degree of alienation between the two classes.

Ironically, this social divide within the black community constituted a precondition for the eventual triumph of an entrepreneurial spirit of individualism that began to take root between the two social groups in the black community during the 1920s. The mass migration of blacks from the rural South to northern cities during the First World War was certainly a major contributing cause of this change. In fact, as unwitting scabs who had been wooed to the North to replace striking workers in various wartime industries, these newcomers gradually adapted themselves to the norms of urban life. Their traditional communal orientation to life did not function well in cities characterized by anonymity and alienation. Thus, the communitarian spirit was gradually privatized and relegated largely to the realms of family and church life. That is to say, these recent immigrants (like first-generation immigrants everywhere) maintained close ties with their families in the

South and with the churches that either followed them to the cities or were new ones that they later founded there. In due time, however, the forced concentration of blacks in the large urban centers constituted a necessary condition for the gradual development of political power.

Clearly, the spirit of individualism, which in many ways can be viewed as expressive of the spirit of urbanism, had a profound effect on the rise of a new form of black leadership. As noted above, the earlier leaders comprised a social elite within the walls of racial segregation. They were deeply devoted to the aims of building a surrogate world for their people, on the one hand, while struggling with the white community to effect social justice for their people, on the other hand. Beyond a shadow of doubt, these early leaders were greatly respected and trusted by their people because of the measure of communal dedication they embodied. The highest praise for such people was that of being dubbed "race men," a term that also signified the predominant patriarchal character of black leadership in spite of the presence of an increasing number of black female leaders at the time.

This massive migration of unskilled rural blacks to the cities represented the largest internal migration in the history of the nation. Its impact on the previously small black urban community was enormous. Removed from the communal ethos of the rural South, these newcomers had migrated to the cities in search of better jobs and decent civil treatment. In the process of adapting to urbanism, they gradually assimilated the culture of competitive individualism. That is to say, they found themselves driven primarily by the principle of self-interest rather than seeking to discern, establish, and promote the community's good. Following World War I any careful observer would have been able to see this gradual change in the character of many black leaders.

No one had ever questioned the motives of such leaders as Booker T. Washington, Monroe Trotter, Bishop Henry McNeil Turner, Daniel Payne, Alexander Crummel, Frederick Douglass, Harriet Tubman, Mary McLeod Bethune, W. E. B. Du Bois, Marcus Garvey, A. Philip Randolph, Ida Wells-Barnett, Mary Church Terrell, and a host of others. All such persons were trusted leaders who would never betray the community's good in favor of their own personal gratification. Not true, however, with the newer brand of leaders, who often seemed vulnerable to accusations of pursuing their own self-aggrandizement even if they were not guilty of the violation. Their vulnerability was due in part to the conditions of urbanism, the rapid rise of many colorful charismatic leaders, their flamboyant lifestyles, and the competitive nature of persons and groups in virtually every dimension of city life.

This newly emergent ethos of individualism among urban blacks did not imply the complete demise of the African communal spirit. In spite of its shrinkage to the private realm of family and church, a residue of this spirit was retained and often drawn upon effectively in mobilizing the people to respond to the many and varied racist attacks that threatened all black people. Various forms of brutality by both the police and mobs invariably reunited the black community in protest. But, after the immediate crisis had ended, the community often returned to the diverse activities that had contributed to its apparent disunity in the first place.

Another sign of these diverse initiatives among urban blacks is evident in the many and varied religious associations that emerged among them. These were often founded and led by charismatic leaders who had little or no interest in cooperative activity with other leaders. Since the cities were large enough for them to have sufficient space and followers without impinging on the preserves of others, they were able to coexist with little friction, not unlike the diversity of tribal groups in Africa that exist in close proximity to one another.

Conflicts emerged here and there whenever the groups openly competed with one another or some of them assumed an attitude of ideological hegemony. This occurred at various times, the most notable examples being the rise of Booker T. Washington's so-called Tuskegee Machine and the rapid growth of Marcus Garvey's back-to-Africa movement. Both endeavors appealed to masses of poor blacks in the rural South and urban North respectively. Both threatened the nascent civil rights organizations that had been founded and led by the black social elite, which, in turn, relied heavily on a racially integrated community of cooperation and support. Such organizations included the National Association for the Advancement of Colored People and the National Urban League, as well as black universities and colleges and many churches, especially those that either continued association with predominantly white denominations or patterned their liturgical life in accordance with white ecclesiastical norms.

Finally, we should also mention that a potential conflict always existed between those charismatic churches that appealed mostly to the poor (e.g., Daddy Grace's Universal House of Prayer for All People, Father Divine's Peace Mission Movement Church) and those that appealed largely to middle-class, educated congregants (e.g., Adam Clayton Powell's Abyssinian Baptist Church in Harlem and William Holmes Borders's Wheat Street Baptist Church in Atlanta, to mention only two). The social distance between the two has prevented overt conflict from arising.

The rise of the civil rights movement under the charismatic leadership of

Martin Luther King Jr. provided the occasion for a major reunion of all the progressive forces in the black community for social justice. Though the movement was interracial in its orientation, the initiative for it originated from blacks themselves. Even though its internal conflicts often threatened to split it apart, the genius of Dr. King's leadership in helping the movement keep its focus on the goal of eradicating racial segregation and discrimination preserved its unity. Thus, its final victory was attained by the Civil Rights Act of 1964 and the Voting Rights Act of 1965. Some viewed that as the greatest victory for civil rights since the Emancipation Proclamation one hundred years earlier.

Finally, it seems abundantly clear to this writer that African peoples who are minorities within predominantly white environments in the United States, Canada, and various European countries must rely on the following strategic initiatives in order to make progress: (a) developing diagnostic clarity concerning their issues and control of their votes in such a way as to gain reciprocal commitments from political candidates for the empowerment of the group rather than benefits for individuals alone; (b) developing a strong sense of spiritual solidarity with African peoples globally and especially those in the ancestral African homeland for the sake of collective identity, the pride of belonging, and self-respect; (c) developing the art of becoming self-critical of black leaders in all spheres of life including politics, religion, sports, entertainment, business, and the professions; (d) developing significant ways to praise men and women publicly for the good they do for the community as a whole and, concomitantly, blaming those who serve only their own interests; (e) developing the necessary strategies to conquer the psychological and social obstacles to a good education for the children; (f) developing appropriate methods for assessing everything in terms of its good for the empowerment and liberation of African peoples at home and elsewhere.

The Problem of Poverty in Africa Today

As mentioned above, poverty constitutes the paramount moral issue of the twenty-first century. It excludes people from the necessary resources to sustain life and impoverishes people in ways analogous to seeds that are planted in infertile soil. The poorer the soil, the less likely the plant will survive; certainly, the plant will never flourish under such conditions. Similarly, where there are no public policies supporting and promoting the well-being of the people, the latter will gradually perish unless they are able to seize the initiative and overthrow their cruel rulers and greedy overseers. But, even if they are unable to effect the necessary change by themselves, they will need the assistance of others.

Unmistakably, the poor and destitute are ubiquitous throughout Africa. They comprise children; orphans; widows; the sick, disabled, diseased, and destitute; street children; and countless others who are abused in every conceivable way—including such customary practices as child marriages; the degradation of women by traditional practices such as clitorectomies, domestic violence, rape, and prostitution; unequal educational opportunities for boys and girls; the wanton exploitation of natural resources; and the stark prospects for refugees and the victims of the HIV/AIDS epidemic, to mention only a few.

Unfortunately, the dawn of African sovereignty in the second half of the twentieth century did not lead to a corresponding economic empowerment. Rather, a syndrome of economic dependency was nurtured and fostered by both sides of the cold war, the end of which left material emptiness in its wake. Even countries with vast oil, gold, diamond, tin, cobalt, and agricultural resources continue to have very low status in the global economy. The Organization of African Unity, which recently changed its name to the African Union, has not been able to develop effective strategies on the continent for economic development.

Yet, the African Union has done notably well in providing peacekeeping military forces in several troubled regions of the continent even while seriously lacking technological equipment. Nonetheless, there remains the question of how African countries in need of economic empowerment will take the initiative in determining a true diagnosis of the common causes of their impoverishment and jointly developing effective policies for controlling their resources and using them for the well-being of their respective peoples.

Several decades ago various church leaders in Africa called for a moratorium on Christian missions, which sent shock waves throughout the Western world. It may be that a similar moratorium needs to be declared on all exports from Africa for a period of time. Such an act would shock large parts of the world into realizing their indebtedness to Africa for a variety of material resources. Further, it might provide African countries with sufficient leverage that could be used for various types of domestic development.

Let us recall once again Mercy Oduyoye's challenging question: "Africa is rich. Why, then, are Africans poor?" Some of the causes of this problem are obvious: (a) African leaders who betray the trust of their peoples by using their power to serve their own selfish interests while oppressing their peoples; (b) the lack of freedom to protest against social injustices and advocate social justice; (c) the lack of democratic structures guaranteeing the accountability of public leaders; (d) the lack of effective control mechanisms to guarantee a fair exchange for all exports; (e) the failure to develop appropriate infrastructures to support economic enterprises aimed at national self-sufficiency and the demise of all forms of economic dependency.

Contemporary Challenges

As we have seen above, in the midst of their oppressive conditions, it has been characteristic of Africans both on the continent and in the diaspora to devise the means to seize the initiative and assert themselves courageously and creatively in the quest for social change and liberating possibilities for themselves and their respective communities.

Throughout our travels during the Pan-African Seminar, we were conscious of the two forms of poverty that our colleague Elizabeth Amoah discussed in the first meeting in Ghana, namely, what she calls "anthropological poverty" and "material poverty." The former designates a deficit of the highest order because it refers to the absence of human dignity, which has ontological significance in traditional African life and thought. That is to say, the most important value in African society pertains to who one is, rather than what one possesses. Since the community bestows value on the person, the most valued person is the one whom the community holds in the highest esteem. Traditionally, such persons were given titles. Thus, such a titled person might have few material possessions but be viewed as the richest of all. Consequently, in those contexts, material poverty has subordinate status.

This understanding of poverty may explain in large part why the masses of African peoples seen daily on the streets of most African cities rarely bear the marks of clinical depression or despair. Rather, one is impressed with the throngs of people scrambling seemingly everywhere, buying and selling merchandise of every conceivable type for very minimal profits. Unending amounts of energy seem devoted to such ubiquitous pursuits. Invariably, such people are not working for themselves alone but for their families and, hence, fulfilling their obligations to their respective communities.

Yet, throughout our travels we have been constantly aware of the message we learned from Samuel N. Ashong, research fellow at the Centre for Policy Analysis in Accra, who addressed us at the start of our meeting. He argued that an effective alliance between government and the private sector needs to take hold in order for sub-Saharan Africa not to be left behind in the global economy. From his point of view the global economy is here to stay and Africa is presently excluded from it by an overdependency on imports and a lack of human capital. Without skilled persons to manage technology, Africa will continue to be left behind. Most important, he contended that Africa must greatly increase its exports.

Each of the countries we visited (Ghana, Kenya, South Africa, and Jamaica) bear the marks of so-called "third-world" or "underdeveloped" countries. Admittedly those terms are derogatory, but they do serve as sociological indicators of national economies that exhibit a privileged ruling elite at the top, a small middle class, and the poor masses at the bottom. In countries like Kenya and South Africa, people of European descent continue to be the owners of wealth; Asians largely control the small retail businesses; black Africans comprise the elected politicians, a slowly rising middle class, and the masses of poor people. In all of these situations one must not forget the presence of an underclass of people composed of those who have no viable means of livelihood: abandoned orphans, refugees, and those who are mentally ill.

Few people in America can imagine the expansive conditions of poverty as seen in the slums of Alexandria, South Africa; in Mathari in Nairobi; or in various sections of Kingston, Jamaica. Also, everywhere in Africa one encounters thousands of street children, unsafe drinking water, open sewers, poor hygiene, an epidemic-level health crisis produced by HIV infections and AIDS, and heavy death tolls from malaria and many other curable diseases. Most important, one also encounters disproportionate numbers of illiterate and semiliterate people, whose possibility for self-improvement is severely limited.

Though often provided with the assistance of the government, nongovernmental organizations, overseas missions, and local churches, various self-help initiatives are present in Africa:

(a) *Government-supported and privately managed assistance programs*: Examples are small grassroots cooperative projects in the Homeland of Ga Rankuwa outside of Pretoria, South Africa, where we visited a sewing and knitting project organized and managed by blind people; also in the Homeland of Ga Rankuwa, a youth development program organized for former street youths, where they are making money bags under contract for a bank; a project run by disabled people who package room deodorizers for the Johnson Wax Company.

(b) *Independent service missions*: These help people in need and include rescue missions for women like the Potter's House in Johannesburg, South Africa, for victims of domestic abuse; the Rehabilitation Center for Disadvantaged Girls in Kajiado, Nairobi, who are being rescued by the Seventh Day Adventists from being sold by parents into early marriages because of their poverty; a similar program for young teenage women in Johannesburg who have been rescued from prostitution and other forms of criminal activities on the streets; numerous services for children born with HIV, like the Nyambani Center for Children with HIV/AIDS in Nairobi, which is run by a group of nuns from India; various orphanages in Ghana, South Africa, and elsewhere for similarly afflicted children; services provided for street children like those offered by the Catholic Action Service for Children in Accra; homes for the elderly who are destitute and homeless, for instance, the one provided by the Little Sisters of the Poor in Nairobi, where the former Cardinal Morris Otunga, the first bishop in Kenya, has chosen to live out his last days as a way of honoring the work of those sisters.

(c) *Informal networks for cooperative savings and small loans:* These include the *susu* network, which operates both in Jamaica and among the Suthu in South Africa, and a small loan program in the Trinity United Church in Legon for market women in their congregation.

(d) *Various governmental cooperative endeavors:* These are aimed at poverty alleviation and include governmental grants for small business initiatives undertaken by not-for-profit organizations and government programs undertaken in cooperation with the Family Services System in Jamaica for the care of HIV-infected children and the mentally disabled who have the potential for learning.

(e) *Governmental contracts:* Examples include those with the World Bank and the International Monetary Fund, which, however, need serious critical evaluation as to their helpfulness in resolving the problem of poverty.

(e) *Governmental programs:* The major programs undertaken involve land redistribution and construction of roads, waterways, housing, schools, and other infrastructures.

Clearly, the evidences of poverty are similar everywhere: rapid expansion of HIV/AIDS; numerous orphans, child soldiers, and street children; unhygienic environmental conditions in general and the lack of clean water; high infant mortality; malnutrition; inadequate health care; and numerous untreated diseases. Further, the steady brain drain of African peoples via emigration to Europe and North America is also a consequence of poverty— though the extent to which the latter is a liability or an asset for the extended family needs to be explored.[20]

Conclusion

My reflections on the subject of religion and poverty among African peoples on the continent and in the diaspora have led me to the following conclusions. First, by continuing to exploit the natural and human resources in Africa, many individuals, corporations, and nations continue to grow richer and richer while the masses of African peoples continue to grow poorer and poorer. Second, it is a moral travesty of the first order that approximately one-fifth of the world's population owns and controls four-fifths of the world's resources. Third, while there are signs that the poor and their allies are seizing the initiative to achieve their destiny, the forms that that initiative takes seriously lack the capacity to be effective means for economic empowerment. Fourth, since many powerful though hidden forces benefit from the unequal distribution of the earth's resources, all advocacy for the eradication of poverty from our society and world at large is destined to meet enormous resistance. Fifth, and most important, since the initiative for the antislavery movement did not originate among slaveholders, since the initiative for the eradication of racial segregation did not originate among segregationists, since the initiative for independence from colonialism did not originate among the colonialists, and since the initiative to destroy apartheid did not originate among its supporters, so the initiative to rid the world of poverty will not come from the rich: it must come from the poor themselves. They and their allies must seize the initiative in order to become empowered economically. How this goal can be accomplished justly and effectively is the major challenge of the twenty-first century.

Notes

1. For a full discussion of this concept of initiation as a theory of action, see Hannah Arendt, *The Human Condition* (Chicago: University of Chicago Press, 1958).
2. Bishop Sigqibo Dwane, *Issues in the South African Theological Debate: Essays and Addresses in Honor of the Late James Matta Dswane* (Braamfontein: Sikotaville Publishers, 1989), 107.
3. For a full analysis of the Bible translation process and its implications, see Lamin Sanneh, *Translating The Message: The Missionary Impact on Culture* (Maryknoll, N.Y.: Orbis Books, 1996).
4. Readers should be mindful that the missionary secondary schools prepared students to pass the Cambridge examinations at both the ordinary and advanced levels. The latter assured them of entrance to university. Thus, each year a select number of African students passed those exams, which demonstrated that they were the academic equals of the best of English students.
5. Meyer Weinberg, *W. E. B. Du Bois: A Reader* (New York: Harper Torchbook, 1970), 392.

6. Ibid., 393.
7. Ibid., 400–401.
8. At the time of this writing, one of the most tragic events in African independence history is the evidence that Robert Mugabe, the father of the independence movement in what is now Zimbabwe, chose to become a dictator bent on rejecting all the nation's democratic traditions.
9. My operational definition of racism is any principle of exclusion, subordination, segregation, discrimination, or prejudice based on racial characteristics alone.
10. Leonard Curry, *The Free Black in Urban America, 1800–1850* (Chicago: University of Chicago Press, 1981), 81.
11. Ibid., chap. 2.
12. Ibid., chap. 4.
13. Ibid., 86.
14. Ibid., 94.
15. Robert Weisbrot, *Freedom Bound: A History of American's Civil Rights Movement* (New York: Penguin Books, U.S.A., 1990), 5.
16. Kevin K. Gaines, *Uplifting the Race: Black Leadership, Politics, and Culture in the Twentieth Century* (Chapel Hill: University of North Carolina Press, 1996), 2.
17. These black elites included the clergy, teachers, black intelligentsia, businesspersons, and black clubwomen.
18. Gaines, *Uplifting the Race,* 3.
19. Ibid.
20. Time and again this writer has encountered recent African immigrants to the United States who are sending monies home to their families and villages in support of important community projects such as schools, churches, senior citizen homes, community wells, and housing programs. A more precise measure of such activities is worthy of investigation.

CONTRIBUTORS

ELIZABETH AMOAH, B.A., M.A., Ph.D., is a senior lecturer in religion at the University of Ghana, Legon. She is also the author of "African Spirituality, Religion and Innovation," in *Religion: Empirical Studies*, ed. Steven Sutcliffe (2004); and "Femaleness: Akan Concepts and Practices," in *Women, Religion and Sexuality*, ed. Jeanne Becher (1990).

KOSSI A. AYEDZE, M.Div., Th.M., Ph.D., is the principal of the Presbyterian Theological Seminary at Atakpame, Togo, and a professor of church history at the Protestant University of West Africa, Porto-Novo, Benin.

BARBARA BAILEY, B.Sc., B.Sc.Med., Dip.Ed., M.A., Ph.D., is the university director of the Centre for Gender and Development Studies at the University of West Indies, Mona, Jamaica. She is also the editor (with E. Leo-Rhynie) of *Gender in the Twenty-First Century: Caribbean Perspectives, Visions and Possibilities* (2004); and (with G. Tang-Nain) of *Gender Equality in the Caribbean: Reality or Illusion* (2003).

KATIE G. CANNON, B.Sc., M.Div., Ph.D., is the Annie Scales Rogers Professor of Christian Ethics at Union Theological Seminary–PSCE, Richmond, Virginia, and the author of *Teaching Preaching: Isaac R. Clark and Black Sacred Rhetoric* (2002) and *Katie's Cannon: Womanism and the Soul of the Black Community* (1995).

NOEL LEO ERSKINE, Dip.Th., M.Th., S.T.M., Ph.D., is an associate professor of theology and ethics at Emory University, Atlanta, Georgia, and the author of *From Garvey to Marley: Rastafari Theology* (2005) and *Decolonizing Theology* (1998).

DWIGHT N. HOPKINS, B.A., M.Div., M.Phil., Ph.D. (from both Union Theological Seminary, New York, and University of Cape Town), is a professor of theology at the University of Chicago Divinity School. He is the author of *Black Theology USA and South Africa: Politics, Culture, and Liberation* (1989; 2005) and *Shoes That Fit Our Feet: Sources for a Constructive Black Theology* (1993).

SIMEON O. ILESANMI, B.A. (Hons.), J.D., Ph.D., is an associate professor and director of the Graduate Program in Religion at Wake Forest University, Winston-Salem, North Carolina. He is the author of *Religious Pluralism and the Nigerian State* (1997).

LAURENTI MAGESA, D.Th., Ph.D., is a senior lecturer at the Maryknoll Institute of African Studies, Nairobi, Kenya, and the chaplain at Baraki Sisters' Farm, Musoma, Tanzania. He is the author of *Anatomy of Inculturation: Transforming the Church in Africa* (2004) and *African Religion: The Moral Traditions of Abundant Life* (1997).

MADIPOANE MASENYA (NGWAN'A MPHAHLELE), B.A., B.A. (Hons.), H.E.Dip., M.A., D.Litt. et Phil., is a professor of Old Testament and ancient Near Eastern studies at the

University of South Africa, Pretoria. She is the author of *How Worthy Is the Woman of Worth? Rereading Proverbs 31:10–12 in African-South Africa* (2004).

TAKATSO A. MOFOKENG, B.A., Th.M., D.Th., is a technical advisor to the National African Farmers Union in South Africa; the resident theologian at the Motsweding FM radio of the South African Broadcasting Corporation; a former vice chancellor of the University of North West, Mafikene, South Africa; and the author of *The Crucified among the Cross Bearers* (1983).

ESTHER M. MOMBO, B.D., M.Phil., Ph.D., D.D., is an academic dean at St. Paul's University, Limuru, Kenya; a lecturer in African church history and women's theologies; and a member of the Circle of Concerned African Women Theologians.

NYAMBURA J. NJOROGE, B.D., M.A., Ph.D., is the project coordinator of Ecumenical HIV and AIDS Initiative in Africa (EHAIA), World Council of Churches, Geneva. She is the author of *Kiama kia Ngo: An African Christian Feminist Ethic of Resistance and Transformation* (2000); and the editor (with Musa Dube) of *Talitha Cum! Theologies of African Women* (2001).

JACOB OLUPONA, B.A., M.A., Ph.D., is a professor of African religious traditions at Harvard University Divinity School and a professor of African and African American studies in the Faculty of Arts and Sciences. His current research focuses on the religious practices of recent African immigrants to the United States. His book *Kingship, Religion and Rituals in a Nigerian Community: A Phenomenological Study of Ondo Yoruba Festivals* (1991) is a model for ethnographical studies. In 2007 he received Nigeria's National Order of Merit for distinguished contributions to the humanities.

PETER J. PARIS, B.A., B.D., M.A., Ph.D., D.D., is the Elmer G. Homrighausen Professor of Christian Social Ethics at the Princeton Theological Seminary. He is the author of *Virtues and Values: The African and African American Experience* (2004), *The History of the Riverside Church in the City of New York* (2004), *The Spirituality of African Peoples: The Search for a Common Moral Discourse* (1995), *Black Religious Leaders: A Conflict in Unity* (1991), *The Social Teaching of the Black Churches* (1985), and *Black Leaders in Conflict: Joseph H. Jackson, Martin Luther King, Jr., Malcolm X, Adam Clayton Powell, Jr.* (1978). He is the editor (with Max Stackhouse) of *God and Globalization: Religion and the Powers of Common Life* (2000) and (with Douglas A. Knight) *Justice and the Holy: Essays in Honor of Walter Harrelson* (1989).

ANTHONY B. PINN, B.A., M.Div., M.A., Ph.D., is the Agnes Cullen Arnold Professor of Humanities, a professor of Religious Studies, and the director of graduate studies at Rice University, Houston, Texas. He is the author of *African American Humanist Principles* (2004) and *Terror and Triumph* (2003).

LINDA E. THOMAS, B.A., M.Div., Ph.D., is a professor of theology and anthropology at the Lutheran School of Theology at Chicago, Illinois. She is the author of *Under the Canopy: Ritual Process and Spiritual Resilience in South Africa* (1999) and "Anthropology, Mission and the African Woman: A Womanist Approach," in *Black Theology: An International Journal* 5.1 (January 2007).

LEWIN L. WILLIAMS, Dip.Th., M.Div., M.A., Ph.D., was the president of the United Theological College of the West Indies and the author of *Caribbean Theology* (1994). Williams passed away in September 2006.

Caribbean/African American Dialogue (CAAD), 13, 280

Caribbean Community (CARICOM), 9, 104–6

Caribbean Conference of Churches, 106, 280

Caribbean Council of Churches (CCC), 9, 56–61

Caribbean islands, 272–91; African American connections to, 276–80, 284–86, 289–91; collective self-reliance in, 290–91; colonial exploitation in, 274–75; common history of, 272–75; Cuba, 284–89; cultural identity in, 282–83; culture of resistance in, 273–76, 278–80; economic democracy in, 283–84; Haiti, 273, 276–77; role of the church in, 280–81, 284–91; tourism in, 282. See also Jamaica

Caribbean Ship Rider Agreement, 101, 104

Caribbean Theology (L. Williams), 171

Carmichael, Stokely, 276

Carter, Jimmy, 233

Castro, Fidel, 284–88

Catholic Action Service for Children, Accra, 337

Catholicism, 251, 254, 268n6, 300. See also Nyerere, Julius K.

Cayton, Horace, 328

Centre for Community Change, 59

Chang, Grace, 46, 50–51

chattel slavery, 30

Chewa of Malawi, 316n80

children, 115, 337; in Ghana's trokosi system, 77; with HIV/AIDS, 52–53, 60, 78, 175, 256, 337; as HIV orphans, 50, 78, 256; income earning activities of, 73, 75; mortality rates of, 234, 299; sexual exploitation of, 52, 234–35; substance abuse among, 234; urban street life of, 234–35, 240, 245n28

Christaller, J. G., 116

Christianborg Castle, Ghana, 171

Christian Community Services (CCS), 218–19

Christian faith-in-practice, 258

Christianity, 77; affluence of churches and leaders in, 196, 202, 205–6, 212n58, 255, 283; ambiguous relationship to poverty of, 7, 11, 193–209; commercial activities of, 76, 202, 207–8, 214; ecumenical social justice movements in, 56–61; faith-based organizations of, xv–xviii; gender equality in, xviii–xix; growth in Africa of, xv, 16n11, 25, 195; impact of traditional religion on, 79–80; in Jamaica, 79–80; koinonia principle of, 9, 89, 91–92, 99–106; Nyerere's views on, 253–55; political activism within, 56–61, 178–86, 236–38, 246n40; the prosperity gospel approach to, 93, 139, 194, 197, 214, 242–43; role in apartheid of, 153–54; role in the slave trade of, 24–25; theologies of poverty in, 44–47, 286–89. See also Africanized Christianity; evangelism; liberating theologies; missionary enterprises

Christianity, Poverty, and Wealth in the 21st Century project, 47, 53

Christian Methodist Episcopal Church, 144

Christian political activism, 179–80. See also social activism

chronic poverty, 229, 235–36. See also cycles of poverty

Chrysostom, John, 197, 204

civil rights, 318; African struggles for, 320–22; constitutionalism in, 306; interconnections with human rights of, 295, 302–11, 315nn65–67; as negative rights, 305–6, 315n60; U.S. civil rights movement, 13, 284–85, 328, 332–33

Civil Rights Act of 1964, 333

civil society, xvii. See also social activism

class contexts: in African American communities, 330–33; bosadi approaches to, 160–63; homogenization theories of, 263–64; of Rastafarianism, 141; rituals for empowerment in, 130–31

Clendenen, Clarence, 36n8

Clinton, Bill, 209n3

Coker, A. Soyemi, 323

cold war, 263–64, 306

colonialism, xii, 3–4, 106, 111, 319–20; apartheid as legacy of, 133, 153; in the Caribbean, 272–75; civil service practices of, 321–22; destruction of traditional economies by, 4, 11; divide-and-rule approach of, 173; extraction of natural resources of, xiii, xiv, 45–46, 70; feminization of poverty in, 54–57; Jamaican slave economy of, 138–39; logic of colonialism of the postcolonial era, 170–74, 178, 184, 298; loss of cultural identity under, xiii; mercantilism of, 26–27, 37n19, 70; modernizing projects of, 215–16; psychology of dispossession in, 169–70. See also independence movements; slavery/slave trade

Colored Methodist Episcopal Church, 144

Commission on Christian Action for Development in the Eastern Caribbean (CADEC), 57–58

communal life, 14–15; among African Americans, 326–28; festivals of, 113, 123–24; focus on group well-being in, 111–12, 120, 126–27, 283–84, 302, 318–19; land and property in, xiv–xv, 118–21, 126; sociocentricity of, 100, 180–81; ujamaa village system, xv, 7, 12–13, 249–55. See also koinonia principle; rituals for empowerment; traditional practices

community of spirit powers, 114–15, 134–35

Congo, 126, 199, 310

constitutionalism, 306

consumption-based poverty, 43

cooperative efforts, 7, 336–37. See also communal life

Council of Anglican Provinces of Africa (CAPA): on gendered aspects of poverty, xviii; Nairobi Conference of 2000, xvi, 223–25

covenant, 91–92

creation stories, 115

Crisis of the Global Economy (Soros), 85–86

Crummel, Alexander, 331

Cuba, 103, 284–89

Cuffy, 273

cultural anthropology, 89

cultural assimilation, 329

cultural hermeneutics, 182–84

cultural poverty, 43–44

currency devaluations, 97

current status of poverty, x–xii

Curry, Leonard, 326

Curtin, Philip, 279

Cuthbert, R. W. M., 56–58

cycles of poverty, 91, 125, 166–67, 229, 235–36

dancing in the spirit, 241

Davies, Omar, 79–80, 86n9

Davis, Kortright, 289–90

debt: expenditures on, 299; Jubilee 2000 movement, 214, 220–23, 226n4; national debt levels, 97, 102–3, 232, 298–99, 313n22

Declaration on Human Rights of 1948, 301

decolonization of the mind, 170–74, 178, 184, 298

Decolonizing Theology: A Caribbean Perspective (N. Erskine), 170–71

definitions of poverty, 40–44, 90–92, 193, 209n1, 317–18; anthropological poverty, xi; changes in, 124–25; Gutierrez's three-part definition, 15on4; in Iliffe's classifications, xi; the poverty line, 41; rich nation/poor nation categories, 91; structural/material poverty, 128–30, 144, 194, 317–18; in traditional culture, 14–15, 116–18; UN measures of, 40–44

De Haeresibus (Augustine), 203

deindigenization, 315n67

deMarrais, K. B., 45

Democratic Republic of Congo, 126, 310

Dent, Martin, 220

Derrida, Jacques, 252, 261, 265

development, 98–99, 297–300, 310, 312n15. See also North-South dichotomy

dialectical responses to oppression, 9–11

diaspora Africans, 5, 259

Dictionary of the Asante and Fante Language (Christaller), 116

disease, 179, 234–35. See also HIV/AIDS

dispossession, 169–70, 173–74

Divine, Father, 332
Divine Tag on Democracy, The (Njoya), 172–75, 188n30
Divinity School at Freretown, 176, 188n40
"Doing Theological/Religious Education" (Dube), 183–84
domestic abuse, 60, 334, 337. *See also* sexual violence
Dominica, 273
Donnelly, Jack, 304
Dostoevsky, Fyodor, 258
Double Standards: Women's Property Rights Violations in Kenya (Human Rights Watch), 175
Douglas, Mary, 238
Douglass, Frederick, 331
Drake, St. Clair, 328
dreadlocks, 142–43
drug abuse and trafficking, 96, 145
Dube, Musa, 171–72, 183–84, 188n39, 189n44
Du Bois, W. E. B., 171, 322, 328–29, 331
Duchrow, Ulrich, 83
Duignan, Peter, 36n8
Dutch Curacao, 273
Dutch West India Trading Company, 26, 37n18
Dwane, Sigqibo, 320

ecological contexts: corporate farming, 121; environmental pollution, x, 231, 234; slash-and-burn farming, 121
economic cooperatives, 336–37
economic democracy, 283–84
economic migration, 50–51, 126
economies of affection, 61, 65n49, 137–38
Ecumenical Council of Cuba, 284
Ecumenical Service for Socio-Economic Transformation (ESSET), 59
education: gender differences in, 55, 178, 215; of girls, 78; illiteracy, 178, 210n10, 299; Kenya's church-led systems of, 217; meritocracy in, 45; missionary systems of, 54–55, 175, 215–16, 320–22, 338n4; Monrovia Symposium on, 298; origins of the independence movement in, 321–22; recreation of,

178; of theologians, 176, 184–85, 188n40, 238; by worker self-training, 81
Effutu of Winneba, Ghana, 123
Eliot, T. S., 294
Elmina, Ghana: *bakatue* festival of, 123; slave trade in, 6, 25–27, 36n17
emancipation, 54–56, 333
Emancipation Proclamation, 333
empowerment, 132, 319. *See also* rituals for empowerment
Ennis, Errol, 79
environmental crises, x, 231, 234
Erskine, Glenda, 2
Erskine, Noel Leo, 2, 7, 13, 170–71
Ethical Approach to the International Debt Question, An, 300
Ethiopia, 21–22, 141–42
ethnic music, 85
ethno-religious identity, xiii–xiv, 160–63
Etwatwa township, South Africa, 44
evangelism: in Kenya, 168; prosperity gospel in, 93, 139, 194, 197, 214, 242–43; televangelism, 197. *See also* missionary enterprises; Pentecostal (IAG) churches, South Africa
evil eye, 114–15

Facing Mount Kenya (Kenyatta), 170
faith-based organizations, xv–xviii. *See also* poverty alleviation; social activism
Family Services System, Jamaica, 337
Fanon, Frantz, 166, 289
farming, 95; corporate farming, 121, 126; of milk, 103; of rice, 105; slash-and-burn farming, 121; of sugar, 101, 103–4; in the United States, 150n3
Feinberg, Joel, 305
feminist hermeneutics, 183–84
feminization of poverty, xviii–xix, 6, 8, 39–40, 47–53; access to education in, 55, 178, 215; church's response to, 62–63, 196–97; economic migration in, 50–51; during emancipation, 54–57; gender-neutral discourses of, 61; in households headed by women, 49–50, 78; in informal economic settings, 74–75; international women's movement

feminization of poverty (*cont.*)
impact on, 61–62; in Kenya, 168–69, 174; labor protests targeting, 55–56; Nairobi Conference agreements on, 223–25; political perspectives on, 45–47; prostitution industry in, 51–52; social indicators of, 43–44; social justice movement responses to, 56–61; in subsistence farming, 71; theological perspectives on, 44; work patterns of women, 48–49

Fernandez, Paul, 284

fertility, 115

festivals, 113, 123–24

First Inter-Continental Consultation of Indigenous, African/American, and African/Caribbean Peoples on Racism in the Americas, 280–82

"Forgive Us Our Debts" letter, 300

Free Black in Urban America, 1800–1850, The (Curry), 326

G. I. Bill, 229, 243n2

Gaines, Kevin, 328–30

Galbraith, John Kenneth, 252–53

ganja, 143

Garvey, Marcus Mosiah, 141–42, 289, 331–32

Gas of Ghana, 113, 123–24

gender contexts: in access to education, 55, 178, 215; of *bosadi* readings of the Bible, 6, 10, 154, 157–63; in oppression of black males, 274; of Rastafari, 143–44; rituals for empowerment in, 130–31. *See also* feminization of poverty; women

gender studies, 62–63

General Agreement on Tariffs and Trade (GATT), 261

Ghana: Christian activity in, 21–22; European commerce in, 25–30, 36n17, 37n19; globalization in, 84, 97; HDI rating of, 1, 70; independence era of, 216–17, 325; independence movement of, 323; indigenous fishing industry of, 28–30; informal economy (*makola*) in, 69–71; moral values in, 23; oral tradition of, 20; poverty indicators for, 41–

43; slave trade in, 6–8, 19–25, 29–34, 34n3, 36n8, 37n28, 70, 171; traditional festivals in, 113, 123–24; *trokosi* system of, 77, 84

Gibb, Brother, 278

Gikuyu of Kenya, 170, 176–77

gleaning, 161

globalization, 46–47, 88–94, 213–14, 268n7, 335–36; CARICOM's response to, 104–6; development consensus on, 98–99; economic migration of, 50–51, 126; economic stratification under, 88–89, 91, 93, 95; feminization of poverty under, 48; focus on individual success of, 80, 93–94, 100, 125; homogenizing impact of, 84–85, 94, 140, 264; indigenized sources of legitimacy of, 82–84; informal economies under, 69–86; *koinonia* as response to, 89, 91–92, 99–106; market as centerpiece of, 94–97, 178; national debt under, 97, 102–3, 232, 298–99, 313n22; North-South dichotomy of, 259–62, 260n38, 269n33, 299–300; Nyerere's warnings about, 259–60; people-centered consensus on, 99; political agenda of, 259–60; as religion, 83, 94; role of consumers in, 81–83; sex industry under, 51–53; structural adjustment policies of, xiv, 8, 46–53, 97, 218, 261, 306–7, 315nn66–67; Washington consensus on, 98

global village, 88–89

global *vs.* local challenges, 6, 8–9

glue, 234

Goncalvez, Antam, 34n3

Gordon, David, 231

Gospel of Luke, 44

Gospel of Matthew, 44

Goudzwaard, Bob, 83

government programs, 337

Grace, Daddy, 332

grassroots cooperatives, 336–37

Gregory the Great, 204

Grenada, 273

gross domestic product (GDP) per capita, 41–42

Group of 77, 260

Guadeloupe, 273

Guinea Company, 26
gun crimes, 140
gunpowder, 125
Gutierrez, Gustavo, 150n4
Guyana, 105, 273

Haenger, Peter, 31
Haile Selassie I, emperor of Ethiopia, 141–42, 149
Haiti, 273, 276–77
harambee system, 126
hard work, 120, 123–24
Harm, Robert, 37n19
Harrington, Michael, 235
Hart, Keith, 69, 71–72
healing practices: power of the divine in, 240–41; in traditional religion, 23–24, 120, 135–37, 147, 149
health challenges, 230–36, 337; disease and malnutrition, 179, 234–35; life expectancy rates, 299; mortality rates, 234, 299; psychological problems, 235–36; U.S. reform efforts in, 233–34. *See also* HIV/AIDS
Henry the Navigator, prince of Portugal, 21, 35n6
hermeneutics. *See* Bible-reading
Higgins, Charles Isaac, 280
Hinchliff, Peter, 198
Hinduism, 273
HIV/AIDS, 8, 14–15, 125, 337; in the Caribbean, 140; child-headed households due to, 50, 78; children with, 52–53, 60, 78, 175, 234–35, 256, 337; education programs on, 15; feminist Biblical hermeneutics on, 183–84; in Kenya, 173, 188n31, 232; Nairobi Conference agreements on, 223–25; *State of World Population*, 2002 report on, 53; support groups for, 181–82; women's rates of, 52–53, 174–75
HIV/AIDS and Children's Rights in Kenya (Human Rights Watch), 175
holistic approaches: in development programs, 218–19; to theological education, 184–85; of traditional religion, 63, 162–63
Holly, J. C., 277

Holy Spirit, 240–41, 246n51, 262
Holy Spirit churches, 239–40
Home and Exile (Achebe), 170
Homeland of Ga Ranuwa, South Africa, 336
homogenization theories, 263–64
homowo festival, 113, 123–24
Hopkins, Dwight, 2, 6, 61, 65n49, 83, 150n5, 151n15
Houphouet-Boigny, Felix, 323
Houston, Texas, 231
Howard, Rhoda, 304
Human Development Index (HDI), 1
Human Development Report (UNDP), 40–44
humanism, 302
human poverty, 43
human rights, 13, 294–311, 318; Banjul Charter of 1981, 13, 295–303, 312n13, 314n55; connections with civil-political rights of, 295, 302–9; interdependence theory of, 295–96, 309–11, 316n80; as a luxury, 295, 304–6; moral validity of, 296; O.A.U. Charter of 1963, 312n13; positive and negative rights, 305, 310–11, 315n60; right to development, 297–300, 304–6, 312n15; social and economic focus of, 295, 300–306, 314n55
Human Rights Watch, 175
humility, 121
hybridized religion. *See* Africanized Christianity
Hylton, Edward, 278

idione/the individual, 80, 93–94, 100, 125
Ilesanmi, Simeon, 2, 7, 13, 234
Iliffe, John, xi
Imago Dei, 89
incarceration levels, 144–45
income-based poverty, 43
independence movements, xiv, 3, 13, 56–57; educational origins of, 321–22; leadership of, 322–25. *See also* postcolonial era
indigenous Christianity. *See* Africanized Christianity
individual/family poverty, 252
individualism, 331–32

industrialization, 45–46

inequality of poverty, x, 152, 193, 338; downward marginalization of the poor, 129, 150n3, 275; Iliffe's classifications of, xi; narratives of, xi–xii; U.S. "black-white gap," 4, 129, 229–31, 325

infant mortality, 234

informal economies, 6, 8–9, 82–86; of Ghana's makola market, 69–74; global market's interest in, 80–83; ideological resources of, 75–77; in Jamaica, 77–80; of Kenya's jua kali, 71–74; principles of reciprocity in, 73; religious constructs in, 73–74; of South Africa's spaza, 74–76, 81

Institute for Contextual Theology, 154

Institute for the Study of the Bible and Worker Ministry Project (ISB&WM), 181–82

intellectual commodities, 95

interdependence theory of rights, 295–96, 309–11, 316n80

Interim Poverty Reduction Strategy Paper, 2000–2003 (Kenya), 71, 168–69

International Assemblies of God (IAG), South Africa. See Pentecostal (IAG) churches, South Africa

International Conference on Popular Participation in the Recovery and Development Process in Africa of 1990, 225n1

International Covenant on Economic, Social, and Cultural Rights, 301, 313n33

international financial institutions. See International Monetary Fund; World Bank

International Labour Organization (ILO), 49, 52, 72

International Monetary Fund (IMF), 12, 337; debt classifications of, 298, 313n22; hegemonic policies of, 46; Jubilee 2000 movement, 220–23, 226n4; political agenda of, 101–3, 306–7; poverty-reduction partnerships with, xvii–xviii; Standby Agreement with Jamaica of, 140; structural adjustment policies of, xiv, 8, 46–53, 97, 218, 261, 315nn65–67

international women's movement, 61–62

Inter-religious Foundation for Community Organization (IFCO), 285–86

Introducing Feminist Cultural Hermeneutics (Kanyoro), 182–83

Isichei, Elizabeth, xi

Islam, 21, 35n6, 195

Jackson, Jesse, 285

Jamaica, 255–56, 284, 292n19; African American settlers in, 276–80; African majority of, 77; Baptist war of 1831 in, 278–80; church's role in, 256–57; colonial legacy of, 138–39; cooperative endeavors in, 337; cultures of resistance in, 13; debt crisis in, 102–3; emancipation in, 280; evil eye in, 114–15; formal economy of, 78–79; globalization in, 97, 101–4; HDI rating of, 1; hierarchies of color in, 139; HIV/AIDS in, 140; indigenous Christian practices in, 139, 149; informal economy of, 77–80; labor struggles in, 55–56; neo-evangelism in, 139; poverty indicators for, 40–44; Rastafarianism in, 141–44, 149; reggae music of, 80, 276; religious practices in, 79–80; rituals for empowerment in, 130–32, 138–44; social ministries in, 60; structural adjustment and liberalization in, 139–40; sugar industry in, 103–4

Jamaica Council of Churches, 80

Jary, David, 45

Jary, Julia, 45

Jaycox, Edward, 296–97

Johnson, James Weldon, 328–29

Johnson Wax Company, 336

Joseph, Richard, 302

jua kali (self-employment) system, 12, 71–74, 217

Jubilee 2000 movement, 214, 220–23, 226n4

Justice for Working Women Group, 60

Kairos Document of 1985, 77, 153, 164n4

Kanyoro, Musimbi, 182–84

Kariuki, James Mwangi, 187n28

Katongole, Emmanuel, 275

Makola, Akosia: on African religious life, 22–24; on Fort Elmina, 26–27; on Ghana's indigenous fishing industry, 28–30; on the slave trade in Ghana, 19–20, 23–24, 29–30; on variability in slavery practices, 31–33
Malcolm X, 289
malnutrition, 179, 234
Mandela, Nelson, 225n1, 267n4, 323–25
Mandi, Carol, 213
Manicheans, 203
manufactured goods, 95
Maphori, M. T., 157, 164n8
marijuana, 143
marked black bodies, 239
market women's protests, xiii
Marley, Bob, 276
marriage, 159–60, 165n17
Martin, Jennifer, 77–78, 86n7
Martínez, Sergio Arce, 272
Marx, Karl, 76, 266–67
Masai of Kenya, 119
Masenya, Madipoane, 2, 6, 10, 76, 150n8
mass poverty, 252–55
material dimension of life, 144, 194, 317–18, 335. See also poverty alleviation
Mathare slum, Nairobi, 216, 255, 260
Mau Mau war, 170, 176–77, 187n27, 189n42
Maurain, Peter, 62
M'Baye, Keba, 300
Mbeki, Moeletsi, 305
Mbeki, Thabo, 268n13
Medicaid, 233
Medicare, 233
Meeks, M. Douglas, 94
Meer, Fatima, 152
Mendieta, Eduardo, 75–76
mercantilism, 26–27, 37n19, 70, 319
meritocracy, 45
metanoia, 266
micro-credit programs, 218, 337
migration, 50–51
milk, 103
Millennium Declaration, xix, 3
Mirii, Ngugi wa, 187–88n29
missionary enterprises, 111, 319–22; charitable activities of, 195; conversion and

control in, 54–57, 133, 138–39, 173, 197–203, 214–15, 249; cultural stratification under, 92; ecumenical social-justice activities of, 56–61; education systems of, 54–55, 175, 215–16, 320–22, 338n4; failure of, 321–22; of IAG in South Africa, 155–56; manipulation of spiritual poverty in, 130; mercantile role of, 197–200, 207–8, 215–16, 249; moratorium on, 334; psychology of dispossession in, 170; responses to traditional religion of, 133; teachings on wealth and poverty of, 139, 194, 197–203, 210n8
"Missionary Theology as Theology of Domination" (Williams), 171
modernization, 215–16, 219–20
modesty, 121
Mofokeng, Takatso, 2, 6, 8–9
Moi, Daniel Arap, 172, 187–88nn28–30
Mokgokong, Pontifus, 157
Mombo, Esther, 2, 7, 11–12, 234
money laundering, 96
Monrovia Symposium, 298
Morales, 273
morality and values, 5, 16n15; in human rights, 296; moral well-being, 318; in traditional religion, 122–23
Mosoma, David, 2
Mothers Union, xix
Mugabe, Robert, xv, 339n8
Mugambi, J. N. K., 260
Multilateral Clearing Facility, 104–5
Murphy, Joseph, 246n45
Mustard Seed Community, 60
mutual obligation systems, 19–34
Mveng, Father E., xi
Mwaura, Philomena, 262
Myal religion, 141

Nairobi Conference of 2000, xvi, 223–25
Nanny, 273
Naomi, 158–63
narratives of poverty, xi–xii
Nasimiyu, Anne, 261–62
National Association for the Advancement of Colored People (NAACP), 332
National Council of Churches in Kenya (NCCK), 177–78

National Council of Churches in the USA
(NCC USA), 59–60
National Poverty Reduction Program
(Rwanda), xv
National Urban League, 332
Native Baptist Church of Jamaica, 278–80
natural resources, xi, 338; aluminum,
105; colonial control of, xiii, 45–46;
corporate appropriations of, 121, 126;
development of, xiv, 70; exports of,
334–35; missionary roles regarding,
199–200; oil, x, 105; synthetic replace-
ments for, 97; traditional management
of, 115, 121–22
Navigation Act (Britain), 34n3
Ndambuki, Berida, 166–70, 173–75, 181,
184, 186n2, 186n8
negative rights, 305–6, 310–11, 315n60
Negro Education Grants, 54–55
neoliberal economics, 89, 90, 94. See also
globalization
Nettleford, Rex, 80, 86n12
Network lobbying group, xvi
Nicaragua, 288
Nigeria, xi, 69, 311n1, 323–24
Njoroge, Nyambura, 2, 6–7, 10–11,
62–63
Njoya, Timothy, 172–76, 179–80, 182,
184, 187n28, 188n30
Nkrumah, Kwame, 216–17, 267n4, 323
Nku, Mother Christina, 133–34
nongovernmental organizations (NGOs),
218–19
North-South dichotomy, 259–62,
269n33, 269n38, 299–300
Not Yet Uhuru (Oginga), 187n28
Nozick, Robert, 315n60
Nyerere, Julius K., xv, 12–13, 220, 250–
55, 267–68nn5–6, 323; defense of
ujamaa of, 264–66; economic policies
of, 259–61, 270n38, 302; on human
equality and socialism, 257–58, 262,
267nn2–3, 268n12, 269n32; legacy of,
252; on transformative faith-in-
practice, 253–55, 257–58, 266. See also
ujamaa village system
Nyumbani, 256

Obasanjo, Olusegun, 301–2
Ochieng, William Robert, 175–76
Odotey, Irene, 1
Oduyoye, Mercy Amba, 171, 317, 334
odwira festival, 123
Oginga, Odinga, 187n28
Ogoni people of Nigeria, x
oikonomia, 94
oil development, x, 105
Okonkwo (character), 319–20, 324
Okullu, John Henry, 218
Oladeji, S. I., 219
Olupona, Jacob, 189n46
Olusanya, G. O., 312n15
Ongonga, Jude, 260
"On the Development of Peoples" (Pope
Paul VI), 254–55
Open Sore of a Continent, The (Soyinka), 308
Operation Crossroads Africa, 5, 16n16
Organization of African Unity (OAU),
298, 312n13, 323–24
Orlando Uniting Reformed Church,
Soweto, 60
othering of poverty, 61
Otunga, Morris, 337
"Out of the Temple" (Maurain), 62
Owens, Ray, 2

Padmore, George, 323
Palmer, Colin A., 34n3
Pan-African Congresses, 322–23
pan-African perspectives, xix–xx, 4, 16n13
Pan-African Seminar on Poverty and Reli-
gion: country visits of, 1, 3, 5, 150n10,
188n40, 209n4, 213, 249–50; essays of,
5–6; findings of, 14–15; goals of, 4,
250; members of, 2, 5, 16nn11–12;
methodology of, 5–7
Parham, Charles E., 155
Paris, Adrienne Daniels, 2
Paris, Peter, 2, 7, 13, 311
Pastors for Peace Project, 13, 285–86, 289
Patterson, Orlando, 229
Paul VI, Pope, 254–55
Payne, Daniel, 331
Peace Mission Movement Church, 332
Peel, J. D. Y., xii
Pelagians, 203

Pentecostal (IAG) churches, South Africa: *bosadi* Biblical hermeneutics of, 6, 10, 154, 157–63; compartmentalization of injustices in, 153–57, 164n8; focus on salvation in, 156–57, 164n8; Jeseocentricity of, 153–54; normative role of marriage in, 159–60, 165n17; origins of, 155–56; speaking in tongues in, 155; spiritualist Biblical hermeneutics of, 158, 163

Pentecostalism in Kenya, 77, 84, 239–41

people-centered consensus, 99

personalist character of African religious ethics, 311

Philadelphia Negro: A Social Study, The (Du Bois), 328

Pinn, Anthony, 2, 7, 12, 61

Pinto, Jean, 187n28

political perspectives: on feminization of poverty, 47–53; of independence movements, 56–57; on the role of power, 45; on the slave trade, 46; of social justice movements, 56–61; of structural adjustment policies, xiv, 8, 46–53

positive rights, 305, 310–11

postcolonial era, 1–4; corruption of, 11–12, 324–25; growth of civil society in, xvii; independence movements of, xiv, 3, 13, 56–57, 321; indigenization in, 315n67; Jubilee 2000 movement, 214, 220–23, 226n4; leadership in, 330–33; logic of colonialism of, 170–74, 178, 184, 298; poverty levels of, 217; self-initiation principle in, 325–33. *See also* poverty alleviation

Potter's House program, Johannesburg, 60, 337

poverty. *See* definitions of poverty

poverty alleviation, xix, 12–15, 213–25, 336–38; CAPA's Nairobi conference of 2000, xvi, 223–25; grassroots cooperatives in, 336–37; holistic approaches to, 218–19; independence-era approaches to, 216–20; Jubilee 2000 movement, 214, 220–23, 226n4; micro-credit programs, 218, 337; missionary approaches to, 214–16; by non-governmental organizations, 218–19; of Nyerere's ujamaa village system, 12–13, 249–55, 264–67; religious commercialization approach to, 214; role of the church in, 214, 256–58; self-initiation principle in, 7, 13, 325–33, 338; through social activism, 236–38, 246n40

poverty gospel, 197

poverty indicators, 41–43

poverty line, 41

Powell, Adam Clayton, 332

praxis, 228–29, 275. *See also* rituals for empowerment

prebendalism, 302

precolonial era. *See* traditional practices

Prester John, 21, 35n6

primary poverty, 40

prisons, 144–45

privatization, xiv–xv

propheting, 134

prosperity gospel, 93, 139, 194, 197, 214, 242–43

prostitution, 51–52

proverbs, 112–13; about material things, 122; about poverty, 116–18; about work, 120

"Proverbs 31:30–31 in a South African Context" (Masenya), 157

Prudentius, 197

psychological dimensions of poverty, 116, 262–63

psychology of dispossession, 169–70, 173–74

Pukumina revivalism, 142

purchasing power parity (PPP), 41–42

race men, 330–31

racial uplift, 328–30

racism, 339n9; "black-white gap" in the United States, 4, 129, 229–31, 325; *bosadi* approaches to, 160–63; in the Caribbean, 280–82; empowerment responses to, 130–31; homogenization theories of, 263–64; in Jamaica's hierarchies of color, 139; Rastafari responses to, 141; in South Africa, 133, 136–37, 152–54, 303; in the United

States, 326–33. See also bodies of the poor
Raiser, Konrad, 58
Randolph, A. Philip, 331
rape, 175, 178, 182, 189n54, 274–75
Rape—The Invisible Crime (Amnesty International), 175
Rastafarianism, 80, 141–44, 149
Rawlings, Jerry, 325
Reagan, Ronald, 233
reciprocity, 119–20
"Redemption Song" (Marley), 276
reggae music, 80, 276
Rehabilitation Center for Disadvantaged Girls, Nairobi, 337
relative poverty, 40
religion, 4, 11–12, 317; as opium "for the people," 76–77, 130, 197; role in informal economies of, 75–77; role in slave trade of, 21–25. See also Africanized Christianity; Christianity; Islam; traditional practices
Religion, Wealth, and Poverty (Schall), xv
religious commercialization, 214
Renquin, Jules, 199
rice production, 105
righteousness, 100
rights. See civil rights; human rights
ring shouts, 246n51
rituals for empowerment, 128–49, 275, 320; aesthetic recovery of black bodies in, 228–29; baptism as, 136; of black bodies in energetic worship, 238–41, 246n45, 246nn50–51; characteristics of, 131; connections to the land in, 142; festivals as, 113, 123–24; healing practices in, 135–37, 147, 149; in Jamaica, 138–44; of the Rastafari, 142–43, 149; rite of passage rituals, 147; through social and political activism, 148, 236–38, 246n40; in South Africa, 133–38, 149; through support networks, 137–38, 146–48; syncretic practices in, 134–36, 141–48; in the United States, 144–48; use of the Bible in, 152–63
Riviera Pagan, Luis, 24
Robertson, Claire C., 166, 169
Robinson, James H., 16n16, 35n6

Roosevelt, Franklin D., 243n2
Roper, Garnet, 79–80, 86n10
Royal Adventures in Africa, 26
rum, 36n8
Ruth, 10, 158–63
Rwanda, xv

Sachs, Jeffrey, 3
Sacks, Jonathan, 220–21
Salvation Army Home, 60
Sanghera, Jyoti, 51–52
Sanneh, Lamin, 320–21
Santa Ana, Julio de, 83
Sao Jorge da Mina, Elmina, 25–27, 36n17
Schall, Father James, xv
scientific socialism, 266–67
secondary poverty, 40
Sedler, Robert, 35n5
segregation, 325–28. See also racism
Seleoane, Mandla, 294, 301, 307
self-employment, 12, 71–74, 217
self-initiation principle, 7, 13, 325–33, 338
Sen, Amartya, 1, 307–8
Senghor, Leopold, 297, 323
Sese Seko, Mobutu, 310
sex industry, 51–53, 234–35
sexual violence, 175, 178, 182, 189n54, 274–75
sharing, 119–20
Sharp, Sam "Daddy," 273, 278–80
Sherman, William, 35n5
Ship Rider Agreement, 101, 104
Shorter, Alyward, 195
shrines, 22, 29, 124
Shue, Henry, 310
Sierra Leone, 126
Simmons, Angelin, 2
Sing, Horst, 268n6
slash-and-burn farming, 121
slavery/slave trade, xii, 15n2, 34n3, 46, 111, 259, 319–20; Africanized Christianity of, 144; African practices of, 30–33, 37n28; asylum in Haiti from, 277; in the Caribbean, 273–80; chattel slavery, 30; cultures of resistance in, 13, 273–75; depopulation of West Africa

slavery/slave trade (*cont.*)
  by, 70; emancipation, 54–57, 333;
  freed blacks under, 326–27; in Ghana,
  6–8, 19–25, 29–34, 125, 171; in Kenya,
  176; manipulations of spiritual poverty
  in, 130; reparations movement, 20–21,
  35n5; role of religion in, 21–25; use of
  rum in, 23, 36n8
"Slave Trade and Its Continuing Impact
  on Ghana, The" (Makola), 19–20
small-loan programs, 218, 337
social activism, xv–xix, 10–11, 179–80,
  236–38, 320–22; in Kenya, 178–86,
  237–38; Nyerere's views on, 253–55;
  social and economic justice movements, 15, 56–61; through transformation of existing relationships, 237–38,
  246n40. *See also* civil rights; human
  rights
social indicators of poverty, 42–44
socialism, 257–58, 262, 266–67, 267n4,
  268n7, 302
societal dimension of life, 318
Soros, George, 85–86
South Africa: apartheid system in, 133,
  136–37, 153–54, 303; Basic Income
  Grant program in, 60; *bosadi* approach
  to the Bible in, 6, 10, 154, 157–63;
  Christianity in, 77, 84; HDI rating of,
  1; human rights debates in, 303; indigenous Christian practices in, 130–38,
  149; informal spaza economy of, 74–
  76, 81; *Kairos Document* of 1985, 77, 153,
  164n4; poverty indicators in, 41–44;
  poverty reduction programs in, 307; racialized poverty in, 152, 336; social
  ministries in, 60; squatter camps in,
  74; St. John's Apostolic Faith Mission
  Church in, 133–38; Truth and Reconciliation Commission of, 325; white
  wealth in, 336
South African Council of Churches, 59,
  154
South African National Development
  Agency, 74
Soyinka, Wole, 308
spaza economy, 74–76, 81
speaking in tongues, 241

spirit powers, 114–15, 134–35, 240–41,
  246nn50–51
spirit shrines, 22, 29, 124
spiritual aspects of poverty, 112, 116
spiritual dimension of life, 318
spiritualist hermeneutics, 158, 163
spiritual poverty, 130–31, 145, 150n4, 318
squatter life, 14–15
St. Andrews Presbyterian Church of East
  Africa, 188n30
St. James Cathedral Anglican Church of
  Kenya, 177
St. John's Apostolic Faith Mission Church
  of South Africa, 133–38
St. Lucia, 273
St. Paul's United Theological College,
  188n40, 238
Standby Agreement of 1977, 140
State of World Population, 2002 report (UN-
  FPA), 53
Sterling, J., 54–55
Strauss, Anselm L., 233
structural adjustment policies (SAPs),
  315n65; economic impact of, xiv, 8,
  46–53, 97, 218, 261; in Jamaica, 139–
  40; political reform agenda of, 306–7,
  315nn66–67
structural functionalist theory of social
  transmission, 45
structural/material poverty, 128–30, 144,
  194, 317–18, 335. *See also* poverty alleviation
subeconomies. *See* informal economies
subsistence values, 99
Sudan, 126
sugar markets, 101, 103–4
Sunstein, Cass, 306
support groups and networks, 137–38,
  146–48, 181–82
Suriname, 105
sus network, 337
Swiegle, Nicholas, 278
syncretism. *See* Africanized Christianity

Tainos of Jamaica, 138
Tamar Campaign, 182, 189n54
Tanzania: independence movement of,
  323; Nyerere's presidency of, 250–51;

ujamaa village system of, xv, 7, 12–13, 249–55, 302
televangelism, 197
Terrell, Mary Church, 331
Terror and Triumph: The Nature of Black Religion (Pinn), 228
theological perspectives on poverty, 44–47, 286–89
Things Fall Apart (Achebe), 319–20, 324
Thiong'o, Ngugi wa, 170–73, 187n29
third world, 336
Thomas, Linda E., 2, 6, 10, 61, 65n49, 150n5, 151n15
Tillich, Paul, 240
Toure, Ahmed Sekou, 323
tourism, 51–53, 282
Toussaint L'Ouverture, François-Dominique, 273
Townes, Emilie, 230
Townsend, Peter, 116
toxic waste, x, 231, 234
traditional practices, 111–27, 321; community of spirit powers in, 114–15, 134–35, 240–41, 246nn50–51; festivals and rituals of, 113, 123–24; focus on communal well-being of, 111–12, 120, 126–27, 283–84, 302, 318–19; Ghana's *trokosi* system as, 77; healing practices in, 23–24, 120; holistic worldview of, 63, 130, 162–63; impact of slave trade on, 22, 125; in Jamaica, 79–80; morality and values of, 121–23; negative sanctions in, 123; proverbs of, 112–13, 116–18, 120, 122; as response to globalization, 85–86; sacredness of life in, 121–22; sharing and reciprocity in, xii–xiii, 19–34, 119–20, 296; spirit shrines of, 22, 29, 124; synthesis with African Christian practices of, 133–35, 139; use of land and resources in, 118–21; witchcraft in, 112, 114–15; work in, 120, 123–24. *See also* Africanized Christianity; communal life; rituals for empowerment
translation of the Bible, 195, 321
Treaty of Utrecht of 1713, 34n3
trickle-down economics, 98, 260
Trimiew, Darryl M., 304

Trinidad, 105, 273
Trinity United Church of Christ, Chicago, 145–49, 151n15
Trinity United Church of Legon, 337
Tristo, Nuno, 34n3
Trotter, Monroe, 331
Truth and Reconciliation Commission of South Africa, 325
Tubman, Harriet, 331
Turner, Henry McNeil, 331
Turner, Nat, 273
Tuskegee Machine, 331
two-thirds world, 259–60, 269n33, 270n38

Ubudehe Mukurwanya Ubuduken Program, xv
ubuntu, 320
ujamaa village system, xv, 7, 12–13, 249–55, 264–67, 268n12, 302; Arusha Charter, 213, 225n1, 254; critiques of, 264–66; foundation in equality of, 257–58, 266–67, 267nn2–4; as response to mass poverty, 252–55; as traditional African approach, 251
unemployment, 97, 125
United Church of Christ, 144–48, 149
United Nations Declaration on Human Rights of 1948, 301
United Nations Development Programme (UNDP), 40–44
United Nations Economic Commission on Latin America and the Caribbean (ECLAC), 47–48
United Nations Human Development Index (HDI), 1, 70
United Nations Human Development Report, 40–44, 70
United Nations Millennium Declaration, xix, 3, 59
United States: Africanized Christianity in, 144–48; "black-white gap" in, 4, 40–41, 129, 229–31, 244n3, 325; blockade of Cuba by, 284–85; Caribbean connections of, 276–80, 284–86, 289–91; Caribbean surveillance activities of, 104; chronic poverty in, 229, 235–36; Civil Rights Act of 1964, 333;

United States (*cont.*)

civil rights movement in, 13, 284–85, 328, 332–33; farm workers in, 150n3; G.I. Bill of, 229, 243n2; great migration in, 331–32; HDI rating of, 1; health care in, 230–31, 233; history of racism in, 4, 325–33; HIV/AIDS in, 230; mortality rates in, 234; poverty line in, 41; rituals for empowerment in, 130–32; slave reparations in, 20–21, 35n5; spiritual poverty in, 130–31; structural poverty in, 128–29; Trinity United Church of Christ, Chicago, 145–49, 151n15; Voters Rights Act of 1965, 333; War on Poverty and Great Society in, 233. *See also* slavery/slave trade

Universal House of Prayer for All People, 332

uplift, 328–30, 339n17

urban poverty, 216, 260; exposure to toxic waste in, x, 231, 234; in Kenya, 216, 240, 255; street children in, 234, 240, 245n28

Valentín, Dora, 272

values. *See* morality and values

Vernon, Evelyn, 58

Vesey, Denmark, 273

village intellectuals, xi–xii

Voters Rights Act of 1965, 333

Wallace-Johnson, I. T. A., 323

Wanaume Kwa Sala (WKS), 146–49

Wariboko, Nimi, 189n46

Washington, Booker T., 329, 331–32

Washington consensus, 98

water rituals, 135–37, 149

weapons, 125

Weber, Max, 76, 208

Weisbrot, Robert, 327

welfare approaches, 63, 91

well-being: as focus of African communal life, 111–12, 120, 126–27; HDI measurement of, 1

Wells-Barnett, Ida, 331

We Only Come Here to Struggle (Ndambuki), 166–70, 173–75

Wesley, John, 206–7

West, Gerald, 181–82, 184, 189n52

West Indian Federation, 105

"We the Peoples: The Role of the United Nations in the Twentyfirst Century" (Annan), 3

Wheat Street Baptist Church, 332

Wilberforce, Samuel, 206–7

Williams, Joyce, 2

Williams, Lewin L., 2, 6, 9, 47, 171

Wilmore, Gayraud, 237

Wilmot, S., 55–56

witchcraft, 112, 114–15

Witter, Michael, 78–79, 86n8

Wolfensohn, James, 222

women, 144; access to land of, 119; *bosadi* approach to the Bible, 6, 10, 154, 157–63; childcare roles of, 196; economies of affection of, 61, 65n49; education of, 78, 215; feminist hermeneutics of, 183–84, 189n54; in Ghana's *trokosi* system, 77; HIV/AIDS among, 52–53, 174–75, 181–82; human rights of, 33; illiteracy levels among, 178, 210n10, 299; international women's movement, 61–62; market women's protests, xiii; rape and sexual violence toward, 175, 178, 182, 189n54, 274–75, 337; sex work and prostitution, 51–52; subordination in Rastafari practices of, 144; support networks for, 60–62, 137–38, 181, 337. *See also* feminization of poverty

Women's Guild, xix

women theologians, 182–84

Women Watch, 47

work, 120, 123–24

World Bank, 12, 337; debt classifications of, 298, 313n22; hegemonic policies of, 46; Jubilee 2000 movement, 214, 220–23, 226n4; Nairobi Conference of 2000, xvi, 223–25; political reform agenda of, 306–7; poverty-reduction partnerships with, xvii–xviii; structural adjustment policies of, xiv, 8, 46–53, 261, 315nn65–67

World Council of Churches (WCC), 58–59, 188n31, 280–82

World Health Organization, 188n31
World Trade Organization, 70, 84, 101–2
Wright, Jeremiah A., Jr., 146
Wright, R. R., 277

Yoruba people of Nigeria, xii–xiii, 21
Young, Andrew, 292n19

Zambian humanism, 302
Ziervogel, David, 157
Zimbabwe, xv, 339n8
Zion Christian Church of Soweto, 61
Zion revivalism, 142
Zwingli, Huldrych, 206

PETER J. PARIS is the Elmer G. Homrighausen Professor
of Christian Social Ethics at the Princeton Theological
Seminary. He is the author of *Virtues and Values: The African
and African American Experience* (2004), *The History of the
Riverside Church in the City of New York* (2004), *The Spirituality of African Peoples: The Search for a Common Moral Discourse*
(1995), *Black Religious Leaders: A Conflict in Unity* (1991), *The
Social Teaching of the Black Churches* (1985), and *Black Leaders in
Conflict: Joseph H. Jackson, Martin Luther King, Jr., Malcolm X,
Adam Clayton Powell, Jr.* (1978). He is the editor (with Max
Stackhouse) of *God and Globalization: Religion and the Powers
of Common Life* (2000) and (with Douglas A. Knight) of *Justice
and the Holy: Essays in Honor of Walter Harrelson* (1989).

Library of Congress Cataloging-in-Publication Data
Religion and poverty : Pan-African perspectives / Peter J. Paris, ed. ;
foreword by Jacob Olupona.
p. cm.
Includes bibliographical references and index.
ISBN 978-0-8223-4356-1 (cloth : alk. paper)
ISBN 978-0-8223-4378-3 (pbk. : alk. paper)
1. Christianity—Africa. 2. Church and social problems—Africa.
3. Religion and civil society—Africa. 4. Poverty—Africa. I. Paris, Peter J., 1933–
II. Olupona, Jacob Obafemi Kehinde.
BR1360.R45 2009
261.8'325096—dc22   2009030090